the irish
renaissance

RICHARD FALLIS

 SYRACUSE UNIVERSITY PRESS   1977

Copyright © 1977 by Syracuse University Press
Syracuse, New York 13210

All Rights Reserved

First Edition

Library of Congress Cataloging in Publication Data

Fallis, Richard.
    The Irish renaissance.

    Bibliography: p.
    Includes index.
    English literature—Irish authors—History and
criticism.   I.   Title.
PR8750.F34   820'.9   77-24576
ISBN 0-8156-2186-8
ISBN 0-8156-2187-6 pbk.

Manufactured in the United States of America

for Jean
"brightness of brightness"

Richard Fallis is associate professor of English at Syracuse University. His special interests include modern poetry, Yeats, and Irish traditional music. He received a B.A. degree from Wake Forest University and a Ph.D. from Princeton University. He has been on the faculty at Syracuse University since 1971, often teaching courses in modern Irish literature.

contents

PART III   PHOENIX IMPERILLED

preface

I STILL REMEMBER vividly the first time I read a poem by William Butler Yeats. I was a junior in college, taking a course on Yeats and some other visionary poets. We had spent several weeks on William Blake, and I had been thoroughly confused. Blake's ideas made very good sense to me, but the poems themselves, for the most part, had seemed almost unreadable. The assignment for the next week was some early poems by Yeats. Late one wet Sunday afternoon, I settled in to read, opened the text at random to "Cuchulain's Fight with the Sea," and had a sensation much like that of Keats looking into Chapman's Homer. I had no idea who Cuchulain was, or Emer, or what a dun was, or what "raddling" meant, but I knew enough to be enthralled by the music of Yeats's language and the power of the situation he describes, and the last line of that poem still rings in my ears.

Because the teacher of that course was a master of his art, I learned much about Yeats during that semester. I learned to understand his ideas and his poetic methods; I learned, too, something of his inner vision. The teacher rightly emphasized biography in his approach to Yeats, and that led me to want to know more about the man and the world he lived in. Yeats was, I learned, a central figure in a literary movement called "the Irish Renaissance," and I wanted to know something about that movement. I found it easy enough to read the important works that the writers of that movement produced. I went through *The Playboy of the Western World*, *A Portrait of the Artist as a Young Man*, *The Plough and the Stars*, and stories by Frank O'Connor and Sean O'Faolain with growing enthusiasm. That was all very satisfying, but I still wanted to know more about the Irish Renaissance itself: who wrote what? when? who knew whom? what ideas did they share? I assumed that if I went to my college's library I could find an up-to-date history of the Irish Renaissance which would answer those questions, but it was not that simple. I found two histories, but both were quite old, and neither seemed to tell the entire story. When I was in graduate school, I learned that, in fact, no one had written a fairly full history of modern Irish writing. There were good books on Yeats, Joyce, and the others, and interesting studies of such things as the Dublin literary scene, the influence of nationalism, and the development of Irish fiction, but there was no general history. During the last five years, I have frequently taught an undergraduate course called "The Irish Renaissance," and repeatedly I have had to explain to curious students that, no, there really is not a basic history of modern Irish writing.

Finally, I decided to write one myself. I knew that I could do no more than sketch men, women, and events, but that seemed something well worth doing. Nevertheless, I immediately encountered some serious problems, and some of the questions they raised need to be dealt with here. For example, "What is Irish literature?" Many scholars and critics have argued over that one by trying to decide if there were some special qualities which make a writer or a work distinctively Irish. In a novel or play, an Irish setting and Irish characters certainly help, but the matter becomes more confusing with lyric poetry. Generally speaking, Irish literature ought to deal with Irish themes, but the best Irish themes—isolation, exile, the power of external forces, frustration, the power of a self-enclosed community, and several others—are simply universal themes expressed in an Irish context, so that matter of theme can become a very cloudy one. Thus it seems to me that the best definition of Irish literature, and it is only a makeshift one, is "Irish literature is any literature written by a person of Irish birth or a person born elsewhere who chooses to live in Ireland, identify himself or herself with Ireland, and write in a way which seems particularly meaningful in an Irish context." There are problems with that definition, but it is broad enough to include all the important Irish writers yet narrow enough to exclude some of Irish birth or Irish extraction who hardly belong in Irish literature. It will, for example, include James Joyce, who spent most of his life outside of Ireland, and include Mary Lavin, who was born in the United States; it will, on the other hand, exclude George Bernard Shaw and Oscar Wilde, Dubliners both, but writers whose work is no more than peripheral to Irish literature.

"What was the Irish Renaissance?" To answer that, I need to define another term, "Anglo-Irish literature." The literary heritage of Ireland is in two languages, Irish and English. The Irish language, which I prefer to call Gaelic simply to avoid confusing circumlocutions, has a long and significant history and a very valuable literature. Nevertheless, it has been virtually extinct as an ordinary spoken language for more than a century. Ireland's other language, English, has been the predominant one in its literature since about 1800. It is convenient and accurate to call the writers in Ireland who use English "Anglo-Irish," even though the term may in some nonliterary contexts have connotations about religion or politics. Still, that hybrid term, "Anglo-Irish," reminds us that the writers in English belong to two literary traditions, the general one of the English-speaking world and the more specific one of Ireland. The Irish Renaissance, then, was a literary phenomenon involving, mostly, Anglo-Irish writers. It began sometime in the last quarter of the nineteenth century as an effort to give lasting and worthy expression in literature to the experience of the Irish people. During a period between, roughly, 1885 and 1940, a considerable number of Anglo-Irish writers produced works of importance in each of the literary genres. Yeats became the greatest poet of his time in the English-speaking world. Augusta Gregory, John Millington Synge, and Sean O'Casey were outstanding figures in drama; they, with Yeats and some others, helped make Dublin's Abbey Theatre one of the most important dramatic experiments of the first third of our century. James Joyce became the greatest writer in fiction in English of the first half of the century; Frank O'Connor and Sean O'Faolain became masters of the realistic short story. They were the most important figures in a varied and exciting school of Irish fiction. Not every writer of the Irish Renaissance was a genius, and not every work was a masterpiece, but the Irish writers made their little island the home of a major literature.

This book is intended to give an overview of those writers, their works, and the literary movement in which they participated. Yeats appears in almost every one of the following chapters, and that is appropriate, for he more than anyone else created and sustained the Irish Renaissance. We begin our narrative with his efforts to begin a literary movement in Ireland; chapters 1 and 4 describe the gradual development of the movement in the 1880s and 1890s. The other two chapters in the first part are necessary digressions, brief descriptions of the Irish history and the Irish literature, in Gaelic and English, to which Yeats and the others who began the Irish Renaissance were heirs. The second part of the book describes the writers and their works during the period, roughly, between 1900 and 1923. Chapter 5 sketches the nationalist agitation which finally culminated in a war with England, independence for twenty-six of Ireland's counties, and a tragic civil war. Chapter 6 describes Irish drama during this period, dealing largely with the Abbey Theatre and its playwrights. Chapter 7 discusses Anglo-Irish poetry in this time, while chapter 8 describes the development of fiction. The third unit discusses Irish writing since 1923, but the focus is on the period between 1923 and 1940. Chapter 9 describes the social and political background to Irish writing of the last fifty years. Chapter 10 deals with the slow decay of Irish drama in the years up to 1940. Chapter 11 deals with the remarkable achievements in fiction; chapter 12 deals with the poetry from these times. The final chapter is a very rapid survey of Irish writing since 1940 which attempts to show the relationship of recent writing to the Irish Renaissance itself.

Because this book can provide only an overview, it seems to me especially important to direct interested readers to other books providing more detail. Thus a section with suggestions for further reading is included. These provide some information on biographical and critical studies and background works. This is far from a complete bibliography of scholarship and criticism on Anglo-Irish literature, but every item has been of help to me in preparing this history. If this book sends readers out to find books by the writers of the Irish Renaissance and books about them, and if it answers some of the questions I wanted answered ten years ago and students in my classes want answered today, it will have served its purpose.

Syracuse, New York   Richard Fallis
Spring 1977

acknowledgments

IN THE PROCESS of writing this book, I have accumulated debts to many persons and institutions, and some of those ought to be acknowledged here.

The book owes its existence, ultimately, to two superb teachers who created and encouraged my interest in Yeats and Anglo-Irish literature, Edwin G. Wilson of Wake Forest University and A. Walton Litz of Princeton University. It has been a long time since one introduced me to Yeats and the other urged me on to finish a dissertation on his criticism, but I continue to owe much to both.

Colleagues in the English Department at Syracuse have helped by reading and arguing over manuscript and ideas; among those to whom I feel special debts are Steven Cohan, Donald Dike, Jean Howard, Donald Morton, Walter Sutton, and Judith Weissman. I am grateful as well to the Department and its current chairman, Arthur W. Hoffman, for encouraging me to teach courses in Anglo-Irish literature frequently. I have learned something from almost every student in the undergraduate courses and graduate seminars, but special thanks for ideas shared and talked out should go to Joyce Bloom, Bart Finucane, Kenneth Gelburd, Mary Gordon, Carol Williams Jackson, Ralph Lombreglia, Perry McHugh, Steven Rasmussen, Jay Rogoff, and Michael Tallon.

Colleagues at other institutions have helped sharpen my ideas and avoid errors, and I owe special debts to Mary FitzGerald of Fordham, Richard J. Finneran of Tulane, James MacKillop of Onondaga Community College, Phillip Marcus of Cornell, and William H. O'Donnell of Penn State. I want to acknowledge also the help and advice of friends and colleagues in Ireland, especially Terence Brown and Brendan Kennelly of Trinity College, David Marcus of the *Irish Press*, Peter Fallon, and David Berkeley. I owe a special debt to Gerald and Josie Kilfeather of Sligo, two warm friends who have taught me a good deal about Ireland and the Irish.

I am indebted, as well, to the libraries of Syracuse, Cornell, and Princeton Universities, the National Library of Ireland, and the British Museum. The staffs in each have been helpful even with absurd queries, and I am especially grateful to members of the staff of the National Library of Ireland who helped me on some particularly difficult matters. Generous research grants for the writing of the manuscript came from the National Endowment for the Humanities and the Syracuse University Research Fund.

My thanks, too, to Emily Kessler, a patient and careful typist who labored through some complicated manuscript.

I feel a special debt to parents who have provided all kinds of support for so long, nor must I forget an infant son who has had less attention than he deserved while his father finished up the last chapters. And, especially, I must acknowledge the unceasing support and encouragement of my wife. She bore with me through a long summer of writing, corrected many errors, and talked me out of some misinterpretations. The errors and misinterpretations that remain are entirely of my own making.

For permission to quote from copyrighted materials, acknowledgment is gratefully made to the following:

To Mr. Simon D. Campbell for quotations from the poems of Joseph Campbell.

To The Viking Press for a quotation from James Joyce's *A Portrait of the Artist as a Young Man,* © 1916 and 1959.

To Martin Brian and O'Keeffe, Ltd., for quotations from *The Collected Poems of Patrick Kavanagh,* © 1964.

To the Dolmen Press for quotations from Thomas Kinsella's *The Tain,* © 1970.

To A. D. Peters and Co., Ltd., for quotations from Frank O'Connor's *Kings, Lords and Commons,* © 1959. Reprinted by permission of A. D. Peters and Co., Ltd.

To Colin Smythe, Ltd., publishers of the Collected Edition of AE's writings, for a quotation from AE's "On Behalf of Some Irishmen Not Followers of Tradition."

To the Macmillan Publishing Co., Inc., for quotations from *The Collected Poems of James Stephens* by James Stephens, © 1909 and 1918 by Macmillan Publishing Co., Inc., renewed 1946 by James Stephens.

To the Oxford University Press for quotations from *J. M. Synge: Collected Works, Vol. III and IV: Plays,* edited by Ann Saddlemyer, © Oxford University Press, 1968, and used by permission of the Oxford University Press.

To the Macmillan Publishing Co., Inc., for quotations from W. B. Yeats, *The Collected Plays of William Butler Yeats*, © 1934, 1952 by Macmillan Publishing Co., Inc., and from *Essays and Introductions* by W. B. Yeats, © Mrs. W. B. Yeats, 1961.

To the Macmillan Publishing Co., Inc., for the following selections from the poems of W. B. Yeats: "A Coat" and "September 1913," reprinted with permission of Macmillan Publishing Co., Inc., from *Collected Poems* by W. B. Yeats, © 1916 by Macmillan Publishing Co., Inc., renewed 1944 by Bertha Georgie Yeats; "A Prayer for Old Age," reprinted with permission of Macmillan Publishing Co., Inc., from *Collected Poems* by W. B. Yeats, © 1934 by Macmillan Publishing Co., Inc., renewed 1962 by Bertha Georgie Yeats; "To Ireland in the Coming Times" and "The Hosting of the Sidhe," reprinted with permission of Macmillan Publishing Co., Inc., from *Collected Poems* by W. B. Yeats, © 1906 by Macmillan Publishing Co., Inc., renewed 1934 by W. B. Yeats; "The Fascination of What's Difficult," reprinted with permission of Macmillan Publishing Co., Inc., from *Collected Poems* by W. B. Yeats, © 1912 by Macmillan Publishing Co., Inc., renewed 1940 by Bertha Georgie Yeats; "In Memory of Major Robert Gregory," reprinted with permission of Macmillan Publishing Co., Inc., from *Collected Poems* by W. B. Yeats, © 1919 by Macmillan Publishing Co., Inc., renewed 1947 by Bertha Georgie Yeats; "Easter 1916," "The Second Coming," and "A Prayer for My Daughter," reprinted with permission of Macmillan Publishing Co., Inc., from *Collected Poems* by W. B. Yeats, © 1924 by Macmillan Publishing Co., Inc., renewed 1952 by Bertha Georgie Yeats; "Meditations in Time of Civil War," "Two Songs from a Play," and "Among School Children," reprinted with permission of Macmillan Publishing Co., Inc., from *Collected Poems* by W. B. Yeats, © 1928 by Macmillan Publishing Co., Inc., renewed 1956 by Bertha Georgie Yeats; "I Am of Ireland," reprinted with permission of Macmillan Publishing Co., Inc., from *Collected Poems* by W. B. Yeats, © 1933 by Macmillan Publishing Co., Inc., renewed 1961 by Bertha Georgie Yeats; "John Kinsella's Lament for Mrs. Mary Moore," reprinted with permission of Macmillan Publishing Co., Inc., from *Collected Poems* by W. B. Yeats, © 1940 by Georgie Yeats, renewed 1968 by Bertha Georgie Yeats, Michael Butler Yeats, and Anne Yeats; "Mourn—and then Onward!" reprinted with permission of Macmillan Publishing Co., Inc., from *The Variorum Edition of the Poems of W. B. Yeats*, edited by Peter Allt and Russell K. Alspach, © 1957 by Macmillan Publishing Co., Inc.

To the Dolmen Press for quotations from the *Collected Poems of Austin Clarke*, © 1974.

To the Oxford University Press, New York, for quotations from Seamus Heaney's *Death of a Naturalist*, © 1966.

To Mrs. F. R. Higgins for a quotation from F. R. Higgins' poetry.

To the St. Martin's Press for quotations from *Three Plays by Sean O'Casey*, © 1966, and *Three More Plays by Sean O'Casey*, © 1965.

To Methuen and Co., Ltd., for quotations from *The Plays and Poems of J. M. Synge*, edited by T. R. Henn, © 1963.

Part I

phoenix resurgent

the Beginnings of a movement

The 1880s

There is no great literature without nationality,
no great nationality without literature.

John O'Leary

Know, that I would accounted be
True brother of a company
That sang, to sweeten Ireland's wrong,
Ballad and story, rann and song.

W. B. Yeats, "To Ireland in the Coming Times"

SOMETIME toward the middle of 1885, a young poet and an aging revolutionary met each other for the first time at a club in Dublin. The revolutionary was John O'Leary, recently returned from years of exile for his political activities and a famous man among Irish nationalists; the young poet was William Butler Yeats, then only twenty and an unknown. We do not know what they talked about at that first meeting, but we do know that each made a strong impression on the other. Soon after, Yeats went to visit O'Leary at his modest house in Leinster Road, and on that first visit he found O'Leary's sister and a group of middle-aged women playing cards. The young caller was given a glass of sherry and invited to join them. Thanks to the sherry, he lost sixpence at the game. Later on, Ellen O'Leary told Yeats something of her brother's life. John O'Leary was born in 1830, the son of a well-to-do shopkeeper in Tipperary. As a medical student in Dublin, he had read the poems and essays of Thomas Davis, a nationalist writer of the 1840s. These had changed his life, and soon he had turned to journalism and revolution. In 1865, as the editor of the revolutionary newspaper, *The Irish People*, he had been arrested and sentenced to twenty years' imprisonment. After five years he had been released and exiled, choosing to go to Paris, then the great center of all kinds of European revolutionary activity. The experience in prison and exile had aged him prematurely so that at fifty-five he seemed a very old man, and Yeats's imagination was stirred by his noble profile and gentle eyes, a countenance which seemed purified through suffering.

But as Yeats came to know O'Leary better, he was affected by more than the man's appearance and history. In an Ireland in which patriotism, cant, and expedience were sometimes synonymous, O'Leary was a remarkable example of moral courage. He had suffered for his country, but he insisted to Yeats that there were some things a man must not do even to save his nation. Vague talk of "philanthropy" and "humanitarianism" offended him deeply. Though he had devoted his life to freeing Ireland from British rule, he had a genuine respect for the character and intelligence of his enemies and argued that there were good men with worthy motives who fought for even the worst causes. But O'Leary's patriotism ran deep, and so did his interest in literature. He had an excellent collection of Irish books, and he urged these on Yeats, although he freely admitted that some of the patriotic verses which had changed his own life were very poor poetry. Yeats soon became one of O'Leary's enthusiastic disciples, and it is not really an exaggeration to say that the Irish Renaissance came out of that friendship. If Yeats had not met O'Leary at the right time, he might never have begun to discover his own Irishness. Yeats became the first great figure in modern Irish literature and the chief organizer of a new and powerful literary movement. The Irish Renaissance *could* have occurred without Yeats or O'Leary, but it would have been a different and poorer movement if they had not met: Lady Gregory might have remained the mistress of a great house in County Galway; John M. Synge might have remained a failed Parisian journalist; James Joyce might have become a Jesuit; Sean O'Casey might have remained a laborer and journalist; Frank O'Connor might have died a Cork librarian.

This is not meant to suggest that Irish literature did not exist before Yeats and O'Leary met. In 1885 there was already a tradition of literature in the Gaelic language which was more than a thousand years old, and there was a tradition of literature in English—Anglo-Irish literature—which went back several centuries. Even so, the Ireland of the 1880s seems in retrospect a country waiting for a new and distinctive national literature. The Great Famine of the 1840s had wiped out almost all that was left of Gaelic-speaking Ireland and its literature with it. The Anglo-Irish literature of the nineteenth century had been too much a matter of patriotic ballads and colorful tales of conniving peasants. Ireland had been for too long almost an inarticulate province of the English-speaking world—but all that was about to change.

Historians could argue at great length as to when the Irish Renaissance actually began, and some might want to say that Anglo-Irish literature was already beginning to speak with its distinctive voice well before the middle of the 1880s. One could say that the Irish Renaissance really began in 1842 when Thomas Davis, the first great ideologue of Irish nationalism and the writer whose work so affected John O'Leary, began to publish *The Nation*, a Dublin-based newspaper which quickly became popular throughout the country. In *The Nation*, Davis and other members of a group of young writers and thinkers which called itself "Young Ireland" first spoke of an Irish literature in the English language which would be "racy of the soil," nationalistic in that it reflected Irish life and Irish values. Or one might want to date the Renaissance from 1878, the year in which Standish O'Grady published his *History of Ireland: Heroic Period*, a book which excited the imaginations of Irish writers. O'Grady's *History* is hardly history in the conventional sense; instead, it is a stirring retelling in vigorous prose of some of the legends of ancient Ireland, particularly the stories associated with the heroic Cuchulain. O'Grady's great fighting man was an important imaginary figure in the developing sense of Irish self-identity: a nation which had seen itself as oppressed and politically impotent found in him a figure of heroic strength and virtue. But Davis's Young Ireland movement died in a few years and O'Grady's book was not enough to sustain a movement. Before it could develop, Anglo-Irish literature needed a writer of genius and a thinker who could clarify the relationships between literature and nationalism. It found the writer in Yeats and the thinker in O'Leary.

O'Leary provided Yeats with practical support—he lent him money, lent him books, helped him find work as a journalist, and helped raise the money to pay for his first volume of poems—but, more importantly, he taught Yeats a set of ideals about Irish literature. A lasting Irish literature in English, O'Leary said, could not develop unless writers were willing to commit themselves to Irish nationalism. No great literature could exist without nationality; no nationality could define itself without great literature. If Ireland were ever to gain her political and cultural freedom from Britain, the Irish writers would have to provide the climate for it by helping create a national imagination which was distinctively Irish. Irish writers should write about Ireland (some of Yeats's early poems had been about India), and they should write in a recognizably Irish style (most of Yeats's early work had been imitations of Spenser, Shelley, and the English Pre-Raphaelites). Because the Irish language was virtually dead, Irish writers would have to use English, but by studying the mythology and legend of ancient Ireland as well as the folklore and history of modern Ireland and by listening to the English actually spoken in Ireland, the writers could find a subject and a style which were distinctively their own. O'Leary was an ardent nationalist, but he insisted that Irish literature had to be purged of politics. The idea that Irish literature ought to be overt propaganda for the nationalist cause was, he said, one of things which had made it so mediocre in the past. Irish literature had to further the cause of nationalism, but it should do so not by creating propaganda but by creating a literature so essentially Irish, so reflective of the national imagination, that it would prepare the country spiritually for the coming day of political liberation.

It was largely because of O'Leary's influence and the wisdom of his teaching that Yeats and some of his friends set out on the business of creating a new national literature. O'Leary saved Yeats and some others for Ireland, and this in itself was important. Irish literary history is full of the names of writers of great talent who can be called Irish only because they were born there; they made their careers in England. Goldsmith and Sheridan are two outstanding examples from the eighteenth century, and in the nineteenth, Dion Boucicault had a long career as one of the most popular "English" playwrights. He wrote and produced more than 140 plays, and his natural talent was so strong that *London Assurance,* produced when he was only twenty-one, became one of the great hits of the century. Although he wrote three famous Irish plays, even in these he was an exploiter of English prejudices towards Ireland, and he helped keep alive the traditional figure of the "stage Irishman," loud, drunken, violent, and sentimental. Two of Yeats's own older contemporaries, Oscar Wilde and George Bernard Shaw, were also good examples of Irishmen who had to go to England to develop their talents. Wilde's mother had been a well-known Young Ireland poetess, but her son found little in Ireland or Irish literature which meant anything to him. Shaw, like Wilde and Yeats a native Dubliner, played a minor role later in the Irish Renaissance, but the focus of his life, too, was the London stage. Neither had an O'Leary to interpret Ireland for him, and O'Leary's kind of literary nationalism was valuable simply because it provided a way to be an Irish writer and a serious artist at the same time.

The Yeats O'Leary met in 1885 was still a young man and malleable. Born in 1865 in a suburb of Dublin, he was the son of J. B. Yeats, a painter, and Susan Pollexfen Yeats, a withdrawn woman who would slip into early senility after a series of strokes. Yeats spent much of his boyhood in Dublin and London, the cities in which his father tried to earn a living, but the crucial days of the childhood were the ones spent in Sligo, the little port on the west coast of Ireland where his mother's parents lived. His autobiography tells us that much of his childhood was unhappy, but the summers in Sligo were full of intense experiences as he watched the sailors on the docks, heard stories of fairies and ghosts, and learned to love the starkly beautiful countryside surrounding the town. Sligo remained for him always an imaginatively potent place, a place to be loved in remembrance perhaps more than in fact, as Irishmen are prone to remember "home." Although he was taunted at his English school as a "mad Irishman," both sides of his family were thoroughly Anglo-Irish, Protestant and reasonably well off. The men in the Yeats family had often been clergymen of the Protestant Church of Ireland; the Pollexfens and their relations had been merchants, mill-owners, and landlords. The boy who spent the summers in Sligo often came into contact with elements from the Catholic, Gaelic peasant culture which was all around his grandfather's house, but some of his earliest memories were of flying the British Union Jack in front of that house and dreaming of a heroic death fighting Irish rebels. Even his first experience with poetry came through a collection of "Orange rhymes," poems full of that same patriotism which today sends Protestants in Belfast out to fight with their Catholic neighbors and makes them Britain's most vociferous subjects.

The vacations in Sligo helped form Yeats more than any formal schooling. He went to schools in London and Dublin, but he was an erratic student, interested in zoology, good in geometry, mediocre in English (spelling and punctuation would remain problems for him all his life). His real literary education was conducted by his father, who taught him early on to love poetry and drama for their moments of high passion. Together they read Shakespeare, Shelley, and Rossetti, and J. B. Yeats told his son that in the greatest literature "All must be an idealisation of speech, and at some moment of passionate action or somnambulistic reverie."[1] When they saw *Hamlet* together, the Danish prince became the boy's "image of heroic self-possession for the poses of youth and childhood to copy, a combatant of the battle within myself."[2] As a teen-ager, he decided that his life's work was to be poetry, but the poetry he

---

[1] W. B. Yeats, *The Autobiography of William Butler Yeats* (New York: Collier, 1965), pp. 42–43.

[2] *Ibid.*, p. 30.

had come to love was all English. In his autobiography, Yeats describes himself and his poetry at about the time he met John O'Leary by saying: "I wanted to be wise and eloquent, . . . and when I was alone I exaggerated my blunders and was miserable. I had begun to write poetry in imitation of Shelley and of Edmund Spenser, play after play—for my father exalted dramatic poetry above all other kinds—and I invented fantastic and incoherent plots. My lines but seldom scanned, for I could not understand the prosody in the books, although there were many lines that taken by themselves had music. I spoke them slowly as I wrote and only discovered when I read them to somebody else that there was no common music, no prosody."[3]

The two years or so between his first meeting with O'Leary and June of 1887, when his family moved to London, were vitally important ones in Yeats's development. Slowly, he began to master the art of poetry. At the same time, with O'Leary's encouragement, he began to learn something about Irish history and literature in a remarkable exercise in self-education. He studied translations of the ancient Irish myths and legends and, because of his interest in the supernatural, became expert on Irish folklore. He was discovering that the "other" Ireland, the Ireland of the peasantry and folk traditions, the Ireland of the Celt, was his Ireland, too. In the 1880s, though, Ireland and Britain were full of groups of young men and women who were trying to rediscover and reinterpret what it meant to be Irish, and it is only in retrospect that O'Leary's circle of young friends appears to be the most important. Yeats may have been the only potential genius in the O'Leary circle, but some of the old man's other disciples were also to be important figures in the development of Irish writing.

Katharine Tynan, for example, a young woman whom Yeats once thought he might marry, was already a poet with more reputation than Yeats himself. Early in her career, she had been encouraged as a writer by Anna Parnell, the sister of the great political leader, and Father Matthew Russell, who sponsored many of the younger Irish writers. Her first volume of poems, the first of some eighty titles she would publish, had had good reviews even in Britain when it appeared in 1885, and during her long career she published many collections of poems and several novels, many of them imbued with a gentle but intense Catholicism. Stephen Gwynn, another of O'Leary's friends, would grow into a capable minor poet and novelist and an important authority on eighteenth-century Ireland. T. W. Rolleston, the editor of a little magazine, the *Dublin University Review*, in which Yeats and other members of the O'Leary circle

3 *Ibid.*, p. 43.

published some of their work, would eventually become an authority on German literature and the author of poems based on ancient Irish legend. But, aside from Yeats, the two members of the group who would achieve the most lasting reputations were Douglas Hyde and George William Russell.

Hyde, born five years before Yeats, was by 1885 an expert scholar of the Gaelic language and its literature, and during the 1890s he would become a leader of the movement to reestablish the old language through the Gaelic League. When he and Yeats met at O'Leary's, Hyde had already produced more than a hundred original poems in Gaelic, and he was working on *Leabhar Sgéulaigheachta*, a large collection of tales in Irish. A man who said he dreamed in Gaelic, Hyde had a gift for turning Gaelic into English in translations which were marked by a lucid idiom very different indeed from the exaggerated language of earlier translators. When Yeats first met Hyde, he mistakenly assumed that he was a Gaelic peasant, so thoroughly had this Anglo-Irish son of a Protestant clergyman become immersed in Celtic Ireland. George William Russell was immersed in Celtic Ireland, too, but Russell's Ireland then was a land of fairies and supernatural beings rather than the Gaelic-speaking peasants of Hyde's imagination. A mystic and visionary, Russell, who called himself AE, for "aeon," found in Ireland a rural society still in touch with the supernatural that industrial civilization had obscured elsewhere in Europe. AE took the folk stories of the supernatural very seriously indeed; he was often certain that the ancient gods were about to return to Erin. Yeats, too, had a strong interest in the supernatural and the occult; he and AE agreed that this shared interest could be developed in an Irish context. The early occult teachings Yeats had encountered had had mostly to do with Indian philosophy, but with AE's encouragement, he began to see that Ireland had its own traditions of the supernatural and the visionary, traditions which could also be used to help create a distinctively Irish literature. For all his esoteric interests and apparent otherworldliness, AE would become, later on, an able agricultural organizer and man of practical affairs as well as the spiritual and personal guide for generations of young Irishmen. He never became a great poet, as Yeats had hoped, but he did become an idiosyncratic saint, and he, as much almost as Yeats, would become also the exemplar of the "Celtic twilight" phase of the Irish Renaissance, the phase which in the 1890s would find in magic and folk beliefs one of the central definitions of Irishness.

O'Leary's circle was by no means the only active group of young Irish writers at the time, but, in the long run, it became the most important because O'Leary's ideals for Irish literature were potentially so powerful and because

Yeats, Hyde, and AE were talented men. Moreover, we ought to remember that
O'Leary's followers were, by and large, more receptive to complex beliefs than
were many of the other young nationalists at home and in America and Britain
who cared deeply about Ireland and Irish writing. O'Leary's Anglo-Irish followers came out of what was really an Irish genteel tradition; they may have
wanted to become like peasants in some ways, but they wanted to because they
had the economic and imaginative freedom to do so. They were not burdened,
as some young writers were, with the long tradition of cramped education,
narrow piety, compulsive nationalism, and restrictive morality which for too
long had been part of the fundamental Irish experience. To a certain extent,
the history of the Irish Renaissance is the history of conflict between Anglo-
Ireland and Celtic Ireland, and many later figures who came from the Celtic
peasant or bourgeois backgrounds would right the balance, but for the time
being, the future of Irish writing was with men such as Yeats, Hyde, and AE,
men who would have to work to become what the world calls "typical Irishmen."

In the 1880s, though, Dublin and London, the home of thousands of Irish
immigrants, were full of groups who had high hopes for the future of Ireland
and Irish writing. In London, Francis A. Fahy and some other Irishmen
founded an Irish Literary Club in Southwark, then an Irish enclave on the
south bank of the Thames. Its original purpose was to foster an awareness of
Irish culture and history among Irish people living in "the capital of the
enemy," and it sponsored lectures on Irish subjects, ran a patriotic Sunday
school for Irish children, and built up a library of Irish books. In a way, it was
typical of the self-help movements then common among immigrants and working people ambitious to better themselves. In turning the pages of the history
of this group, there is something genuinely moving in the pictures of the earnest
clerks and laborers who organized and promoted the club; they were sincerely
concerned with preserving the Irish culture they had brought with them from
home and with developing it. But their club, like so many others of the time,
had its eyes on the past, on a nostalgic remembrance of an Ireland all had left
behind. Their tastes were sentimental and philistine, but their patriotism was
fervent and intense. Eventually, the Southwark club would be taken over by
Yeats and his friends in the 1890s, and it did good work in its time, but it
lacked the imaginative energy and the freedom from parochialism out of which
a real literary revival could come. In fact, the constricting vision of Ireland it
represented, a vision which equated nationalism and virtue, would come to pose
a serious problem for later Irish writing.

The Southwark club had its "Original Nights" when members would read and perform their own work, as did many other groups, but it was O'Leary's circle which produced the book which announced most convincingly that a new literary movement had arisen. *Poems and Ballads of Young Ireland* (1888), edited by O'Leary and his sister, was a small anthology, but it contained one of Yeats's best early poems, "The Stolen Child," and poems by Hyde, Rolleston, and others of real merit. Much of the poetry, though, was mediocre, and the book's real importance was not in its achievements but in its ambitions. The title of the volume would have had a double meaning for Irish readers at the time. Of course, the "young" in it is an allusion to the youth of its contributors, but it is also a reminder of the Young Ireland movement of forty years before, the movement which had argued that Irish poetry ought to be the servant of political nationalism. O'Leary's disciples identified themselves as the descendents of this old Young Ireland, but their work also made it clear that they had absorbed some of O'Leary's lessons: craftsmanship was more important to them than patriotic sentiment; ancient Ireland and the Ireland of folklore would be a more important subject for poetry than topical political matters; Irish nationalism would be construed as something more than allegiance to dogma or political party. Examined in terms of 1888, the best that can be said for the collection is that it was promising, but the promise in it was real, and the attitudes upon which it was based were to be central to the best writing of the Irish Renaissance.

The first years of the Irish Renaissance had produced no masterpieces, but a good deal of basic work for a literary revival had been done. Talented people had been brought into contract; ideals had been clarified; methods had been analyzed. It was becoming apparent that the literary revival, however it developed, would be a group effort. One of the continuing strengths of the movement would remain the close personal contact among the writers. Sometimes this led to discord and even feuds, but the continuing cross fertilization would be immensely useful. Moreover, it was becoming clear that the new movement would find a great source of imaginative energy in myth, legend, and folklore. Eyes could not remain fixed on the ancient past or the cottages of the west of Ireland forever, but at least the first phase of the Irish Renaissance would find a continuing sustenance in the Gaelic Ireland that was past or passing. Two fundamental questions remained to be answered, though, as Phillip Marcus observes in his study of Yeats and the early Irish Renaissance. How far could Irish literature develop by being national and not nationalistic?

What were the boundaries of Irish writing?[4] A strong national literature must be both particular and general; it must speak directly out of a particular place to a particular people, but it must also have a significance which goes beyond that place and those people. If the literature goes too far away from its place and people, it loses its nationality, but if it focuses exclusively on one place and one people, it will quickly become too narrow. The literary nationalism of the 1880s was a good start toward a literature which would be both particular and general, but it was only a start, a first step on a very long journey.

[4] *Yeats and the Beginning of the Irish Renaissance* (Ithaca, Cornell University Press, 1970), p. 3.

past and present
The Burden of Irish History

'I am of Ireland,
And the Holy Land of Ireland,
And time runs on,' cried she.
'Come out of charity,
Come dance with me in Ireland.'

W. B. Yeats

Let my memory be left in oblivion, and my tomb
remain uninscribed, until other times and
other men can do justice to my character.
When my country takes her place among the
nations of the earth, *then*, and *not till then*,
let my epitaph be written.

Robert Emmet

MORE THAN TWO CENTURIES ago a German visitor to Ireland observed, "It seems as if there were something peculiar in the nature and condition of Ireland that prevents her wounds from ever healing."[1] As the violence continues today in Northern Ireland, that traveler's comment still seems depressingly relevant. The hatred which yields today's killings goes back beyond 1690, and it is difficult for those of us who are not Irish to understand how any feud could last so long. We may, in fact, feel that the Irish, like the Bourbon kings of France, are able to forget nothing and learn nothing. Feuds of such length and intensity can exist, we may think, only in legend and myth;

[1] Johann Georg Kohl, quoted in Desirée Edwards-Rees, *Ireland's Story* (New York: Barnes and Noble, 1967), p. 86.

13

they hardly seem part of the twentieth century. But that points to a basic problem in dealing with Irish history: it is, in many ways, not a series of facts and
events in a chronological order of cause and effect, but a potent and often
murderous myth. Although this chapter is largely concerned with facts and
dates, it should be remembered that these are the stuff of myth in Ireland and
that myth is often more powerful than fact. The history of Ireland given here is
perhaps not the one the professional historian would give, but it is an attempt
to sketch some of the facts behind the myths, the facts of Irish history which
were the inheritance and the burden of the writers of the Irish Renaissance. To
understand their Ireland, let us begin by looking briefly at geography before we
move to examine the Irish environment of 1885 and the history which formed it.

Ireland is a fairly large island of about 32,000 square miles (roughly
the size of Indiana) on the edge of western Europe. The sea between Ireland
and Wales is only about 350 feet deep, and the European continental shelf
extends some 150 miles to the west of the island, but geographically Ireland is,
like Norway and the Iberian peninsula, one of the Atlantic edges of Europe.
The island itself is relatively hilly around the coasts and flat in the center,
forming a sort of natural bowl, but there are some significant internal divisions.
A range of knobby hills called drumlins separates the northern quarter of the
island from the rest. South of that, the River Shannon divides the country on a
north–south and then an east–west axis. These basic geographical facts account
for the traditional division of Ireland into four provinces: Ulster north of the
drumlin belt, Connacht west of the Shannon, Munster south of the Shannon,
and Leinster east of it. Much of the best farmland is found in Leinster and
Munster, and because their coasts are gentler than those of Connacht and
northern Ulster, these are the provinces which were most heavily settled and
most often invaded. The cities have all grown up around natural harbors:
Dublin in Leinster, Cork and Limerick in Munster, Belfast and Derry in Ulster;
most of the larger towns, Galway, Sligo, and Waterford, for example, are also
ports. In fact, there is no town in Ireland today with a population of more
than 20,000 which is not on the sea. Nevertheless, the Irish have never been
great sailors, and the fishing industry is still undeveloped. Nor are the Irish
really city folk. Today, Dublin, with a population of more than 700,000,
contains more than a quarter of the inhabitants of the Irish Republic, but in the
island as a whole more than 60 percent of the population lives on farms, in
villages, or in towns with fewer than 10,000 residents. Northern Ireland is
fairly heavily industrialized, but in the Republic only a few cities have much
major industry. Instead, life centers on the farm and the market town.

Life centered on the farm and market town in 1885, too, but the Ireland in which Yeats and John O'Leary first met was in several important ways a different country from the Ireland of today. Then, the British Union Jack flew over all of Ireland rather than just the six counties of Northern Ireland. Then, most of the land was owned by Protestant landlords rather than the farmers who actually worked it. Then, something close to 60,000 people were emigrating from Ireland each year. The Ireland of 1885 was neither prosperous nor happy, but many of the millions who emigrated from Ireland during the nineteenth century would have preferred to stay at home. That they could not was, ultimately, the result of a human and economic disaster, the terrible famine of the 1840s and its aftermath.

The famine that raged through Ireland from 1845 until 1850 was one of those overpowering events almost impossible to comprehend after the fact. The basic history of those tragic years is simple enough. Although Ireland produced other crops, the potato was the basic staple of the diet, especially among the poor; the potato crop failed partially because of blight in 1845. It failed utterly in 1846. Typhus, dysentery, and scurvy killed thousands of the hungry. In 1847 the blight seemed to relent, but the next year it returned in full force, and again the potato crop was lost. Perhaps a million people died of starvation and disease, while hundreds of thousands, often the young, the strong, and the bright, emigrated to Britain and America. By 1851 one person in four of those who had been in Ireland ten years before was gone. The government attempted relief, as did charitable organizations, but these efforts were grossly inadequate, and, in the long run, probably only increased the suffering. The 1840s were hungry years in Britain, too, and the British Prime Minister, Peel, did not dare stop the export of needed grain from Ireland. Consequently, hungry peasants had to watch as the grain was taken from their land to the seaports, sometimes under armed guard, to be sold for profit overseas.

These cold facts are the things historians tell us about, but what burned into the imagination of the Irish people was not facts and figures but a hideous everyday reality. In December of 1846, before the famine was even at its worst, a Cork magistrate, Mr. Nicholas Cummins, paid a visit to the town of Skibbereen and the area around it; horrified by what he had seen, he sent a public letter to the Duke of Wellington, himself an Irishman, Britain's great military hero, and a leader of the Tory party. Mr. Cummins reported that in the first house he visited "six famished and ghastly skeletons, to all appearances dead, were huddled in a corner on some filthy straw, their sole covering what seemed a ragged horsecloth, their wretched legs hanging about, naked above the

extremely powerful figures in a culture which was highly conservative, respect-
ful of the spoken word, and concerned that self-identity and corporate identity—
both defined by law, memory, and legend—not be lost.

By the time Caesar defeated the Celts in Gaul, Celtic civilization on the
European continent was on the defensive, and gradually the Celts were driven
back to the Atlantic edges of Western Europe. In France, the Romans subdued
them and later the Franks pushed them back into Brittany; in Britain, the
Anglo-Saxons eventually forced them back into Wales and parts of Scotland.
But Ireland remained essentially untouched, its continuous Celtic civilization
lasting long after the fall of Rome. Nevertheless, the fifth century after Christ
brought a fundamental change in Irish culture; the agents of that change were
Christianity and St. Patrick. There were already enough Christians in Ireland
by 431 to make it necessary to appoint a bishop for them, but it was St.
Patrick who remains the great symbol of the Christianization of the country.
Patrick was a native of Roman Britain; at sixteen, Irish raiders took him to
their country where they made him a slave for six years. Eventually, he escaped
from slavery, but a vision soon sent him back to Ireland as a missionary. We
cannot be entirely sure when he returned (432 and 462 are both plausible
dates), but he spent some thirty years preaching, teaching, and founding
churches and monasteries. Most of the legends about him are probably untrue,
but he, his disciples, and other Christian teachers transformed the country,
turning it into a bastion of Christian piety.

In terms of later Irish history, the monasteries Patrick and the others
founded were centrally important, and by the end of the sixth century there
were monasteries all over the country from Glendalough in its pleasant valley to
Aran on the wild west coast. The monasteries in Ireland were quite unlike those
on the continent. Instead of living in a communal residence, the monks built
individual cells, and the Irish monks emphasized solitary contemplation and
solitary labor considerably more than their European brethren. Discipline was
exceedingly strict, and the Irish monks soon became famous even outside
Ireland for their piety and enthusiasm. From early times the monks were much
given to wandering, seeking secluded spots in Ireland and in Europe for morti-
fication, self-sacrifice, and prayer. St. Columba went to Scotland as early as
563, while his namesake, Columbanus, went as far as Italy where he founded
a monastery at Bobbio in 613. As the years passed, the monks in Ireland and
abroad mastered the art of illumination, the technique of making beautifully
illustrated manuscripts, and the Book of Kells together with dozens of other
manuscripts are still a glowing testimony to their piety and sense of beauty.

For a few centuries, Irish Christianity was a light in a darkened Europe; King Alfred welcomed the Irish monks who washed up on his English shore, and Charlemagne was delighted by the learning they brought to his court. At home, Irish Christianity remained highly idiosyncratic with its emphasis on monasticism at the expense of parochial and diocesan organization and its unconventional ecclesiastical calendar, but we owe the monks a great debt for their willingness to transcribe the traditional literature of Celtic Ireland and for the churches, towers, and high crosses they built all over the island.

Yet even as Irish Christianity was exerting a powerful influence on Europe, invasions of Ireland were beginning again. The Vikings came in the end of the eighth century, despoiling the monasteries of their wealth and causing havoc among the people. Ireland, still politically disunified, was unable to fight them off, and gradually the Norsemen turned from regular raids to trading and establishing settlements. They founded Dublin in 840, Waterford, Wexford, Cork, and Limerick soon thereafter; in fact, most of Ireland's ports were originally Viking towns. The Irish tried to resist them, and gradually Norse power receded until Brian Boru, who had forced many of the local Irish rulers to acknowledge him as overlord, defeated them decisively at the battle of Clontarf in 1014. Although Brian was killed in the battle, before it took place he had also established himself as the high-king of Ireland, and his defeat of the Vikings was no more important than the measure of political unity he brought to the country. Three families fought for the high-kingship after his death, but the defeat of the Vikings and the new sense of political unity gave Ireland about a century and a half of relative peace—not really good times, perhaps, but a breathing spell.

Still, dissension among the local warlords remained, and it finally helped bring about the first invasion from England and the first attempt to establish English hegemony in Ireland. In 1152 Dermot MacMurrough, the warrior king of Leinster, abducted Devorgilla, the wife of Teirnan O'Rourke. Although O'Rourke recaptured his wife the next year, he waited until 1166 for his final revenge on MacMurrough, when he attacked his town and destroyed his palace. MacMurrough then went with a few followers to England's Henry II. Anxious to find allies to help him get revenge on O'Rourke, MacMurrough made himself Henry's vassal in exchange for a promise of Norman support in Ireland. Henry himself did not come to Ireland then, but he encouraged his followers in Britain to go, and gradually many of the Norman warriors realized that they could make their fortunes there. MacMurrough gave his daughter, Aoife, to the leader of the Normans, Richard FitzGilbert de Clare, "Strongbow," and it was

Strongbow and his Norman warriors who became a new and frightening power in Irish affairs. The Norman warriors, like so many invaders before them, settled in to stay, building stone guard towers and castles throughout much of the country, and turning parts of Ireland into an Anglo-Norman colony. Gradually, the Normans themselves were partially absorbed into the country like so many invaders before them, becoming eventually the "Old English." They and the Gaelic aristocracy lived together in an on-again, off-again peace; much of the east of the Ireland became Anglicized, most of the west remained Gaelic.

Some of the subsequent English kings took little interest in the island they supposedly ruled, but in the sixteenth century the Tudor monarchs began to think seriously about what to do with Ireland. In 1541 Henry VIII had himself declared King of Ireland, becoming the first English king to carry that title, and Henry, anxious for power to be centralized in his own hands, began to devise ways to break the power of the Anglo-Irish aristocracy as well as the Gaelic. By the 1580s his daughter, Elizabeth I, concerned by the continuing infighting in Ireland and the fact that it was a Catholic island entirely too close to her Protestant England, began to take an active hand in Irish affairs. Edmund Spenser, the English poet, was only one of many Englishmen sent over to help subdue the natives; Spenser found the countryside beautiful but the Irish savages, and he was not the only Englishman to have his house burned by rebels. Rebellion was especially common in Ulster until 1603, when Hugh O'Neill, the Irish leader, and his followers were finally defeated. That defeat was the last gasp of the old Gaelic aristocracy; O'Neill, his brother, and their families fled from Ireland, thus opening the way for a new solution to the nagging Irish question by James I, Elizabeth's successor. The new solution was an attempt, quite simply, to repopulate Ulster with people loyal to the crown. Many of the Irish were expelled from the province; land was confiscated in six of Ulster's nine counties and then given out on cheap rents to Protestant tenants. Some people from England and many from Scotland came to take advantage of this "Plantation of Ulster," and they introduced a new way of life into Ireland. The earlier invaders from Britain had been aristocrats; these people were farmers, and they cleared the forests, built towns, villages, churches, and schools, turning parts of Ulster from Ireland's wildest province into neat, prosperous townlands. Thus was founded the Scots-Irish colony that has played so tragic a role in Irish history and such an important one in American.

Bloodshed and terror marked the seventeenth century in Ireland, and after James I's son, Charles I, was defeated in the English Civil War, the victorious

Oliver Cromwell used an even more drastic means than repopulation to deal with the recurring Irish problem. Catholic Ireland had stayed essentially loyal to the crown during the Civil War, and in 1649 Cromwell came to settle accounts. The Catholic citizens of Drogheda and Wexford were massacred in retaliation for massacres of Protestants in Ulster, but all over the country people were killed, towns and churches destroyed. Catholic landholders who had fought against Cromwell were dispossessed of their property; landowners who had not actually fought against the new regime were moved off their estates and given land in barren Connacht or County Clare instead. The Cromwellian settlement was not all-inclusive, but it furthered the breakdown of Gaelic Ireland. A significant portion of the old Gaelic aristocracy had left Ireland after the defeat of O'Neill at Kinsale in 1603; after the confiscations of 1652–53, the stabilizing power of the Catholic gentry, Gaelic and Old English, began to go. Peasant Ireland was left in place, but with a new aristocracy of English soldiers and gentlemen of fortune to rule it.

The last battle of Gaelic Ireland against English rule came some forty years later. A second revolution in England, the "Glorious Revolution" of 1688, displaced James II, the last Stuart king and the last Catholic to sit on the English throne. After James was deposed, he fled to Catholic Ireland where Dublin welcomed him as the rightful Irish king. When he tried to claim authority over the entire island, however, Protestant Ulster rebelled. The apprentices of Londonderry closed the gates of their city against him, and for fifteen weeks his army laid siege to the town. During the siege, his son-in-law, the new English king, William III, had time to raise an army to invade Ireland. At the Battle of the Boyne, on July 1, 1690, he defeated James so thoroughly that he fled to France, leaving Ireland to William, but, led by Patrick Sarsfield, the Irish kept up a guerrilla war against the victorious Protestant monarch. The Irish were defeated in a bloodbath at Aughrim in July of the next year; Sarsfield then fell back on Limerick, defending it under siege for six weeks. After Sarsfield finally surrendered, he and about eleven thousand of his followers, the best of that generation of Irishmen, fled abroad to become soldiers of fortune.

This "Flight of the Wild Geese" left Ireland open entirely to English mastery and Protestant domination. The new Protestant English aristocracy, the Anglo-Irish Ascendancy, was firmly in control of an island which now became a virtual colony of Great Britain. Since Gaelic Catholics made up the vast majority of the population, the new ruling class realized that its power could be insured only by stringent religious and economic measures. Catholics were excluded from the Irish Parliament in 1692, and three years later the first of a long series of "penal laws" intended to hold the Irish majority in check went into effect. Catholic bishops were exiled on the belief that without bishops to ordain them, the priests and their religion would eventually vanish. The Catholic laity was excluded from participation in government, the army, and the legal profession. No Catholic could keep a school, own a firearm, or keep a horse worth more than £5. Catholics could not buy land or lease it for more than a fairly short period; by requiring that the property a Catholic owned be divided among his sons at his death, unless one of them became Protestant, the old Catholic estates were made to grow smaller and smaller. Technically, the practice of the Catholic faith was not forbidden, and Catholics retained a few civil liberties, but many priests refused to register with the government as was required and, in effect, went underground. Yet the faith of Ireland could not be broken: new churches, "chapels" they had to be called because only the buildings of the Protestant Church of Ireland could be given the name "church," went up behind storefronts; courageous priests and bishops came back from exile in Europe to reform and restaff a church which had fallen into ecclesiastical disorder during the seventeenth century; the old tradition of Irish learning may have grown tenuous during the eighteenth century, but Irish piety remained and grew more intense under persecution. Nevertheless, the "penal laws" were an apparent success. The Anglo-Irish landlords prospered, and Ireland had more peace than she had enjoyed for centuries; there was no significant rebellion against English rule for more than a hundred years after the Battle of the Boyne. The almost feudal control of the Ascendancy over the land meant that peasants were required to pay rents to their landlords and tithes to the Protestant church according to an inflexible timetable, whether or not these payments were realistic in terms of what was actually earned. Landlords could arrange short leases and could evict almost at whim; the rights of the peasants to transfer the land they leased were severely restricted.

Ireland became in the eighteenth century three nations. The nation of the Catholic peasants was poor, unstable, and oppressed; life for them was often brutal and degrading as they tried to raise enough on their patchy farms to pay the tithes and rents and have something left over, often only potatoes, to feed themselves. The nation of the Ascendancy, on the other hand, enjoyed a world of exploitation and luxury. Some landlords were absentees who lived in England, but those who stayed in Ireland built the Georgian great houses which still can be seen around the country, and they became a squirearchy not unlike that Fielding portrays in England in *Tom Jones*. There was always something a little crude and raw about the Ascendancy, but Dublin gradually became a beautiful city full of handsome townhouses and such imposing public buildings as the Four Courts, the Customs House, and the Irish Parliament (now the Bank of Ireland). It was a city full of rakes, fashion, and elegance, and Anglo-Ireland sent a succession of remarkable men across the Irish Sea to make their reputations in London—Congreve, Sheridan, Burke, Goldsmith among them. Until 1744 the dean of Dublin's Protestant cathedral, St. Patrick's, was that most astonishing of prelates, Jonathan Swift, and in Swift we can see some of the tensions in the Ireland of his time. As a Protestant, he despised the Catholicism which surrounded him; as a gentleman who had known London, he sometimes scoffed at provincial Dublin's pretensions to grandeur. Nevertheless, Swift was a true patriot who made himself see what most members of his class refused to see—that Ireland was a miserable country. He supported the "penal laws," but vigorously attacked the poverty which they helped create and the landlord class which benefitted from them. One of his pamphlets, "A Modest Proposal," suggests that since the Catholic peasants had nothing else, they might well try selling their children for food as a way to get some income: "this food will be somewhat dear, and therefore very proper for Landlords, who, as they have already devoured most of the Parents, seem to have the best Title to the Children."[4] Swift's fame as a patriot came largely, though, from his "Drapier's Letters," vitriolic attacks on an attempt by the English to debase the Irish coinage. Attempts to restrict Irish trade in such ways occurred repeatedly, and they were of the greatest concern to the merchants and small businessmen.

This third Ireland, the Ireland of the shopkeepers, made up a small part of the population, but played an important role in the eighteenth century and later. As Dublin, Belfast, and other towns gradually developed into strong manufacturing and trading centers, the Protestant and Catholic middle classes grew larger and more powerful. Towards the end of the eighteenth century, both Ascendancy and the middle class became restive under the continuing colonial status. In 1782, as Britain was reeling from the loss of her empire in America, Ascendancy leaders secured the establishment of an independent Irish Parliament in Dublin; there had been some sort of Irish parliament for centuries, but under this new system Ireland was, theoretically at least, an independent kingdom sharing a monarch with Britain. Nevertheless, British rule had only become Ascendancy rule, and the two were largely interchangeable. Some middle-class leaders, excited by the ideals of the French revolution, wanted more than this

---

4 *The Prose Works of Jonathan Swift*, edited by Herbert Davis (Oxford: Blackwell, 1955), X, 112.

titular independence, and they wanted social reform. A young Protestant lawyer, Theobald Wolfe Tone, argued, Dublin parliament notwithstanding, that Ireland was still essentially a British colony and would be until two under-privileged groups in Irish society, the Catholics and the middle class, cooperated in a program of reform and emancipation from the "penal laws." Tone was a founder of the United Irishmen, a group seeking Catholic emancipation, re-form, and real independence. Working with republican France, which was then at war with Britain, the United Irishmen staged a rebellion in 1798. A small French fleet landed at Killala in Connacht, but its soldiers were defeated soon after they landed, and the revolt itself failed. With painful irony, Wolfe Tone's rebellion produced just the opposite effect from what he had hoped. Alarmed by unrest in Ireland, the British Prime Minister, Pitt, cajoled and bribed the Irish Parliament into putting itself out of business; an Act of Union was passed, and in 1801 Ireland joined Britain in the United Kingdom of Great Britain and Ireland.

It took more than a century to overturn the Act of Union. Irish history in the nineteenth century could be described as a continuing debate over who would govern Ireland and who would own its land. At first, it seemed that Britain was more thoroughly in control than ever in the past. The Anglo-Irish Ascendancy continued to own the land; Ireland was governed from London through a viceroy in Dublin and an English and Anglo-Irish bureaucracy. But Ireland was given a hundred or so seats in the British Parliament, and some Irish politicians, even early in the century, saw them as a powerful weapon. So long as those seats remained exclusively in Protestant hands, Catholic Ireland could turn only to violence as a means of gaining power, but if Catholics could be permitted to sit in Parliament, then those Parliamentary seats could be used to exert some real influence. In 1823 Daniel O'Connell, a Catholic lawyer, founded the Catholic Association to bring about that desired electoral reform. The worst of the old "penal laws" were gone by then, and Catholics had the vote. In 1828 the voters in County Clare used that privilege to elect O'Connell himself to Parliament. This brought the issue of Catholic emancipation to the decisive stage, and the British government caved in, changing the law so that Catholic O'Connell could take his seat.

Catholic emancipation was a major development in Irish politics because it meant that the majority of the population began to have an active voice in government; nevertheless, it also pointed to some serious problems. To win his point, O'Connell had organized Irish mass opinion very effectively, but no one, including O'Connell, could be certain that he could control the masses he led.

Moreover, Catholic emancipation was a political rather than an economic development, and even Catholic members of the British Parliament would not be strong enough to change the old economic pattern of landlord control. Finally, any failure in the gradualist means O'Connell had used would almost certainly lead to a renewed interest in violence and revolution as a way for Ireland to rid itself of British domination. O'Connell had, in other words, upped the ante in Irish politics, and the new game turned out to be a very dangerous one. O'Connell himself learned this in the 1840s when he led a movement for repeal of the Act of Union; his "monster demonstrations" in favor of repeal eventually terrified the British authorities. O'Connell was jailed, and his repeal movement collapsed. During the agitation, O'Connell came into conflict with a younger generation of patriots, the members of a group called "Young Ireland" and associated with a weekly newspaper, the *Nation,* founded in 1842 to aid the repeal movement. The Young Ireland movement of Thomas Davis, Charles Gavan Duffy, John Mitchel, and James Fintan Lalor did not last long, but, in a sense, these men were the first real Irish nationalists, and each of them had a lasting influence on Irish history.

O'Connell and Young Ireland quarreled essentially over the methods of gaining repeal; they wanted more drastic measures than he was willing to undertake. Davis, strongly influenced by the rising nationalism in Europe, was the first great prophet of Irish nationalism, and his vision of a united Ireland undivided by religion or ethnic background became a powerful idea for generations that followed. In the past, O'Connell had worked closely with the English parties in the British Parliament, but Gavan Duffy advocated a policy of remaining independent of both Whigs and Tories; this notion of parliamentary independence was one which the Irish members of Parliament later learned to use very effectively. John Mitchel, on the other hand, insisted that parliamentary politics were not enough; Irish independence could only be won by rebellion and "physical force." Lalor, himself the son of a farmer, wrote an important series of letters to the *Nation* and other newspapers in which he argued that the question of who would possess the land was a more crucial one than the matter of political independence. The *Nation* became the first articulate voice of the new nationalism in Ireland, and in the varying tactics of Young Ireland we can see the seeds of subsequent attempts to resolve the perennial Irish question. From Davis' ideas came all those who stressed the sense of Irishness above everything else; from Gavan Duffy came the tactics of generations of Irish members of Parliament. Mitchel and Lalor represent something more potent than political manoeuvre; Mitchel's insistence on armed uprising would remain the possibility, the eventual solution, when political pressure failed, while Lalor's focus on land possession reminded his readers then and later generations that political independence without economic independence would be meaningless.

The Young Ireland movement itself collapsed after an abortive armed uprising in 1848, but that rebellion was almost insignificant in the face of the famine which had ravaged Ireland in the preceding years. We have already looked at the way in which the famine became a watershed in Irish history, but it should be added that it simply made the economic and political situations that much more unstable. That the famine could occur at all was a result of the ramshackle economy which had developed in Ireland after the Napoleanic wars. Ireland in the eighteenth century had not been the most poverty-stricken country in Europe, and it could be argued that around 1800 Ireland was actually in very good shape economically. A century and more of peace had brought prosperity to the port towns, and linen making had become a major industry. Roads and canals had been built, as well. Even so, the economic situation in rural Ireland was not good. Landlords, emulating the style of their English brethren, tended to live beyond their means, and the landlords rarely encouraged their tenants to make better use of the land they worked. During the Napoleanic wars, Ireland was encouraged to produce grain to feed a Britain economically strained by a wartime agriculture. Grain became the cash crop for Irish farmers, the crop that paid rents and tithes, while the potato, easy to grow and nutritious, became the base of the Irish diet. In wartime prosperity, many farmers subdivided their land, leasing small patches out to poor laborers who needed only enough ground to plant potatoes to feed themselves and their families. After a century and more of peace, the population of Ireland was increasing rapidly. The increase in the early nineteenth century was frighteningly Malthusian: 5 million Irish people in 1800, 6½ million in 1821; 8 million in 1841.

All that prepared the way for economic disaster; the blight that killed the potatoes only brought the disaster on more quickly and terribly than anyone could have expected. In retrospect, one wonders why the Young Ireland rebellion of 1848 failed; surely it would have been as well to die in a battle against British troops as to starve by the roadside. But the rebellion did fail, and Ireland immediately after the famine was a pathetically demoralized country. Those who had suffered worst were, of course, the poor—the thousands of people who had never had homes of their own, and the thousands of small farmers who had access only to enough land to feed themselves scantily in even the best of times. The economic effects of the famine could be seen in the crowded "coffin ships" that carried hundreds of thousands of emigrants to England and America. The effects could be seen, too, in the staggering increase in the numbers of people so poor that they could do little but wander the roads or enter the grim workhouses; in 1849 almost a million people in Ireland, a sixth of the population, were virtual beggars. Ireland was to remain a desperately poor country for most of the rest of the century. For at least two decades after the famine it remained politically stagnant as well. Irish emigrants in New York and Irishmen in Dublin founded a secret organization to foment rebellion in 1858, the Irish Republican Brotherhood, but the rebellion this Fenian movement led in 1867 was a failure. For all the nationalistic talk and all the raising of money to buy arms, nothing seemed to change the facts of life of landlordism, urban slums, and rural poverty.

Nevertheless, political change was coming, if very slowly. William Ewart Gladstone, a leader of the British Liberal party, had found his conscience stirred by the Fenian rising and Gladstone's conscience was a powerful thing. When he took office as Prime Minister the next year, he intended to do something to ameliorate conditions in Ireland. He led the way to disestablishment of the Church of Ireland, thus finally freeing Catholics from the burden of paying tithes to a church they did not attend, and in 1870, he introduced an act which brought the first slight reform in the conditions of tenant farmers. Its protections against eviction were ineffective, but they were a step in the right direction. Meanwhile, the effort to solve the constitutional problem of the Act of Union was aided in 1870 by the founding of a home-rule movement by Isaac Butt, a Dublin lawyer. Thanks to the introduction of the secret ballot in 1872, Butt's party won more than half the Irish seats in Parliament in the next election. What Butt advocated was not necessarily complete Irish independence but a situation in which Ireland would administer its own internal affairs, and "home rule" became an attractive idea indeed. Butt was a good parliamentarian; he was not a charismatic leader. His successor as leader of the Irish Party, Charles Stewart Parnell, was; with the advent of Parnell, the postfamine political stagnation ended and new Ireland began to emerge.

Like so many Irish leaders before him, Parnell was a Protestant, the son of a landowner in County Wicklow. Initially a poor public speaker, he made himself into a powerful orator; fundamentally conservative, he mastered the technique of seeming to be an extremist while still using politic caution. A brilliant political operator, he organized most of the Irish members of Parliament into an effective coalition and found an ally in Gladstone, again the

British Prime Minister. Or, rather Gladstone found a tool in Parnell, for Gladstone realized that Parnell was the only Irish leader through whom some solution to the Irish problem could be realized. When in 1885 an election produced a situation in which Gladstone had to depend on Parnell's Irish party for support to stay in office, he introduced a bill which would have provided a limited amount of home rule. But Gladstone's own Liberal party refused to support its chief; in 1886 enough Liberals voted against the Home Rule bill to defeat it, drive Gladstone from office, and by the establishment of a Conservative government, eliminate the possibility of Home Rule for several years. Even so, moderate nationalists rightly saw in Gladstone's conversion to Home Rule a clear sign that an amelioration of the Irish situation was in sight. Gladstone, they knew, would remain committed to their cause, and that meant not only a political advantage but, perhaps more important, a moral advantage. At the same time, the radical groups which advocated armed rebellion tended to be discredited by Parnell's successes. John O'Leary, for example, an aggressive old republican, sensed that the moment for his kind of political action was passing and turned to sponsoring literary groups.

Meanwhile, the question of the control of the land remained, literally, a burning issue. Ever since the famine, the warfare between the peasants who worked the land and the landlords who owned it had been fierce. Evictions remained distressingly frequent, as did rural violence, and the tenants rightly demanded what was called "The Three F's," fair rent, fixed tenure, and free sale, basic safeguards of tenant farmers in most western European countries but unguaranteed in Ireland. In Michael Davitt, they found a leader of immense courage and resource. Davitt's Land League organized the tenants to campaign against the landlords, Davitt himself working against the tradition of rural violence by preaching peaceable means of protest. His work produced results in 1881, after a "Land War." The Second Land Act assured that fair rents would be determined by special tribunals, that no tenant could be evicted if he paid his rent on time, and that aid would come from the government in buying the land tenants worked. The Land Act provided only a modest beginning of agrarian reform, but it was an important step in the establishment of economic justice in rural Ireland.

The Ireland in which the literary revival began was, then, a troubled land with far too long a history of injustice and far too strong a tendency to look to the past. Optimists could have felt, though, that Ireland was finally beginning to come out of the long night of chaos and disaster. Education was improving; the economic situation was deteriorating less rapidly; in Parnell, moderate nationalism had found a powerfully effective leader; and in Davitt, the rural proletariat had found a leader who was able to free it from the injustices of the past and, also, from its own mythology of violence. But it is a truism of politics that when an oppressed society begins to feel some liberation it will begin to demand more and more; the achievements of the recent past will not satisfy. And that is precisely what happened in Ireland. The Anglo-Irish landlords may have known as early as Catholic Emancipation in 1829 that their days as a ruling class were numbered, but it was the events of the seventies which told them that in no uncertain terms. Increasingly, they seemed to lose faith in themselves and in their caste; what had been a fairly firm consensus of political and social views as late as the famine years began to fall apart. Protestants in Ulster began to be increasingly frightened by the power which the Catholic majority in the remainder of the island demonstrated it could employ effectively. Out on the farms or in the urban slums things may have been much as they had always been for the peasants and the poor who made up the majority of the Catholic population, but acute observers knew that radical change was coming. The economic and social situation since 1691 had enforced a kind of stability on Ireland, or, at least, a kind of stagnation, but that could not last. Irishmen at home were slowly polarizing into groupings— Protestant/Catholic, peasant/landlord, unionist/nationalist—which eventually had to produce a realignment of the realities of Irish life and would probably produce that realignment in violence. There was too much money coming in from Irishmen overseas to support political agitation at home, too little imag- ination in the ruling classes, too many social imbalances for it to be otherwise.

The sense that change had to come was fundamental to the development of the Irish literary revival. Young Ireland, in the 1840s, had been devoted to a cause which had little chance of political success, and that, as much as a lack of talent, had doomed it as a literary movement. But, somehow, in the 1880s it finally seemed that history was on the side of Irish nationalism and, also, on the side of Irish writing. The writers could not avoid the burden of Irish history, and no writer of any significance sought to avoid it, but increasingly the writers, and ordinary Irishmen as well, began to sense that Irish history was not so much a burden as a powerful weapon. Gladstone spoke of the treatment of Ireland as the blackest stain on British history; Irishmen began to sense that the long litany of defeat and martyrdom could be turned to potent moral effect. Ireland in the 1880s was, without quite knowing it, a prerevolutionary society, precisely the sort of society which can, if the chemistry works, produce literary explosions as well as political.

3

Before the Irish Renaissance
Literature in Gaelic and English

> The poets of Ireland one day were gathered around
> Senchán Torpéist, to see if they could recall the
> 'Táin Bó Cúailnge' in its entirety. But they all
> said they knew only parts of it.
>
> from *The Tain*, translated by Thomas Kinsella

ACCORDING TO AN ANCIENT TALE, the greatest Irish saga, the *Táin*, was only remembered in fragments when Senchán Torpéist the poet sent out two of his disciples to try to recover it whole. The disciples succeeded in recovering the complete saga, not by reading it in a book or finding a learned man who could tell it to them, but by stopping at the grave of Fergus mac Roich, one of the heroes of the old tale. As one of them chanted by his grave, Fergus' ghost arose "in fierce majesty" and recited "how everything had happened, from start to finish."[1] This legend of the recovery of the *Táin* embodies a basic experience in literary Ireland, the act of recapturing the past, and Yeats and the others who began the Irish Renaissance had a good deal in common with those disciples of Senchán a thousand years ago. They, too, went out, found ghosts from the past, and recovered their lost inheritance.

Their literary inheritance was an extraordinarily rich one involving two different literatures in two different languages: Gaelic and English. The Gaelic heritage went back more than twelve centuries and included everything from ancient sagas, tales, and poems to the folklore which was still current in the west of Ireland. The English or Anglo-Irish inheritance went back only about two centuries, and in quality it was much inferior to the Gaelic. Even so, Yeats and the others were committed to writing an Irish literature in English, and they had to learn to deal with the Anglo-Irish tradition as well as the Gaelic. The Irish Renaissance in unique among nineteenth-century nationalist literary move-

---

[1] *The Tain*, translated by Thomas Kinsella (London: Oxford Univ. Press, 1970), pp. 1-2.

ments in that its writers mostly chose to use something other than the traditional language of their country. It is impossible to imagine a Tolstoy or a Dostoevsky choosing to write in the French of the Russian aristocracy rather than in Russian, but the Irish writers were faced with a more complex linguistic problem. The traditional language of Ireland, Gaelic, was virtually dead by 1880; millions of people had spoken it before the Famine, but, by the time Yeats began to write, only about one person in a hundred in Ireland was exclusively Gaelic-speaking. Yeats himself did not know the language, and he rightly observed that "Gaelic is my national tongue, but it is not my mother tongue."[2] Like many of the other writers of the first generation of the Irish Renaissance, he came out of an Anglo-Irish background which was openly contemptuous of Gaelic. "A gentleman does not speak Gaelic" was a basic rule of Anglo-Irish life, and Edward Dowden, the distinguished professor of English literature at Trinity College, was only reflecting the opinion of his class when he commented in 1882 that "I am infinitely glad that I spent my early enthusiasm on Wordsworth and Spenser and Shakespeare and not on anything that Ireland ever produced."[3] Dowden was a friend of Yeats's father, and Yeats himself grew up reading Shakespeare, Shelley, and Blake. To people of their class, Gaelic literature was the preserve of scholars, most of them foreigners, who examined it for its philological or anthropological interest, and the Irish literature in English was crude and vulgar, consisting, it seemed, mostly of comic tales and absurdly patriotic poems.

Yeats discovered Anglo-Irish literature under the influence of John O'Leary, O'Leary playing the role of Fergus' ghost for him. Through the books the old man lent him, he discovered that Ireland in the nineteenth century had produced a fairly extensive literature in English. There had been many Irish-born writers in English in the eighteenth century, of course, but a *national* literature in English had developed only with the rise of nationalism itself in the nineteenth century. Maria Edgeworth's *Castle Rackrent* (1800) was the first real Irish novel of any quality, while Anglo-Irish poetry began with popular ballads and the sentimental songs of Thomas Moore, Edgeworth's contemporary. There had been dozens of Irish novels and hundreds of Irish poems since, but Yeats and even O'Leary, for all their nationalistic enthusiasm, knew that most of it was very poor stuff indeed. The problem for the writers of Yeats's generation was not only to write better than their predecessors in

---

[2] *Essays and Introductions* (London: Macmillan, 1961), p. 520.

[3] E. D. and H. M. Dowden, eds., *The Letters of Edward Dowden* (London: Dent, 1914), pp. 183–84.

English but also to write in what seemed a more genuinely Irish way. The Anglo-Irish literature of the nineteenth century was too full of sentimentality, uncritical patriotism, and crude exploitation of the local scene to be a strong foundation for a new Irish literature in English.

Gaelic literature, on the other hand, had all the things Anglo-Irish literature lacked: a long tradition of superb craftsmanship, a wealth of fresh stories, situations, characters, and images, and what was, by definition, an Irish point of view. The great problem with Gaelic, of course, was that even in its modern form it was an unknown and very difficult tongue for Yeats or anyone else who had not grown up in a Gaelic-speaking home, and the older forms of the language, in which most of the best literature was written, were spectacularly complicated. Standish O'Grady's *History of Ireland* (1878) provided one entry into the imaginative world of Gaelic literature and the scholarly translators of the old writings provided others, but these could never take the place of a first-hand knowledge. Nevertheless, the encounter with the Gaelic tradition was the first great discovery of the Irish Renaissance—and many of the writers described the encounter almost as though it were a religious conversion—but the inheritance from the literary past posed serious problems for all of them. Given their ignorance of Gaelic, the difficulty of learning it, and the fact that most Irish people did not understand it anyway, how could the Gaelic inheritance best be used? It was probably quixotic to write in Gaelic, but was it possible to use material from the language in English in such a way that it kept its essential Irishness? Given the weakness of the Anglo-Irish tradition and the close proximity of Ireland to Britain, how could a new Anglo-Irish literature be created which would be still distinctively Irish and imaginatively fresh? Finally, how could the new techniques in European literature which were neither Irish nor British be adapted? There were no easy answers to these questions, and no committee could sit down to work out solutions. Instead, each writer had to come to his own way of dealing with the problems. Yeats, for example, during a very long career moved from poems in something like the old Anglo-Irish style through a mixture of Celtic imagery and French symbolist technique eventually to a final style which had some of the vigor and compression of Gaelic folksong. Synge combined an extensive knowledge of European dramatic technique with folklore from Wicklow, Kerry, and Aran. Lady Gregory, always closer to the ordinary life of Gaelic-speaking Ireland than most of her contemporaries, adapted the English and the experience of her part of County Galway to the form of the French farce in some of her best work. Joyce found in Continental symbolism and naturalism methods to embody much of the popular culture of the Ireland of his time, while the masters of the Irish short story have often used Turgenev and Checkhov as models for stories which still speak with the distinctive voice of provincial Ireland.

All of these techniques were, metaphorically, ways of giving English-speaking Ireland a distinctive literary language. In spite of the problems posed by a bilingual tradition, most Irish writers have benefitted from the fact that theirs is a highly verbal and indeed highly oral culture. The Irish are, proverbially, great talkers, and the visitor from abroad is always impressed by the fluency and brilliance of Irish conversation, and also by the curious way English is used in Ireland. Even among non-Gaelic speakers in Ireland, the syntax of Gaelic is never too far away. English pronounciation, inflection, and sentence construction in Ireland all owe something to the Gaelic heritage. In fact, there are several English dialects in Ireland. The most distinctive are the clipped and Scots-influenced dialect of Ulster, the heavily Gaelicized English of Connemara, and "Anglo-Irish," really a new dialect created about the time of the Famine by the wholesale shift of Gaelic-speakers to English. This "Anglo-Irish," with its Gaelic grammar and English vocabulary, became something close to the standard dialect of modern Irish drama and can be found in differing forms in the plays of Synge and Lady Gregory. A less distinctive dialect, but a no less real one, comes out of the midlands of Ireland and may be found in the plays of Padraic Colum. Gaelic itself still exists as a spoken and literary language in Ireland, too, although the number of persons who speak it exclusively is very small.

Nevertheless, there is something remarkably tenacious about Gaelic and its literature, and the history of Gaelic literature is a remarkable story of survival and achievement under intense pressure. Irish literature began long before the Celts knew how to read and write. By the fifth century they had developed a primitive script, Ogham, but it was too clumsy to record anything more than simple inscriptions. Instead, early Celtic literature was essentially an oral tradition, one in which stories and poems were handed down by word of mouth for generations. All Celtic peoples had a learned or priestly caste, the druids, one of whose functions was to chant magical invocations. In ancient Ireland, these "literary" men played an enormously important role, and they were carefully divided into classes according to their functions. There were seers or prophets, historians, and eulogists, poets who devoted themselves to praising the leaders of the tribes. The very oldest kinds of Irish literature are the chants which were used for religious purposes, but the descriptive poems about certain locales are very ancient, and a saga such as the *Táin* reflects the life of more than fifteen hundred years ago. Gaelic literature is, in fact, the oldest vernacular literature north of the Alps, and some of the oldest works clearly take us back to a way of life as old or older than Homer's.

Because the poets and storytellers of ancient Ireland had to carry their memories in their heads, they tended to be very conservative about technique. It was their duty to remember, not to innovate, and they found useful mnemonic devices in alliteration and elaborate metrical patterns. Even as late as 1000 A.D., when writing had been known for centuries in Ireland, the young poet still underwent an extensive training in the devices of oral composition and remembrance. He would learn the ancient traditions of his people and the elaborate techniques which permitted him to continue the process of tribal memory. Bardic poems often ran as long as fifty quatrains, and each quatrain was extraordinarily complicated. One common form, *sétna mór*, used the following techniques: within the four lines of the stanza, two words alliterated in each line; there was alliteration between the last word of line one and the first word of line two, as well as the last word of line three and the first of line four; the last word in lines one and three had to have two syllables; the last word in lines two and four had to have three syllables; the first syllable of the last word in lines one and three and the last syllable in the final word in lines two and four had to assonate; finally, every line had to have seven syllables.[4] Anyone who wishes to speak of ancient Gaelic poetry as "primitive" ought to try to write one of those quatrains!

Mnemonic devices such as these may have stifled personal creativity, but the necessity of remembering was considered vastly more important than any single poet's desire to express himself personally. But as a means of remembrance, the best mnemonic devices are always inferior to writing; thus most of ancient Gaelic literature would have been lost to us if the Christian monks had not introduced reading and writing into Ireland, probably during the sixth century. The earliest known Irish manuscripts date from the end of that century. By the end of the seventh century, however, the monasteries had become centers of literary activities. Some of the most attractive poems in the Gaelic of the time, Old Irish, were written by monks, and they also did a splendid job of preserving the traditional literature of Ireland. The eighth and ninth centuries were a golden age of Gaelic literature with an enormous amount of beautiful poetry and many written versions of the old oral literature. Un-

---

[4] This description comes from Patrick C. Power, *A Literary History of Ireland* (Cork: Mercier, 1969), p. 33.

fortunately, the raids of the Vikings interrupted much of this literary activity, and there is no surviving manuscript of Old Irish written before the eleventh century, when the Viking terror had finally abated. In the eleventh and twelfth centuries, however, there was a resurgence of Gaelic literature. The monks did what they could to preserve the older literature they had inherited, but, after the upheavals of the Viking times, much of it came to them in fragmented forms. Too often they stitched narratives together without quite understanding what they were doing; we owe these antiquarians of the eleventh and twelfth centuries a great debt for preserving much of Gaelic storytelling for us, but they often made a mess of what they preserved. While these works of preservation were going on in the monasteries, the traditional poets or bards of the Irish kings remained at work, although their religious functions had been taken over by the Christian priests and monks. The poetry of these professional poets maintained a very high technical level; perhaps it was too high a technical level because some of it is so involuted as to be mechanical and uninteresting. Nevertheless, the period between about 800 and 1200 was the golden age of Gaelic writing. The Irish monks did a great work in preserving sagas and tales that might otherwise have been lost, and the monks in Ireland and those who wandered through Europe created a great deal of fine lyric poetry. Meanwhile, the professional storytellers and poets of the courts continued the development of an ever more complex oral and written literature of remembrance and praise.

There are three major types of early Irish poetry: court poems (panegyrics, epitaphs, satires, and so on) made by the professional poets attached to the tribal kings; religious poetry which derives partially from the Latin poetry then common to all of medieval Europe; and the incidental poems which appear in the prose sagas and romances, or even in the margins of the monks' manuscripts. To the modern reader, these incidental poems are usually the most attractive of all. The court poems often seem a tedious kind of journalism and the overtly religious poetry is often unremarkable, but the little incidental lyrics have the "freshness of spirit and perfection of form" which one distinguished scholar has called hallmarks of all the best of Irish poetry, ancient or modern.[5] As Professor Myles Dillon suggests, these lyric poems, mostly written by monks, deal with three of the basic experiences of the Irish churchmen: contact with nature, life as a hermit, and exile: "The hermit, indeed, rejoices in being alone with nature, and the same ascetic ideal that

[5] Gerard Murphy, quoted in Myles Dillon, "Early Lyric Poetry," *Early Irish Poetry*, edited by James Carney (Cork: Mercier, 1965), p. 9.

inspired the hermits led other monks to go into exile for Christ's sake, *peregrinam ducere vitam.*"[6]

In the nature poetry, there is very little of the fuzziness and yearning which we sometimes associate with the Celtic Twilight. Instead, there is a sense of wonder in the natural world, a sense that the poet is seeing a world freshly created. That is nowhere better felt than in one poet's description of the month of May:

> The wind awakes the woodland's harp,
>   The sail falls and the world's at rest,
> A mist of heat upon the hills
>   And the water full of mist.
>
> The corncrake drones, a bustling bard,
>   The cold cascade that leaps the rock
> Sings of the snugness of the pool,
>   Their season come, the rushes talk.[7]

The love of animal nature was very strong among these poets, as the exquisite "Blackbird of Belfast Lough" shows:

> What little throat
> Has framed that note?
> What gold beak shot
>   It far away?
> A blackbird on
> His leafy throne
> Tossed it alone
>   Across the bay.[8]

The joy in the natural world often turned almost imperceptibly into praise of the hermit life which permitted such close contact with nature. In one of the

---

[6] *Ibid.*, p. 10. Dillon makes essentially the same argument in his fine survey, *Early Irish Literature* (Chicago: University of Chicago Press, 1948), pp. 149ff.

[7] "May," translated by Frank O'Connor in his *Kings, Lords, and Commons* (Dublin: Gill and Macmillan, 1959), p. 18. I have used O'Connor's translations exclusively in this section, but Kuno Meyer and Gerard Murphy, among others, have also provided attractive translations of many of these poems.

[8] *Ibid.*, p. 27.

most beautiful poems in the Gaelic tradition, a hermit, Marbhan, praises his
life to his brother, King Guaire of Gort:

> A hiding tuft, a green-barked yew-tree
>   Is my roof,
> While nearby a great oak keeps me
>   Tempest-proof.
>
> I can pick my fruit from an apple
>   Like an inn,
> Or can fill my fist where hazels
>   Shut me in.[9]

Exile, the "white martyrdom" of living and dying away from friends and
family, is also a constant theme in these poems, and that reminds us that not all
early Irish poetry is cheerful or gentle. We can sympathize with the monk who
wrote in the margin of a manuscript during the Viking invasions:

> Since tonight the wind is high,
> The sea's white mane a fury
> I need not fear the hordes of Hell
> Coursing the Irish Channel.[10]

The court poets, like the monks, knew the sufferings of warfare, and there is
still a shiver in the epitaph one of them wrote for King Hugh of Connacht:

> 'Have you seen Hugh,
> The Connacht king in the field?'
> 'All that we saw
> Was his shadow under his shield.'[11]

The depredations of old age are also a frequent theme, and they are nowhere
better expressed than in the lament of the Old Woman of Beare, now awaiting
death with other hags in a convent:

9 "The Hermit's Song," *ibid.,* p. 7.
10 "Storm at Sea," *ibid.,* p. 22.
11 "The King of Connacht," *ibid.,* p. 44.

For my hands as you may see
Are but bony wasted things,
Hands that once would grasp the hand
Clasp the royal neck of kings.

Oh, my hands as may be seen
Are so scraggy and so thin
That a boy might start in dread
Feeling them about his head.[12]

Early medieval Ireland produced much poetry but none of it is quite so attractive as these lyrics. The religious epics, the praise-poems, the poems on geographical locations were all important, but in these lyrics we can feel and hear the speaking voice, and that makes them especially a part of the continuing tradition of Irish poetry.

The speaking voice is sometimes apparent in the prose writings, too, although the confused transcriptions of so many of them gave us more the impression of a babel of voices. But in spite of the limitations of the pedantic transcribers and the problems caused by the bewildering variety of manuscripts they left, the early Gaelic prose narratives remain the great achievement of the literature, greater even than the poetry. There are scores of stories, myths, legends, and "histories," and the great number of them itself makes them difficult to catalogue. Even so, they may be classified in the following categories:

1. the mythological cycle dealing with the Celtic gods and their relations with men;

2. the stories dealing with the legendary hero, Finn Mac Cumaill, and his followers;

3. satiric writings;

4. narratives of visions and imaginary journeys;

5. stories of the ancient tribal kings, sometimes historical figures, and their deeds;

6. stories of the early Christian saints;

7. the stories which deal with the heroic acts of Cuchulain and the men of Ulster.

Some of these categories are more important than others, but each has something of interest in it, though we should remember that the categories

[12] "The Old Woman of Beare," *ibid.*, p. 35.

themselves are artificial. Often the content of the stories is strikingly primitive—many of these tales are very, very old and go back to prehistoric experience—but their techniques of storytelling are often surprisingly sophisticated. They are full of those often miraculous and sometimes grotesque motifs common to many kinds of folklore: magical weapons, supernatural births, exaggerated genitalia, fantastic physical strength, special charms and incantations. Like the poems, the prose narratives are also full of elaborate oral-formulaic devices, standardized verbal patterns which helped the storyteller remember his material. They often deal with family and tribal relationships, explaining who was who and why things were, frequently in that way which mixes the ordinary and the supernatural that so appealed to primitive men.

The mythological cycle details the relationships of the old pagan gods to men. As one commentator has observed: "In comparison with the other cycles, few tales remain and those which we possess are frequently quite vague. The main trouble with this cycle is its basic lack of human interest. While it is full of fantasy, wonder, magical gods and marvellous exaggerations, it cannot be said to be directly related to human experience. This cycle stands strangely aloof in its bewildering world of primitive wonder and magic."[13] The stories largely deal with the affairs of the Tuatha Dé Danaan, the local gods or "divine magicians" who had supposedly inhabited Ireland in prehistory and had been driven underground to become the fairies of Christian times. The stories tell us, as mythological cycles usually do, about the loves of the gods, the cycle of birth, death, and rebirth, and encounters of mortals with supernatural powers. The most important stories in the group are the "Wooing of Étain," the amazingly complex story of how the beautiful mortal, Étain, was finally won by Midir, the king of the elf-mounds of Brí Léith; "The Second Battle of Moytura," which describes the war between the Tuatha Dé Danaan and their dark enemies, the Fomorians; and "The Children of Lir" which recounts how the children of a chieftain of the Tuatha Dé Danaan were turned into swans.

Like the mythological stories, the cycle centering on Finn Mac Cumaill, his son Oisín, and the adventures of Finn's soldiers, the Fianna, is often full of fantasy, exaggeration, and even grotesque comedy. Finn was, and still is, a folk hero, and the stories about him were composed not for a noble or learned audience, but for the common people.

In the great love story of Diarmuid and Gráinne, for example, he appears as the jealous and cuckolded husband of a beautiful woman much his junior.

---

13 Brendan Kennelly, "Mythology," *Encyclopaedia of Ireland*, edited by Victor Meally (Dublin: Allen Figgis, 1971), p. 400.

Gráinne had married him when he was old and widowed, and she had married him without seeing him. When she did see him, she decided immediately that she wanted a younger and more attractive man. Through magic, she caused Diarmuid to take her away from the marriage feast after she had put Finn and the guests to sleep. When Finn awakened, he pursued them and eventually brought about Diarmuid's death. The magic employed by Gráinne is typical of the Finn stories, and the stories are full, too, of primitive folk beliefs, grotesque exaggerations, and ribald comedy. Finn had a magical thumb which, when he bit it, permitted him to know the truth about any situation. He is almost always described as a figure of gigantic size and strength and sometimes also as a figure of gigantic cowardice. One late story about the Fianna is a good example of the ribald comedy which appears often in this cycle. Finn and his men, including Conán Moal who is often the butt of the humor, had been visiting a fairy dwelling. While there, all became stuck to their seats. When they were released by magical intervention, the skin of Conán's buttocks remained glued to the bench, and he had to use a sheepskin in place of what he had lost. Eventually, he grew enough wool on his bottom to provide stockings for all of his companions! Other stories about the Fianna involve the magical journey of Finn's son, Oisín, to *Tir na nÓg*, the marvel-filled land of youth. There are many versions of this, but the most remarkable is the *Colloquy of the Old Men* which dates from the twelfth century. In it, the last survivors of the Fianna, Oisín and Caoilte, encounter St. Patrick, the representative of the new Christian Ireland which has replaced the heroic world they once knew. The encounter is, psychologically, a basic Irish myth of the encounters of two civilizations, both claiming to represent the best that is in Ireland.

Satiric elements appear constantly in the Fenian stories as do tales of imaginary journeys and visions, but these two categories of Gaelic fiction exist in such abundance elsewhere that they deserve separate attention. In his classic study of Irish comedy, *The Irish Comic Tradition*, Vivian Mercier notes that "the most striking single fact about Irish literature in either Gaelic or English is the high proportion of satire which it contains."[14] For about sixty years scholars have understood that Gaelic satire originated in the magic which the ancient poets were assumed to be able to practice through their incantations. The ancient poet's *aer*, a word which came to mean "satire" but earlier meant "attack in prose or verse" or "curse," was something which early Irishmen

---

14 *The Irish Comic Tradition* (1962; New York: Oxford University Press, 1969), p. 103.

feared; it was the dangerous side of the poet's magical power.[15] Gaelic satire tended to remain personal, and it was often no more than abuse directed against inhospitable kings, impious clergymen, and pedantic scholars. But the finest narrative satire, *The Vision of Mac Con Glinne*, while it attacks both clergy and scholars, is something more than just abuse. With its complicated parodies of literary forms and religious beliefs and its exuberant narration, it is the first sustained example of the Irish talent for ironic fantasy and an antecedent to both Joyce and Flann O'Brien. Like the satires, the tales of visions and imaginary journeys are based on the power of magic; in this case, the power to pass from the real world to the super-real. As an island, Ireland was a logical place to produce stories of imaginary voyages, and there are many of these stories. Some are similar to the mythological stories of humans lured away by supernatural creatures; they include such stories as that of Oisín, the voyage of Bran, and the voyage of St. Brendan which permits Irishmen to claim that one of their number discovered America. Like the satires, these stories often contain a good deal of social commentary in the description of other worlds and in the complaints of the returnees about how things have fallen off at home in their absence. The visions, on the other hand, are exclusively religious works, stories also of imaginary travel, but travel to Heaven, Purgatory, or Hell. The vision literature is largely based on Christian and Jewish sources, but there is sometimes a strong dose of pre-Christian Irish belief.

The cycle of the kings involves, as the mythological and Fenian tales do not, a mixture of legend and history. It probably preserves some of the tales of the court historians who always accompanied the Irish kings; although some of the stories are clearly very old, they tend to focus on kingship as a social responsibility more than on specific heroic acts. Thus the finest story in the series, "The Destruction of Da Derga's Hostel," turns on the failure of King Conaire to observe ritual taboos, while "The Frenzy of Suibhne" describes how that king's cowardice in battle was punished by madness. The stories of the Christian saints are, in a way, similar to the cycle of the kings because the saints, too, must fulfill the requirements of heroism, though on their own Christian terms. St. Columba, for example, becomes just as much a heroic warrior for his faith as any pagan warlord.

But the greatest of all these cycles of tales is the "Ulster" or "Red ✓

---

[15] The classic study of the matter is F. N. Robinson, "Satirists and Enchanters in Early Irish Literature," in D. G. Lyon and G. F. Moore, eds., *Studies in the History of Religions Presented to Crawford Howell Joy* (New York: Macmillan, 1912), pp. 95–130.

Branch," the cycle of stories which is the closest thing Ireland has to a national epic and a collection which was immensely important to many writers of the Irish Renaissance. The stories of the Ulster cycle, some of which probably existed orally before the fifth century, survive in fragmentary and confused written versions, but the central narrative is the *Táin Bó Cúailnge* (*The Cattle-Raid at Cooley*). Like the heroic stories of other traditions, the *Táin* is essentially an aristocratic story (as the Finn stories are essentially peasant tales), but it tells of a very primitive aristocracy indeed. Its world is strikingly a world of individuals. The gods may sometimes appear in the narrative, but their role is inconsequential; groups wage war on each other, but the fighting itself is usually single combat. It is a world made for the prowess of the single hero, and that hero is Cuchulain, the immensely powerful and cunning champion of Ulster. His battles take place in the context of a feud between his king, Conchobor of the Red Branch of Ulster, and Medb, the wife of Ailill, the king of Connacht. The bulk of the story deals with the consequences of Medb's desire to steal a great bull from Ulster, but before that narrative begins, we must be told something of the background, and that is given in a series of fore-tales. These tell us first how Conchobor gained the kingship of Ulster through his mother's craftiness. Then they recount the story of Noisu and Derdriu, the greatest of Irish love stories. Conchobor was once feasting in the house of his chief storyteller when, amid evil portents, the storyteller's wife gave birth to a daughter, Derdriu. Because of the portents, the king's warriors wanted to kill the girl, but Conchobor decided instead to have her raised in seclusion and kept to become his wife. But, when she had grown up, Derdriu fell in love with Noisu, one of Conchobor's warriors whom she happened to meet. Noisu, his two brothers, and Derdriu fled from Conchobor's wrath, eventually going to Scotland, but the king still wanted his bride and wanted vengeance on Noisu and his brothers. Eventually, he sent word to them by Fergus mac Roich that they would be welcomed if they returned to Ireland; it was, of course, a trap, though Fergus did not realize this. When they returned at Fergus' urging, Conchobor had Noisu and his brothers killed and tried to make Derdriu his wife. But, in the blunt words of the *Táin*, "A big block of stone was in front of her. She let her head be driven against the stone, and made a mass of fragments of it, and she was dead."[16] Fergus, furious at the deception, left Conchobor's court at Emain Macha and went to the court of Medb and Ailill in Connacht.

16 Kinsella, *The Táin*, p. 20.

Cuchulain himself was born magically. In time, he was trained in arms, performed some amazing deeds of valor as a child, then courted and married the beautiful and clever Emer, the daughter of Forgall Monach, himself a very cunning man. Cuchulain rapidly established himself as the greatest of Conchobor's warriors. Meanwhile, Medb, off in Connacht, decided she wanted a brown bull which had once belonged to her but was now in the possession of Conchobor. To recover her bull, she invaded Ulster, placing the Fergus of the Derdriu story at the head of her army. At first, the Ulstermen were unable to fight, being overcome by a strange sickness from which only Cuchulain and his father were exempt. Cuchulain, though, went alone to head Medb's army off at the ford of a river. There he performed a long series of feats of valor in one-to-one combat, but to no avail, for Medb turned north and took the bull from Cúailnge where it was being kept. At this point, though, the god Lug came to Cuchulain's aid by causing him to sleep for three days during which he healed his wounds; meanwhile, the Ulstermen, recovered from their illness, fought with the men of Connacht. When Cuchulain awoke, he fell into a frenzy like that of Achilles in the *Iliad* and killed 130 kings in a terrible slaughter on the battlefield at Murtheimne. At last, in desperation, Medb called on Cuchulain's foster brother, Ferdia, to fight him. Ferdia lamented the fact that he had to fight his brother, but because he could see no honorable alternative, he went out to find him. The heroic code of the world of the *Táin* is embodied in conversation between Ferdia and his charioteer when they approach Cúchulain:

> 'How does Cúchulainn look?' Ferdia said to his charioteer.
> 'He and his charioteer look as if all the men of
> Ireland meant nothing to them,' he said.
> 'Enough, my friend,' Ferdia said, 'you praise him
> too much.'[17]

And the modern reader gets something of the ancient storyteller's delight in cataloging the facts of his culture in the description of Ferdia's battle-dress:

> This was his battle-harness: a filmy girdle of silk
> with a speckled-gold hem next his bright skin, a dark
> supple apron of leather over that on the outside, and

---

17 *Ibid.*, pp. 179–80.

a stout strong stone outside that again, the size of
a millstone. . . . He set on his head his war-like
crested battle-helmet, finely decorated with forty
precious carbuncles and inlaid with red enamel and
crystal and carbuncle and gleaming stones from the
East. He took in his right hand his furious spear,
stout and fierce. In his left he took his battle-
sword with its gold grip and its hilt of red-gold.[18]

Cuchulain and Ferdia fought for several days, but they fought always with
heroic courtesy. Each night, Cuchulain would send amulets and charms to
heal his brother's wounds, and Ferdia would send some of his food back in
return. After a day of fighting which lasted "from the grey of early morning
until the evening sunset," Cuchulain said to Ferdia.

'Let us break off now from this, Ferdia, for our
horses are spent and our charioteers are dazed, and
if they are finished why shouldn't we be finished too?
He said further:
    'Why suffer the chariots' plunging
    or struggle like Fomorian giants?
    Hobble the horses.
    Let the turmoil die away.'
'Very well, let us break off if it is time,' Ferdia
said.

They broke off and threw their weapons into their
charioteers' arms. They came up to each other and
each put his arm around the other's neck and gave him
three kisses.[19]

The battles end, finally, when Cuchulain kills Ferdia with the *gae bolga*,
his magical weapon. Cuchulain kills his brother because his code demands it,
but after he is dead, he mourns intensely:

Misery has befallen us,
Scáthach's two foster-sons
—I, broken and blood-red,
your chariot standing empty.

18 *Jbid.*, p. 193.
19 *Jbid.*, pp. 189–90.

> Misery has befallen us,
> Scáthach's two foster-sons
> I, broken and blood-raw,
> you lying stark dead.

> Misery has befallen us,
> Scáthach's two foster-sons
> —you dead and I alive.
> Bravery is battle-madness.[20]

The terrible beauty of Cuchulain's combat with Ferdia and his great, tragic lament for his brother with that wonderful final cry helps make the entire story so central to the Irish tradition. After that battle, the men of Ulster continue to fight the men of Connacht, Cuchulain himself defeating the last of the enemy forces. Cuchulain has the chance to kill Medb, the cause of all the trouble, when he comes upon her during her menstrual period, but, "not being a killer of women," he spares her. To Fergus, her general, she says, "We have had shame and shambles here today," and Fergus replies, "It is the usual thing for a herd led by a mare to be strayed and destroyed."[21] But the *Táin* does not end with Fergus' bitter jest. Instead, in a great and moving analogue to all of the combat, the bull of Ulster and the bull of Connacht fight each other. The Ulster bull kills his rival and madly rushes through Ireland carrying the remains of the Connacht bull on his back until he drops dead. That final image of the fighting animals makes a wonderfully fitting conclusion to a story full of violence, passion, and tragic nobility.

By the time the maker of the *Book of Leinster* transcribed his version of the *Táin* around 1160, the golden age of Gaelic literature was already passing. By 1350 literary men were creating a new standard language, what we now call Early Modern Irish, which could have been the medium for a great new literature, but history was running against Gaelic Ireland. The Norman invasions put the old culture on the defensive, and even after it recovered a century and more later, Gaelic literature was past its best days. Nevertheless, the period from about 1200 to about 1600 produced some important writing. The court poets, the old *filid*, reorganized themselves into a hereditary literary caste and supported themselves by writing poems in praise of the remaining Gaelic aristocracy. Their technique was flawless, but the poets of this bardic system too often had little to say. Although original prose, much of it religious, con-

20 *Ibid.*, pp. 203-204.
21 *Ibid.*, pp. 250-51.

tinued to be produced during these centuries, this period was especially important for its work in preserving the literature of the past. Most of the compilations of Irish myth and saga date from this time, and Fenian stories, increasingly popular as the heroic world of Cuchulain faded into the past, were especially valued.

By the beginning of the seventeenth century, the century which saw the final destruction of the Gaelic aristocracy and the beginning of English landlordism, the old Gaelic literature was almost a thing of the past. The destruction of the bardic system was brought about by the end of the Gaelic aristocracy. Gaelic scholars driven abroad to Louvain worked hard to salvage what was left of their culture while in Ireland the "Four Masters" in Donegal and Geoffrey Keating in Tipperary wrote their annals and histories. Their desire to summarize and catalogue was a sure sign of the end of aristocratic Gaelic culture, but it was by no means the sign of the end of Gaelic literature. Gaelic literature after about 1690 became that of an oppressed peasantry and a dispossessed aristocracy. Folk tales abounded, but there was often no one to write them down; poetry was still written, but its audience became increasingly small as larger numbers of Irishmen forgot their native tongue. Even so, there are some splendid, if isolated, poems from the eighteenth century. Eileen O'Leary's lament for her husband, Art, murdered because he would not sell a horse to a Protestant landlord, is a very moving poem, and Bryan Merryman extended the traditions of anti-feminism and vision literature by his hilarious and grotesque satire, "The Midnight Court." Egan O'Rahilly, writing in the early part of the eighteenth century, produced in "Brightness of Brightness" an exquisitely beautiful poem on what was to become a standard theme of Irish writing, how Ireland the beautiful lady had been seduced by loutish Britain. And his "A Grey Eye Weeping" deals with another convention of the time, the feelings of the dispossessed Irishman towards the new Protestant landlords who have made him a beggar. But no Gaelic poem from the period has quite the poignancy of the anonymous "Kilcash," a lament for the lost past as symbolized by Kilcash house, the home of one branch of a now landless noble family driven into exile:

> My grief and my affliction
>   Your gates are taken away,
> Your avenue needs attention,
>   Goats in the garden stray.

> The courtyard's filled with water
> And the great earls where are they?
> The earls, the lady, the people
> Beaten into the clay.[22]

Towards the middle of the eighteenth century, the Gaelic poet Peader Ó Doirnin wrote of his native tongue:

> Oh Gaelic, most sweet and soft of sound,
> Swift, robust, as the waves of the sea,
> Trodden and trampled, despised by all—
> That you live at all is a wonder to me![23]

And the survival of Gaelic language and literature was a wonder. Both were in a maimed condition in Ó Doirnin's time, but both survived until the 1840s when the famine killed perhaps as many as a million of its native speakers.

After the famine, there was almost no original writing in Gaelic, but, ironically, by that point the ancient literature had already become the subject of considerable popular interest and scholarly investigation both inside Ireland and out. The great success of James Macpherson's bogus renderings of Fenian stories in the 1760s began a fad for all things Celtic, even though reputable scholars agreed that Macpherson's "ancient" epics were hardly the products of third-century Scotland as he claimed. Goethe, and thousands of other Europeans, shared their century's sentimental interest in primitivism, the lays of a lost culture, and nostalgic pathos, all of which the Celtic world seemed to offer. Macpherson, a good Scot, had some unkind things to say about Ireland and the Irish literature, though the stories of Finn and Oisin he retold were more Irish than Scottish; Irishmen quickly began to defend themselves from his attacks. In the process they began to recover their own past. At first, the investigations were hardly scholarly; it was easier, and more satisfying, to write songs and stories about the lost world of the Celts than do the hard work of scholarship and archaeology. Thomas Moore and Lady Morgan, whose novel, *The Wild Irish Girl* was a best seller in 1806, cashed in on the fascination with Celtic Ireland, but some of the "scholars" produced works of such oddity that

---

[22] *Kings, Lords, and Commons*, p. 100.
[23] Quoted in Power, *A Literary History of Ireland*, p. 109.

sentimental, and most of it is deservedly forgotten. One writer, though, had a kind of crude genius, and he has been fairly called "the peasant Chaucer of a new tradition."[27] This was William Carleton, the first great realist of Irish fiction, and a father figure for the fictional realists of the Irish Renaissance itself. Because Carleton was perfectly willing to write for whomever would pay him, there is an astonishing inconsistency in his choice of themes. Within one year he produced novels which attack, in turn, the Protestant landlords, the peasant organization created to fight them, and the peasants themselves. "Attack" is a basic word for describing Carleton, and two strains run continuously through his varied work: a bitter hatred of the ills of Irish life, and a nostalgia for the simple and passionate peasant life of his own childhood. He was an erratic artist, often clumsily mechanical, but the tales in *Traits and Stories of the Irish Peasantry* (1830–33) have a melodramatic power and effective comedy; they take the Irish peasant seriously as a human being rather than as a stock type. In a better time, Carleton could have been a major writer; as it is, he remains particularly important because he was the first storyteller to express that love-hatred for Ireland which is so central to the Anglo-Irish literary consciousness.

By the end of the 1840s, the first phase of the Anglo-Irish tradition in fiction was ending; distinctively Anglo-Irish novels would continue to be written during the remainder of the century, perhaps the best being Charles Kickham's *Knocknagow* (1879), but they became increasingly formulaic and stereotyped. But in the 1840s the "Young Ireland" movement, that oddly quixotic and oddly heroic effort toward Irish freedom and cultural regeneration, produced the beginnings of an important Anglo-Irish poetry. And, in general, the imaginative energy of Anglo-Ireland went into poetry in the latter half of the century. There had been Anglo-Irish poetry before, of course. Thomas Moore, for one, had made a fortune and an immense reputation with his songs and ballads, but his poetry was essentially poetry of exploitation, a verse analogue to some Anglo-Irish fiction. Exploiting the Ossianic fad, he created works of easy sentiment and escape; he knew better, and he sometimes employed rather subtle English versions of Gaelic poetic techniques, but he also knew where fame and fortune lay. Moore is an important figure in the development of Anglo-Irish poetry, however, particularly in the way in which he helped make a combination of pathos and patriotism central to the tradition. The poets of Young Ireland employed that combination, too, when their newspaper, *The Nation*, became for several years in the 1840s a center of poetic

27 W. B. Yeats in *Uncollected Prose*, edited by J. P. Frayne (London: Macmillan, 1970), p. 364.

activity. Thomas Davis, their leader, sought to create a national literature in
English for Ireland, and, like the German Herder, he urged his followers to go
back to the traditions and cultural heritage of their forefathers to find the basis
for a new Irish culture. He was, historically, extremely important because he
was the first to argue effectively that the future of Irish writing lay in bridging
the gap between Celtic, Catholic Ireland and Protestant Anglo-Ireland, but he
was no more than a mediocre poet. His newspaper tended to encourage ballads
(Davis himself wrote some fairly good ones) and patriotic poetry which had
more sincerity than artistry. To Irishmen of the time, who saw themselves as the
oppressed victims of British imperialism, artistry was less important than
patriotic sentiment, but the emphasis on political statement retarded the real
growth of Anglo-Irish poetry for decades. Too much of the poetry of *The
Nation* was, to put it bluntly, junk.

Nevertheless, there were some poets of real merit in nineteenth-century
Ireland, and it was no accident that most of these were essentially nonpolitical.
The generation of Young Ireland produced one fine, if erratic, poet in James
Clarence Mangan. He had an intense, sometimes undisciplined imagination and
the ability to make poems of powerful emotion. Some of his work is overtly
Irish, the beautiful "Dark Rosaleen" and "O'Hussey's Ode to the Maguire"
for example, but his best work is private and visionary, and one critic has aptly
described his as a sort of Irish Nerval.[28] Mangan's Irish poems, like so much
of the work of his time, are full of nostalgia for the lost world of Celtic
Ireland, but where some poets were simply exploitive, Mangan often produced
something more. A stanza from his "Kinkora" is a good example with its
moaning refrain:

> They are gone, those heroes of royal birth,
> Who plundered no churches, and broke no trust;
> 'Tis weary for me to be living on earth
> When they, O Kinkora, lie low in the dust!
>
> Low, O Kinkora![29]

The death of Davis in 1845, the famine which began the next year, and the
death of Mangan in 1849 terminated Young Ireland as a poetic movement

28 Harold Bloom, *Yeats* (New York: Oxford Univ. Press, 1970), p. 85.

29 "Kinkora"; this poem, along with a good selection of other Gaelic and Anglo-Irish poems,
appears in the *Penguin Book of Irish Verse*, edited by Brendan Kennelly (Harmondsworth, Middlesex:
Penguin, 1970).

before it had time to mature, but its influence was long-lasting, especially in popular poetry. Davis became the type of the patriotic poet as Mangan became that of the frustrated Irish artist.

Between the death of Mangan and the 1880s, Anglo-Ireland continued to produce some capable poets, but no geniuses. Aubrey DeVere, disciple of Wordsworth, produced some superficially "Irish" poetry, but he rarely gives the impression that he is more than a conventional Victorian who occasionally successfully exploits material from his Irish homeland. The same could be said of William Allingham, another minor poet, but it would not tell the whole story. In most ways, Allingham's creative affinities were with the English Pre-Raphaelite movement, but his *Lawrence Bloomfield in Ireland* (1864) is an interesting verse novel which focuses on the problems of tenant–landlord relations. Moreover, Allingham was a native of Ballyshannon, a little town north of Sligo, and some of his best work, a series of ballads, celebrates his birthplace, some of them in a poetic style which is a direct antecedent to the metres and images of the "Celtic Twilight" phase of the Irish Renaissance. Allingham had, in fact, a considerable influence on Yeats, not only in terms of technique but also in that Yeats decided to follow the example of Allingham by making himself a poet of his native locale. It was hardly Allingham's fault that Yeats's "native" place, Sligo, was full of much richer poetic resonance—or that Yeats was a genius and Allingham was not.

But the most important poet of the period between the death of Mangan and the rise of Yeats was Sir Samuel Ferguson, an Ulster Protestant and antiquarian who became a national poet without becoming a nationalist, in itself an important breakthrough. Turning to Irish legend for much of his subject matter, he tried to imitate the manner as well as the content of the ancient literature. His ways of dealing with saga and legend in *Lays of the Western Gael* (1865) and his "epic," *Congal* (1872), have a certain authenticity, and his poetic language often has a clumsy strength, but he was basically a dull poet. Nevertheless, his work demonstrated that the ancient literature could be used by modern writers for something more than evocative exploitation, and Ferguson himself, by avoiding religious and political controversy in his poetry, intended to demonstrate that "national" poetry could be written by confining oneself to the Irish countryside and Irish legend. The intentions of Ferguson, the man and his work, were ultimately more important than his limited imaginative achievement; those intentions made him another important figure for younger poets who were looking for ways to express what they understood to be their national consciousness without falling into political topicality. Yeats, as a young man, admired Ferguson excessively, but his instincts were right, at least, in telling him that Ferguson was the sort of poet Ireland needed.

Yeats's own first important volume, *The Wanderings of Oisin and Other Poems* (1889) must be viewed as the culmination of a century of Anglo-Irish poetry, and that volume, far more than the spotty *Poems and Ballads* of O'Leary's disciples, was in reality the first sign that something important was afoot in Anglo-Irish literature. It is also an important bridge between the old Anglo-Irish tradition and the new one which Yeats helped create. Although he still owed a great deal at this point in his career to Shelley and Morris, Yeats's title poem, "The Wanderings of Oisin," is a fine example of Ferguson's technique of dealing with Irish legend, in this case the Fenian stories, coupled to Yeats's own sensibility. Overtly, it is the long narrative of three imaginary journies of Oisin, Finn's son, in the company of Niamh, the fairy who seduces him away from the heroic Ireland of the sixth century. In the tradition of Gaelic voyage literature, Oisin visits three magical lands, all clearly allegorical as many of Mangan's poems are allegorical. But Oisin eventually tires of wandering and returns to an Ireland which, through St. Patrick, has become Christianized and, in Oisin's view, diminished. Oisin's defiant praise of ancient pagan Ireland to Patrick is in line with the tradition of revenant nostalgia in Anglo-Irish poetry, and Oisin himself is an interesting development of the convention of the pathetic hero, a convention which appears in much formal Anglo-Irish poetry and in the popular ballads.

Other poems in the volume also suggest Yeats's debt to the Anglo-Irish tradition and the rediscovery of folklore and legend. "The Madness of King Goll" is an important early example of Yeats's way of dealing with Irish legend for what are, in reality, personal reasons. The poem tells us how an ancient king gave up his royal power to become a wanderer in an Irish landscape so alive with suggestion for him that he becomes mad, and there are analogies here to the story of Sweeney in the Gaelic Kings' stories cycle, but the poem really deals with the dangerous intersection of reality and imagination, the world of men and the world of the supernatural. This theme is one which recurs frequently in Yeats's poetry, and in the 1889 volume Yeats deals with it in a different way in one of his most perfect early poems, "The Stolen Child." Using a common *donnée* from folklore—the stealing of a child by the fairies—the poem employs a nostalgic tone familiar from English translations of Irish folk poetry and a style derived from Ferguson's "The Fairy Thorn." With its haunting refrain, this poem is an excellent example of Yeats's way, in his early work, of making a poem which has the appearance of folk art but is, in fact, very highly and consciously wrought.

The popular "Down by the Salley Gardens" is, as so much Anglo-Irish poetry was, a free translation of a Gaelic folksong, while the ballads of Father O'Hart, Moll Magee, and the foxhunter are all in the tradition of the Anglo-Irish ballad, if rather less vigorous than "The Night Before Larry Was Stretched." Yeats kept in this collection the best of the non-Irish poems he had written before he knew John O'Leary and came under his influence, a series of Indian poems and lyrics from a play, but he excluded a great deal of his early work. What was left out is generally rather mediocre apprentice work, but it was also poetry which did not fit in Yeats's new image of himself as an Irish poet, and that was the image he was determined to present to the world. *The Wanderings of Oisin* was not the best volume of poetry to appear in the English-speaking world in 1889 (there was formidable competition in Tennyson and Swinburne), but it was unquestionably the best volume the Anglo-Irish tradition had ever produced. It was the capstone of that tradition in the nineteenth century, and it was, simultaneously, the foundation for the poetry of the Irish Renaissance.

So we end where we began. As Senchán Torpéist's disciples went to the grave of Fergus to rediscover their ancient literary heritage, so John O'Leary's disciples had to go back to the graves and monuments of the literary past to find theirs. The ancient poems, the Gaelic narratives, and the *Táin* in particular, the Gaelic poetry of the eighteenth century, the scholarly translations, and the bumbling achievements of Anglo-Irish writing in the nineteenth century were all the inheritance from which the writers of Irish Renaissance fashioned one of the great national literatures of modern times. Irish literature has repeatedly had a history of achievement, loss, and regain as, in Auden's phrase, the words of dead men are modified in the guts of the living.

the years of the celtic twilight
The 1890s

We hold the Ireland in the heart
More than the land our eyes have seen,
And love the goal for which we start
More than the tale of what has been.

AE

We are not content to dig our own potato patch in
peace. We peer over the wall at our neighbour's
instead of making our own garden green and
beautiful. And yet it is a good garden. . . .

W. B. Yeats

THE 1890s was the first full decade of the Irish Renaissance, a decade of
only modest literary achievement, but a period in which the new movement gathered force and began to find self-definition. Considering its modest
origins in John O'Leary's parlor and the small nationalist clubs in London and
Dublin, the Irish Renaissance actually developed with remarkable rapidity.
What had been even in 1890 only a parochial effort in literary nationalism
grew by 1900 into an internationally important phenomenon. Yeats remained
the movement's *de facto* leader and its best-known figure, an enthusiastic
propagandist for Irish writing as well as a poet with a growing reputation.
Appropriately, the decade's lasting achievements in terms of published work
were in poetry and folklore, two areas of central concern to Yeats himself, but
the importance of the nineties to the Irish Renaissance lay in more than the

books that were published. In a series of literary controversies, the writers came more clearly to understand the relationships between literature and nationalism, and toward the end of the decade there was the beginning of a dramatic movement which would strongly influence the future of Irish writing.

Two developments helped give the Irish 1890s their distinctive tone. One was the disastrous climax to the remarkable career of Charles Stewart Parnell, the great political leader. Parnell's fall and the subsequent controversy changed the course of Irish nationalism, embittering a generation. As Yeats wrote years afterward, "Everywhere I saw the change take place, young men turning away from politics altogether, taking to Gaelic, taking to Literature, or remaining in politics that they might substitute for violent speech more violent action. . . . From that national humiliation, from the resolution to destroy all that made the humiliation possible, from that sacrificial victim I derive all that is living in the imagination of Ireland today."[1] Yeats was surely right to see the fall of Parnell as a crucial event, and we will need to return to it to understand some of the tone of the nineties. Even so, another development had at least as strong an effect on Irish writing, and perhaps, in some ways, it was a response to the Parnell political tragedy. This was the rising increase in interest in the idea of Celticism, the idea that there was among the Celtic peasantry of Ireland a distinctive kind of national or racial imagination. All through the 1890s Irish writers tried to come to terms with what they understood to be the Celtic imagination. It was in fact, the Anglo-Irish writers who were Yeats's friends who became the most intense Celtophiles. In the 1880s the young Irish writers had tended to identify with the nationalistic ideals and means of expression of the Anglo-Irish nineteenth century. In the 1890s, perhaps because they sensed in the Parnell tragedy an indictment of Anglo-Irish nationalism, they tended to associate themselves with Ireland's older Celtic inheritance. Even so, most of the definitions of what it meant to be a Celt or write from a Celtic perspective were hazy indeed. Katharine Tynan did about as well, or badly, as anyone when she wrote: "By the Irish note I mean that distinctive quality in Celtic poetry the charm of which is so much easier to feel than to explain. . . . Some of the parts which go to make up its whole are a simplicity which is *naive*—a freshness, an archness, a light touching of the chords as with fairy-finger tips; a shade of underlying melancholy as delicately evanescent as a breath upon glass, which yet gives its undertone and its shadow to all; fatalism side by side with bouyant hopefulness; laughter with tears; love with hatred; a rainbow of all

---

[1] "Modern Ireland," *Irish Renaissance*, edited by Robin Skelton and David R. Clark (Dublin: Dolmen Press), p. 15.

colours where none conflict; a gamut of all notes which join to make perfect harmony."[2]

Because the fall of Parnell was the crucial political event in modern Irish history, the facts of the matter and the myths which grew up around it need some close attention. The "facts" are, unfortunately, none too clear. What is clear is that for several years in the 1880s, Katharine O'Shea had been Parnell's mistress. Her husband had been aware of their relationship and had more or less condoned it. But in December of 1889 he filed for divorce, naming Parnell as the third party. Parnell had earlier in the year been cleared of charges that he had sympathized with the Phoenix Park murderers back in 1882, charges that were proved to have been based on forged letters, and many Irishmen assumed that the charge of adultery was just another attempt to discredit "the Leader." Parnell himself said that he would emerge from the divorce case with his reputation unstained, and most people took him at his word, even after the trial on November 15 and 17, 1890, found him, in effect, guilty. Within a week, though, trouble was brewing. Cardinal Manning, the Catholic primate of England, urged Prime Minister Gladstone to repudiate his alliance with Parnell. Gladstone was also warned that his Liberal Party was not happy about the situation. Nonconformist laymen in the Midlands of England were the backbone of the party, and many of them had seen the justice in Gladstone's calls for Irish Home Rule in the past. On the Sunday after the trial, however, Parnell was condemned from scores of nonconformist pulpits. Finally, on November 24, Gladstone conferred with Justin McCarthy, an important figure in Parnell's party, warning him that if Parnell remained the leader of the Irish it would produce "consequences disastrous in the highest degree to the cause of Ireland." Gladstone also wrote a letter, which apparently neither Parnell nor McCarthy saw, saying that Parnell's continued presence would render Gladstone's own leadership of the Liberals "almost a nullity."[3]

In spite of the furor, the Irish Party reelected Parnell as its leader on November 25. Gladstone's letter with its "almost a nullity" phrase was published the next day, and a special meeting of the party then asked Parnell to reconsider his position. Meantime, the Catholic hierarchy in Ireland had been completely silent on the matter. After Michael Davitt condemned it for not speaking out on the moral issue of adultery, a meeting of the hierarchy was called for December 3. Before that meeting took place, though, Parnell himself

---

2 "The Poetry of William Allingham," *The Irish Fireside* (30 October 1886): 261–62.
3 Quoted in Conor Cruise O'Brien, *Parnell and His Party* (Oxford: Clarendon Press, 1957), p. 293.

confused the situation by issuing a manifesto in the Irish newspapers which attacked some of his followers for bowing to Gladstone's pressure, suggested that the Prime Minister had acted deceitfully on the matter of home rule, and ended by claiming that it was necessary for the Irish Party to remain independent of all the English parties. This was a strange argument indeed, coming from one who had worked closely with Gladstone and the Liberals in the past, and it made it obvious that even if he retained his position, Parnell would never be able to work with Gladstone again.

The Irish Party met in Committee Room 15 of the House of Commons in London on Monday, December 1, to consider the questions of Parnell's continuing leadership. With the press giving the meetings enormous attention, the debates dragged on through all of that week. On Wednesday, the Catholic hierarchy met in Dublin to urge the party to depose Parnell. In London, Parnell and his followers insisted that English wolves were howling for the Leader's blood. The anti-Parnellites replied that the divorce had ended his moral authority and his manifesto had ended his political usefulness. Finally, on Saturday, December 6, the debates ended with a walkout by the anti-Parnellite majority; 44 members rejected his leadership, 27 followers remained. Parnell was ruined politically, and so was the Irish Party.

Then began a series of conflicts in Ireland between the two factions. There were physical battles for control of *United Jreland*, the Parnellite newspaper, and bitterly fought elections to Parliament in which mud-slinging became more than a metaphor. When Parnell himself died in England in October of 1891, the passions were hardly abated. His body was brought back to Dublin for burial. Standish O'Grady insisted that he saw super-natural signs in the sky as the Leader's remains was interred, and Parnell had surely become as much a mythic figure as O'Grady's own Cuchulain. Parnellites could claim, and justly, that their leader has been overthrown at the bidding of Gladstone and the Irish hierarchy. Anti-Parnellites could claim, and justly, that the divorce and Parnell's subsequent behavior had ended his right and ability to lead his party. Both were correct, but the cry of betrayal on both sides led toward mythmaking. The anti-Parnellite myth was that he had betrayed the cause; the Parnellite myth was that the cause had betrayed Parnell. In either case, the Parnell tale fitted that eternal Irish political myth of betrayal on the eve of victory.

Timothy Healy, one of the leading anti-Parnellites, observed, after being attacked by a group of small boys, that his side had the voters, but Parnell had their sons. Healy was right. Writers who were children or young adults in the 1890s would come to see Parnell as a totem of tragically self-destructive

Ireland. James Augustine Joyce, nine years old in 1891, produced his first known literary work a few days after Parnell's death, a poem which compares Parnell to Julius Caesar and Healy to Brutus, the murderer-friend. Yeats, twenty-six in 1891, wrote his own elegy, "Mourn—And Then Onward," a wretched poem, but striking in its final image of Parnell's memory as "a tall pillar, burning/Before us in the gloom!"[4] O'Grady's falling stars, Joyce's comparison to the betrayed Caesar, Yeats's to the divine fire which had led the Hebrews through the desert all suggest the anguish caused in Parnell's fall, but nothing describes it better than the famous scene in Joyce's *A Portrait of the Artist as a Young Man* in which the Christmas dinner of 1891 at the Dedalus house is ruined by an argument between Dante Riordan, an anti-Parnellite and devout Catholic, and Mr. Casey and Mr. Dedalus, heart-broken followers of the dead leader:

> At the door Dante turned round violently and shouted
> down the room, her cheeks flushed and quivering with rage:
> —Devil out of hell! We won! We crushed him to death!
> Fiend!
> The door slammed behind her.
> Mr. Casey, freeing his arms from his holders, suddenly bowed his head on his
> hands with a sob of pain.
> —Poor Parnell! he cried loudly. My dead king![5]

The Parnell debacle ended, for the time being, the chance that parliamentary politics would win a change in the Irish constitutional situation. Some who cared intensely about Irish political freedom turned to the Irish Republican Brotherhood, the secret organization committed to the violent overthrow of British rule. Others turned to other sorts of organizations—literary societies, groups for the improvement of social conditions, the Gaelic Athletic Association, and the Gaelic League. The Parnell crisis had profoundly shaken the national self-confidence, and perhaps there was a sense of safety in groups as there was a distrust of the idea of the single leader. There was also in groups a sense of identity, and the nineties became the decade in which Irish writers desperately sought to come to some sense of identity, some way of defining what it meant to be an Irish writer. One obvious way to define oneself as an

4 *The Variorum Edition of the Poems of W. B. Yeats,* edited by Peter Allt and Russell K. Alspach (New York: Macmillan, 1956; rpt. 1966), p. 738.

5 *A Portrait of the Artist as a Young Man* (1916; New York: Viking, 1964), p. 39.

Irish writer was in terms of race. Now, in fact, neither Yeats nor Douglas Hyde nor AE was a Celt by birth, but for all three the notion of Celticism became a fundamental way of defining Irishness. Theories of ineradicable racial differences between Celt and Saxon went back at least as far as Thomas Davis in the 1840s, but for many of the younger writers it was enough to have been born Irish, even Anglo-Irish, to qualify them as spokesmen for Celtic Ireland.

The international interest in Celticism was already long established; Macpherson's Ossianic poems had helped begin it as early as the 1760s. As Professor Ann Saddlemyer suggests, the "Celtic revival" of the 1890s was really no more than a "re-naming or re-ordering of a familiar trait, the 'folk spirit,' marked by the heightened passions and superstitions common to all literature rising from the people, and given new life by recent scientific studies of folklore and myth culminating in Sir James Frazer's *The Golden Bough* of 1890."[6] Ernest Renan, the great French scholar and critic, had rediscovered Celtic poetry in Brittany in the 1850s, and, for English readers, Matthew Arnold had given the interest in Celticism respectability in 1867 with his Oxford lectures on the Celtic movement in literature. Arnold, though oddly ignorant of real Celtic literature, had found certain basic characteristics in the Celtic imagination: a sense of natural magic and the mystery of life, melancholy titanism coupled with a love for lightness and brightness, generosity, and a continuing rebellion against the despotism of fact.[7] Arnold used his theory of Celticism to attack the dullness and stolidity he saw in the Saxon temperament, though it could be argued that he saw in the Celts an imaginative and inept people who needed to be ruled by sturdy Saxons. Nevertheless, his view was, in its time, insightful and sympathetic. His definition of Celticism became a commonplace in the last third of the nineteenth century, but it was vague enough that even self-professed Celts could interpret the racial description to suit their own interests.

For Douglas Hyde, Celticism meant particularly the Irish language, to the study and propagation of which he devoted most of his adult life. In 1892 he gave an influential lecture, "The Necessity for De-Anglicising Ireland," in which he said that by giving up their native language and customs the Irish had thrown away their best claim to be recognized as an independent nation. The soul of the nation could be rediscovered in the Gaelic-speaking peasantry which

---

6 "The Cult of the Celt: Pan Celticism in the Nineties," *The World of W. B. Yeats*, edited by Robin Skelton and Ann Saddlemyer (Seattle: University of Washington Press, 1965), p. 3.

7 See "On the Study of Celtic Literature," *Lectures and Essays in Criticism*, edited by R. H. Super (Ann Arbor: University of Michigan Press, 1962), pp. 291–386 but especially pp. 335–51.

still remained, a soul simple, passionate, and sincere. All during his career, Hyde made much of the idea that the Celtic peasants were an oppressed people whose sufferings had given them a special virtue; they were the suffering and redemptive servants of an Anglicized Ireland. For AE, in contrast, Celticism was a way of coming into contact with the supernatural. He found in the tales told him by peasants and the stories of ancient Irish literature the same figures who inhabited his own dreams. Celticism became for him a means for dealing with ancestral memory, with an imagined past full of mystical power. As William Irwin Thompson observes, AE was a rebel against modernism whose "atavism was as clear a rejection of civilization as Hyde's resuscitation of a language in which abstract thought was impossible."[8] Yeats, too, was an atavist. His vision of Ireland, largely based on Arnold's theories, was of an ideal rural society in which peasant and landed gentry were united by common virtues of instinct and passion. He was not especially sympathetic to Hyde's efforts to revive Gaelic, but he agreed with AE that it was the visionary quality which made the Irish imagination unique in western Europe. In "The Celtic Element in Literature" (1898), he approvingly quoted Renan's claim that "compared with the classical imagination the Celtic imagination is indeed the infinite compared with the finite," and adds that the Celtic imagination has never lost its mythmaking qualities.[9] Like AE, Yeats believed the Celts had a special access to supernatural wisdom because they remained passionate and instinctive; in addition, they lived and thought in a symbolically charged world beyond the ken of urban civilization, a world which Yeats, with his elaborate symbolism, also inhabited.

It would be easy to be cynical and assert that all three writers were merely talking romantic nonsense and nostalgia—and exactly what all these theories have to do with the facts of life on an Irish farm is indeed unclear. It would be more accurate to say that each was imposing on a mythical Celtic race his own desires for a different world: Hyde for one full of Gaelic-speaking peasants, AE for a visionary utopia, Yeats for a pastoral society of mythmakers. Even so, the varying visions of the Celt had considerable influence in their time. They gave the Irish a sense of self-worth, a way of saying that they were a special people who were morally and imaginatively superior to the English oppressor. Nevertheless, Celticism was also a potentially dangerous business, as racial theories almost always are. How dangerous would become apparent only at the end of the nineties when the beliefs of these Anglo-Irishmen began to clash

[8] *The Imagination of an Insurrection* (New York: Harper, 1967), p. 172.

[9] *Essays and Introductions* (London: Macmillan, 1961), p. 173.

with the values of some real Celts who valued nationalism above theorizing. In
the meantime, Celticism provided a temporary definition for the Irish writer
and a sense of meaning for the developing literary revival.

The interest in Celticism had been encouraged by the study of Irish
folklore; it, in turn, was further encouraged by the Celtic revival. Earlier in the
nineteenth century there had been, of course, a great deal of attention to
the traditional literature of Ireland. The scholars had produced their editions of
the ancient tales and translations of Gaelic materials and the popularizers,
writing often for Irish emigrants around the world, had published green-bound
volume after green-bound volume of quaint tales. Yet the gap between scholarship and popularization long remained unbridged; readers who would put down
hard cash for *Tales from Irish Hearths and Homes* had little interest in the
scholarly translations and dictionaries of Gaelic, and vice versa. Editing and
philological study do not interest the ordinary reader, but we should not
forget the good work of John O'Donovan, George Petrie, and Eugene O'Curry
who had begun the scholarly study of Irish antiquities in the 1830s. Nor
should we forget the German scholars, Ernest Windisch, Heinrich Zimmer, and
Kuno Meyer among them, who continued the work of recovering the old texts
and the old language. It is easy, too, to be contemptuous of popularization, but
all those popular collections of songs and stories were an important means of
preserving Irish culture after the depredations of the Great Famine, even though
these versions of folklore often misrepresented their material through ignorance
or the desire to be amusing. One such book, and there were scores of others,
carried the title, *Irish Wonders, The Ghosts, Giants, Pookas, Demons,
Leprechauns, Banshees, Fairies, Witches, Widows, Old Maids, and Other
Marvels of the Emerald Isle*. Its stories were harps-and-shamrocks hokum told
in a dialect more stage-Irish than any English spoken in Ireland.

The publication of Standish O'Grady's *History of Ireland: Heroic Period*
in 1878 demonstrated that it was possible to combine the work of the scholars
with the techniques of popularization and so produce a work which would
become part of the living Irish imagination. O'Grady believed that Irish history
and legend needed to be treated imaginatively, and he was willing to use the
work of the scholars as the raw materials, but no more than the raw materials,
for his re-creation of ancient Irish life and legend. He was no great prose
stylist, but his *History* and the many other books he wrote had a contagious
enthusiasm for the life and literature of Gaelic Ireland. He had himself grown
up in Cork unaware of the ancient literary heritage of his country, and it was
only in his late twenties that he discovered a history of Ireland which changed

his life. His enthusiasm was that of the late convert; if he sometimes over-
stated his case, as when he claimed that all ancient Gaelic writing was deeply
moral, those overstatements were simply an extension of his passionate
enthusiasm. Although he made numerous and sometimes prudish changes in his
originals, his *History* deserves its place as a modernized Irish epic. His great
achievement lay in weaving scores of episodes into a believable whole so that
even if his version of the *Táin* is not really accurate, it makes exciting reading.
At the time of its publication, O'Grady's *History* received less attention than it
deserved, but by the nineties, it had become almost a bible for young Irish
writers and nationalists. They found in it stirring retellings of the ancient tales,
and they also found in his Cuchulain an exemplar of the Irish spirit, manly,
courageous, extravagantly emotional, and genuinely noble.

O'Grady's work provided a model for a way to deal with the Gaelic inheritance of heroic legend, the way of imaginative re-creation. O'Grady's methods
had their problems, though (his prose idiom was no more Irish than any other
Victorian journalist's, for one thing), and what was a good method for dealing
with ancient stories would not do for folklore that was still current in the
countryside. Douglas Hyde, for one, realized that Irish folk literature would be
either an arcane scholarly subject or the stuff of cheap popularization unless it
were presented in a responsible but interesting way. In 1890 he published
Beside the Fire, with fifteen tales in English versions facing their Gaelic
originals. The book presented to English-speaking readers for almost the first
time unvarnished versions of real Gaelic storytelling. In addition, Hyde used in
his translations a dialect which actually reflected the English spoken in Ireland.
In his introduction, he notes that English and Gaelic are radically opposed
languages in spirit and style, but he also observes that the English spoken by
most Irish people is influenced heavily by the idioms and sentence constructions
of Gaelic. By using a dialect for his translations, Hyde made *Beside the Fire*
both a preservation and an innovation, a preservation in that it helped give yet
another generation some sense of what real Gaelic story-telling was like, an
innovation in that it used for the first time an accurate Anglo-Irish dialect based
on an acute ear and a good knowledge of Gaelic. Three years later Hyde followed his work on Irish prose with *Love Songs of Connacht*, a collection of
texts and translations from the traditional poetry of the west of Ireland. These
songs, often of love frustrated by custom and poverty, are strikingly beautiful,
and again Hyde continued his process of preservation and innovation. He
saved songs that might otherwise have been lost to non-Gaelic speakers, but
translated them into an idiom, particularly in his prose versions, which catches

much of the spirit of the originals. The prose versions of these songs did a good deal to help those who were ignorant of Gaelic understand that real Gaelic poetry was tough, specific, and quirkily imaginative, strikingly different from what had passed for "Irish" poetry with Moore, Mangan, or even the younger Yeats. Hyde followed these collections with several others, but these two were perhaps his most valuable. By preserving and translating traditional tales and songs, he helped remind Anglo-Irish writers of the wealth of the Gaelic world. By helping create an Anglo-Irish literary dialect, he led the way toward the development of an idiom that was distinctively Ireland's own and perhaps the best possible way to translate the Celtic consciousness into English.

Hyde was the great folklorist of the nineties, but he was only one of many writers who devoted themselves to the subject. Yeats was no trained folklorist and was almost entirely ignorant of Gaelic, but his collections were popular and significant. Yeats's approach to folklore was rather like O'Grady's to the ancient texts. Folklore was, he thought, the very voice of the people, and he saw in it almost a sacred oral tradition. Although he published several collections of folklore, his most important was *The Celtic Twilight*, which appeared in 1893. This little book is a set of short sketches of Irish storytellers and their tales, many of the stories having to do with magic and the supernatural. Yeats's tales of magic and his elaborate prose style combined with the title of his collection to give readers, non-Irish ones especially, the idea that all the new Irish writers spoke out of a gray and magical mist. Yeats himself said, though, that his purpose in the book was "to create a little world out of the beautiful, pleasant, and significant things of this marred and clumsy world, and to show in a vision something of the face of Ireland to any of my own people who would look where I bid them."[10] The word "vision" was the important one here, for Yeats hoped that his book would add to the development of a "symbolical" language for Ireland which would reach into the past as well as the present. Looking back at the book after seventy years, we can see three things that are especially significant about it. In terms of Yeats himself, it is a sort of fragmented autobiography of his own discovery of himself as an Irish writer and his discovery of his affinities with the illiterate storytellers he met around Sligo and elsewhere. In addition, Yeats's was the first popular book of Irish folklore to take seriously the beliefs of the peasants in the supernatural. For him, the fairies and the banshee were no joke or quaint survival, but part of the living imagination of the country. And, finally, the subject and tone of the *Celtic*

10 *The Celtic Twilight* (1893; New York: Signet, 1962), p. 31.

Twilight did much to create the popular impression of what Ireland and Irish writing could and should be like.

Folklore and poetry were closely tied together in the Irish Renaissance of the 1890s; Yeats was only one of several poets who gathered folk materials to use in poetry and only one of several who hoped that his own work would eventually become a part of the living folk tradition. Even with the help of folklore, though, Anglo-Irish poetry was only starting to find its real voice during this decade. Too many of the poets, having discovered their native land and its Celtic inheritance, proceeded to write worthy but feeble poems. John Todhunter, for example, an Irishman living in London, produced some suave and competent work on Irish subjects as well as some poetic dramas which probably influenced Yeats, but his work is no more Irish than, say, Aubrey de Vere's. T. W. Rolleston wrote at least one fine poem, "The Dead at Clonmacnoise," but he was a better critic than poet. AE had a powerful imagination, but he never became a first-rate poet perhaps because his imagination was too powerfully visionary to be disciplined into the mundane business of poetic craft. His first volume, *Homeward: Songs by the Way* (1894), carried "I know I am a spirit" as its epigraph, and there was almost nothing overtly Irish about the poems that followed. Filled with a love of beauty, humanity, and what he saw as the divine in human nature, AE valued Irish folklore because he saw in it an expression of the ancient desire to come into communion with the real but invisible spiritual world. He was interested, too, in Irish myth because he sensed in the ancient gods and heroes expressions of his own pantheistic religion of the Earth Mother.

In 1896 AE wrote to Yeats that he believed that the old gods were returning to Erin and that an apocalyptic moment in world history was near. Soon thereafter, Yeats invited him to participate in preparing the rituals for a mystical Irish spiritual order which was to have its headquarters in an abandoned castle in Lough Key. We may find it odd that poets would plan such a project—and it came to nothing—but Yeats agreed with AE in seeing Ireland as a land of mystical symbolism, as his poetry from the nineties clearly demonstrates. His first volume of poems, *The Wanderings of Oisin and Other Poems* (1889) had in its title poem and several others shown his debt to nineteenth-century Anglo-Irish poetry. The volumes of poetry he published in the 1890s showed an even stronger debt to the idea of Celticism. *The Countess Kathleen and Various Legends and Lyrics* (1892) contained, in addition to his first major play, a set of poems which weave together themes and images from folklore and Gaelic legend. These lyric and narrative poems, reordered and republished in his *Poems* of 1895 as "The Rose," fall, basically, into two categories: poems about frustrated love, clothed often in the imagery of the Celtic tradition, and a group of overtly legendary or folkloric poems which are also commentaries on the dangers of the poetic imagination. Both sets show Yeats's remarkable talent for blending personal concerns and Celtic imagery. The poems of frustrated love arose out of his own frustrated passion for the beautiful nationalist, Maud Gonne. Yeats had first met her in 1889 and had immediately fallen in love. Throughout the nineties his emotions turned to her, but she reciprocated his love only in certain ways. Committed to the cause of Irish nationalism and involved with another man, she valued Yeats for his usefulness to the cause, but she had no intention of marrying him, as he so ardently hoped. His love for her tortured him, but it also produced such beautiful lyrics as "The Sorrow of Love," "When You are Old," and "A Dream of Death." These poems of personal emotion appear to have little in common with such poems as "Fergus and the Druid" and "Cuchulain's Fight with the Sea," poems based on Irish legend. But the poems to Maud Gonne and the legendary poems are similar in their concern with the dangers to the self posed by the passionate imagination. As Yeats's life was blasted by his hopeless love, so Fergus is driven to all-knowing madness by the druid's bag of dreams and Cuchulain is driven mad by druid enchantment and his accidental killing of his only son. Yeats's emphasis on even the destructive power of the imagination needs to be understood in terms of his interpretation of Irishness in this volume. The Irish belief in the supernatural which had been seen by others as a quaint Celtic trait becomes in his poems an immensely powerful force. "The Rose" is a particularly valuable sequence because in it we find the first of his mature poetic styles and his first series of major poems. As a collection of poems, it was the best he was to write for nearly a quarter of a century, and it was surely the best to come from Ireland in the 1890s.

Yeats remained the dominant figure in the growing Irish movement throughout the nineties, and he did as much as anyone to gain a reputation for it in England. Actually, he spent about as much time there and in France as he did in Ireland, and it was to Yeats that the movement owed much of its increasing sophistication, as well. Between 1890 and 1896, he was often in London, helping, among other things, to make a link between the Irish movement and some of the young English poets. He was a member of the Rhymers' Club, a group of young poets in London, and to a certain extent he turned this club into an extension of the Celtic revival. Lionel Johnson, a young, Oxford-educated Irishman and disciple of Walter Pater, the mentor of the Aesthetic movement, came to terms with his Irishness through Yeats's influence. A characteristic "decadent" poet of his time, Johnson had had little interest in Irish matters until he met Yeats, but with Yeats's encouragement he began to study Irish writing. He lectured widely in Ireland in 1894, urging the young Irish poets to be better artists and to avoid the dangers of provinciality. His own Irish poetry was often a more sophisticated version of the patriotism of the Young Ireland movement of the 1840s, but the best of his work combined nationalism and Catholicism successfully, and in a way Yeats could not.

Johnson, an able critic, wrote some good essays on Anglo-Irish literature, becoming one of several voices in literary debates which were to sharpen the goals of the Irish movement. The literary and nationalist clubs in London and Dublin provided a good forum for such discussion; Yeats and some friends took over the old Southwark Irish club in 1891, and a year later, he was in Dublin for the founding of a new national literary society there. Yeats himself was more than a little ambivalent about these organizing forays, for he was never really comfortable with the clumsy and earnest nationalists who would regularly come to the meetings. The poet who was an editor of Blake, student of the occult, and friend of Oscar Wilde must have seemed an exotic figure to these ordinary Irishmen, and one of them has provided an amusing description of Yeats's first speech at the Southwark club: "In appearance he was tall, slight, and mystic of the mystical. His face was not so much dreamy as haunting: a little weird even—so that really if one were to meet him on an Irish mountain in the moonlight he would assuredly hasten away to the nearest fireside with a story of a new and genial ghost which had crossed his path. He spoke in a hushed, musical, eerie tone."[11]

For the National Literary Society in Dublin, Yeats prepared one of his most important lectures, "Nationality and Literature," given in May of 1893. In it, he suggested that every national literature must go through three basic stages in its development: epic, dramatic, and lyric. He argued that English literature was reaching the degenerate end of its lyric phase, but that Anglo-Irish literature was only in the prime of its epic. Insisting that Irish writers should take up the challenge of this phase, he told them to reject the attractions of writing on non-Irish subjects and to perfect their styles. The emphasis on the perfecting of style was a valuable reminder to Irish poets who had too often valued patriotism over craft in the past, but Yeats himself almost became too involved with style in his writing in the later nineties. He defended his elitism

---

11 W. P. Ryan, *The Irish Literary Revival* (London: no publisher; 1894) p. 29.

and obscurity by saying that there was a need for a literature for the spiritual aristocracy which would have to lead the new Ireland, but the poems and stories he published at the end of the decade seem now as thin as they are intricate. *The Secret Rose* (1897) is a collection of stories using some Irish settings and themes, but it has very little indeed to do with the earlier kinds of Anglo-Irish short stories. The collection's dominant concern is the conflict between spiritual values and ordinary ones, a theme which Yeats used often, but one which had little to do with the peasants and landlords of traditional Anglo-Irish fiction. "Rosa Alchemica" uses thought and imagery from the occult Order of the Golden Dawn, of which Yeats was a member, while "The Adoration of the Magi" is a tale of the search of apocalyptic transformation in the bohemian Paris of the 1890s. The stories are interesting period pieces, but Yeats was being overly optimistic in thinking that these stories added much to the development of Irish fiction. *The Wind Among the Reeds*, the second collection of poems he published during the nineties, is a group of exquisitely beautiful lyrics, but there is something airlessly artificial about too many of them. The Celticism is very strong, but it is world-weary. Yeats appended a ponderous set of notes to these fragile poems to explain their mythological and anthropological references and so freight them with more significance than might appear on a first reading. Too often, though, the notes try to explain poems which are unreasonably obscure and private. Even so, the best of them still exhibit Yeats's astonishing lyrical gifts, and the handling of the theme of magical metamorphosis (the volume could be read as Yeats playing Ovid) is often excitingly imaginative.

It is hard to imagine the unworldly poet of *The Wind Among the Reeds* as a literary organizer and debater, but Yeats was an exceedingly complex man, and he was right in the midst of several important literary discussions, quarrels even, during the nineties, discussions which were useful in clarifying the goals and methods of the new Irish movement. One, in 1895, between Yeats and his friends on one side and Edward Dowden, the professor of English at Trinity College and a scholar-critic of international reputation on the other, dealt with the basic question of the value of Irish writing. Dowden, an exponent of "West-Britonism," believed that Ireland would do well to become as English as possible, and the faster the better. He maintained that most Irish poetry was worthless because it was sentimental and rhetorical. Yeats agreed that sentimentality and empty rhetoric were serious problems, but he attacked Dowden's apparent belief that Irish literature, the new as well as the old, was unworthy of serious attention. Most literary nationalists agreed with Yeats in this debate, but two other quarrels divided them. One was a bitter controversy in 1893 over the publication of a series of Irish books. Yeats had hoped to control the project himself in order to publish books which met his criterion of artistry over nationalism, but the project fell into the hands of the ancient Sir Charles Gavan Duffy, a survivor of the Young Ireland group of the 1840s. Duffy proceeded to edit a series of nationalistic titles which reflected old-fashioned patriotism and were mostly worthless as literature. If nothing else, this quarrel showed that the nationalist belief that any patriotic writing was in itself a good thing had not died yet. Later, in 1899, Irish writers were again divided by a quarrel between those who believed that they should restrict themselves to Irish themes and those who believed that Irish literature could only grow by joining in the great international literary movements of the time, urban realism in particular. These "cosmopolitans" argued that the attempt to create a national literature was anachronistic. To a certain extent, this was a debate over method: Symbolists vs. Realists. In another way, it was an argument between writers of rural Ireland and those from the cities. The writers who glorified Celticism and the peasantry were naturally drawn toward rural themes and images and, usually, toward the techniques of Symbolism. The urban writers were just as naturally drawn towards international Realism and the themes and images which are common to all urban cultures, Irish or otherwise. This last quarrel was one which was never really resolved, and that may have been just as well for Irish writing because much fine work was produced in both modes for decades. "Cosmopolitan" attitudes would eventually support the work of Joyce, some of the masters of the Irish short story, and some later poets. "Localism" had already produced Yeats and the writers of the Celtic twilight; it would later reinforce the work of a whole school of dramatists. But that was all in the future.

Healthily enough, the argument between cosmopolitans and localists showed that by 1899 the Irish Renaissance had matured to the point that its writers could hold divergent views without giving up their concern for the future of Irish writing. Even though the mists of the Celtic twilight seemed as deep as ever in 1899, the first phase of the Irish Renaissance was ending. A movement had been organized and books had been published; one definition of Irish writing, the definition based on Celticism, had been created and exploited. The relations between literature and nationalism had been clarified, and some varying theories about how Irish writing had to be put forward. The nineties did no more than build a foundation for the new Irish literature, but it was a good foundation. Still, an impartial observer looking at the situation in 1899 might have decided that the Irish revival was beginning to lose its impetus; too much writing was beginning to look too much like what had already been done. But that observer would have been wrong. When Yeats had argued in his lecture on "Nationality and Literature" that a literature naturally developed from its epic phase to its dramatic, he was, without knowing it, prophesying the future for the Irish Renaissance. After the turn of the century, drama would become a major genre in Ireland, and gradually the enormous energy of the dramatic movement would spill over into poetry and fiction. The great days of the Irish Renaissance were yet to come.

Part II

phoenix triumphant

the patriot game
Politics and Revolution, 1891–1923

> Irishmen and Irishwomen: In the name of God and
> of the dead generations from whom she receives her old
> tradition of nationhood, Ireland, through us,
> summons her children to her flag and strikes for her freedom.
>
> Proclamation of the Irish Republic, 1916

> I'm telling you . . . Joxer . . . th' whole worl's
> . . . in a ter . . ible state o' . . . chassis!
>
> Sean O'Casey, *Juno and the Paycock*

IRELAND in 1891 was a nation stunned. For almost a year, the Parnell debacle had been its obsession, and even the death of Parnell did not end the arguments and recriminations among his followers. Those quarrels poisoned Irish political life for a full generation, and even the genuine organizational ability of John Redmond, Parnell's eventual successor as leader of the Irish Party, was not enough to bring unity and purpose again to the Home Rule cause. In the two decades after Parnell's death, Irish politics remained largely fragmented with a majority of the Irish people still willing to work through parliamentary channels for home rule, but an increasingly vocal minority insisting that it would take something stronger than parliamentary politics, even bloodshed, to make Ireland truly a nation once again. Meanwhile, the real initiative in Irish political and social life passed back to the British government and its Unionist supporters in Ireland. Under a program of "constructive Unionism," which joined amelioration of Irish social conditions and political

73

coercion, the government began some important social reforms. Control of the land remained the pressing economic problem in Ireland, but the truly revolutionary Wyndham Land Act of 1903 forced landlords to sell their entire estates to their tenants if three-quarters of the tenants wished to buy. That remarkable piece of social legislation accelerated the pace of native control of land, and its benefits were augmented by the work of the Congested Districts Board, a governmental agency devoted to the development of industry, public works, and land redistribution in the parts of the country most densely populated by the poor. At about the same time, an Irish Unionist, Horace Plunkett, began the hard and valuable work of establishing agricultural cooperatives to help stabilize the incomes of Irish farmers; AE, visionary turned social reformer, became one of his organizers.

Valuable as they were, even these reforms were too little too late in terms of satisfying Irish people with British rule. Despite the national humiliation of the fall of Parnell and its aftermath, the sense of Irish nationalism continued to rise. The Irish politicians squabbled and made themselves ineffectual, but the people developed almost daily their growing sense of Irish self-identity. The literary revival played a central role in that process, of course, but in historical terms it was only one of several important movements. The Gaelic Athletic Association reached far more Irishmen than the writers. By stressing the importance of Irish sports, hurely and football especially, and by urging Irishmen to play no English games, the GAA exerted a remarkable influence in what was and is an intensely sports-loving country. The Gaelic League, founded in 1893 by Douglas Hyde, Father Eugene O'Growney, and Eoin MacNeill, caught the popular imagination, too, with its mixture of adult education and entertainment through language, history, and dancing classes, drama groups, and colorful national meetings. The League did much to encourage national self-reliance and self-respect; by 1908, it had 600 branches throughout the country. Because of its efforts, Gaelic came to be taught in hundreds of primary schools and a knowledge of the language was made a prerequisite for admission to the new National University. The Gaelic League and the GAA owed a good part of their success to effective publicity, and the Irish genius for journalism expressed itself, too, in newspapers which were convincing proponents of nationalist ideas. D. P. Moran, the brilliant editor of *The Leader*, summed up the views of many of his generation by insisting that there were in Ireland two civilizations, one Irish, one English, which could never really reach a rapprochement. To Moran, too much nationalist energy in the past had gone into what were really Anglo-Irish concerns; the time had come, he preached, for Irish Ireland to assert itself.

The failure of the conventional Irish politicians to achieve much at the Parliament in London was symbolized by the Irish Council Bill of 1907, a wishy-washy piece of legislation which would have given local Irish authorities some control over internal matters. That was a far cry from independence or even home rule. Disappointed in the failure of parliamentary politics, a new generation grew up in Ireland after the fall of Parnell believing that it would take more than legislative debate to achieve the goals of nationhood and social justice. Especially after the turn of the century, more extreme nationalist organizations began to emerge, frequently led by men and women whose patriotism had been fired by the books of the Irish Renaissance and whose organizational expertise came from experience in the GAA or the Gaelic League. Some turned to the Irish Republican Brotherhood, the secret revolutionary society which was the offspring of the Fenian movement of the 1860s. The IRB believed that only a revolution could free Ireland of British rule and that parliamentary tactics were essentially a waste of energy. Until the time was ripe for another rising, the IRB could do little but organize, publicize, and conspire. Like most secret organizations, it was often harmed by internal intrigue, and even in the headily nationalist atmosphere of the 1900s, it grew slowly with only 2,000 members in 1912.

Two other organizations, Sinn Fein and the Irish Transport and General Workers' Union, had greater mass appeal than the IRB. Sinn Fein, formed soon after the turn of the century out of several small nationalist groups was dominated by Arthur Griffith, a brilliant ideologue and publicist. Sinn Fein meant "ourselves," and that, in a word, was Griffith's theory of nationalism. He urged Ireland for the Irish through the development of Irish industry and agriculture with tariffs to protect both, and he argued that the constitutional problem could best be resolved by turning the United Kingdom of Britain and Ireland into a dual monarchy on the model of Austria-Hungary. Inspired by the Hungarian Franz Deak's policy of keeping the Hungarian members of the Austrian parliament at home until Hungary was given its own parliament, Griffith urged the Irish members of the British parliament to stay away from it so that eventually an Irish parliament could be established which would be answerable only to a figurehead king Ireland and Britain both acknowledged. The Hungarian model was not really applicable to the Irish situation, and Griffith's dual monarchy was impractical, but his notion of Ireland for the Irish was its strong emphasis on Irish self-reliance and self-definition made a great deal of sense in its time. Griffith, a former member of the IRB, kept close ties with militant nationalism, and in the years before World War I, Sinn Fein became an increasingly attractive alternative to a Home Rule movement which seemed to be losing its effectiveness.

Irish labor unions could have provided a strong support for nationalism, for Ireland was becoming increasingly industrialized and many workers were ardent nationalists. But the Irish labor movement was slow in developing after its real beginnings in the 1860s. After the turn of the century, however, Irish labor found immensely effective leaders in James Connolly and James Larkin, with Connolly providing the intellect and Larkin the brawn and charisma. Connolly's Irish Transport and General Workers' Union began the difficult task of organizing urban workers. Connolly was a nationalist and would eventually die for it before a British firing squad, but to him the cause of Irish nationalism was basically an economic question. A legally independent Ireland which still permitted one class to exploit another would be free in name only, he believed, and he worked for the day when Ireland would become a socialist republic. In the meantime, there was organizing to be done in the slums and factories of Dublin and Belfast, for workers in both cities, and most smaller cities too, lived in the midst of terrible economic exploitation. Working conditions were often appalling and poverty was rampant with many workers enduring conditions all too reminiscent of the famine years on the farms. In Dublin, a fifth of the population lived in tenement houses which were judged unfit for human habitation, most of these families living in one room each. One eight-room tenement house had almost a hundred occupants, and usually there was neither running water nor decent sanitation. More than half the population of Dublin was sporadically employed or out of work; for those with jobs, ninety-hour work weeks were not uncommon. There was a great task for the unions to do, and Connolly and Larkin threw themselves into it passionately. Eventually, in 1913, Larkin's union came into conflict with the Dublin employers led by William Martin Murphy, the owner of the city's street-car system. Murphy organized the employers so that by the end of September, 24,000 workers who were members of Larkin's union had been locked out of their jobs. What followed was a bitter autumn and winter of riots, arrests, police brutality, and strikes by other unions. With their parents on strike, thousands of children went hungry, and a benevolent plan to send them to England for the winter to avoid starvation was opposed by the Catholic clergy on the grounds that the children might lose their religion in Protestant England. As F. S. L. Lyons tells it, "So emphatic and well-organized was the hostility that the rescue operation had to be abandoned and the children left to wither in the sanctity of their slums."[1]

1 *Ireland Since the Famine* (1971; London: Fontana, 1973), p. 283.

Eventually, time, hunger, and quarrels with the British unions which had supported the strike led to failure as the workers drifted back to the sweatshops. Labor had lost the immediate battle, but the great general strike of 1913 dramatized the shocking conditions in Ireland and made the labor movement itself far more militant. One lasting effect of the strike was the formation of the Irish Citizen Army to protect strikers from harassment by police; in a few years, James Connolly and his Citizen Army would play an important role in the armed rising of Easter, 1916.

At the time of the Dublin strike and for several months thereafter, Irish people were as much interested in the revived matter of home rule as they were in labor troubles. After the general election of 1910, the British Liberal Party, short of a majority, had to depend on the Irish Party for the votes to make a majority in the House of Commons. With chances of success better than they had ever been for Parnell, Redmond and his followers were determined to make the best of a wonderful opportunity to secure home rule. Redmond had little of Parnell's force, but he was an effective politician, and he had done a good job of rebuilding the Irish party after the bad years of the 1890s. It seemed for a time that his steady and careful statesmanship would succeed where Parnell had failed. A Home Rule Bill was introduced, and slowly made its way through Parliament. Redmond's apparent success undermined more militant nationalist groups for a time, and Sinn Fein, for one, seemed to be losing its popularity. Nevertheless, the success of the Home Rule movement frightened Protestant Unionists, especially in the north of Ireland. The real crisis began in 1912, when the Home Rule Bill passed the House of Commons. Under British parliamentary procedures, it could be delayed in becoming law for as much as two years by opposition in the House of Lords, but passage in the Commons made its eventual enactment almost as inevitability. Opposition to it in northern Ireland was rising daily, and the opposition found a powerful spokesman in Edward Carson, a Unionist from Dublin who had had a brilliant legal career and was a superb public speaker. As the leader of the opposition to Home Rule, Carson became as much a charismatic figure to his followers as Parnell had been to his twenty years before. Under the slogan, "Ulster will fight and Ulster will be right," a paramilitary force of more than 100,000 men was organized among Ulster Protestants, the Ulster Volunteers. With a well-organized military force behind him, Carson urged in January of 1913 that the nine counties of Ulster be excluded from any Home Rule legislation. Catholic nationalists in the south replied by organizing their own paramilitary force, the Irish Volunteers. By the spring of 1914 there was a military crisis as well as a constitutional one. If the politicians could not find a way to solve the Irish question, it seemed certain that civil war would come.

Tension was extremely high all during the spring and summer of 1914. British Army officers stationed at the Curragh, a major base in Ireland, threatened to resign rather than enforce home rule. An enormous number of guns for the Ulster Volunteers was landed in April without any interference by police or military authorities. A few weeks later, another huge load of armaments arrived, these destined for the Irish Volunteers. This time the police did act, and civilians in Dublin were killed in the ensuing melee. As the summer of 1914 dragged on, the Irish crisis dominated the newspapers in Ireland and Britain. The Ulster Volunteers threatened to fight even the British Army to remain British subjects; Redmond, nominally the leader of the Irish Volunteers, tried desperately to find a compromise which would keep his followers from fighting either the Ulster Volunteers or the British. He reluctantly agreed to a formula that would exclude Ulster from the provisions of the Home Rule Bill for a time, but before the crisis could be fully resolved, the murder of an Austrian prince in far-off Sarajevo intervened. Britain, and Ireland, went to war with Germany and Austria in August of 1914, and attention shifted away from the Irish crisis. Nevertheless, soon after the outbreak of World War 1, the Home Rule Bill became law. Even though Ulster was to be excluded from its provisions for six years after it took effect, Redmond could congratulate himself because he had achieved more than any Irish leader of the previous century.

Yet home rule was not to take effect immediately; in passing the new legislation, Parliament also agreed that it would be suspended for the duration of the war. Thus a potentially explosive situation came into being. British rule in Ireland was undermined by the fact that everyone knew that it would soon end, at least over most of the island. The Ulster Unionists gained an even longer breathing period to try for more concessions from the Redmondites and the British government. Moderate nationalists were tantalized by the possibility of home rule, but militants could argue that all Redmond had achieved was a vague promise about future change. For those who wanted a united, independent, and republican Ireland—the IRB and its sympathizers—the uncertain situation during wartime provided a remarkable opportunity. The Irish Volunteers split between those who followed Redmond's line of accepting the compromise and supporting the British war effort and those who argued that England's difficulty was Ireland's opportunity. The majority of the Volunteers supported Redmond, but a minority of about 15,000 men, led by Professor Eoin MacNeill, disavowed his leadership, and this group kept itself in training for any eventuality. However, without MacNeill's knowledge, his Volunteers were gradually taken over by men with connections to the IRB. The IRB itself had been a flabby and ineffectual organization for more than a decade after the fall of Parnell, but by 1914, with support from America, it was again becoming a potent revolutionary organization. After some complex negotiations, the IRB men who secretly ran MacNeill's Volunteers and James Connolly, the leader of the Irish Citizen Army, reached an agreement to act together. They then waited for an opportunity to make a military strike against British rule, assuming that Britain involved in a world war would be less able to deal with an uprising in Ireland.

Sir Roger Casement, a former member of the British civil service, a distinguished social reformer and an Irish nationalist, went to Germany to buy arms and try to interest the Germans in the Irish cause. The Germans, astonishingly, failed to realize the possibilities of a rising in Ireland as a stab in the back to the British war effort, but eventually they agreed to supply some arms. Casement was scheduled to return to Ireland with his arms in April of 1916, and plans were set in motion in Dublin for a rising. The bungling of the Casement mission was only one of a series of bungles connected with that rising. Because MacNeill learned what was afoot only at the last minute, there was incredible confusion in commands to the Volunteers. MacNeill felt that he had been used by the IRB, and he was entirely right. Nevertheless, the men who were now preparing for armed rebellion had done what they believed they had to do, and they were an extraordinary group. Some of them were able revoluntionary organizers who genuinely thought they had a chance of driving the British from Ireland. Others were visionaries who sensed that a heroic action, even a futile one, would galvanize public opinion, and they were ready to die as a moral gesture. The most effective of these men was Padraic Pearse, a remarkably complex figure by anyone's reckoning. A minor poet and an important educational theorist, Pearse probably knew that a rising at this point was doomed, yet he drove on toward the inevitable bloodshed. Pearse believed that only blood sacrifice could redeem Ireland and Irish nationalism, and he preached that doctrine in a remarkable series of speeches and newspaper articles. He was a mystical nationalist, and to some extent his views were shared by Thomas MacDonagh and Joseph Mary Plunkett, two of his closest colleagues, both poets and literary men. Yet MacDonagh was also a shrewd political organizer and Plunkett, for all his love of extravagant dress and melodramatic intriguing, had given some imaginative thought to how to conduct urban guerrilla warfare. Thomas J. Clarke, on the other hand, was an old-time revolutionary, a survivor from the Fenian movement and the new group's strongest link with the past. And James Connolly, the labor leader, was a Socialist who only slowly came to believe that nationalism was as worth fighting for as social change. The other men and women who led the rising, Sean MacDermott, Eamonn Ceannt, Eamon de Valera, Constance Markievicz and the rest, came to their militancy from a variety of motives, but it is worth noting how much the 1916 rising was a continuation of the ideas of the Young Ireland movement of seventy years before. Those who believed in the necessity of violence reflected John Mitchel's prayer to send war in our time, O Lord; those who saw an armed rising as a means towards social justice were the heirs of Fintan Lalor. Those who believed in mystical nationalism owed a good deal to the Celticism of the 1890s, but even more to Thomas Davis.

The 1848 rising by Young Ireland was a military disaster; the 1916 rising was, in the short run, a failure, too, but it changed the course of Irish history far more than the rising of 1848. Still, it began badly. The load of German armaments Casement was bringing was sunk off the Kerry coast, and Casement himself was captured. The confusion over orders to the Volunteers meant that the rising was largely restricted to Dublin; there were some military operations outside the capital, but they were disorganized and ineffectual. About 1,600 men and women "went out" on Easter Monday of 1916 in Dublin, though, and they made a surprisingly effective rebellion. On the morning of that April 24 they occupied some crucial positions around the city, but they failed to establish themselves firmly at Dublin Castle, which they captured with astonishing ease, and valuable time was wasted elsewhere. The center of the rising became the General Post Office in Sackville Street (now O'Connell Street). The holiday crowds in Dublin were, for a time, almost oblivious to what was going on, and only a small group was present in front of the post office to hear Pearse read the proclamation of the Irish Republic. One man who was there, a casual bystander, remembers thinking how slight a figure Pearse seemed and how high-pitched his voice was as he read that "the Irish Republic is entitled to, and hereby claims, the allegiance of every Irishman and Irishwoman."[2] It all seemed, this bystander recalled sixty years later, a most extraordinary lark; fourteen then, he ambled on down Sackville Street wondering if this were only a patriotic charade. It was not, and the shooting over the next few days proved it. One real advantage the rebels had was their desperation, and Connolly had rightly judged the situation when he told a

2 Quoted in *Ireland Since the Famine*, p. 369.

friend, "We are going out to be slaughtered."[3] Yet the rising lasted for five full days. On Tuesday the British had to use artillery to sweep barricades off the streets. On Wednesday a gunboat was brought into the Liffey; Sackville Street and the area around it was almost completely destroyed. The post office, gutted by fire, had to be abandoned, and on Saturday Pearse finally sent out the order to surrender. By the time it was all over, 450 persons had been killed, 2,614 wounded. The damage to the city of Dublin must have amounted to several million pounds.

The failure of the rising and the destruction it created should have worked to the advantage of the British. Once again Britain had demonstrated that armed rebellion in Ireland was doomed. Moreover, many Dubliners were outraged because the center of their beautiful city had been destroyed in a fruitless act. As the rebels were marched away to internment, they had to face often hostile crowds of their fellow Irish men and women. Nevertheless, having won this particular battle, the British then made an extraordinary series of blunders. 3,430 men and 79 women were interned in a harsh military effort to root out militant nationalism, but many of the people arrested had not been involved in the rising at all. The time they spent in prison helped make rebels out of many of them, and nationalist leaders later observed that the British prisons and internment camps provided a wonderful training school for new revolutionaries. More dramatically, the British began to court-martial and shoot the leaders of the rising. Had that been done all at once, it might have had the desired effect of frightening the Irish. But the executions dragged out for nine days, beginning on May 3, and they had a tremendous effect on public opinion. Pearse and the other signers of the proclamation of the republic must have expected to die, and so perhaps did the other military leaders. Nevertheless, it seemed brutal to shoot men like Eamonn Ceannt and Sean Heuston who had fought as chivalrous soldiers. Willie Pearse, Padraic's gentle brother, died simply because he was his brother. The most brutal of all the executions, though, was that of James Connolly. Wounded in the fighting, Connolly was among the last to die, and his wounds were so serious that he had to be tied into a chair to face his firing squad. Martial law prevailed in Ireland for quite some time; it, together with the executions, simply compounded hatred of the British. Pearse had been right: blood sacrifice was what was needed to change the course of Irish history.

Nevertheless, the situation after 1916 was out of anyone's control. The British government dithered; militant nationalism became ever a stronger force.

3 Quoted in *ibid.*, p. 366.

Lloyd George, the British prime minister after 1916, tried a conference in Dublin to resolve the situation, and it produced nothing. The men and women arrested in 1916 were gradually released from prison, and most of them came home committed revolutionaries. In February of 1917 Count Plunkett, the father of the executed rebel, was elected to Parliament as a Sinn Fein candidate; five months later Eamon de Valera, the senior surviving military officer from the rising, was also elected. In the elections of December 1918, the old Irish parliamentary party was destroyed. It had held 68 seats previously; after the election, it held only 6, and 73 seats went to Sinn Fein. Following Arthur Griffith's dictum, these new members of the British Parliament did not go to London. Instead, they met in Dublin on January 21, 1919, to found their own Irish parliament, Dáil Éireann.

That first Dáil almost immediately produced a declaration of independence, and a few weeks later it elected Eamon de Valera its president. Arthur Griffith, the architect of Sinn Fein's policy of passive resistance, became his deputy, and Michael Collins, from the IRB, was named director of military operations. Griffith had long taught that the surest way to independence was simply to act independent, and that policy produced some remarkable results. Even though the British administration remained in place and the Royal Irish Constabulary and the British Army carried out its orders, the bulk of the Irish people, especially outside Ulster, acknowledged the Dáil as the legitimate authority in Ireland. Collins was spectacularly successful in raising money for the new "government," and in short order Sinn Fein took over much of the local administration in Ireland. Meanwhile, the level of violence between the British and the Irish nationalists slowly heightened. The revived Irish military force, the Irish Republican Army with perhaps 15,000 men at most, and about 3,000 for day-to-day operations, faced a well-organized Royal Irish Constabulary and a fairly sizable British Army in Ireland. Nevertheless, the advantage lay with IRA. The police were dispersed through about 1,500 barracks around the country; the IRA, often not in uniform, could melt into a crowd at will, and it had in Michael Collins a brilliant master of guerrilla warfare. During most of 1919 and into 1920, the Anglo-Irish War as the Irish officially called it, or "the troubles" as they euphemistically referred to it in ordinary conversation, consisted primarily of sporadic IRA raids on police barracks. Even though only eighteen policemen were killed during 1919, the tension steadily mounted. Things turned particularly ugly after March of 1920. The mayor of Cork, Thomas MacCurtain, an IRA sympathizer, was killed by a squad of masked gunmen whom everyone assumed to be from the British Army. Soon thereafter, the IRA murdered a civil servant, Alan Bell, because he had been entirely too successful in finding out about the IRA's finances. Religious riots broke out in northern Ireland, and British public opinion wanted the trouble in Ireland ended. More British Army forces appeared, and two groups of soldiers were brought in to help defeat the IRA, the "'Black and Tans" and the Auxiliaries. Both consisted largely of men who had fought with the British Army in World War I, men who found it difficult to readjust to civilian life, and both brought a new level of brutality to the situation. Midnight raids on private homes by the Black and Tans became ordinary experiences for nationalist families, and bloody reprisals became too common. MacCurtain's successor as mayor of Cork, Terence MacSwiney, died on a hunger strike in a British prison and that stirred Irish opinion deeply, as did the execution of Kevin Barry, a young student charged with an IRA murder. The bloody climax of the war came on November 21, 1920. Early on that morning, eleven British intelligence officers were murdered by IRA men on orders of Collins, some of the murders occurring with their wives watching. That afternoon, the Black and Tans had their revenge by firing indiscriminately into a crowd gathered to watch a Gaelic football match at Dublin's Croke Park. Twelve people died and sixty were wounded. A few days later, the Cork IRA ambushed two lorries of Auxiliaries, killing all but one of them. In reprisal, the Black and Tans and "Auxies" raided Cork itself in a binge of looting and burning that left the center of the city destroyed. Although November of 1920 was the worst month of the war, it went on until June of the next year. Finally, with both sides exhausted and frustrated, a truce was arranged.

For months after the truce, representatives of the British government and the Dáil met to try to work out a solution to the crisis. The negotiations were immensely complex, but, in essence, they turned on several basic problems. The British, under the old Home Rule bill and the Government of Ireland Act (1920), were committed to a partition of the island. Before the negotiations had even begun, a new parliament for Northern Ireland had met in Belfast, and British Prime Minister Lloyd George was in no position to renege on the promises to the Ulster Unionists of separation from any state created in the rest of the country. Moreover, Lloyd George was determined that at least some nominal British rule would remain in southern Ireland. On the other hand, British public opinion was sick of the Irish war. The Irish negotiators, Arthur Griffith and Michael Collins the most prominent, were committed to the traditional aspirations of militant Irish nationalism: full independence, a unified Ireland, and a republican form of government. The differences seemed almost irreconcilable, but both negotiating teams knew that the only alternative to compromise was the continuation of a war neither seemed able to win.

The tale of the negotiations has been superbly told in Frank Pakenham's *Peace By Ordeal*, and it need not be retold here. Finally, on December 6, 1921, the two sides signed a treaty after Lloyd George had delivered an ultimatum of renewed war. The treaty provided for the establishment of an Irish Free State comprising the twenty-six counties of Munster, Leinster, Connacht, and part of Ulster. There was to be no republic; instead, the Free State would be a dominion within the British empire. An oath of allegiance to the king would be required of members of the Dáil. Seeing no other way, Griffith, Collins, and the others accepted the partition of Ireland into Free State and Northern Ireland, hoping that a boundary commission would find a solution to the problem of the Catholic nationalists now stranded in Northern Ireland under Protestant Unionist rule. In general, the British got about all they could out of a bad situation. The Irish got the greatest measure of independence they had known in centuries, and that seemed the best they could do. Michael Collins wrote to a friend after signing the treaty: "Think—what I have got for Ireland? Something which she has wanted these past seven hundred years. Will anyone be satisfied at the bargain? Will anyone?! I tell you this—early this morning I signed my death warrant. I thought at the time, how odd, how ridiculous—a bullet may just as well have done the job five years ago."[4] Collins' words were prophetic, for he would indeed be dead in only a few months because an important part of the Dáil and the IRA felt betrayed. For completely inexplicable reasons, the negotiators in London neglected to transmit the text of the treaty they were signing to de Valera, the president of the Dáil. When they returned to Dublin, they found that he and many others were bitterly disappointed and angered by what their colleagues had done. The Dáil began a long and rancorous debate on the treaty. Partition and dominion status were fought over, but the real fight was over the oath of allegiance to the king, an oath de Valera and many others were utterly unprepared to take. Eventually, in January of 1922, the Dáil voted to accept the Treaty, but only by a vote of 64 to 57.

The Free State then began to slide towards civil war. Because of the transition to dominion status, the governmental situation in Ireland was intensely complicated for a while, and a general election in June of 1922 did not do much to clarify matters. Sinn Fein supporters of the treaty won 58 of the 128 seats in

---

4 Quoted in Frank O'Connor, *The Big Fellow* (1937; London: Corgi Books, 1965), p. 170.

the new Dáil; anti-Treaty Sinn Fein candidates won only 35, but 35 others were held by candidates of other parties. The election results almost seem to suggest that the Irish people were saying they really cared much less about the Treaty than their leaders since candidates from non–Sinn Fein parties took more votes than either the pro- or anti-Treaty elements in Sinn Fein itself. With the election, though, the Free State had a government, and immediately that government was under pressure to assert its authority. An anti-Treaty faction had occupied the Dublin legal complex, the Four Courts. Some of these men kidnapped the deputy chief of staff of the Free State's army; that, together with pressure from the British, made Collins send his army against some of his old comrades. The anti-Treaty men were driven from the Four Courts, but this attack by the National Army was the opening round in a depressing and pathetic civil war. Now it was not Irishman against Briton but Free Stater against Republican. As with the Anglo-Irish war, this was not a war of fixed battles and entrenched lines. The Republicans tried to hold southern Ireland from Limerick to Waterford, but both cities fell to the Free State in July of 1922, and the war rapidly became a matter of ambush, reprisal, and street-corner murder. In August, Arthur Griffith, the head of the Free State, died of pure exhaustion; ten days later, Michael Collins was killed in an ambush. Gradually, though, the power of the Free State wore down the rebels. After the murder of a member of the Dáil in December, the government began a series of reprisal executions, and that had some of the desired psychological effect. Nevertheless, there was a terrible irony in the fact that the government shot seventy-seven Republicans, almost five times as many as the British shot after the 1916 rising. Thousands of Republicans were jailed or interned, and about 4,000 people lost their lives during the course of the war, considerably more than died in the Anglo-Irish war. By May of 1923 it was all over, de Valera having ordered his followers to cease resistance, though he also told them to hide away their guns in case another chance came.

Thus by the spring of 1923, Ireland had been changed, changed utterly. In the twenty-six counties of the Free State, a new tricolor, orange, white, and green, flew over public buildings—tangible evidence of a new nation's independence. Yet the new nation was not entirely independent; members of the Dáil had to take that oath to the British king, and it would be several years before de Valera and his followers would find a way to take the oath and thus rejoin Irish public life on a legal basis. The civil war was a bitter fruit of decades of nationalist aspiration. It had given the lie to much lofty rhetoric about the holiness of Irish aspirations, and it disillusioned a generation and

more. The struggle against the British and the struggle among the Irish themselves had robbed the country of scores of good men and able leaders; Pearse,
McDonagh, Connolly, Griffith, Collins, and too many others were dead before
the Free State could finally begin to govern peacefully. The economic problems
after years of "the troubles" were almost overpowering; the social dislocations
were as great. The six counties of Northern Ireland remained partitioned off
from the Free State; given the large Protestant majority there and the effectiveness of the Unionist government, there was little any politician in the Free
State could do about Northern Ireland except wring his hands and mutter pious
platitudes. Some sober thinkers could well wonder if it were all worth it. Would
Wolfe Tone or O'Connell or Parnell have been happy with the Ireland of
1923? Quite possibly not. Too much hatred, too little room, as Yeats observed
of the Irish situation; political freedom was one legacy of Irish nationalism,
and a precious one, but hatred, disillusionment, and generations of soul-
scarring bitterness were others.

the rise of the abbey
Anglo-Irish Drama, 1900–1923

We will show that Ireland is not the home of
buffoonery and of easy sentiment, as it has been
represented, but the home of an ancient idealism.

Prospectus for the Irish Literary Theatre, 1898

In Ireland, for a few years more, we have a popular
imagination that is fiery, and magnificent, and
tender; so that those of us who wish to write
start with a chance that is not given to writers
in places where the springtime of local life has been
forgotten, and the harvest is a memory only, and the
straw has been turned into bricks.

J. M. Synge

O N A WET AFTERNOON in the summer of 1897, three people sat talking in
the office of a country house in the west of Ireland: W. B. Yeats, Edward Martyn, a well-to-do landowner, and Augusta Gregory. Martyn had
written two plays which he had been unable to get produced in London; both
he and Yeats lamented the fact that there was no theater in Ireland willing to
present serious Irish drama. Lady Gregory knew little about the theater, but she
was interested in writers and was already making her house, Coole Park, into a
refuge for Yeats and some others. Lady Gregory was also a great organizer, and,
as she tells it, that afternoon's conversation about the theater turned into something more than idle talk: "We went on talking about it, and things seemed to

grow possible as we talked, and before the end of the afternoon we had made our plan. We said we would collect money, or rather ask to have a certain sum of money guaranteed. We would then take a Dublin theatre and give a performance of Mr. Martyn's *Heather Field* and one of Mr. Yeats's own plays, *The Countess Cathleen*. I offered the first guarantee of £25."[1]

For Augusta Gregory, nothing she believed in was impossible, and once she came to believe in it, an Irish theater was no impossibility. A public letter was written with which she began the work of asking wealthy and interested friends and acquaintances to guarantee the funds. The public letter said that the plan was to perform "Celtic and Irish plays, which whatever be their degree of excellence will be written with high ambition, and so to build up a Celtic and Irish school of dramatic literature." The letter went on to assert that the "passion for oratory" in Ireland ought to provide these plays with an "uncorrupted and imaginative" audience, one which would be tolerant and anxious to support plays which would portray the true Ireland, "the home of an ancient idealism."[2] The letter also insisted that the plays would be apolitical, and the list of subscribers who eventually offered support certainly shows that contributions were solicited from people of every kind of politics. Nationalists like Maud Gonne and John O'Leary were subscribers, but so was Parnell's heir, John Redmond, and Parnell's fiercest opponent, T. M. Healy; AE and Douglas Hyde signed up, and so did members of the Anglo-Irish aristocracy.

The idea of regular performances of serious Irish plays by Irish playwrights was indeed a new and attractive one, but drama had existed in Ireland for centuries before the first performances of the Irish Literary Theatre in 1899. Dublin's first theater had gone up in 1637, and it was there that the first historical play on an Irish subject, James Shirley's *St. Patrick for Ireland*, had been staged in 1640. In the latter part of the seventeenth century and on through the eighteenth, Dublin had a lively theatrical tradition, producing such splendid comic playwrights as George Farquhar and William Congreve, both graduates of Trinity College, as well as actress Peg Woffington, the Elizabeth Taylor of the mid-eighteenth century. Goldsmith and Sheridan, too, in that century continued the tradition of Irish comic writers of genius, but all these figures made most of their careers in London, as did Dion Boucicault, the enormously popular Irish playwright of the nineteenth century. After the Act of Union in 1800, Ireland had become increasingly a theatrical backwater. Dublin was an important stopping place for traveling companies from England,

---

[1] *Our Irish Theatre* (London and New York: Putnam, 1913), pp. 6–7.
[2] *Ibid.*, p. 7.

and most of the major Irish towns had their occasional theatrical presentations, but what Irish drama there was existed primarily for the English stage. Even so, Boucicault had some spectacular successes in Ireland as Irish audiences found in his *Colleen Bawn* and *Arrah-na-Pogue* "colour, romance, high-sounding words, deeds of daring, and the spirit of sacrifice."[3] They found the same in the patriotic melodramas of J. W. Whitbread toward the end of the century, while Dublin audiences loved the farces which regularly filled the Queen's Theatre and the spectacular productions of English touring companies which played at the Gaiety. Still, none of these really made for an authentic national drama, and Lady Gregory, Yeats, and Martyn had their work cut out for them.

But if a national drama were to be created, what sort of drama should it be? Even as people of all sorts of political views agreed to subscribe their money to support the Irish Literary Theatre out of feelings of national pride, an interest in drama, or just friendship for Lady Gregory, the two playwrights themselves were fundamentally at odds over the sorts of plays they thought ought to be the basis for an Irish dramatic movement. Edward Martyn, strongly influenced by Ibsen, believed Ireland needed plays which dealt with social and personal problems as the plays of the Norwegian master and the new school of "problem plays" did. Yeats, just as strongly influenced by French symbolism, found the realism of much of Ibsen repugnant and dull. Yeats believed that Ireland needed myth, symbol, and high poetry so as to appeal to what he understood to be the Celtic imagination. The play Martyn planned to stage, *The Heather Field*, tells the story of an Irish landowner, Carden Tyrrell, who is obsessed by his estate and his desire to turn a tract of unproductive heather into good farmland. His wife and his close friend fear that he will ruin himself financially with his reclamation project, but he goes on with it, even though it turns him into a tight-fisted landlord, hated by his tenants, who eventually sinks to madness and ruin. *The Heather Field* is a strong play, if sometimes stilted and derivative, in which the conflict of idealism and realism together with some effective handling of symbolism and dream make for more than an ordinary "problem play." Nevertheless, its setting, language, and theme are very different from Yeats's play, *The Countess Cathleen*, an elaborate poetic tapestry shaped into a modern version of a medieval morality play. It, too, has a landowner as its central figure, but Cathleen is by no means a realistic figure nor is the world she inhabits. In Yeats's tale, there is famine in medieval Ireland and two demons,

[3] Andrew E. Malone, *The Irish Drama* (London: Constable, 1929), p. 16.

disguised as merchants, come to Cathleen's peasants offering to buy their souls in exchange for gold the peasants need to buy food. Cathleen, moved by the peasants' plight, gives the merchants her own soul instead, but she is redeemed from her Faustian compact with evil by the nobility of her intention, for "the Light of Lights/Looks always on the motive, not the deed."[4] The play was one of a series of symbolic dramas Yeats then planned to write about the history of Ireland, choosing stories which would somehow define and exemplify the soul and experience of the Irish people. Of the two plays, Martyn's is arguably the better, but what was important at the time and for the future of Irish drama was the fundamental difference between them. Martyn saw the theater as a place of intellectual argument and social commentary on the problems of the contemporary world; Yeats saw it as a place of reverie and imagination about the timeless world of eternal truth. There was room enough for both kinds of drama, and more, but the differences between the two show that the intention of portraying a "true" Ireland was going to be a very complicated matter.

The two plays were scheduled for production in Dublin on May 8 and 9 of 1899, with actors mostly brought over from England, at the Antient Concert Rooms, a large hall seating about 800 people. Because Lady Gregory and both playwrights were almost entirely ignorant of stagecraft, Martyn's cousin, George Moore, hired the actors and organized the rehearsals. Moore was already a famous man; although born into a prominent Irish family, he had made his reputation as a novelist in England, and had only recently begun to see himself also as an Irish writer, one who might have a role in the burgeoning literary revival. Moore was an odd and difficult character, a man who prided himself on his knowledge of the world and his sophistication, but a congenital liar and exceedingly erratic in his behavior. His years as a collaborator in the Irish movement were to prove him at least as much a nuisance as a help.

Even so, the problems Moore sometimes helped make and the usual problems with actors, sets, and costumes were as nothing compared to the problems created by Yeats's seemingly harmless play, *The Countess Cathleen*. Martyn, a devout Catholic, became alarmed when he was warned that the play's action of bartering souls was theologically unacceptable. Moore and Yeats eventually convinced him, with the help of letters from prominent clergymen, that the play was not heretical, but then an old enemy of Yeat's from the nationalist movement, F. Hugh O'Donnell, published a pamphlet, *Souls for Gold*, which brought the theological controversy out into the open. A political controversy

4 *The Collected Plays of W. B. Yeats* (London: Macmillan, 1966), p. 50.

sprang up when ardent nationalists began to insist that the play was a slander on the Irish peasants, honorable folk who even in time of famine would never be so base as to sell their souls. Cardinal Logue, the Catholic primate of Ireland, entered the controversy (without having read the play) by charging in a public letter that "an Irish Catholic audience which could patiently sit out such a play must have sadly degenerated both in religion and patriotism."[5] Intentionally or not, the Cardinal was almost asking for a riot at the first performance. With one newspaper charging that *The Countess Cathleen* was "a blasphemous perversion" and "a hideous caricature of our people's mental and moral character,"[6] Yeats, fearing violence, arranged to have police present at the premiere. There was some hissing and booing from students at the Catholic university (young James Joyce refused to join them), but they did not really interfere with the performance. One viewer wrote in his diary, "I watched enraptured, as if I were in fairy land" as "a spiritual, half-mystic, visionary sensation crept over my senses."[7] *The Countess Cathleen* worked its intended magic on a good section of the audience, but there was no question that Martyn's *Heather Field*, done the next night, was the greater success. Yeats, with his Protestant background and long immersion in Blake, the occult, and Celticism, misjudged his audience. Believing that the Irish were a naturally mystical race whose highest visions could be embodied on the stage through elaborate poetry, complex symbols, and passionate speech, he was out of touch with Dublin and perhaps with the real Ireland. A poet's theater such as he imagined could not succeed, and his plays never exercised the power over a large audience of which he had dreamed. Instead, Martyn's play was the forerunner of the type which would become the basis of much Irish drama, a play dealing with recognizably real people in real situations but in a balance of realism and idealism.

Meanwhile, the first season of the Irish Literary Theatre had generated plenty of publicity, including some favorable reviews in the English newspapers, and a sense of accomplishment. As an Irish movement, it was somewhat tainted by the fact that the police had been called on the first night and that almost no Irish actors had participated. It was very much an Anglo-Irish theater, and the seasons of 1900 and 1901 did not do much to change that. In 1900 the Irish Literary Theatre presented three new plays, *The Bending of the Bough*, a

5 Quoted in Lennox Robinson, *Ireland's Abbey Theatre* (1951; Port Washington, N.Y.: Kennikat Press, 1968), p. 6.

6 Quoted in Peter Kavanagh, *The Story of the Abbey Theatre* (New York: Devin-Adair, 1950), p. 14.

7 *Joseph Holloway's Abbey Theatre*, edited by Robert Hogan and Michael J. O'Neill (Carbondale and Edwardsville: Southern Illinois University Press, 1967), p. 7.

satiric comedy about Irish politics originally written by Martyn but rewritten by Moore, Martyn's *Maeve*, and *The Last Feast of the Fianna* by Alice Milligan. The newspapers still grumbled about the absence of Irish actors, but there was no real controversy, and the productions, considerably more adept than in 1899, took place before a fashionable audience in the huge Gaiety Theatre. October of 1901 brought the final performances of the Literary Theatre, the new plays being a jerry-built collaboration between Yeats and Moore called *Diarmuid and Grania* and a play in Gaelic, *Casadh an tSúgáin*, by Douglas Hyde. Even with a splendid production and incidental music by the greatest living English composer, Edward Elgar, *Diarmuid and Grania* failed to rouse much enthusiasm. Much of the audience seems to have left when it was over, thus missing Hyde's play—the more important of the two—a retelling of a folktale, neatly constructed if amateurishly acted. Its importance, though, was that it was a play in Gaelic, something never before seen in Dublin, and a play acted entirely by Irishmen, something not before seen in the Irish Literary Theatre and a portent for the future. After these performances, the Irish Literary Theatre ceased to exist. It had produced two or three good plays, but it was essentially a toy for some theatrical innocents. A real Irish drama would take more than plays by Yeats, Martyn, and their friends and more than the occasional two- or three-night season.

The next step in the development of Irish drama takes us from the relative splendors of the Gaiety Theatre to a very modest and drafty room, St. Theresa's Hall, in a back street. It was there, on a stage 30' x 21' in a hall seating only 300 that the National Dramatic Society staged AE's *Deirdre* and Yeats's *Kathleen ni Houlihan* in April of 1902. No longer were the actors English professionals; instead they were enthusiastic Irish amateurs led by Maud Gonne as the heroine in Yeats's one-acter. The moving forces behind these productions were William Fay and his brother, Frank, an electrician and an accountant's secretary. Both had been involved in theatricals in Dublin for years; as early as 1891 their "W. G. Ormonde Combination" had presented a comic "screaming sketch" at a temperance hall. Later on, they organized groups to play in "coffee palaces," places of wholesome entertainment operated by total-abstinence organizations. The brothers were amateurs, and most of what their groups had performed had been very amateurish stuff indeed, but both were already expert theater-men. Frank was interested in acting techniques and in the new movements in the theater in his time; he read and took careful notes on all he could learn about Ibsen's National Theatre in Norway, the Théâtre Libre André Antoine had organized in Paris, and J. T. Grein's Independent Theatre in London, the first serious theater there in a century. He became a commentator on drama for the nationalist newspaper, *United Jreland,* where he preached that the Irish Literary Theatre would never really take root until it used Irish actors and created a truly Irish style. His work for the newspaper brought him into contact with Maud Gonne and the Daughters of Ireland, a nationalist women's group she led. Helping them with some tableaux and plays probably brought him to Yeats's attention. At about the same time, AE had written a one-act play, *Deirde,* which the Fays were interested in producing. With encouragement from them and Yeats, AE slowly turned it into a full-length drama, the last act having to be almost squeezed out of him. The Fays' company of amateurs began rehearsals of *Deirdre* with the enthusiasm that only amateurs can have; one of the actors later recalled: "Everybody learned everybody else's part for sheer love of the thing. The lack of a curtain-raiser worried the management. But their worry disappeared when it was whispered that Yeats had had a dream, and had put it into a one-act play, and that Maud Gonne would have the central part."[8]

Finally, on April 2, 1902, the curtain went up on these productions. The audience had to hear the plays over the noise of popular songs, dancing, and billiard balls from the room next door. St. Theresa's Hall was small and uncomfortable; the stage was too small, and the sets were crude. But AE's play was discovered to be rather effective anyway, and Yeats's a good deal more than that. *Cathleen ni Jhoulihan,* which was really a collaboration between Yeats and Lady Gregory, was, in fact, the first masterpiece of Irish dramatic nationalism. It tells the story of a family in the west of Ireland in 1798, the year of the French invasion and the rebellion against British rule. As the family prepares for the wedding of a son, Michael, to a wealthy girl, a haggard old women enters their cottage. Asked why she is poor and vagrant, she replies that strangers have stolen her four green fields, and Michael offers to help her recover them. A shiver of recognition must have gone through the audience as it recognized that the old woman (played by Maud Gonne) was Cathleen ni Houlihan herself, the embodiment of Ireland; the four green fields were the provinces of Ireland; and that the robbing strangers were the British. "It is a hard service they take that help me," the old woman tells Michael. "They that have red cheeks will have pale cheeks for my sake, and for all that, they will think they are well paid." As she leaves the cottage, Michael stands entranced by the door, watching her. His brother enters with the news that the French have landed at Killala to aid the rebellion, and his father asks him, "Did you see an old woman going down the path?" "I did not," Patrick answers, "but

8 Quoted in Robinson, *Jreland's Abbey Jheatre,* p. 26.

I saw a young girl, and she had the walk of a queen."[9] The Irish dramatic movement was conceived on the afternoon Yeats talked with Martyn and Lady Gregory in the great house in County Galway, but it was born at that production of *Cathleen ni Houlihan*.

The success of these performances encouraged the Fays and the others to go on with more plays. They rented a small hall in Camden Street to give them a permanent home for rehearsals and productions and organized themselves into the Irish National Theatre Society with Yeats as president, Maud Gonne, Douglas Hyde, and AE as vice-presidents, and William Fay as stage manager. In spite of the impressive name and the roster of notables, things sputtered for a while. The Camden Street hall was good enough for meetings and rehearsals, but its stage was only six feet deep and a mere fifty spectators could sit on its wooden benches. The company, all amateurs still, worked up a program of four short plays, three in English, one in Gaelic, which it presented for a nationalist organization at the Antient Concert Rooms in October. Thanks to a sympathetic audience, these were well received, but when the company put on three of these plays at its own hall in December, the audiences were small, the theater was bone-chillingly cold, and the reviews unfriendly. The movement could have died right then, but these were determined people and they kept going. In March of 1903, they were back on the stage, but the stage was now the more adequate one of the Molesworth Hall, rented for the occasion. The plays were Yeats's ornate morality, *The Hour-Glass*, and a funnny little farce by Lady Gregory, *Twenty-Five*. Between the two plays, Yeats gave a lecture, "The Reform of the Theatre." Joseph Holloway, an incurable theater-goer who was present that night as he was present at virtually every theatrical production in Dublin for more than forty years, found Yeats's lecture a ridiculous bit of posturing, and so it must have seemed to listeners accustomed to traditional theories of drama. Yeats began by observing that the commercial theater of 1903 was in a "deplorable condition" and that it was necessary to reform it so as to make it again "an intellectual institution." To do this, three basic reforms were necessary: a new emphasis on the importance of "beautiful speech," a simplified acting style which would not detract from speech, and the development of scenery which would be "inexacting to the eye, so that the great attention might be paid by the ear."[10] Yeats probably owed some of his ideas to the Fays,

9 *Collected Plays of W. B. Yeats*, pp. 86 and 88.

10 Quoted in Robinson, *Ireland's Abbey Theatre*, pp. 32–33. See "The Reform of the Theatre" in W. B. Yeats, *Explorations* (London: Macmillan, 1962), pp. 107–10, for a full statement of Yeats's views.

but they were also a logical extension of his own belief in the power of language and his father's emphasis on drama as intense reverie. Yeats was thinking, of course, of reforms which would be necessary for the successful staging of his own symbolist plays, but his emphases on language and simplicity became the governing ones in the best of Irish drama. Even today, good actors trained in the modern Irish tradition are notable for their ability to handle language and their ability to make small gestures count for much. In 1903, with the commercial theaters dominated by ranting actors, extravagant sets, and plays which turned on conventionally "effective" situations, all this was revolutionary talk.

With the development of a theory and practice of performance, the training of some actors, and the development of a sympathetic audience in Dublin, the Irish movement was on the way to success. What it still needed, though, were more first-rate plays and a permanent home. Both came in remarkably short order.

Only two-and-a-half years after the premiere of *Cathleen ni Houlihan*, Irish drama had its home in the Abbey Theatre, the gift of an Englishwoman who insisted she cared nothing about Irish nationalism, Annie E. F. Horniman. Annie Horniman did care about drama though—care enough to give Ireland the Abbey and encourage in England the development of the Manchester Repertory Theatre and the Old Vic. Miss Horniman was a wealthy woman, from a family which had made a fortune in tea, and she shared Yeats's interest in the occult. She had helped him as his secretary and had occasionally come over to Dublin to help also with the Irish National Theatre Society's productions. As the productions continued during 1903 and 1904, she must have become increasingly impressed by the work being done in Dublin. According to one story, she had some stock which she promised the Fays she would use to pay for a theater if its value increased; according to another, in 1903 she heard Yeats make an appeal to the audience at the Molesworth Hall for financial support for the drama group. He had hoped that she might give a small donation; instead, she said, "I will give you a theatre." Both stories may well be true, for both seem characteristic of her impulsiveness and her generosity. Certainly, performances by the Irish players in London in 1903 and 1904 helped her make her decision. For the first time, the company acted in a real theater on those whirlwind tours, and the English critics were much impressed by the plays and the acting. In any event, in April of 1904 she wrote a formal letter to Yeats and the company to say that she had bought a theater in Dublin which she proposed to give to them.

What she gave them was part of the old Mechanics' Institute in Dublin's Abbey Street and another building which had once been a morgue. With the advice of Joseph Holloway, who was an architect as well as a theater buff, she turned these into the Abbey Theatre. For more than forty years it would remain essentially unchanged, the cradle of Irish drama. The renovation of the buildings cost her £1,300, a huge sum in those days, and what she got for her money was a small and adequate theater, but hardly, in view of the Abbey's subsequent fame, a luxurious one. The theater-goer entered through a small vestibule which with its paneling and stained-glass windows looked more like the anteroom to a Presbyterian church than a theater. In the theater itself were, downstairs, rows of plain wooden theater-seats, pit and stalls, and upstairs, a rather narrow, horseshoe-shaped balcony. Altogether, the room would hold about 500 patrons. The stage was forty feet wide and about sixteen feet deep. That meant that it was too small for a cyclorama, but the stage lighting was fairly good for its time. It was all a great improvement on the hired halls the company had used previously. The backstage facilities were limited at first, but, by adding more space, Miss Horniman eventually provided acceptable dressing rooms, a good scenery dock, and a pleasant green room for the actors. To the gift of the building itself, she added an annual subsidy to keep the company going. Her generosity was to prove very great; before her association with the Abbey ended in 1910, she had given it more than £12,000. She was amazingly free with the money, but she was also cantankerous and much given to inter-ference. She subjected the actors and management to a barrage of advice, harassed the Fays continuously, bickered with Lady Gregory, and sometimes drove Yeats to distraction. But though she must sometimes have seemed to be the Wicked Witch of the East, she was also Irish drama's fairy godmother. Without her gift of a theater, the Irish movement could not possibly have prospered and developed as it did.

By the time the company moved into the Abbey in December of 1904, it was already developing its other necessity, more good plays and good play-wrights. Martyn and Moore were no longer part of the movement, but with Yeats, Lady Gregory, J. M. Synge, Padraic Colum, and William Boyle writing plays for it, the company in the new theater could look to the future with a good deal of confidence. Yeats's best play so far, *On Baile's Strand*, and Lady Gregory's little masterpiece, *Spreading the News*, had their premieres on the night the Abbey opened, December 27, 1904. Later that season, a strong play by Synge, *The Well of the Saints*, Lady Gregory's first tragedy, *Kincora*, and a funny comedy by William Boyle, *The Building Fund*, were added to the repertory. The move to the Abbey, and the subsequent decision to go from an amateur group to a largely professional company, cost the Irish National Theatre Society some of its actors and actresses, mostly nationalists who wanted to serve the cause through an amateur group rather than become professionals. Nevertheless, a company that included Frank and William Fay, Arthur Sinclair, George Roberts, and Sara Allgood had plenty of talent and dedication.

Yeats remained a dominant figure in the theater. He was gradually learning the playwright's craft to add to his immense talent as a poet. Too often in his earlier plays, the poet got the best of the playwright, but through seeing his plays on the stage and by continuous revision, he was making himself into a fine dramatist. *The Countess Cathleen* benefitted from that process of revision, though even more revision never turned *The Shadowy Waters*, first produced in January of 1904, into a stageworthy piece. Too much symbolism and too much beautiful language suffocated it. But one of Yeats's strengths as a playwright was his willingness to continue to experiment, and in the early days before and after the opening of the Abbey, he contributed a number of strikingly different plays to the Irish reportory. *Cathleen ni Houlihan*, the patriotic tragedy, and *The Pot of Broth*, a farce, were produced in 1902; both owed a good deal to Lady Gregory for their effective dialogue and peasant speech. Yeats's first attempt to tell a story from heroic legend, *Diarmuid and Grania* (1901) was a fiasco, but free of George Moore's collaboration, he went on to write increasingly effective plays based on this kind of material. *The King's Threshold* (1903) is a striking allegory of the relation of the artist to society cast into the days of the legendary King Guaire of Cort, and *On Baile's Strand* (1904) is a masterpiece. It is Yeats's first dramatization of the Cuchulain legends, telling the story of Cuchulain's battles with his son and the sea, but telling the story through the very effective ironic distancing provided by a fool and a blind man who are commentators on the central plot as well as agents in it. *Deirdre* (1906) treats the greatest of Irish love stories very beautifully and with a good attention to characterization, while *The Golden Helmet* (1908) was an amusing demythologizing of another Cuchulain tale. With the exception of *At the King's Threshold*, Yeats's best plays from this period were the ones in which he did not attempt to work out his own myths about himself as a personality and artist but found his overt subjects elsewhere. Personal plays such as *The Shadowy Waters* and *The Unicorn from the Stars* (1907) were too private and involuted to make effective drama; *The Hour-Glass* (1903), for all the beauty of its language, does not quite hang together.

Yeats was a consummate literary artist who had to learn the craft of the stage by trial and error; Lady Gregory was a natural mistress of dramatic situations who sometimes had difficulty in being more than merely effective. Few of the Irish playwrights had more inherent talent, but it was a talent Lady Gregory discovered only after she was fifty. When she was a very old woman, Sean O'Casey wrote to her: "You can always walk with your head up. And remember you had to fight against your birth into position and comfort, as others had to fight against their birth into hardship and poverty, and it is as difficult to come out of one as it is to come out of the other, so that power may be gained to bring fountains and waters out of the hard rocks."[11] O'Casey, whose childhood in the rough Dublin slums was utterly different from Augusta Gregory's in a well-to-do-house in County Galway was exactly right. Born into the Persse family of the Anglo-Irish Ascendancy at Roxborough in 1852, she grew up a typical member of the Protestant aristocracy. In 1880, she married Sir William Gregory, a retired civil servant who was thirty-five years her elder, and until his death she devoted herself to him and their only son, Robert. Through her connections and his, she knew all sorts of people from Robert Browning and Henry James to William Ewart Gladstone, and she spent much of her time in London or abroad. After her husband died, she settled at their Irish country house, Coole Park, to supervise her property and raise her son. In the early nineties, living at Coole, she came face to face with the Irish world around her, the world of servants, peasants, and the little nearby town of Gort. She had once opposed home rule, but she gradually became a convinced nationalist; she learned Gaelic and became interested in folklore, the stories she heard reminding her of the ones her Irish nurse, Mary Sheridan, had told her during her childhood at Roxborough. Gradually, she made Coole a haven for Irish writers, and after 1897 Yeats, among others, came every summer to write, talk, walk in the woods around the estate, and fish its lake.

When Lady Gregory first asked Yeats what she could do to help the Irish literary movement, he merely told her to buy its books, but soon she began to write them as well. Her interest in folklore and legend led her to think of re-telling the stories of Ireland in a style and dialect like the one she had heard in childhood and heard around her at Coole every day. *Cuchulain of Muirthemne* (1902) was her first important effort, a very successful version of the stories of Cuchulain and the Red Branch in a good approximation of west of Ireland dialect. Her retelling lacks the flamboyance of Standish O'Grady's, but it is a more coherent narrative and less diffuse than O'Grady's *History*; moreover, it

11 Quoted in Hazard Adams, *Lady Gregory* (Lewisburg, Pa.: Bucknell University Press, 1973), p. 27.

is invaluable for its dialect—clear, sensible, but with the swing of authentic Irish speech. Lady Gregory was claiming her due when she said, "I have told the whole story in plain and simple words, in the same way my old nurse Mary Sheridan used to be telling stories from the Irish long ago, and I a child at Roxborough,"[12] and Yeats only exaggerated a little when he called it the best book to come out of Ireland in his time. It and *Gods and Fighting Men* (1904), a retelling of Irish mythology and the stories of the Fianna, became basic source books of Irish legend for many writers who could not read the tales in their Gaelic originals. Both books, and others which followed, showed that Lady Gregory was very skillful in adapting the work of scholars to the style, point of view, and idiom of native storytelling; she was, in fact, the best popularizer of legend and folklore the Irish Renaissance produced.

These books proved her to be a superb storyteller, and it was not long before she began telling stories for the stage. She was a woman who was always willing to do the work at hand which needed doing, and in the early days, the dramatic movement needed short plays, comedies preferably, which would be effective curtain-raisers for the longer and more serious plays. Lady Gregory took to writing these, and she quickly developed into a fine playwright, one who could tell a good story, create strong characters, and handle dramatic situations. *Spreading the News* (1904) was the first play to show her true merit. It is an excruciatingly funny little farce in which deaf Mrs. Tarpey, an apple-seller from the mythical village of Cloon (the town based on Gort which Lady Gregory frequently used as her setting) creates a crazy disturbance through her talk. Working from Mrs. Tarpey's misinformation and using what Lady Gregory once called the incorrigible genius of the Irish for mythmaking, half a dozen other characters decide a murder has occurred, a belief which is not thoroughly discredited even when the supposed victim casually ambles back on stage. *Spreading the News* develops a farcical situation deftly, and it also presents a series of characters, all stereotypes in one way or another, who have the breath of life in them: Mrs. Tarpey herself, the typical village gossip; the English magistrate, always referring to his valuable experience from service in the Andaman Islands and blind to what is going on around him; guillible Shawn Early; frightened Bartley Fallon who makes a life out of bemoaning his misfortune; Tim Casey, a man most adept at adding two and two to make five. *Spreading the News* is characteristic of her farces, a deft, funny play made out of the experiences of small-town Ireland, a world full of isolated person-

12 *Cuchulain of Muirthemne* (1902; Gerrards Cross, Bucks.: Colin Smythe, 1970), p. 5.

alities who are resistant to alien authority and exuberant in their disregard of mere fact.

In one sense, Lady Gregory's comedies are further exploitations of stage Irishmen and conventional aristocratic attitudes towards "the natives," but there is a truth and rightness in them, too, as well as a consistent comic vision of Ireland as a land of mad sanity in which order can be restored, but not for long. *The Gaol-Gate* (1906) and *The Rising of the Moon* (1907) show that she could also write strong plays of sentiment, plays sensitive to the darker side of the Irish experience. *The Gaol-Gate* is a very moving study of women waiting for a man to be released from prison and a passionate cry against British oppression; *The Rising of the Moon* is a surprisingly effective play of patriotism in which the old revolutionary ballad which gives it its title causes a policeman to let a rebel slip away from him. Both plays turn on what is really stage irony, and an O. Henry-like sense of irony informs much of her work. In *Hyacinth Halvey* (1906), it makes for hilarious comedy as Hyacinth, the new Sub-Sanitary Inspector in Cloon, is trapped in the myth of his own virtue; in *The Wrens* (1914) it makes for a kind of bitter amusement as we watch a quarrel in the street cause a servant to forget to tell his master to return for a vote in the Irish House of Commons, a vote on the Act of Union which brought so much trouble to Ireland. The focus on these ironies restricts Lady Gregory's artistic vision, but it makes her small world theatrically effective and involving. Although she constantly experimented—"Desire for experiment is like fire in the blood,"[13] she wrote—she was at her best in small forms. Her big tragedies tend to sprawl, and some of her historical plays are clever ideas which do not quite come off. But she was an acute satirist, as *The White Cockade* (1905), *The Canavans* (1906), and *The Image* (1909) show. Later in her career, she wrote some attractive childrens' plays, clever parodies, many of them, of the conventions of fairy tales, and her last play, *Dave* (1927), is one of her several sentimental but touching religious plays.

She was a very productive writer during a career which began when she was almost fifty and only ended with her death at eighty, producing several books of legend and folklore, more than twenty original plays plus almost as many collaborations and translations, books on the Irish theater, and autobiographies. All this was the product of constant hard work, hard work which also extended to years of day-to-day management at the Abbey, an enormous correspondence, the upkeep and supervision of Coole, and constant attention to

[13] *Our Irish Theatre*, p. 91.

her family and to younger writers. Those who knew her often describe her strength and purposefulness, and she must have been a rather daunting figure at times. Yet there is a controlled twinkle in the eye in her best photographs; control of herself and amusement at the world's foibles were two of the secrets of her career. A third secret was her passionate love for Ireland, the Ireland of Coole with its beautiful house and deep woods, but love also for the Ireland of dull little Gort, the Ireland of urgent nationalism, and the Ireland which the Abbey embodied. She was a persistent and courageous woman, fearless in defending her friends, the theater company she nurtured and sustained, and the ideals she came to believe in. One night during the Anglo-Irish War, when she was in her late sixties, she was waiting for a tram with the secretary of the Abbey after the night's performance. Shots rattled in the street, and she was begged to lie down on the pavement. "Never!" she answered as she shouted out encouragement to the rebels. That courage carried her through "the troubles" in Ireland, the death of her son in World War I, and the eventual sale of Coole. She was herself a great rebel against her background and her class, a fighter determined to do all she could for Ireland and Irish drama, a rebel who knew that every cause worth fighting for has its funny side. Only a person of great courage and great humanity could write as she did toward the end of her life, "Loneliness made me rich—'full' as Bacon says."[14]

Lady Gregory's early plays did much to define the direction of modern Irish drama. Many of the good but unremarkable plays which made up the bulk of the Abbey's repertory owed more to her than to Yeats's symbolism or Martyn's earnest Ibsenism. Today it is fashionable to undervalue the plays which can be categorized as peasant and village comedies or tragedies, yet these plays, pictures of a life any Irish person could recognize, were central to the dramatic movement and the process of national self-understanding it fostered. From its early days, these were the Abbey's most successful plays, and two of the Abbey's most successful early playwrights, William Boyle and Padraic Colum, were masters of the genre. Boyle caught the flat facts of life in Louth and Meath in several of his plays. His work was fairly conventional in style, but *The Building Fund* (1905) with its wonderful old miser, Mrs. Grogan, is still amusing as is *The Eloquent Dempsey* (1906), a satire on the double-dealing politicians. His situations were stock ones, but he had a good control of acidulous irony, and his plays had a professional competence some other Irish plays of the period lacked. In the early years of the century, it

14 Quoted in Adams, *Lady Gregory*, p. 42.

seemed that Padraic Colum might develop into the best of the younger Irish playwrights. He was only in his early twenties when he had his first success with *Broken Soil* (1903), the first impressive play of that kind of peasant realism which was to help make the Abbey famous. His next play, *The Land* (1905), was a strong study of a recurring problem in Ireland: who will inherit the little patches of land on which a farm family lives? In Colum's play, as too often in reality, the weak and conniving eventually inherit the property the older generation has ruined itself striving to preserve, while the strong and imaginative emigrate to America. Colum's command of a realistic dialect and his ability to deal interestingly with serious social problems ought to have made him a continuing figure in Irish drama, but after *Thomas Muskerry* (1910) he wrote no more for the Abbey. Conn Hourican, the central figure in *The Fiddler's House*, the revised version of *Broken Soil*, is a fiddler with equally strong instincts for wandering and artistic creation; Colum's own instincts were very much like his Conn's. He left Ireland for America when he was only in his thirties, and spent much of the rest of his life wandering and writing. He wrote some fine poems and many books of folklore, but his promise as a dramatist remained unfulfilled. Given his talent, there is something disappointing about his later career.

Colum, Boyle, and Lady Gregory all wrote good plays about the Irish farms and villages and helped establish one kind of modern Irish drama, but nothing better illustrates the difference between the good and the great in drama than comparing their work with that of John Millington Synge. Lady Gregory's *Hyacinth Halvey*, for example and the Christy Mahon of Synge's *Playboy of the Western World* are rather similar characters in somewhat similar situations, but Hyacinth is an amusing stage-figure while Christy is alive as few people we know in real life are alive. His creator, John Synge, was a complex man and a complex playwright, but Yeats probably came closest to defining him when he wrote: "He was a solitary, undemonstrative man, never asking pity, nor complaining, nor seeking sympathy . . . knowing nothing of new books and newspapers, reading the great masters alone; and he was but the more hated because he gave his country what it needed, an unmoved mind where there is a perpetual Last Day, a trumpeting, and coming up to judgment."[15]

Yeats's emphasis on the hatred Synge's plays aroused reminds us that Synge's entire career at the Abbey was controversial. His masterpiece, *The Playboy*, provoked riots after its premiere in 1907, but even his first play, the

[15] "Preface to J. M. Synge's *Poems and Translations*," *Essays and Introductions* (London: Macmillan, 1961), p. 310.

one-act *In the Shadow of the Glen* (1903), created its share of trouble. It tells a simple story of a tramp seeking shelter for the night at a lonely cottage in County Wicklow. He is welcomed by a woman whose husband has just died, and the corpse is laid out on the table for the wake. The woman leaves the tramp and the corpse alone in the room while she goes out to find the young farmer she loves. Terrified, the tramp sees the "corpse" rise from the dead; he explains that he has pretended to die so that he can catch his wife and her lover together. The husband again pretends to be dead. When the wife and her farmer return, he "rises from the dead" a second time. He drives his wife from the house, but her cowardly lover stays behind to drink with her husband, and the tramp and the young wife set out into the world together. The story is, of course, a traditional folk tale found in many cultures, but to the good Irish nationalists of 1903 it was a slander on the virtues of the Irish peasantry. No peasant woman would be unfaithful to her husband; there was no such thing in Ireland as a loveless marriage, or so they said. More sensitive viewers than these nationalists might have been delighted by the play's powerful evocation of the dark glens of Wicklow and its subtle symbolism, but Synge's characters seemed too real and his language too idiomatic for much of his audience to believe that *In the Shadow of the Glen* was anything more than a realistic "slice of life" created to offend them.

For Synge, though, the wild and chaotic life of the peasantry was a source of constant wonder. Born in 1871 into an Anglo-Irish family fearfully contemptuous of its Catholic tenants, Synge had originally hoped to be a musician. That career never developed because of his intense shyness, but by the time he finished his education at Trinity College in 1892, he had learned Gaelic and already had a good knowledge of Irish rural life. There seemed to be no career in Ireland for him, so he went abroad, first to Germany and then to Paris, to try to make his way. Yeats encountered him in a cheap hotel in Paris in 1896, supporting himself as a literary journalist. Somewhere in their conversations Yeats told him, "Give up Paris. You will never create anything by reading Racine, and Arthur Symons will always be a better critic of French literature. Go to the Aran Islands. Live there as if you were one of the people themselves; express a life that has never found expression."[16] It was, in fact, two years before Synge went to Aran, but when he did go he began to discover himself as an artist just as so many Irish writers did, by encountering the peasant life of the country. Beginning in 1898, Synge spent parts of five summers on these

[16] "Preface to the First Edition of *The Well of the Saints*," *ibid.*, p. 299.

isolated, primitive islands. Almost untouched by the rest of the world, they then preserved the closest possible approximation of traditional Irish life: Gaelic was the native language, and modern comforts were few indeed. Men still fished from the high cliffs, took cattle to the mainland in small, frail boats and farmed tiny, rock-enclosed fields. Synge learned to love the islanders for their openness and their passion, and from their English dialect he partially made the language which gives his plays their life and poetry. He made good friends on the islands, and during his winters abroad (he continued to try to get along in Paris), letters full of simple eloquence came from them. In February of 1902, for example, Martin McDonagh wrote to him: "Johneen, Friend of My Heart. A million blessings to you. It's a while ago since I thought of a small letter to write, and every day was going until it went too far and the time I was about to write to you. It happened that my brother's wife, Shawneen, died. And she was visiting the last Sunday in December, and now isn't it a sad story to tell? But at the same time we have to be satisfied because a person cannot live always."[17] Out of McDonagh's letter came the climactic lines of the mother's lament in Synge's *Riders to the Sea,* as out of the peasant world of Aran, Wicklow, and West Kerry came Synge's greatness.

Synge was a genius, but he could be a difficult genius. Neither Yeats nor Lady Gregory, with him the directors of the Abbey in its early days, liked him thoroughly. There was something wild about this quiet man, something danger-ous, something disturbing. Both had difficulty in persuading him to tone down the language in his plays; neither was quite sure of the common sense of one who would talk of writing a play for an Irish audience in which a Protestant woman would choose to be raped by soldiers rather than stay in the house of a Catholic. One of his plays, *The Tinkers' Wedding,* was too roaringly anticlerical for the Abbey to dare produce; all of his plays were too full of a passionate vision of Ireland to make them please complacent audiences. The critics saw *Riders to the Sea* (1904) as "hideous realism," and failed to understand that it was Synge's moving tribute to the indomitable spirit of the Aran women and a tribute to all the Aran peoples' steadfastness in the hands of fate and its agent, the sea. In a single scene it tells how Maurya, an old woman, loses her remaining sons to the eternal tides. The "action" is simplicity itself, but it has the simplicity and force of the greatest tragedies, and *Riders to the Sea* is surely the great short tragedy in our language. Its protagonists are, in T. R. Henn's words, "enclosed in an inflexible circle of destiny."[18] The play reminds us of

17 Quoted in David H. Greene and Edward M. Stephens, *J. M. Synge, 1871–1909* (1959; New York: Collier, 1961), p. 112.

18 *The Plays and Poems of J. M. Synge* (London: Methuen, 1963), p. 37.

tragedy's origins in the lyric; Synge's powerfully plain lyricism and his subtly unified symbolism make the little play a perfect whole. Maurya's concluding lament for her sons is one of those rare moments when dramatic language transcends itself to become a vision of eternal truth:

> Michael has a clean burial in the far north,
> by the grace of the Almighty God. Bartley will
> have a fine coffin out of the white boards, and a
> deep grave surely. . . . What more can we want than that? . . .
> No man at all can be living for ever, and we must be
> satisfied.[19]

In the Shadow of the Glen and *Riders to the Sea* made it clear that in Synge Irish drama had found a new master; *The Well of the Saints* (1905), his first three-act play to be produced at the Abbey, solidified his reputation. Again there were complaints from the nationalists who claimed, rightly, that the action of the play was based on a foreign source and that, therefore, the play could not possibly be Irish. But its characters and its setting are thoroughly Irish, as is its theme, that illusion is often more satisfactory than reality. That theme, one which runs through all his later plays, finds its great expression, though, in *The Playboy of the Western World* (1907), a play which would be a comedy if it were not so close to tragedy, a tragedy if it were not a comedy.

It was his masterpiece, but it was simply too much for most of his audience. Irish nationalists were infuriated by the portrayal of brutal peasants who condoned violence and murder and were vulgar, crude, and small-minded. In three acts of realistic fantasy, Synge more or less destroyed a century of myth about the peasantry of the west of Ireland, myth which had held that their sufferings had made them into quintessential Irishmen, a "saving remnant" which had to be honored for its patience, fortitude, and piety. The myth was based on the modern urban belief that country people who live close to the natural world are somehow made holy by it; in Ireland, the myth had been encouraged by Catholic piety and the nationalist theory of the innate superiority of spiritual Ireland to materialistic England. In fact, centuries of ignorance and oppression had left much of the Irish peasantry degraded, superstitious, and violent. Synge himself also idealized peasant Ireland, but the peasants he loved were the traditionally oppressed: tinkers, tramps, and the poor. In these

---

[19] J. M. Synge: *Collected Works, Plays, Book 1*, edited by Ann Saddlemyer (London: Oxford University Press, 1968), p. 27.

real people, rather than the imaginary mystics of the Celtic twilight or the plaster saints of Irish nationalism, he found his myth of the Irish soul—passionate, hard, unforgiving, and wild. As he wrote to a young admirer who praised *The Playboy*, "In the same way you see—what it seems so impossible to get our Dublin people to see, obvious as it is,—that the wildness and, if you will, vices of the Irish peasantry are due, like their extraordinary good points of all kinds, to the *richness* of their nature—a thing that is priceless beyond words."[20]

The troubles with *The Playboy* began long before the first performance. Yeats, W. G. Fay, and Lady Gregory were all concerned about the strong language in it from the first time they heard it read, and some of the actors objected strenuously to the words they were made to say. Eventually, the company made cuts or emendations in more than fifty speeches. Still, no one expected really serious disturbances, and Yeats, for one, went off to Scotland to lecture. But the opening night's audience erupted during the third act. The next day the newspapers were indignant, the *Freeman's Journal* calling the play a "libel upon Irish peasant men and, worse still, upon Irish peasant girlhood," and the *Evening Mail* saying it implied Irish people were "gorillas."[21] With excitement in Dublin rising, Synge and Lady Gregory thought it might be well to have police in the theater for the next performance, but that only helped incite the audience. The performance turned into a riot. Yeats returned from Scotland, gave a newspaper interview in which he said those who disliked the play were illiterates being led by ignorant patriots, then let into the theater a group of drunken students from Trinity College to shout down the nationalists. For several of the performances, the actors could not be heard over the racket. Ironically, the crowds which came to damn *The Playboy* or praise it made it an enormous box-office success, but at the cost of losing much of the Abbey's position as a national institution. Some nationalists swore never to enter it again; Boyle and Colum withdrew their plays from its repertory in protest against the management's continued defense of Synge. Joseph Holloway, the architect-playgoer, probably reflected much Dublin opinion when he wrote in his journal that *The Playboy* "is not a truthful or a just picture of the Irish peasants, but simply the outpouring of a morbid, unhealthy mind ever seeking on the dunghill of life for the nastiness that lies concealed there."[22] The worst row in Irish theatrical history did not end in

20 Quoted in J. M. Synge: *Collected Works, Plays, Book II*, edited by Ann Saddlemyer (London: Oxford University Press, 1968), p. xxiii.

21 Quoted in Greene and Stephens, *J. M. Synge, 1871–1909*, p. 242.

22 *Joseph Holloway's Abbey Theatre*, p. 81.

1907 or in Dublin. The Board of Guardians of the Gort workhouse hurt Lady Gregory deeply by forbidding its orphans picnics at Coole in retaliation for her support of Synge. In 1911, Irish-Americans in Philadelphia had the Abbey company, then touring the United States, arrested for presenting the "immoral and indecent" *Playboy*. Lady Gregory's life was threatened when the company reached Chicago, but the mayor there, asked to stop performances of the play in his city, read three pages of it and reported, "instead of finding anything immoral I found the whole thing was wonderfully stupid."[23]

What sort of play was it, then, that could cause so much trouble? Its plot is simple enough, as Synge's usually are. Christy Mahon appears in a village in the wilds of County Mayo saying that he has murdered his father. The peasants take him in, admiring what they see as his daring, although we in the audience can see that he is nothing more than a shy, frightened boy. Killing his father was not, Christy insists, your "common, week-day kind of murder," and the legend he and the villagers create around it and him makes a man of him while it simultaneously entraps him. He falls in love with the pub-keeper's daughter, Pegeen Mike, in spite of the efforts of the cantankerous Widow Quin and Pegeen's old boyfriend, the snivelling, pious Shawn Keogh. But Christy's fame and his new-found manhood collapse when his "murdered" father reappears, bandaged yet full of life after the blow from his son's spade. Christy tries to kill him again and apparently succeeds. Now faced with the reality of murder and realizing "there's a great gap between gallous story and a dirty deed," the peasants turn on Christy, bind him, and try to cripple him to make it easier to get him to the police. But Old Mahon revives once more; he and his son go off together with the old man saying, "We'll have great times from this out telling stories of the villainy of Mayo and the fools is here." Pegeen, who has loved and betrayed Christy with equal passion, is left with the knowledge of what she has lost: "Oh my grief, I've lost him surely. I've lost the only playboy of the western world."

Around this series of comic reversals with motifs of ironic resurrection, frustrated romance, and Oedipal conflict, Synge creates a wonderfully extravagant verbal construct. No play of the Irish Renaissance has a richer, more various language, language better fit for cursing or lovemaking. Pegeen Mike assaults the Widow Quin and her scheme for stealing Christy from her by saying of the Widow, "Doesn't the world know you reared a black ram at your own breast, so that the Lord Bishop of Connaught felt the elements of a Christian, and he eating it after in a kidney stew?" Christy, pouring

---

[23] Quoted in Malone, *The Irish Drama*, p. 112.

himself out to Pegeen, cries, "It's well you know it's a lonesome thing to be passing small towns with the lights shining sideways when the night is down, or going in strange places with a dog nosing before you and a dog nosing behind, or drawn to the cities where you'd hear a voice kissing and talking deep love in every shadow of the ditch, and you passing on with an empty hungry stomach failing from your heart."[24]

Yet for all the glory of its language, *The Playboy* is a strange play. In one sense, it is a Dionysiac comedy in which anything goes, a fulfillment of Synge's desire to create what is "superb and wild" in reality. In another, it is a satire on the traditional lawlessness of Ireland and a satire, too, on its patterns of courtship and marriage. It is more than a little a tragedy in which the hero, Christy, discovers his identity and his "fate," but only by leaving Pegeen, the archetype of the strong woman of so much Irish drama, bereft of all comfort. There is that and more in the play, and critics have found everything in it from an allegory of Irish political history to a retelling of the myth of sacrificial expiation with Christy as Christ-bearer. Cyril Cusack, one of the finest of the recent actors who have played Christy, tells how it took him years of performances to realize fully how the play moves through a series of anticlimaxes towards a resolution in which "reality disappears in a balloon-burst of disillusionment and the person of Christopher Mahon suddenly resolves itself into a dew."[25]

The Playboy was the last of Synge's plays to be produced during his lifetime. Two years after those riotous nights in 1907 he was dead. He left unfinished his last play, *Deirdre of the Sorrows*, it is his only full-scale tragedy, a play which misses greatness only because its author did not live to give it the final revisions which would have made it an artistic whole. Even with its imperfections, notably a second act that drags, *Deirdre* is a powerfully moving work. Many other playwrights of the Irish Renaissance tried to tell the story from the *Táin* of Deirdre and Naisi, their flight from the wrath of old king Conchubor who had meant to marry Deirdre, and their eventual deaths through his vengeance, but none did it better than Synge. Still employing his dialect, Synge made what was really a dramatic poem on the themes of love, death, and old age which so obsess him in his lyric poetry. He subtly turns the old tale of fated love into a study in heroic pride; Deirdre is

---

24 All quotations from *The Playboy* from J. M. Synge: *Collected Works, Plays, Book II.*

25 "A Player's Reflections on the Playboy," *Twentieth Century Interpretations of the Playboy of the Western World*, edited by Thomas R. Whitaker (Englewood Cliffs, N.J.: Prentice-Hall, 1969), p. 53.

the last in his line of proud and determined women. She is as much a relation of Pegeen Mike and Maurya as a figure from ancient legend. Her pride and her determination never to lose Naisi's love drive her to return with him to Conchubor and inevitable death. There is no greater speech in Irish drama than Deirdre's last, as she keens over the grave of Naisi and prepares for her own suicide.

> I have put away sorrow like a shoe that is worn
> out and muddy, for it is I have had a life that
> will be envied by great companies. It was not
> by a low birth I made kings uneasy, and they sitting
> in the halls of Emain. It was not a low thing to be
> chosen by Conchubor, who was wise, and Naisi had no
> match for bravery. . . . It is not a small
> thing to be rid of grey hairs and the loosening
> of the teeth. . . . It was the choice of lives
> we had in the clear woods, and in the grave
> we're safe surely. . . .[26]

John Synge, too, found safety in the grave after a career which made Irish drama uneasy and himself immortal. As Una Ellis-Fermor observed long ago, much of Synge's greatness came from the fact that he knew Ireland itself rather than what was written about it. His travel books, particularly his superb memoir of the Aran Islands, show an open-eyed delight in the life around him that is reminiscent of the open wonder of early Gaelic nature poetry. His ear for Irish speech was as fresh. He was surely the greatest playwright Ireland has produced and, in a special way, the most Irish. A decade after his friend's death, Yeats remembered him as one who came

> Towards nightfall upon certain set apart
> In a most desolate stony place,
> Towards nightfall upon a race
> Passionate and simple like his heart.[27]

By the time John Synge died in 1909, modern Irish drama and the Abbey Theatre had passed through its first years of greatness. A disagreement over

26 J. M. Synge: Collected Works, Plays, Book II, pp. 267, 269.
27 "In Memory of Major Robert Gregory," Variorum Poems, p. 325.

the management of the theater had caused the Fays and some others to leave, losing for the company some of its best actors and effective directors. But even if Synge had lived and the Fays had stayed, the excitement and achievement of those first ten years of the movement probably could not have been sustained. It is almost impossible to overestimate the sense of purpose and commitment in those early years of collaboration between some fine playwrights and a devoted group of actors. Lady Gregory would give a party at the end of each week of rehearsals; barmbrack from Gort was always in the green room for snacks between sessions. Miss Horniman would sometimes be there, drinking claret cup and smoking a cigar. In the early days, Frank Fay would come directly from his employer's office to type scripts and teach elocution. Synge would silently sit in the wings during performances, rolling cigarettes to hand to the actors as they came off stage. Yeats would fuss over whether the theater were warm enough for its few patrons; sometimes the box-office take was only a few pounds, and even with Miss Horniman's subsidy there was hardly enough money. The salaries of the company were ridiculously low considering the talent involved; even as late as 1914 Arthur Sinclair, one of the best actors Ireland produced, was earning only four pounds a week. The actors were paid double salaries and the theater took in the amazing sum of £160 during the week of the first performances of *The Playboy*, but, during the week before, a triple bill of *Kathleen ni Houlihan, Spreading the News*, and *Hyacinth Halvey* earned only slightly more than £37. Still, the money was not the important thing, and one actress who played minor roles with the company looked back after forty years to remember fondly Lady Gregory telling the company to be quiet while Mr. Yeats read "his new masterpiece," and, not so fondly, an occasion when Yeats was so rude that one of the actors threatened to push him into the footlights. There were some bitter quarrels and the kinds of personal rivalries that always come in a theater, but there was also a sense of purpose and community.

Both of those continued even after the death of Synge and the Fays' departure, but the Abbey was becoming increasingly an ordinary professional theater. Miss Horniman withdrew her subsidy in 1910, something she had been threatening to do for several years and finally did when the theater failed to close in mourning on the death of King Edward VII. With the subsidy gone, the Abbey had to pay even closer attention to the box office; the "theatre of beauty" Yeats had envisioned or even the theater of dramatic nationalism others had imagined gradually turned into a commercial playhouse. But it was a playhouse which was still committed to Irish drama and Irish playwrights. The

Abbey's acting style remained uniquely its own. The actors who had been trained by the Fays had mastered the art of spare and forceful gesture as well as the technique by which to convey the power of language. Some might cynically observe that the Abbey's small stage and primitive facilities precluded any elaborate sets, but there was still something very effective in the modest and often beautifully simple ones used. The Abbey drew on some of the best experimental stage designers of the day, Gordon Craig being the most important, and many Abbey actors gradually achieved international fame. To the theater buff those old cast lists are still tantalizing: W. G. Fay as Christy Mahon, Maire O'Neill as Pegeen Mike or Deirdre, Sara Allgood as Synge's Lavarcham, or Arthur Sinclair as his Conchubor.

As the Abbey acclimated itself to the loss of Synge, the Fays, and Miss Horniman's subsidy, its new concern with the box office and its continuing interest in finding good Irish playwrights led it to produce more plays that were realistic, more plays that dealt with contemporary problems. Two new playwrights who helped fill the need for those sorts of plays were Lennox Robinson and T. C. Murray, both natives of Cork and sometimes grouped with some other writers as the "Cork realists." Robinson discovered his interest in drama when he saw the Abbey perform in Cork while he was still a young man, and he was only twenty-two when the company did his first play, *The Clancy Name*, in 1908. It was a gritty melodrama of family pride, and all of his early plays were grimly realistic in their recurring theme of the disastrous results to rural life when its values came into conflict with those of urban society. Robinson's career at the Abbey went on for half a century. His most lasting plays were two comedies, *The Whiteheaded Boy* (1916) and *Drama at Inish* (1933), but he could write well in many dramatic forms. His construction was almost always effective and his dialogue alert to the patterns of real speech. He was probably too fluent a writer for his own good, but his plays were very popular with Abbey audiences, and in *Crabbed Youth and Age* (1922) he showed that he could write a clever comedy of manners, something few modern Irish playwrights have been able to do.

Like Lennox Robinson, T. C. Murray tried his hand at several styles, but his best plays were careful expositions of emotional conflicts in provincial life. A Catholic native of Macroom in West Cork, a gray and ugly town stretched out along the road from Cork to Killarney, Murray was the first good playwright of the Irish Renaissance to write of country and village life from the inside, and his portrayals of Catholic farmers and townspeople have a ponderous truth to type. His themes are the permanent ones of provincial life: frustrated ambition, exile, loveless marriage, the persistent care of motherhood, and the dull bleakness of old age. *Birthright*, produced at the Abbey in 1910, is a story of fraternal conflict, while *Maurice Harte* (1912) deals sensitively with the problems of a mother who wants her son to be a priest and the son who feels no vocation for the priesthood. These two and *Autumn Fire* (1924), a powerful study of inevitability and quiet despair, are among his best work; *Autumn Fire* uses much the same situation as Eugene O'Neill's *Desire Under the Elms* and is probably the better play. Murray was a conscientious playwright, but too often his plots were melodramatic and coincidental, and his characters were sometimes talking cliches. Nevertheless, he, Robinson, and some others wrote strong plays which helped define the norms of modern Irish drama. Rather conventional plays such as these can be important in their time, but they do not necessarily last well. A repertory theater such as the Abbey was then needs this kind of drama, but if they become all the theater has to offer, then something is wrong.

Looking back, it seems that something was wrong with the Abbey around the time of World War I. The new plays kept coming and the acting was often excellent, but the old excitement was gone, and too many of the new plays were earnest, worthy, and similar. The tragedies were melodramatic tales of village frustration; the comedies were laughing presentations of Irish stereotypes. Two playwrights, both fantasists, seem sharply differentiated from all this sameness: Lord Dunsany and George Fitzmaurice. Neither had a very long career at the Abbey; both had that remarkable Irish talent for imagining mad and cosmic worlds of fantasy which, psychologically, are alarmingly real. Lord Dunsany's *The Glittering Gate* (1909) is almost Swiftian in its lunatic irony and wisdom. Bill and Jim, two burglars in this life, wait at what they think is the gate of Heaven for it to open. While they wait, they talk out their lives on earth. Beer bottles, reminders of their chief pleasure when alive, rain down on them, but all the bottles are empty, and when the gate finally opens, there is only mocking laughter and "Stars. Blooming great stars."[28]

Dunsany's forte was prose fantasy rather than drama, and he went on to write some of the best fantasies of the century. George Fitzmaurice's forte, unfortunately for him, was drama, but after successes with his first few plays, the Abbey failed to produce any more of his work. Fitzmaurice died in 1963 with a trunk full of unproduced plays, and it is only since his death that he has been recognized as a major Irish playwright and a startling original. He was born in 1877 near Listowel in the northern part of County Kerry. As the child

---

[28] *Five Plays* (1914; Boston: Little, Brown, 1917), p. 99.

of a Protestant clergyman in Catholic Kerry, Fitzmaurice seems to have developed early the sense of detachment which eventually led him to spend his life watching but not participating in the world around him. Kerry is a proverbially old-fashioned and idiosyncratic part of Ireland, and it is from the folklore of Kerry that Fitzmaurice drew his sense of rural fantasy as well as interests in the grotesque and the violent. He spent most of his life, though, in Dublin as a not very successful member of the civil service. In 1907 the Abbey produced his first play to be staged, *The Country Dressmaker;* it enjoyed a great success and remained for more than forty years one of the most popular plays in the reportory. Like most of Fitzmaurice's plays, its setting is Kerry, and its plot involves two factions in a village which are scheming to marry off Pats Connor, a villager who has gone to America and returned. The plot is unremarkable, but Fitzmaurice demonstrated in this play that his mastery of Kerry dialect was as good as Synge's mastery of that of Aran and County Wicklow and that there was a vein of fantastic humor in him.

If Fitzmaurice had continued to write comedies like *The Country Dressmaker,* he might have remained a successful dramatist. But the best of his subsequent plays are private fantasies, plays which begin by being firmly fixed in the real world but quickly veer off into nutty imaginings. *The Pie-Dish* (1908) is that unusual thing, a tragic fantasy, or, perhaps more accurately, a pathetic fantasy. In one very short act, it tells how old Leum Donoghue has spent twenty years making an ornamental pie dish; dying, but in a frenzy to complete his masterpiece, he calls on the devil to give him more time. When he does, he falls dead, and the dish drops from his hands, smashing. This is a strange little play; dead accurate in its dialogue and characterization, and a quirky variation on the Romantic theme of the Faustian desire of the artist to create a perfect work. The audiences of 1908 laughed heartily at it, and perhaps it was the laughter where none was intended that encouraged Fitzmaurice to go on to make wilder fantasies in which abnormality overtaken by the supernatural is the norm. In *The Magic Glasses* (1913), laughing madness ends in death for Jaymoney Shanahan, a thirty-eight-year-old man who spends his time in the loft of his father's farmhouse looking through nine glasses he has bought from a fairy. Through the glasses, Jaymoney can enjoy an immensely satisfying fantasy world, strikingly different from the everyday: " 'tis better than being in the slush—same old thing every day—this is an ugly spot, and the people ignorant, grumpy, and savage."[29] His parents call in Morgan Quille, a quack medical man, to cure him, but Quille's efforts to exorcise Jaymoney's demon

---

[29] *The Plays of George Fitzmaurice: Dramatic Fantasies* (Dublin: Dolmen, 1967), p. 11.

leave the exorcist himself in convulsions; Jaymoney returns to the loft. It collapses with him, and the play ends with Jaymoney dead, his throat slit by his magic glasses. The play is a brilliant parable on the power of the imagination as well as a satire on the escapism of the writers of the Celtic twilight, all this placed in the context of characters and language skillfully drawn from Kerry originals. It was the next to last of Fitzmaurice's to be produced at the Abbey, and its author gradually became as reclusive as Jaymoney himself. Still, he continued to write plays, fantasies as well as realistic ones. *The Dandy Dolls,* which was published in 1914, was probably his masterpiece. Its theme, as in so many of Fitzmaurice's plays, is the intrusion of the supernatural into the ordinary world of County Kerry. Its action and language are a perfect farrago of farce, but just beneath the surface are inexplicable magic, violence, and grotesquerie. Roger Carmody devotes his life to making dandy dolls, what they are Fitzmaurice never really explains; a priest as well as all sorts of supernatural powers would like to get their hands on them, but Roger's most recent creation, like all the others, is eventually stolen by a mysterious figure, the Hag's Son. Roger's earthy wife, Cauth, explains the process: "For the Hag's Son is against them to the death, and so sure as Roger makes a doll, so sure will the Hag's Son, soon or late, come at it, give it a knuckle in the navel, split it in two fair halves, collar the windpipe, and off with him carrying the squeaky-squeak."[30] This time, though, Roger is stolen along with his doll, and we are left to wonder if normality has returned finally or if it ever will.

Fitzmaurice once said the characters in some of his plays were "wicked old children."[31] His best work depends on the conflict of crazy innocence and uncomprehending experience. He was a great tale-teller, one who could spin a yarn as well as any Kerryman by the fire, and there is something absorbing still in his parables of frustrated vision and artistry. Because of his command of peasant character and dialect, he is often compared to Synge, but Fitzmaurice's imagination was more narrow and less disciplined. A few of his characters have the rich humanity of most of Synge's, but the majority are whirling caricatures. During the last forty years of his life the Abbey produced none of his new plays, but that did not keep him from writing, and apparently he did not care whether the plays were staged or not. Increasingly he became a recluse in his own fantasy world, coming out only to go to work and for his regular pints of stout at Mooney's and other Dublin pubs. When he died in 1963, a pathetic note was found in his effects: "Author is prepared to sell outright all

30 *Ibid.,* p. 22.
31 Quoted in *ibid.,* p. viii.

rights in 14 plays dealing intimately with life in the Irish countryside."[32] There had been no buyers in his lifetime, but Fitzmaurice was exactly right in his phrasing: his plays to deal "intimately with life in the Irish countryside," not the day-to-day life of north Kerry farmers, perhaps, but the imaginative life which still exists inside the head of many a village storyteller.

The failure to encourage Fitzmaurice after 1913 is one of the mysteries of the Abbey's history, but by that time the theater was probably too concerned with commercial success to want his work. The years between 1913 and 1923 were a difficult time for it, years in which it took great effort simply to stay in business. The building survived the devastation of the 1916 rising, but one of the actors died in the fighting and a promising writer, Thomas MacDonagh, was among the patriots shot in the aftermath. The new plays continued to come, but the exhaustion of those times is indicated by the fact that most of the 1916–17 season was given over to the plays of George Bernard Shaw, an Irishman, admittedly, but one who was no more than tangentially associated with Irish drama. The "troubles" brought the company to the edge of bankruptcy, and in the spring of 1921, Lennox Robinson, then the manager, had no choice but to tell the actors that the theater was giving up its struggle for survival. But, in spite of all odds, it reopened that fall in the lull between Ireland's war for independence and her civil war, and it kept going. In 1924 the new Free State offered a subsidy, and that seemed to guarantee some financial security for the future. The Abbey had become Ireland's state theater, the first state-supported theater in the English-speaking world.

John Synge would have seen some irony in that. The nationalists who execrated his *Playboy* had become the guarantors of his theater. Yet there was something appropriate in this decision, for the Abbey had done as much and more than any nationalist to prove that Ireland was indeed "the home of an ancient idealism." Yeats's plays spoke to one vision of Ireland in their intricate symbolism and passionate reverie. Lady Gregory's spoke to another, Synge's to yet a third, Colum's, Murray's, Fitzmaurice's to others still. No one vision was complete or perhaps even ultimately true, but each was a kind of truth about the Ireland that was and the Ireland that could be. Those visions, the products of the dramatic genius of Ireland's playwrights, had made drama one of the great and lasting achievements of the Irish Renaissance.

---

[32] Quoted in Arthur E. McGuinness, *George Fitzmaurice* (Lewisburg, Pa.: Bucknell University Press, 1975), p. 16.

peasants, visionaries, and rebels
Anglo-Irish Poetry, 1900–1923

My father and mother were Irish,
And I am Irish, too;
I bought a wee fidil for ninepence,
And it is Irish, too.

Joseph Campbell

I am come of the seed of the people, the
    people that sorrow,
That have no treasure but hope,
No riches laid up but a memory
Of an ancient glory.

Padraic Pearse

T HE IRISH RENAISSANCE began with poets and poetry, and it would not be an exaggeration to say that it produced little significant fiction or drama until at least fifteen years after it began. Nevertheless, once the movement had started in earnest, it gave rise to less poetry of lasting merit than fiction or drama for several decades. There were many poets working in Ireland in the first quarter of this century, but few of them wrote many poems which seem of much significance today. Thomas Kinsella, a distinguished Irish poet of our own time, attributes this to the presence of Yeats as too strong a poetic model: "As to Yeats's contemporaries, my own impression is of a generation of writers entranced, understandably, by the phenomenon of Yeats among them, and themselves going down in a welter of emulation and misunderstanding of his work."[1] Kinsella is probably right, but even if there had been no Yeats, the

---

[1] "The Divided Mind," *Irish Poets in English*, edited by Sean Lucy (Cork and Dublin: Mercier, 1973), p. 217.

Irish poets of this period would have faced some formidable problems. There was, at the most basic level, the problem of recognition; would it be possible for any Irish poet to find an audience inside the country and abroad? Beyond that, the Irish poet had to deal with the problem of Irishness in subject matter and style; how would he define his Irishness? Some poets did it largely by using something like the old style of the poets of *The Nation,* writing poems of patriotic sentiment in high, emphatic language. Other poets, looking to the more recent literary past, continued to find a definition of Irishness in the mysticism, reverie, and wavering rhythms of the Celtic Twilight. A few poets, influenced by the techniques of their English contemporaries, the Decadents and the Georgians, used urban impressionism and elaborate technical forms to portray the Irish experience. Yet others, looking to Douglas Hyde's translations from Gaelic and Gaelic poetry itself for models, found ways to create what came close to folk poetry.

Especially in the years before World War I, there were plenty of theories of how to write Irish poetry, and there were plenty of poets. The Dublin literary world of that time, like the one of today, was small and self-inclusive. Young nationalists and writers would gather at Seumas O'Sullivan's on Sunday mornings; AE held open house at his home in Rathgar Avenue on Sunday nights. Maud Gonne was At Home on Monday nights, Padraic Colum on Tuesdays, and when writers were not at someone's house, they were in the pubs and the newspaper offices. Joyce's description of the newspapers as Aeolian halls of the winds should not make us forget that they took an active interest in the literary revival. The daily papers, even the Unionist *Irish Times,* gave generous space to reviews of the work of the Abbey and the Irish writers. In addition, Ireland was beginning to develop a good range of literary and intellectual magazines. The *New Ireland Review, The Shanachie,* Standish O'Grady's *All-Ireland Review,* John Eglinton's *Dana,* the *Irish Review,* and even AE's farmers' magazine, *The Irish Homestead,* all played parts in the development of a significant literary culture. There was sometimes too much self-congratulation, rivalry, and laxness of standards, but Dublin was becoming an exciting place in which to be a writer.

Yeats used to refer to some of the younger poets as AE's canaries, and the bird image is not far wrong, for AE was a sort of mother hen to many of them, regularly clucking over his chicks. He taught them his philosophy, a pantheistic adoration of nature, and he argued that the essential value of Ireland lay in the primitivity of the country and its people. His own poetry was less an influence than his ideas and his personality. A few of his poems from after 1900 carried on the wavering rhythms and pale imagery of the Celtic

Twilight successfully, but his poetic voice remained a faint one. One of his best poems, "Carrowmore," is attractive enough as an evocation of fairyland, but its images owe too much to the Yeats of "The Lake Isle of Innisfree" and "The Song of Wandering Aengus" for it to seem more than a good pastiche. AE taught his followers that "the province of a national literature" was "to create the Ireland in the heart,"[2] and his prose writings all during this quarter-century were valuable for their intelligent definitions of the relationship between the artist and his nation. The interest in Theosophy which he had shared with Yeats and others in the nineties remained important to him, although his work with Irish farmers taught him that the Ireland of the mystical imagination was a different thing from the Ireland of the bogs and the dairy farms. Nevertheless, his belief in the divinity of nature never wavered nor did his belief in an easy intercourse between the spiritual world and the human. AE's candor about his mystical experiences was sometimes disconcerting, as when he would show friends pictures he had painted of the spirits who visited him, but his spiritual autobiography, *The Candle of Vision* (1918), is a glowing interpretation of the visionary life. His insistence on a relationship between visionary experience and nationalism did much to establish among some of the writers the belief in the "national being" itself as a motive for their lives. It is unkind to charge so good a man as AE with racism, but there is no doubt that his acceptance of the idea of a collective Irish consciousness with emphases on spirituality and immateriality was a dangerous mixture of nationalism and mysticism. AE himself had nothing but good will toward others, but such beliefs could, and did, lead to the violence he deplored.

AE's greatest service to Irish literature, though, came neither in his poetry or his ideas. It came, instead, in his unceasing kindness to younger writers. Some of them may later have disparaged him as "Dublin's glittering guy" and laughed about the "at homes" in which a comment from Mrs. Russell would set him off on an hour's monologue, but he was, as Frank O'Connor said, the father of three generations of Irish poets. Among his "discoveries" were James Joyce, Padraic Colum, James Stephens, Frank O'Connor, Austin Clarke, and Patrick Kavanagh. AE's genius was for dealing with writers at the very beginnings of their careers, and often, as they matured, their allegiances turned from him to Yeats. Yeats was his closest and oldest friend, and yet there was often antagonism between them. Yeats envied his friend's ability to attract the young, and perhaps AE was dismayed by Yeats's toughness and egotism. Yeats's wife described the problem exactly when she told her husband that he was the better

---

[2] Quoted in E. A. Boyd, *Ireland's Literary Renaissance* (1916; New York: Knopf, 1922), p. 234.

poet, but AE was a saint. One friend, when asked what AE was like, replied: "Well, there was the beard and the hair and the glasses and the brown, large clothes. . . . He was very large, he had a sort of wild look, but it wasn't wild with fury, he was wild with warmth and vitality and terrible interest in everything."[3]

His interest in the young led him, in 1904, to sponsor the publication of a collection of poems by younger writers, *New Songs*. Some of the poets who appeared in it are thoroughly forgotten today, but it was an important volume because it introduced some good young talent and because it suggested that a new movement was coming in Irish poetry. The best of the poets in that volume turned away from the style of the Celtic Twilight toward new ways of interpreting the Irish experience. Often they replaced the mazy rhythms of the poetry of the nineties with an energy which came from folk song; in general, they avoided the legends which had attracted the earlier generation and wrote instead of the ordinary experiences of peasants, tinkers, and tramps. For the vague and evocative visions of the older poets, they substituted hard, clear pictures. The interest in peasant life which Yeats, Hyde, and AE had stimulated in the nineties led some of the younger poets to a fuller knowledge of traditional Irish music, Gaelic folk poetry, and English ballads. Love songs such as "My Love is Like the Sun," political ballads, and such masterpieces of the ubiquitous Anon. as "The Night Before Larry Was Stretched" and "The Willow Tree" were a far cry from the highly wrought Celticism of the nineties, and the younger generation benefitted from the concision, firmness, and energy of the old songs.

Padraic Colum wrote several poems which have by now become a part of the folk tradition in Ireland, and Colum was in some ways the best of the poets AE sponsored around the turn of the century. Born in 1881, the son of the master of a workhouse in Longford in the dull center of Ireland, Colum's first successes had come in his plays for the Irish National Theatre. He was a good dramatist, and could have been a better one, but the publication of a little collection of poems, *Wild Earth*, in 1907, was perhaps his most lasting contribution to Irish literature. The influence of Douglas Hyde's translations from the Gaelic is strong in this collection, but the entire volume has a freshness and spontaneity which marked Colum as something more than anyone's imitator. Bryan MacMahon writes that "Colum's view of life is in essence that of the peasant as a noble savage endowed with the secrets of life and death. This valuable but somehow simple viewpoint is projected in poetry where not alone sowers and reapers but honey-sellers, drovers, blacksmiths, ballad-singers,

3 Comment of Lady Glenavy in W. R. Rodgers, *Irish Literary Portraits* (London: BBC, 1972), p. 185.

bird-catchers, and tin whistle-players move in delightful but somehow silent mime."[4] Not all of this is in *Wild Earth,* but Colum shows a good mastery of the dramatic lyric and a striking sense of the wonder in elemental things. "An Old Woman of the Roads," "The Plougher," and "Achill Girl's Song" are all sentimental poems, but their sentiment is the true one of folk song rather than the meretricious one of bad poets and cheap entertainers. As one commentator on Colum's work has written, Colum often shows a "childlike power to see straight to the soul of things" and thus "presents us with poetic experience in its most innocent and naked form." And, he adds, "Often there are no allusions, no symbols, only the simplest images, nothing but the singing tone and the thing itself."[5] From the plainness of such poets as Colum has come one important strand in more recent Irish poetry, a strand of simplicity and openness.

Unlike Colum, Joseph Campbell was not one of AE's proteges, but he shared with Colum the ability to create a simple poem which seems to be the thing itself. He was, in fact, one of a number of writers from Ulster who were involved in a literary revival in their province which drew its inspiration from what was going on in Dublin and other parts of Catholic Ireland. He was involved in the Ulster Literary Theatre, Belfast's counterpart to the Abbey, in its early days. Moreover, Campbell did important work in collecting the folk songs of his province, and these, with their distinctive north of Ireland and even Scottish idiom, colored his creative work. His first collection of poems was unremarkable, but his second, *The Rush Light* (1906), showed an impressive awareness of the techniques and simplicity of folk poetry. The first stanza of one of his early poems aptly expresses his outlook:

> I am the mountainy singer—
> The voice of the peasant's dream,
> The cry of the wind on the wooded hill,
> The leap of the fish in the stream.[6]

There is little of AE's mysticism in his work and less of Yeats's arcane symbolism; his interest in the precise presentation of experience led him to experiment with Imagism, the technique of modernist poetry which values clarity of

---

[4] "Place and People into Poetry," *Irish Poets in English,* p. 66.

[5] L. A. G. Strong, quoted in Zack Bowen, *Padraic Colum* (Carbondale and Edwardsville: Southern Illinois University Press, 1970), p. 29.

[6] "I Am the Mountainy Singer," *Mentor Book of Irish Poetry,* edited by Devin A. Garrity (New York: Mentor, 1965), p. 46.

objective pictorialization above all else. *The Mountainy Singer* (1909) contains much of his best poetry, but *Irishry* (1913), a collection of poetic impressions of peasant types, is perhaps his most characteristic work, a bit sentimental but moving in its honesty of observation.

As much or more than any other Irish poet of his time, Campbell caught the voice of peasant song, and such poems as "The Ninepenny Fidil" and "My Lagan Love" have, in fact, become now part of Irish folksong. Most of his poetry from after about 1914 is disappointing, but his earlier work gives him a place as an important minor poet. Several religious poems, including the well-known "I am the Gilly of Christ," suggest his fundamental strength, the ability to turn the most complex sort of experience into something simple and precise. His most memorable images are often his simplest: the dancer with music in his feet and death on his face, the days of his life as a black valley in which silence is audible. He lacks some of Colum's energy and too often he confused sentimentality with sympathy, but "The Old Woman" is only one of many poems which seems right as only perfected simplicity can be:

> As a white candle
> In a holy place,
> So is the beauty
> Of an agèd face.
>
> . . . .
>
> Her brood gone from her,
> And her thoughts as still
> As the waters
> Under a ruined mill.[7]

If Colum is the representative poet of the midlands of Ireland in these years and Campbell of Ulster, then James Stephens is the representative of Dublin and the dream world of the Dublin slum dweller. Stephens did not appear in *New Songs*, but he was an important follower of AE, and his first collection of poems, *Insurrections* (1909), marked him as a major voice in Irish poetry. His subject is primarily the city; there is little interest in ancient legend or folklore. Natural or racial mysticism is largely absent; vague imagery and the desire for evocation are replaced by colloquialism and the sound of an ordinary voice:

[7] "The Old Woman," *ibid.*, p. 53.

I saw God! Do you doubt it?
Do you dare to doubt it?
I saw the Almighty Man! . . .[8]

Stephens owed a good deal to Browning for this colloquialism, and one of his best poems, "Mac Dhoul," is a kind of Irish revision of the end of Browning's "Fra Lippo Lippi." The plain talk and the almost breezy mysticism are welcome, but like Colum and Campbell, Stephens wore out as a poet too early, and his best work was done by 1920, thirty years before his death. Even so, his second collection, *The Hill of Vision* (1912), had such good poems as "Why Tomas Cam was Grumpy" and "What the Devil Said," and in 1918 he published what may have been his most interesting poetry, a volume called *Reincarnations.* The poems here are based on the Gaelic poets of the seventeenth, eighteenth, and early nineteenth centuries. Stephens did not intend to make scholarly translations; instead, his poems are re-creations in English of the Gaelic originals, and they catch much of their spirit and vigor. "A Glass of Beer," perhaps Stephens's best-known poem, comes from this collection; it is not characteristic of all the poems in it by any means, but its invective against the serving girl in the inn who will not give the poet "the loan of a glass of beer" is unforgettable:

If I asked her master he'd give me a cask a day;
But she, with the beer at hand, not a gill would arrange!
May she marry a ghost and bear him a kitten, and may
The High King of Glory permit her to get the mange.[9]

For even more potent invective, we could turn to J. M. Synge's "The Curse." One of Synge's ablest critics, T. R. Henn, feels that Synge's achievement as a poet was slight, and sometimes the poems do not seem as finished as they ought to be. But slight and casual as many are, they ring true to their maker's vision of life, his glorification of the roughness and energy of peasant Ireland, and his fear of death. Synge wisely observed that the poetry of his own time needed to learn to be brutal in order to become human again. That was good advice; Yeats took it, wrote some brutal epigrams, and then some intensely human meditations and lyrics. Synge himself never moved far beyond brutality,

8 "What Tomas Said in a Pub," *ibid.,* p. 353.
9 "A Glass of Beer," *ibid.,* p. 352.

but his command of imagery is consistently striking, even in the violent tale of how a score of Erris men got "shut" of the Danny who was "playing hell on decent girls" and "beating man and boy." There is no romanticization of peasant life in the ballad of Shaneen and Maurya Prendergast who own just "a cur-dog, a cabbage plot,/A goat, and cock of hay,"[10] and very little Celtic Twilight glamor in "Beg Innish."

"The Passing of the Shee," written, the poet tells us, after looking at one of AE's pictures, is a satiric comment on vague and glamorous Irishism. Poets would continue to write in the Celtic Twilight manner long after Synge's death, but Synge was right in asserting that all that was finished for any real creative purpose:

> Adieu, sweet Angus, Maeve, and Fand,
> Ye plumed yet skinny Shee,
> That poets played with hand in hand
> To learn their ecstasy.
>
> We'll stretch in Red Dan Sally's ditch
> And drink in Tubber fair,
> Or poach with Red Dan Philly's bitch
> The badger and the hare.[11]

Synge's abrupt dismissal of the Celtic Twilight, its gods, its style, and its ethos suggested one important direction Irish poetry would eventually take. But, historically, Synge was as ahead of his time in his poetry as he was in his plays and his vision of Ireland. He had no use for what he saw as nationalistic nonsense about his country, but some other poets still found in nationalism a powerful means of expression. The mystic vision of Ireland, the nationalism religious in its intensity, implicit in the early work of Yeats and AE remained an important factor in Irish verse as well as in Irish politics. For one group of poets and nationalists, in fact, the vision of Ireland was so real that they were ready to die for it. Only an extreme nationalist would now claim that Padraic Pearse, Thomas MacDonagh, and Joseph Mary Plunkett were important poets, but each died to give birth to a free Ireland in 1916, and their poetry and their nationalism were intimately connected.

10 "Danny" and "Patch-Shaneen," *The Plays and Poems of J. M. Synge*, edited by T. R. Henn (London: Methuen, 1963), pp. 291–92.
11 "The Passing of the Shee," *ibid.*, p. 295.

Pearse's place in history is as the creator of the Irish Republic, but he was considerably more than the man who led the troops on Easter Monday of 1916 and read the declaration of Irish freedom. Born in Dublin in 1879, he worked for several years as a journalist and editor for the Gaelic League before founding St. Enda's School in 1908. At ten he had gone down on his knees to vow that he would spend the rest of his life trying to free Ireland, and St. Enda's was one way of carrying out that vow. St. Enda's taught its students in Gaelic and English, and Pearse, interested in educational reform, had even gone to Belgium to study that country's system of bilingual schooling. Nevertheless, St. Enda's real purpose was to teach patriotic idealism. Visitors to the school found in its entrance hall a mural of the arming of Cuchulain because Pearse's aim was to arm a generation of Irish boys with Cuchulain's courage, devotion, and passion for Ireland. A shrewd commentator has noted that Pearse "read the Ulster Cycle as allegory, as an image of the story of Calvary. Emain Macha was a kingdom afflicted with a primal sin that was redeemed by the blood sacrifice of Cuchulain. Pearse's writing, political or literary, is filled with the imagery of apocalypse and one must go to Revelation to encounter the Christ-Cuchulain figure that he envisioned."[12] In his poetry, as in his life, Pearse saw himself as a redeemer, misunderstood and maltreated, who would nevertheless redeem his people from their political bondage to Britain and their spiritual bondage to English materialism.

In Gaelic Ireland he found purity, passion, and purpose, and so he learned the language, bought a cabin in the west of Ireland, and even wrote poetry in Gaelic. Yet much of his poetry is far removed from the usual verse of Gaelic Ireland, for it is really an allegory of his own tortured imagination. There is a strong streak of asceticism, even masochism, in it; it is almost as though the beliefs of the Gaelic League and the most intense antiphysicality of Irish Catholicism had found expression in the language of a Biblical prophet. Such poems as "The Rebel" and "The Fool" have an impressive Biblical cadence in their parallelisms and repetitions, but they are also mawkish and embarrassingly self-pitying. His best play, *The Singer* (not produced during his lifetime), is just as clearly an autobiographical allegory. Pearse himself is surely MacDara, the wandering singer of patriotic songs, "shy in himself and very silent, till he stands up to talk to the people. And then he has the voice of a silver trumpet, and words so beautiful that they make people cry. And there is terrible anger in him, for all that he is shrinking and gentle." At the end of the play,

---

[12] William Irwin Thompson, *The Imagination of an Insurrection*, pp. 121–22.

MacDara's obsessions with his mother, patriotism, and sacrificial death (all obsessions Pearse shared) lead him out to die alone for his nation: "One man can free a people as one Man redeemed the world. I will take no pike, I will go into the battle with bare hands. I will stand up before the Gall as Christ hung naked before men on the tree!"[13] MacDara-Pearse's death is to be, really, suicide, a death consciously sought for its symbolic significance. Padraic Pearse chose just this sort of death, a blood sacrifice which would redeem his people, and perhaps he could be dismissed as nothing more than a neurotic rebel if it were not for the incontestable fact that the death he and his colleagues chose was indeed a symbolic act which led to the liberation of their country. Pearse would rank as an insignificant poet if the idea of blood sacrifice for national redemption, so clearly stated in his poems, had not changed the course of Irish history and made him one of the truly prophetic voices in modern Ireland. Pearse's obsession with Mother Ireland lets him speak as archetypal patriot, a nationalist for whom death for a glorious thing is preferable to any sort of life. And perhaps it is not entirely accidental that the one great poem he wrote does not speak of himself or Mother Ireland but speaks as the voice of a human mother grieving and praying for the sons she has lost in the struggle for liberation; it is a sentimental poem, but a true and moving one. It begins:

> I do not grudge them: Lord, I do not grudge
> My two strong sons that I have seen go out
> To break their strength and die, they and a few,
> In bloody protest for a glorious thing,
> They shall be spoken of among their people. . . .[14]

Pearse was not the only poet to die before the firing squads in 1916; Joseph Plunkett and Thomas MacDonagh died with him. Plunkett, who was only twenty-eight, published a single volume of poems, *The Circle and the Sword* (1911), but his work shows a strongly Catholic mysticism and a Pearse-like concern with personal sacrifice. Thomas MacDonagh was a more considerable poet and a playwright whose *When the Dawn is Come* was produced at the Abbey in 1908. Although he helped Pearse found St. Enda's in that same year, he spent much of his career as a lecturer in English literature at

---

13 *The Singer and Other Plays* (Dublin: Talbot Press, 1960), pp. 16–17, 44.

14 "The Mother," *Penguin Book of Irish Verse*, edited by Brendan Kennelly (Harmondsworth, Middlesex: Penguin, 1970), p. 296.

University College, Dublin. "The Yellow Bittern" shows that MacDonagh was alert to the voice of Gaelic poetry in a way Pearse was not; that poem and "John-John" could almost be by Colum or Stephens. Much of his poetry which comes out of his own imaginative experience rather than the Gaelic is conventional Romantic melancholy, and William Irwin Thompson may be right in suspecting that MacDonagh was fundamentally an intellectual who found that the intellectual can be little more than sacrificed in Ireland. Certainly, he was a shrewd thinker, and his posthumously published *Literature in Ireland* (1916) is an important study of Gaelic and Anglo-Irish poetry. In it MacDonagh rightly observed that any true Irish poetry must draw a significant part of its inspiration from Gaelic literature and that the "Celtic mode" created out of Standish O'Grady and the poets of the Celtic Twilight was based on a misunderstanding of the Gaelic tradition.

Yeats, in his great elegy for the poets and rebels of 1916 wrote:

> Hearts with one purpose alone
> Through summer and winter seem
> Enchanted to a stone
> To trouble the living stream.[15]

But the Yeats of "Easter 1916" was clearly disturbed by the "excess of love" for Ireland which he saw in the rebels, an excess which had given birth to a "terrible beauty." The road of excess may lead to the palace of wisdom, as Blake said, but the seeming excesses of Irish nationalism, of which the Easter Rising was only one climax, frightened Yeats. He had come into the twentieth century with a vision of Ireland based on his own idiosyncratic mixture of Theosophy, occultism, folklore, and Celtic saga, and even the disturbances at the premiere of *The Countess Cathleen* in 1899 had not completely shaken his faith in this vision. Those disturbances were, though, the first quarrel in an increasing controversy between the Yeatsian vision of Ireland and the nationalists' vision of political liberation, material improvement, a peasant-centered culture, and Catholic piety. Yeats would eventually announce furiously that "Romantic Ireland's dead and gone,/It's with O'Leary in the grave,"[16] but, in fact, O'Leary's kind of literary nationalism still had great truth in it, truth which Yeats was sometimes too egocentric to see. With his shyness, his haughtiness,

---

[15] "Easter 1916," *Variorum Poems*, p. 393.
[16] "September 1913, *ibid.*, pp. 289–90.

and his interest in esoteric matters, Yeats was frequently out of sympathy and even out of touch with the Ireland of the first quarter of this century. But his detractors underestimated his immense imaginative power and even his rocky character as they laughed at his mannerisms. It has sometimes been said that the other poets in Ireland during these times had genius but lacked the talent to sustain it; Yeats had both, and through his bitter quarrels with Ireland and himself, he became the greatest poet in English of our century.

He sometimes spoke of his involvement in Irish affairs as a baptism in the gutter; those are strong words, but they are not entirely inappropriate as a description of his experiences in the Irish dramatic movement bewteen 1899 and the death of Synge in 1909. The baptism turned the gentle and dreamy poet of the nineties into a combative man. Through writing plays, Yeats gradually learned to objectify even himself and his own emotions. When AE sent him a copy of *New Songs*, Yeats replied: "Some of the poems I will probably under-rate . . . because the dominant mood in many of them is the one I have fought in myself and put down. . . . an exaggeration of sentiment and sentimental beauty which I have come to think unmanly. . . . We possess nothing but the will and we must never let the children of vague desires breathe upon it nor the waters of sentiment rust the terrible mirror of its blade. I fled from some of this new verse you have gathered as from much verse of our day knowing that I fled that water and that breath."[17] The shift from poetry imaged as water and breath to poetry imaged as sword was immensely important to him, and the image of the sword reflected a new-found toughness in his own imagination. During the years of his day-to-day involvement in the Abbey and its affairs, he demonstrated a surprising particality and harshness. Sometimes his sharp tongue enraged the actors, but he proved himself an adroit manager of theatrical business. He told a friend in 1906 that Dublin needed "some man who knows his own mind and has an intolerable tongue and a delight in enemies,"[18] and his vigorous defense of Synge during the *Playboy* riots showed he was that man.

Some old friends lamented the loss of the gentle Willie Yeats, but in Synge and Lady Gregory he had found powerful reinforcements for his new self. Synge's relentless clarity and his call even for brutality in poetry stiffened Yeats's resolve to remake himself. Lady Gregory's Coole Park offered a place of seclusion and order in his tumultuous life, and Lady Gregory herself was a

17 *Letters of W. B. Yeats*, edited by Allan Wade (London: Hart-Davis, 1954), p. 434.
18 *Ibid.*, p. 474.

firmly supporting presence. In her he saw a living example of an aristocracy which had roots in the past as well as the courage and the stability Yeats sought. His father wisely observed that his son was a conservative at heart, and so he was. The new glorification of Anglo-Ireland was a conservative development of the old theories of the Celtic Twilight days: Anglo-Irish aristocrats and Gaelic peasants had much in common, he decided, and the praise of both, together with the attacks on the supposed materialism and religious narrowness of the urban middle class, became Yeats's way of asserting his primitivism and his belief that simplicity, nobility, and passion were the shared characteristics of aristocrat and tinker. Some of the glorification of aristocratic values was absurd, as when Yeats claimed that he ought to have been the Duke of Ormonde, but it enriched and broadened his imagination even as it made him a snob personally. For his poetry's sake, though, it was not a bad thing; the discovery of a deep-rooted past helped sustain his creativity through some difficult times and it led, eventually, to some of his greatest poetry.

That happened slowly, and admirers of the poet who bought his new collections of poems, *In the Seven Woods* in 1903 and *The Green Helmet* in 1910, were sometimes dismayed by the changes in his work. Much of the intricacy, some of the verbal magic, and almost all of the Celticism of previous volumes were gone. *The Wind Among the Reeds* in 1899 had opened with an evocative description of the Sidhe riding the air and calling, "Away, come away:/Empty your heart of its mortal dream,"[19] but the title poem of *In the Seven Woods* was a compact, freely rhymed sonnet in which vision still hangs in the air but our attention is drawn to the earthly woods of Coole Park and the poet's modest contentment in the Quiet that wanders among the bees and pigeons there. Maud Gonne shocked Yeats by marrying a soldier, Major John MacBride, in 1903, and in place of the earlier passionate love poetry, there is an aging and chastened voice. He insists that there is still folly in being comforted for his lost love, but he knows there are threads of gray now in Maud Gonne's hair, and much of the love poetry concerns old memories. Most remarkably, the Yeats of 1903 was willing to say what the Yeats of the nineties could not possibly have said: "Never give all the heart." The finest poem of *In the Seven Woods*, and one of the finest Yeats ever wrote, "Adam's Curse," is also a poem of disappointed love, but it is most impressive in its command of things which would become central to his later poetry: dialogue, meditation on the craft of poetry, closely controlled irony, beautifully plain language, and, at

---

[19] "The Hosting of the Sidhe," *Variorum Poems*, p. 140.

the end, a coalescence of image, thought, and emotion into a magically right stillness.

"Adam's Curse" has the inevitability of great poetry, but its rightness was something Yeats found only intermittently in these years before World War I. *In the Seven Woods* and *The Green Helmet* are both small collections, and Yeats wrote little lyric poetry during this period. The writing of plays and Abbey business kept him from that work, of course, but his personal and emotional turmoil cost him even more creatively. *The Green Helmet* is interesting for its identification of Maud Gonne with Homer's Helen and for its sharp little epigrams which show Yeats had learned much about concision and clarity from Synge and the poets—Catullus, Ronsard, and Villon—Synge loved. Still, it does seem, as Yeats said, that

> The fascination of what's difficult
> Has dried the sap out of my veins, and rent
> Spontaneous joy and natural content
> Out of my heart.[20]

The death of Synge in 1909, a resumption of the unhappy relationship with Maud Gonne after her separation from John MacBride, increasing bitterness about Irish affairs, and a gradual disengagement from the Dublin scene marked the Yeats of this time. An expensive, multivolume *Collected Works*, published in 1908, looked suspiciously like a handsome end to his career; by 1910 he had accepted a pension from the British government, and there were those who expected him to live out his days as a conventional man of letters in London.

They were wrong, thoroughly wrong. Controversies in Ireland and bitterness over developments at the Abbey did cause Yeats to move back to London, but once there, he began again to rediscover and remake himself once again. The interest in the esoteric revived, leading to a new interest in mediums, spiritualism, and attempts to contact the dead; out of this, he gradually began to find answers to his questions about the supernatural and even answers about human personality, history, and creativity. In London, too, he met Ezra Pound, the American expatriate poet, who became his secretary and adviser. Yeats was furious when Pound edited some of his poems before submitting them to an American magazine, *Poetry*, but gradually he realized that his friend's insistence on precise imagery and clarity was exactly what

---

20 "The Fascination of What's Difficult," *ibid.*, p. 260.

he needed to continue the work of remaking himself as a poet. Pound also
introduced him to some manuscripts of translations of Japanese Noh plays, and
Yeats found in these a model for the sort of drama he now wished to write,
an aristocratic drama of mime and suggestion which came still closer than the
symbolist plays of the decade before to the theater of ritual and intimation he
had always sought. The publications of George Moore's *Hail and Farewell*
and Katharine Tynan's indiscreet autobiography turned his attention, also,
towards his own past and his family's. His next volume of poems, *Responsibilities* (1914) reflected several of these new interests. It opens with an
apology to his ancestors that there is "nothing but a book . . . to prove your
blood and mine."[21] *Responsibilities* has many sorts of poems in it, from the
powerful invective of "September 1913" with its attack on an Ireland turned
grubby and mean to the fragile lyricism of "To a Child Dancing in the Wind,"
but the collection as a whole is notable for a regathering of poetic power.
None of the poems quite equals Yeats's best work, but they clearly show that
the process of remaking was coming towards a successful conclusion:

> I made my song a coat
> Covered with embroideries
> Out of old mythologies
> From heel to throat;
> But the fools caught it,
> Wore it in the world's eyes
> As though they'd wrought it.
> Song, let them take it,
> For there's more enterprise
> In walking naked.[22]

Still, Yeats was hardly ready, then or ever, to walk naked, and around
1917 he began to restitch his coat into a new mythology. In that year, after a
final proposal to Maud Gonne and subsequent a proposal to her daughter,
Iseult, he married an Englishwoman, George Hyde-Lees. Although he had had
an interest in mediums and automatic writing for several years, it seemed to
him almost a miracle when his young bride began to write out for him
messages from the spirit world. At first, the messages seemed confused, but
gradually he pieced them together into a coherent philosophy of life and art,

---

21 "Pardon, Old Fathers," *ibid.*, p. 270.
22 "A Coat," *ibid.*, p. 320.

a philosophy which taught that eternal, preordained change was the condition of history, that all kinds of human personality could be understood in terms of common types, that human creativity was an attempt to work out an understanding of one's self and one's inherent opposite or antiself. The theories Yeats eventually developed in his prose testament, *A Vision* (1925) were complex and esoteric, but their importance for his poetry lay in the fact that he believed them to be at least an approximate answer to the questions of human existence which had troubled him all his life. The theories, and perhaps marriage and its stability, liberated his imagination in an astonishing way.

His next two collections of poems, *The Wild Swans at Coole* (1919) and *Michael Robartes and the Dancer* (1921) were the products of that liberation. In poem after poem, he asserts his greatness. "The Wild Swans at Coole" itself is an exquisitely poised lyric in the Romantic nature tradition; the elegy for Lady Gregory's son, Robert, killed fighting in the British air force in Italy in 1918, is the first of a long series of personal elegies, a complex meditation of death, personality, and the creative imagination. Some of the poems, "Solomon to Sheba," for example, reflect the happiness of the married man. In the later volume, the title poem reveals a new sense of humor, and several poems in both volumes turn the anger and point of the earlier epigrams and invectives toward a new breadth. "Easter 1916" is a triumph of the plain style, an honestly doubting poem which carefully examines the poet's response to the rising in Dublin while admitting that in their deaths the leaders of the rising and Ireland itself have been "changed, changed utterly." Change becomes a dominant theme in *Michael Robartes and the Dancer*, and the poet who once had sought apocalypse now becomes a powerful voice for humane conservatism in a world changing violently and not knowing how or why it changes. "On a Political Prisoner" laments change at the personal level, regretting the politics that have turned Constance Gore-Booth, the old friend from Sligo, from "youth's lonely wildness" to a bitter and abstract mind. In "The Second Coming" Yeats finds the true prophetic voice as he gives us in his image of "A shape with lion body and the head of a man,/A gaze blank and pitiless as the sun"[23] the ruling phantasm of our times. "A Prayer for My Daughter" offers one solution to the problems of a changing world and a pitiless future: let the soul recover "radical innocence" by driving out hatred and learning that it is

23 *Ibid.,* p. 402.

> self-delighting
> Self-appeasing, self-affrighting,
> And that its own sweet will is Heaven's will.[24]

All through the 1920s Yeats's imagination would run free and wide, giving us some of the great lyrics in our language. He was by no means the only valuable Irish poet of his time, but he was the one whose works last. He never quite found the open-hearted simplicity of a Colum, Stephens, or Campbell; Synge was better at bitter invective; Pearse expressed a mystical nationalism Yeats was too complex to accept. Part of Yeats's superiority to his contemporaries lay in his astonishing command of the English language; is there any other poet who wrote so few bad lines? Part of his superiority lay in the intricacy of his mind and emotions; Yeats simply lived and experienced more fully than his contemporaries. In many ways, he was an outsider to Ireland; it is difficult to imagine him at Mass in the parish church, at the races at Fairyhouse, or gossiping in a pub. Often his themes and images seem far outside the mainstream of Irish verse, and yet he seems the most essentially Irish poet of them all, perhaps only because in his poetry he was most essentially himself. His presence on the Irish scene and his mastery of his art probably harmed the development of Irish poetry. He had too many imitators, in all his styles, and too many poets who were not imitators could only react against his work. Still, better one master, with all the problems that implies, than a dozen evanescent talents.

[24] *Ibid.*, p. 405.

mirrors up to ireland
Anglo-Irish Fiction, 1900–1923

It is the spectator, and not life, that art
really mirrors.

Oscar Wilde

My intention was to write a chapter of the
moral history of my country.

James Joyce

ARLY IN James Joyce's *Ulysses*, Stephen Dedalus, a young poet, comments of a mirror a friend is using to shave by, "It is a symbol of Irish
art. The cracked looking glass of a servant."[1] As much as drama, and more
than lyric poetry, fiction has often been seen as a mirror held up to life. A
novel or a story will, we assume, often reflect the time and place in which it
was written, and it will also, necessarily, reflect its author. And, as Oscar
Wilde reminds us, art will also mirror the spectator, the reader who empathizes with one character, dislikes another, finds one plot true and moving,
another inauthentic and uninvolving. Irish fiction from the early part of our
century is a multireflective mirror, a mirror which shows us things about Ireland in the time, Irish concerns and problems, Irish writers, and, when it is
good fiction, something about ourselves as well.

Fiction developed most slowly of all the genres in the Irish Renaissance;
by 1900 there was already some effective poetry and the beginnings of an
important dramatic movement, but there was little worthwhile fiction. By

[1] *Ulysses* (1922; New York: Vintage, 1961), p. 6.

133

1923 Ireland had produced one great master, James Joyce, a writer who towers over Irish fiction as Yeats towers over the poetry. But Joyce spent most of his life in exile from Ireland, and he had much less effect on the development of fiction at home than Yeats had on the poetry. Instead, inside Ireland, things moved slowly. The old Anglo-Irish tradition of tales based on colonialist exploitation of local color and character died hard, and two women who worked as a remarkable collaborating team, Somerville and Ross, wrote the last books of lasting merit in it. While they were still at work, George Moore, in *The Untilled Field* (1903), produced the first collection of short stories in the modern Irish mode, realistic, painstakingly accurate commentaries on ordinary life, stories which use the commonplace details of everyday experience to suggest a universal as well as a local significance. The realistic story gradually became one of the characteristic modes of the Irish Renaissance; Joyce himself added to it with *Dubliners* (1914), and so did a number of other writers, Padraig O Conaire, Seumas O'Kelly, and Daniel Corkery among them. On the other hand, Irish writers produced relatively few novels of lasting merit. Joyce, in his exile, was the great exception with *A Portrait of the Artist as a Young Man* (1916) and *Ulysses* (1922). In Ireland itself, however, the most interesting long narratives from this period are fantasies and autobiographies. James Stephens became the great fantasist of his time, and his work reminds us that the old Irish tradition of wild and wise fabulation was far from dead. Autobiography is not fiction, perhaps, but it, too, is a kind of fabulation, an imaginative re-creation of the writer's past in which mere fact is less important than the imposed patterns of meaning. Joyce's *Portrait of the Artist* is, in some senses, autobiographical; George Moore's *Hail and Farewell* and Yeats's *Reveries Over Childhood and Youth* are overtly so. Together, they helped establish the strong Irish tradition of the autobiography of the artist. These autobiographical works provide one mirror to the Irish scene; fantasy and realism provide others, and the best of all these are considerably more than cracked looking glasses.

Nineteenth-century Anglo-Irish fiction ended with two women who wrote as Somerville and Ross. That seems appropriate enough, for it had begun with Maria Edgeworth, a writer whom they resemble very much in background, attitude, and, sometimes, tone. Edith Somerville and Violet Martin were, like Maria Edgeworth, products of the Anglo-Irish Ascendancy. Like her, they were sharp chroniclers of the failings and foibles of their class. They were second cousins; Edith Somerville had been born in 1858 on the island of Corfu, where her father was stationed with the regiment he commanded;

Violet Martin was born four years later at her family's big-house in County Galway. They met in 1886, and an intense friendship developed quickly. Soon after that first meeting, they began to write together, Violet Martin choosing the name, Martin Ross, as a pseudonym. Their first books, two novels and some travelogues, were not especially successful, but their third novel, *The Real Charlotte* (1894) was a good deal more than the harmless product of gentility and amateurish enthusiasm. It is an engrossing story with a memorable heroine, Charlotte Mullins, a grasping moneylender and intriguer. She is rather obviously based on Balzac's *Cousine Bette*, but she could also be the granddaughter of the Jason Quirk of *Castle Rackrent*. *The Real Charlotte* is more memorable, though, for its insightful portrayal of Ascendancy society, with all its concern for rank and status, in the last years of its dominance over the native population.

The Real Charlotte deserves to rank with *Castle Rankrent* as one of the best Irish novels of the nineteenth century, but the lasting reputation of Somerville and Ross really rests on a series of short stories, *Some Experiences of an Irish R.M.* (1899), *Further Experiences of an Irish R.M.* (1908), and *In Mr. Knox's Country* (1915). These are some of the funniest short stories to come from Ireland. Writing from their own positions safe at the top of Irish society, Somerville and Ross were able to make splendid comedy of the interrelations of the two Irelands of their time, the Ireland of the Anglo-Irish Ascendancy and the Ireland of the Gaelic peasantry. Their sympathies lay with their own class, of course, and it is clear that they saw nationalism and Catholicism as enemies of the established order it represented, but their satiric sketches of tenants and workmen are no more acid than the sketches of their own class or the English who came to administer and straighten out muddled Ireland. The setting for the stories is the archetypal Irish village of Skebawn; the characters are cleverly drawn stereotypes from the world of Anglo-Irish fiction. The R.M. (resident magistrate; then the Irish equivalent of an American justice of the peace) is Major Yeates, innocent but earnest in his expectations of bringing normality and sturdy English values to manic Ireland. His wife, Philippa, is a do-gooder whose benevolence yields all sorts of repercussions. From the Anglo-Irish Ascendancy (the major and his wife are English) come Flurry Knox, the Yeates's landlord, irresponsible friend, and guide to Irish ways, and his remarkable grandmother. Old Mrs. Knox is a brilliant satire on the exuberance and irresponsibility of her class; on first meeting, she astonishes Major Yeates by quoting Virgil, and she astonishes him the more by screeching at her servants, serving splendid meals on cracked china, and wearing diamond rings to feed her chickens. Mrs. Knox is a superb image for the Ascendancy of Somerville and Ross's day, aged, failing, opinionated, and still full of random energy, and the stories themselves provide a vibrantly comic picture of a world that is now gone.

The "R.M." stories are, though, an end, not a beginning—the last significant fictions to come out of the colonizing aristocracy. Making a new beginning was a slow and often frustrating business, even if plenty of Irish fiction was being published early in this century. The newspapers and periodicals were full of it, but it was mostly sentimental pulp or yet more exploitation of local color. On a more serious level, Lady Gregory's versions of myth and legend in *Cuchulain of Muirthemne* (1902) and *Gods and Fighting Men* (1904) showed the possibilities and the limitations of the use of dialect in retelling the ancient stories. Standish O'Grady published a series of historical romances based on the ancient legends and on Irish history, but they were not strong enough to be of more than passing interest. Emily Lawless' *Hurrish* (1886) had indicated what might be done with realism, but it would take more than her limited talent to do it. What was needed was someone who knew Ireland intimately, but was an accomplished artist and a critical observer of people, places, and experiences.

That someone turned out to be George Moore, already a famous novelist in England. How Moore laid the foundations for two major kinds of modern Irish prose narrative, the short story and the autobiography, is a complicated and often absurd story, for when Moore moved back to Ireland in 1899 he had very different things in mind. He was forty-seven when he finally responded to the voice which several years before had told him to cast his lot with the Celtic revival. Born at Moore Hall near Lough Carra in the wilds of Connemara, he was the son of a Catholic landlord, who seemed determined to be even more reckless and foolish than the Protestant Anglo-Irish. When he died, his son was eighteen and equipped for manhood "principally with innocence, ignorance, and independence."[2] As a child, George Moore had gone to a Catholic school in Britain, but his real education occurred after his father's death when he moved to Paris. There he met all sorts of people—Mallarmé, Manet, Degas, Daudet, and Turgenev among them—and came into contact with all sorts of ideas. With amazing panache, he turned himself into a sophisticated man of the world. There may not have been much depth in Moore, but he was an extraordinary mimic and a self-ironic one. Out of the years in

[2] Malcolm Brown, *George Moore: A Reconsideration* (Seattle: University of Washington Press, 1955), p. 12.

Paris came poems in the manner of Baudelaire and a fine novel, *A Mummer's Wife* (1884), as well as a continuing alertness to the literary and artistic trends of the day. All this made Moore far from a conventional Irish writer. Although *A Drama in Muslin* (1886) is a sharply observed novel of Dublin society, the attacks on his native land in *Parnell and His Island* (1887) and *Confessions of a Young Man* (1888) suggest that Moore was happy to have put Ireland far behind him.

In those days, Moore liked to think of himself as a disciple of Émile Zola, the French master of naturalism. Zola had defined the naturalistic novel as one which provided "an account of the environment which determines and completes man,"[3] and Moore himself, in *A Mummer's Wife* and *Esther Waters* (1894), produced the first good naturalistic novels in English. He went on from *Esther Waters* to *Evelyn Innes* (1898), an oddly unsuccessful tale of singers and Wagnerian music. One of the characters in that novel, Ulick Dean, was modeled originally on Yeats, and it was from him that Moore got the information about the occult which he wove into the story. Yeats also helped turn Moore's interest towards the Irish literary revival, but it was Moore's cousin, Edward Martyn the playwright, who was instrumental in bringing him back to Ireland to help with the performances of the Irish Literary Theatre.

In 1901 Moore established himself in Dublin's Ely Place, a permanent convert, so he claimed, to the Irish movement. Convinced that Dublin was the new center of imaginative energy, he threw himself wholeheartedly into the movement. He and Yeats fought bitterly over the rather Wagnerian drama they wrote together for the 1901 season of the Irish Literary Theatre, and *Diarmuid and Grania* became Moore's last contribution to Irish drama. He then turned his energy from drama to Gaelic. In 1900 he had delivered a lecture in Dublin in which he asserted that the future of Irish literature lay not in English but in the old tongue. There was, of course, one basic problem with Moore's passion for Gaelic: very few people, even in Ireland, spoke the language, and George Moore was not among those happy few. There is something patently silly in his suggestion that, although he himself was too old to learn Gaelic, he would insist that his brother's children learn it from a nurse brought straight from the Aran Islands. The difficulty with Moore was that the silliness and the earnestness always went together. While he was saying the words of his speech, he probably meant what he said, but for all his

---

[3] Quoted in Walter Allen, *The English Novel* (New York: Dutton, 1954), p. 351.

passion for the Celtic Twilight, he remained also a disbelieving skeptic. Moore honestly thought that his return to Ireland would revitalize his flagging imaginative energies, but he soon realized that, literary renaissance notwithstanding, all the things he had hated in Ireland were still there: clerical, political, and social repression; brutality, ignorance, and overpowering provinciality.

Out of his enthusiasm for Gaelic, though, came one good result. He suggested to the Gaelic League that the students learning Gaelic from its handbooks ought to have stories to read as well as grammar exercises. He first suggested translations from the *Arabian Nights*, but those tales were too immoral for the League. John Eglinton, an essayist and librarian friend, suggested that Moore himself write some stories and model them on the tales of Russian country life of Turgenev. They could then be translated into Gaelic for the students to read. The Jesuit editor of the *New Ireland Review* agreed to publish these, and Moore set to work. The first three he wrote were harmless sketches, but then real inspiration struck, and as Moore described it later, "Story followed story, each coming into my mind before the story on the blotting-pad was finished, and each suggested something seen or something heard."[4] Although Moore was pleased when T. W. Rolleston did indeed translate two of them into Gaelic, and he was delighted to see his name on the title page as "Seorsa O Morda," their real importance had almost nothing to do with Gaelic.

When Moore gathered thirteen stories together and published them as *The Untilled Field* in 1903, he gave to Anglo-Irish literature its first collection of tales in the modern mode. The influence of Turgenev was very strong; as one critic writes "in the tone and atmosphere of the tales—in the use of sky, cloud, and water to convey mood and character. Above all, it is apparent in the technique—the freedom from conventional dramatic shaping, the lack of an obvious climax, and the gentle dying fall, leaving an effect not of inconclusiveness . . . but of a conclusion infinitely deferred or fading slowly away like wisps of cloud in a sunset sky."[5] Beyond the technical innovations, Moore helped the Irish short story by defining some of its basic themes. Turning from the exaggerated eccentricities which are the basis of humor and pathos in so much nineteenth-century Irish fiction, Moore dealt intelligently with the life around him. The stories are full of sympathy for those oppressed by the Church and the dulling weight of social convention, full, too, of protest against

4 *Salve* (1914; New York: Appleton, 1920), p. 173.

5 Gilbert Phelps, quoted in Charles Burkhart, "The Stories of George Moore," *The Man of Wax*, ed. Douglas A. Hughes (New York: New York University Press, 1971), p. 220.

the stultifying inertia of much Irish life. "Julia Cahill's Curse," which begins as an exercise in the conventional device of the native Irishman explaining the oddness of his country to a stranger (a device Somerville and Ross loved), turns into a moving tale of the conflict between an imaginative and independent woman and a grimly moralistic priest. The "village Venus" of that story is forced into exile, and in several of the stories emigration from Ireland is seen as the necessary act for the imaginative and the independent. Exile is also the predominant theme in "So On He Fares," virtually an allegory of Moore's own emotional experiences with the country of his birth. But perhaps the most remarkable story is "A Letter to Rome," a gently comic story which does turn on Irish eccentricity. The eccentric, Father MacTurnan, is one of Moore's few sympathetic priests, the builder of a theater for mystery plays in his desolate parish and the author of a letter to the ecclesiastical authorities in Rome which asks that Irish priests be permitted to marry because they are the only Irishmen with sufficient incomes to raise healthy and independent children. Despite the smiling comedy, barbs are all through this story, as they are through the other dozen.

Moore probably saw the stories in *The Untilled Field* as ephemera in his life's work, as perhaps they were, but they indicated important new directions for the Irish short story. In style as in themes, they showed how the writer of short fiction could handle the details of ordinary existence in Ireland with balanced irony and close attention to the interaction of setting and character. They were a more lasting contribution to the Irish Renaissance than his big novel, *The Lake* (1905), a rather melodramatic tale of a priest and his efforts to escape out of the limits of his ecclesiastical role. *The Untilled Field* was also a more valuable contribution than Moore's other collection of Irish tales, *A Story-Teller's Holiday* (1918), a set of stories supposedly told by a village storyteller, Alec Trusselby. This set of stories is an interesting exercise in narrative technique, with Trusselby sometimes stopped in mid-narration for a discussion of the techniques of storytelling. The technique used in these stories suggested a way of dealing with traditional tales which some later writers would exploit, but the writing is too diffuse to make the volume itself satisfactory.

No one of the figures pilloried in *Hail and Farewell* (1911–14) would have called that work satisfactory either, but this three-part account of Moore's participation in the Irish Renaissance is one of his lasting contributions to Irish writing. *Hail and Farewell* details Moore's involvement with Ireland from the time in the early nineties when he first heard a voice calling him home to his angry departure from Ireland and Irish literature in 1911. It can be read, and usually is, for its hilarious and scandalous account of Irish writers, and Moore does present a wickedly funny set of caricatures: Yeats as priggishly vague priest of art, AE as fuzzy-faced and fuzzy-headed idealist, Moore's cousin, Edward Martyn, as a walking bog of Catholic fearfulness, and on and on. The characterizations may or may not be accurate, and the same could be said of the "facts" Moore presents, but the pictures of the early days of literary and nationalistic revival are unforgettable. Moore skillfully maintains a double narration with his recent memories counterpointed against those of childhood and a double point of view with himself portrayed as the anointed savior of Irish writing and its sniggering denigrator. It is a brilliant book on its own terms and a superb commentary on the pitfalls of literary nationalism. It is also important as the first in the long series of literary autobiographies which have come out of Ireland. Yeats, infuriated by the account of himself and his friends in *Hail and Farewell*, said that it turned his precious things into a post the passing dog defiles.

His anger with Moore and his increasing interest in his own artistic development led Yeats to begin to write his own autobiography. *Reveries Over Childhood and Youth* appeared in print in 1914, three years after the first volume of *Hail and Farewell*. It is a lyrical and intensely moving evocation of youthful memories, utterly different in tone and manner from Moore's book. Few reminiscences of childhood and adolescence re-create its intensity and wonder quite so successfully, and few readers can forget the grandfather the child Yeats thought was God or the mature poet's sensitive recounting of the awakening of his sexuality. In 1922 Yeats added to the autobiography a long memoir of his experiences in the nineties, a segment which owes something to *Hail and Farewell* for its techniques of characterization and commentary. It has little of Moore's malice, but the presentations of Yeats's friends, John O'Leary, Oscar Wilde, William Morris, and Arthur Symons among them, are as good as anything in *Hail and Farewell*. In its final form, the autobiography, filled out by accounts of the early days of the Irish dramatic movement and accounts of events around the time of Synge's death, is one of the supreme poetic lives in English, in its own way as full an account of a poet's growth and development as Wordsworth's *Prelude*.

Although Yeats moved far away from the techniques of *Hail and Farewell* in his autobiography, he owed to Moore an unacknowledged debt for showing that autobiography, whatever its tone, could be an important part of a creative artist's work. Modern Irish literature is particularly rich in autobiographical writing, and it would be much the less without Sean O'Casey's autobiography, Frank O'Connor's *An Only Child*, Patrick Kavanagh's *The Green Fool*, or Brendan Behan's *Borstal Boy*. These autobiographies are all as different from *Hail and Farewell* as Yeats's memories, but Moore deserves to be remembered as the virtual inventor of the Irish literary autobiography as well as the virtual inventor of the modern Irish short story. Moore himself knew, however, that he dared not stay in Dublin after the first volume of his memoirs appeared; he took himself then to London, where he stayed for the rest of his life, an exile pleased to be exiled.

Self-imposed exile from Ireland was an experience Moore had in common with his younger and greater contemporary, James Joyce, but to move from Moore to Joyce is to move from a clever innovator and painstaking craftsman who never quite fulfilled himself to the greatest writer of prose fiction in our language in this century. Joyce and Moore probably had more in common than either would have wanted to admit, interests in naturalism and autobiography, among other things, but in one fundamental they were utterly different. Moore, in spite of his Connemara birth and years of participation in the politics of the Irish Renaissance, was essentially an outsider to Ireland, one who could never make himself at home in the ordinary experiences of Irish life. Joyce spent most of his life outside Ireland and usually tried to have as little as possible to do with the internal affairs of the Irish movement, but he wrote always as an insider, one who understood all the sensitive calibrations of day-to-day Dublin. For an indicator of that, compare Joyce's short story, "Counterparts," with Moore's "So On He Fares." Both, thematically, are allegorizations of Irish experience, but in its setting and characterization "So On He Fares" is thin and obvious. Joyce's little tale of frustration has, on the other hand, the thickness, feel, and even the smell of reality. This is so because Joyce was the supreme insider of the urban Irish experience; three decades and more of exile in Paris, Zurich, and Trieste could not change that. Writing in a cafe in Zurich years away from home, he knew Dublin and Dubliners more fully than any resident of the Hibernian metropolis who never ventured farther afield than Chapelizod or Dalkey.

That is evident in all of Joyce's work, as his first important publication, *Dubliners* (1914), shows. This collection of fifteen stories, some very slight but one almost a novella, could be interpreted as an urban version of Moore's *Untilled Field*. In his book, Moore had turned to rural Ireland for setting, characters, and themes, as generations of Irish writers before him had done; Joyce reverses that by writing exclusively of Dublin men and women. Even so, Joyce described in his Dubliners much the same frustration and desire for escape that Moore had portrayed in country people. Where Moore had shifted the tradition of the Irish short story by taking ordinary Irish people seriously, Joyce went further still, using incidents from ordinary life to write, as he said, "a chapter of the moral history of my country." The Dublin setting, physical and spiritual, governs the volume. Dublin is still a small city, and in the early days of this century, it was almost an overgrown country town, a place where everyone seemed to know everyone, and lives joined in one complex network. Joyce presents his Dubliners in what he called "a style of scrupulous meanness,"[6] and that last word cuts two ways. The stories are, some of them, mean in their presentations of ordinariness. The political hangers-on of "Ivy Day in the Committee Room" are a particularly shabby lot morally, but many of the other characterizations are etched in acid. But "scrupulous meanness" can also mean precision and exactitude, and in that lies one of the miracles of Dubliners. In these intricate stories every word counts, and so the presentations of frustration and paralysis are just that much more meaningful.

The adolescent hero of "Araby," for example, is paralyzed by his encounter with tangible fantasy at a bazaar, but paralysis is the governing theme of all the stories. Little Chandler in "A Little Cloud" is paralyzed by his own mediocrity; the heroine of "Eveline" by her timidity; Lenehan of "Two Gallants" by a mind stuffed full of cultural junk; Mr. Kernan of "Grace" by alcoholism; Maria of "Clay," by sentimentality. Though some of the characters try or want to try to escape from their paralysis (Eveline would like to leave Dublin for Buenos Aires; Mr. Kernan tries to dry out on a religious retreat), most find in paralysis itself an escape, escape from too dull a present into an imaginary past or future. The great study in paralysis and escape, and the greatest of Joyce's short stories, is the last in Dubliners, "The Dead." In it, setting, character, theme, and technique fuse into one astonishing presentation of life among the living dead. The music-teaching Misses Morkan live in a musical and social mausoleum. Their nephew, Gabriel Conroy, would escape a mediocrity he hates, but his man-of-the-world tastes, ironically symbolized by galoshes, are not enough to keep him from delivering a flowery oration at his aunts' annual party or failing as a passionate lover. His wife, Gretta, is paralyzed by the memory of Michael Furey, a boy she knew when she was growing up in a County Galway her sophisticated husband despises, a boy

---

6 Letter to Grant Richards (May 5, 1906), reprinted in Dubliners, ed. Robert Scholes and A. Walton Litz (New York: Viking, 1969), p. 269.

whom she believes died of his love for her. The image of snow, no common thing in Ireland, governs the entire story. Snow, "general all over Ireland," unites the dead and the living dead under a blanket of cold, freezing regeneration. "The Dead" is an intricately unified story, as *Dubliners* is an intricately unified collection. The intricacy is sometimes almost too great, but in the best of the stories Joyce uses even that as a commentary on the atrophy of the ability to make moral discriminations. He called one of the stories, "A Painful Case," but all of them are studies in "painful cases," whether they are the obvious one of the aging pervert in "An Encounter" or the immensely subtle one of the emotionally dying Gabriel in "The Dead." Taken as a whole, the volume shows a high mastery of the techniques of naturalistic fiction as well as the techniques of symbolism; it is also a triumph of moral observation.

When *Dubliners* was first published in book form in 1914, Joyce was still a young man of thirty-two. He was born on February 2, 1882, the son of John Stanislaus Joyce and his wife, Mary, in the comfortable Dublin suburb of Rathmines. His mother was a paradigm of Irish womanhood in her time— devout, patient, self-sacrificing, and willing to suffer more than was her fair share. John Joyce, too, was a paradigm: irresponsible, sentimental, maudlin, diffusely talented, eventually angry and frustrated. The Joyces were well off when their son was born, but John Joyce's ineptitude eventually pulled them down the social scale from the comforts of Rathmines to addresses on the sleazy north side of Dublin. In 1888, though, the Joyces were still financially secure enough to enter James in Clongowes Wood College, a Jesuit school which liked to think of itself as something like an Irish Eton. It was expensive, but it had high intellectual standards, and it was there Joyce began his fourteen years of education by the religious order which was to temper his mind. But after three years at Clongowes, the Joyces could afford the tuition no longer, and he was sent to the mediocre and unfashionable school of the Christian Brothers in Dublin's North Richmond Street. An escape from that came in 1893 when Father John Conmee, the former rector of Clongowes, arranged for him to attend Belvedere College, a good Jesuit school in Dublin, without charge. These schools would not be so important if it were not for the fact that Joyce was an exceedingly bright and observant student, one who responded well to the pressure of academic competition and the Jesuit style.

He also responded strongly to the pressure of Catholicism. Joyce himself, long after he had lost his religion, told a friend that although he was not a Catholic he was yet a Jesuit, and that sums up the situation nicely. From the atmosphere of Jesuit education came the obsessions with logic and order, the sense that pattern and precision can resolve any intellectual problem. Pattern and precision do not necessarily solve emotional or spiritual problems, though, and even as a student at Belvedere, emotional and spiritual complexities developed. Joyce was apparently about fourteen when he had his first sexual experience in a chance meeting with a prostitute. Sensuality and piety became inextricably mixed in his adolescence. The piety expressed itself in the prefectship of Belvedere's sodality of the Blessed Virgin Mary, an interest in the priesthood and a continuing delight in the sanctity, mystery, and ritual of Catholic observance. The sensuality expressed itself in visits to Dublin's redlight district. Moreover, the Joyce of fifteen or sixteen was doing a good bit of reading that was not on the syllabus at Belvedere—Meredith, Hardy, Shaw, Ibsen—just the sorts of writers who were shaking the pious faith of many young men and not only in Dublin. An interview with the rector of Belvedere confirmed him in his belief that he had no vocation for the priesthood; the encounters with prostitutes confirmed him in the belief the sex was dirty and degrading just as observation of his father's irresponsible antics convinced him that Ireland itself was shoddy and vulgar. Gradually, Lucifer's *Non serviam* became his motto; there would be no service to church, family, or the Ireland of popular patriotism. The only service would be to art, at this point art with a capital A and art as an abstraction. The priesthood of art would replace that of the church; the creative process of the artist would be a holy ritual, an effective surrogate for the sanctity of the ritual of the Mass and the filthiness of the ritual of sex.

In 1898, at sixteen, Joyce entered University College, the Catholic university founded less than fifty years before by John Henry Newman. He learned relatively little in his classes, but the experiences as a student were crucial in his development. He educated himself through reading in the National Library of Ireland, half a mile or so north of University College's buildings beside Stephen's Green, and in conversations with fellow students. His friends from those days remembered him as slim and elegant, striking for his very blue eyes, his square chin, and his arrogant style. They remembered, too, the roll of vellum he carried with him, copies of his small poems written out very carefully in the middle of the huge sheets. AE read the poems and told him that there was not enough chaos in him. But the chaos was there behind the ordered facade. Joyce was a poor drinker, but he consumed more than an ordinary student's share of stout, and loved dancing, games, and charades. The real chaos and the real growth, too, were going on in his mind; his reading continued wide: Ibsen, Maeterlinck, Hauptmann, d'Annunzio,

Dante, Flaubert. His growing intellectual ability was demonstrated by a paper on modern drama, and in praise of Ibsen, for the college's Literary and Historical Society. Even more indicative of his ability was an essay on Ibsen's *When We Dead Awaken* which was published in one of the most prestigious English intellectual journals, *The Fortnightly Review*, when Joyce was only eighteen; Ibsen himself, whom Joyce idolized, wrote from Norway to commend the young critic. For a young Dublin Catholic to be writing in praise of Ibsen was sign enough of independence, but an even more striking sign of that quality was "The Day of the Rabblement," a slashing attack on the Irish Literary Theatre for what Joyce saw as its courting of popular favor. He was writing more than essays, though, and in the long run, the most important writing he was doing at this time was a collection of what he called "epiphanies," little fragments of dialogue or personal experience which seemed to have an intense private significance and the first steps toward becoming a writer of fiction.

The Joyce who graduated from University College in 1902 probably did not realize how significant those "epiphanies" were to become. After graduating he had a brief and desultory career as a medical student in Dublin, met AE, Yeats, Padraic Colum, and Lady Gregory, and seemed to be going nowhere. In December of that year he abruptly left Dublin for Paris, ostensibly to study medicine there. The first trip to Paris was only for a few weeks; the second lasted for about three months. It ended with an urgent telegram from his father, "MOTHER DYING COME HOME FATHER," and Joyce returned to Dublin in time to refuse to pray at his mother's bedside before she died. He stayed in Dublin for more than a year, from April of 1903 until October of 1904. After his mother's death, things grew chaotic at home. John Joyce quarrelled bitterly with his sons; he and they drank hard; family possessions had to be pawned. Joyce escaped the squalor at home with brief employment at a school in Dalkey, friendship with Oliver St. John Gogarty, a cynical, clever young man and a brilliant talker, and extensive bouts of drinking and whoring. Even his best friends thought he was out to destroy himself, and so it seemed until June 16, 1904. Six days before, he had seen a striking girl walking down Nassau Street in Dublin. He spoke to her, learned that her name was Nora Barnacle, and that she was from Galway. They arranged to meet again. They met again on June 16, and Joyce fell in love. Nora Barnacle was an unsophisticated woman with a good sense of humor and a healthy way of accepting life, but she cared little about Joyce's writing. Nevertheless, her affair with James Joyce, an affair which ended only with his death in 1941, is one of the great love stories; what it was that attracted each to the other remains something of a mystery, but the attraction was strong indeed.

Because Joyce was opposed to marriage as an institution but could not live openly with Nora in Dublin, they agreed to leave Ireland in October of 1904. Before they left, Joyce published three of his short stories in a magazine AE ran and had a short essay, "A Portrait of the Artist," rejected by what was then the best journal of arts and ideas in Ireland, *Dana.* For a few days in September he lived with Oliver Gogarty and an Englishman named Trench in an old tower on the coast south of Dublin. None of these events seemed of great importance then, but the stories AE printed were the first of those which would eventually make up *Dubliners,* the rejected essay was the germ of Joyce's first novel, *A Portrait of the Artist as a Young Man,* and the tower at Sandycove would provide the setting for the opening pages of his later and greater masterpiece, *Ulysses.* So, in fact, in the summer and early autumn of 1904, Joyce was remaking himself out of the mess of his recent past into what he would be for the rest of his life: an exile, the lover of Nora Barnacle, and the author of fiction. At twenty-two, he had found himself.

Life in exile was none too easy, though. Joyce and Miss Barnacle (she did not become Mrs. Joyce for almost thirty years, and then only for practical legal reasons) went to Paris, then to Zurich, on to Pola in what is now Yugoslavia, and finally to Trieste, in what was then Austria. Here Joyce found work as a teacher of English in a Berlitz school, and here his son, Giorgio, was born in 1905. The income from the Berlitz school was inadequate for a wildly improvident couple, but Joyce seemed to be making a kind of slow headway as a writer. A little collection of poems went off to publishers in London; it was finally published as *Chamber Music* in 1907. When he left Ireland in 1904, Joyce had carried with him the manuscript of those poems as well as the manuscripts of short stories and a huge semiautobiographical novel. By the end of 1905 he was ready to find a publisher for the collection of stories, and the manuscript was sent to Grant Richards, a publisher in London. Richards and his reader liked what they saw and sent Joyce a contract. But when Joyce added another story, "Two Gallants," to the collection, Richard's printer, legally as responsible as Richards himself for what he printed and Richards sold, complained that he was being made to set type for obscenity. A very complex wrangle ensued, and after several years Joyce withdrew the manuscript, submitting it to Maunsel and Company in Dublin, instead. Believing that it might help matters if he went to Dublin to see about the manuscript, Joyce and Giorgio went for a short visit in August and early September of 1909. Convinced for a time that Nora had been unfaithful to him in the past, he brought a terrific emotional crisis on himself during that visit home, and he later compounded his difficulties by a foolish venture as the operator of Dublin's first movie theater. Maunsel and Company agreed to publish the stories, but then the problems started again. Disagreements over all sorts of trivia dragged on for three more years; at one point, a first edition of the book was actually printed and then destroyed. By 1912 it seemed that Joyce's career was hopelessly bogged down; he was the author of a little collection of poems, a set of apparently unpublishable short stories, and an unfinished novel.

Again, as in 1904, his luck turned, and turned dramatically. Grant Richards had second thoughts about *Dubliners* and agreed to publish it; it appeared in June of 1914. Ezra Pound, the American-born poet and chief organizer of literary modernism, arranged for the serial publication of the novel, *A Portrait of the Artist*, in a little magazine called *The Egoist*. Under the pressure of serial publication, Joyce turned what had been a huge and rather shapeless novel into a masterpiece of concision and rhythmic control. With the publication of *Dubliners*, the revision of *Portrait*, and even the tentative beginnings of a second novel, *Ulysses*, 1914 became Joyce's *annus mirabilis*. The outbreak of World War I stopped the serialization of *Portrait* in *The Egoist* for a while (Joyce had probably not finished the last two chapters, anyway), but it was finished early in 1915, and by the end of 1916 it had appeared in book form. The reviews were mixed, but H. G. Wells, not necessarily a friend of literary innovation, called it a "most memorable novel," and alert readers recognized that in Joyce there was a new master of fiction in the world.[7]

Many early readers, and many since, have assumed that *Portrait* is no more than a fictionalization of Joyce's own childhood and youth. Certainly much of the novel's plot does resemble Joyce's own experiences. His hero, Stephen Dedalus, is born into a family much like the Joyces; he, too, goes to Clongowes Wood School and later to Belvedere. Like Joyce, his adolescence is torn between the Church and the brothel, and, again like Joyce, he achieves his manhood in exile. The general outline of the plot is autobiographical, as is much of the incidental action: the Christmas dinner scene in 1891, the experiences at Clongowes, the terrifying retreat, and the arguments with fellow students at University College. But to turn *Portrait* into mere autobiography is to

7 "James Joyce," reprinted in *A Portrait of the Artist as a Young Man*, ed. Chester G. Anderson (New York: Viking, 1968), p. 333.

distort and misunderstand it. As its title implies, it is one view of the artist, any artist, in youth. Like so many other accounts of the development of the artist, from Rousseau's *Confessions* and Goethe's *Wilhelm Meister* to scores of recent novels, *Portrait's* plot presents a paradigm of the development of an artistic mind. In this case, the mind develops in the Catholic Ireland of the nineties. Each chapter is strongly colored by the facts of that world. Stephen cannot begin to be an artist until he takes as his creed, *Non serviam.* "I will not serve" either religion or nation; I will serve only art. The rhythm of the novel, chapter by chapter, is a rhythm of triumph and failure in the process of self-definition. The first chapter ends with Stephen's victory over injustice at Clongowes, but the next begins with an acidulous sketch of the mediocrity of life after he leaves the school. That chapter ends with Stephen's self-discovery through sexuality, but the following opens with a soul-shattering sense of guilt. The piety Stephen then achieves is broken by spiritual doubt, and back and forth he moves until he realizes that his vocation as an artist can only be realized in "silence, exile, and cunning" and that he must leave Ireland, "the old sow that eats her farrow."[8]

Through a brilliant handling of point of view, Joyce invites us to sympathize with Stephen and yet stay distanced from him. The patterns of symbolism which continue from the first page of the novel to the last further encourage us to see Stephen as a whole creature, not just a speaking voice. The novel opens with baby talk, but baby talk which serves as a catalogue of the senses. As Hugh Kenner has observed: "The audible soothes: the visible disturbs. Throughout Joyce's work, the senses are symbolically disposed. Smell is the means of discriminating empirical realities . . . sight corresponds to the phantasms of oppression, hearing to the imaginative life. Touch and taste together are the modes of sex."[9] From this least of beginnings Joyce develops elaborate patterns of remembrance and intimation: water as figure of death and regeneration, the Church as soothing mother and dulling father, Ireland as ingratiating cannibal, artistic creation as escape and secularized Mass. Stephen's own name symbolizes his predicament. He is Stephen, first martyr to his faith, as well as Dedalus, labyrinth-maker, inventor, flier, and master of "unknown arts." But often father-obsessed Stephen is more Icarus than Dedalus, more the prideful child who will not heed wise warning than the master artificer. He talks brilliantly about aesthetics, and then proceeds to write a dead little poem; he behaves often foolishly, sometimes reprehensibly. He has more than the artist's necessary pride, and more than the necessary insecurity. For some

8 *Ibid.*, pp. 247 and 203.

9 "The *Portrait* in Perspective" (from *Dublin's Joyce*), reprinted in *ibid.*, pp. 418–419.

readers, Stephen and *Portrait* do not wear well on re-reading. One could complain that some of the writing is too intense and almost mechanically hypnotic. Moreover, although we are invited to empathize with Stephen, he can be priggish and tedious in his self-absorption. If *Portrait* is not an entirely satisfactory book, perhaps it is because at the time of its writing, Joyce had not yet found the sure balance of naturalistic and symbolist techniques he needed or the sympathy with ordinary experience. Nevertheless, *Portrait* does achieve much of the wholeness, harmony, and radiance Stephen believes any true work of art must have. Its wholeness lies in the fullness of its narrative; its harmony in the subtle management of patterns of perception and symbol; its radiance in our discovery that Joyce has created a modern myth of the making of an artist.

Even so, *Ulysses,* Joyce's next novel, represents an extraordinary advance. In his art of memory and suggestion, the art of making the particular and even the trivial somehow universal, it is his masterpiece. Its publication in 1922 was one of the landmarks of modern literature, and it remains today the supreme fiction in English in our century. Joyce began work on it almost as soon as he had finished *Portrait,* but put it aside to work on a play for the Abbey, *Exiles,* which was finally not produced. The writing of *Ulysses* eventually took almost eight years, years which were made easier by the remarkable gift in 1919 from Harriet Weaver, the former editor of *The Egoist,* of the income fom a very large sum of money, but years which were made difficult by Joyce's increasingly bad eyesight. In spite of that, the first three episodes of the novel were ready for publication in *The Little Review* in 1918; the completed novel was published in book form in time for Joyce's fortieth birthday, February 2, 1922. But the difficulties with the publication of *Ulysses* were as great as those with *Dubliners.* The first episodes of the novel were found shocking, and Ezra Pound, no literary coward by any means, took the liberty of censoring them. In 1921 the editors of *The Little Review* were fined $50 each for permitting the obscene novel to appear in their magazine, and no British or American publisher would touch the finished work. Again, Joyce was saved by the generosity of an admirer; Sylvia Beach, the American proprietor of a Paris bookstore, Shakespeare and Company, took the risk of publishing it. *Ulysses* achieved its first fame as a "dirty book." Americans smuggled copies of it home in their luggage from Paris, and it would be years before people in Ireland could buy the book there legally. The reviews were by no means universally enthusiastic, and even some highly literate readers, Shaw and Yeats among them, were not especially happy about the novel.

The friends in Paris who celebrated with Joyce on the night of the publication of *Ulysses* knew that their friend had produced a masterpiece. *Ulysses* is, to dirty minds, a dirty book; even to sympathetic minds, it is a difficult book, but in its eight hundred pages and more Joyce came closer than any other novelist in English to doing what every novelist desires: he created a world. The world is Dublin, and the date is June 16, 1904, the day he first went out with Nora Barnacle. The novel has three central characters, Stephen Dedalus, back from exile in Paris and living the sort of chaotic life Joyce himself lived after his own return from Paris in 1903; Leopold Bloom, an advertising agent for a Dublin newspaper, amiable, a little artistic, sometimes sex-obsessed, almost always overflowing with common sense; and Molly Bloom, Leopold's wife, unfaithful, capricious, and Mother Earth. These three characters are fully realized figures from the naturalist tradition in fiction, but they are also modernized archetypes roughly but ironically similar to the three central figures in Homer's *Odyssey*. Leopold is an urban Ulysses whose adventures are trivial compared to his prototype's but essentially similar. Stephen is a sort of Telemachus, physically the son of one father but searching for his psychological father, a father who turns out to be Leopold. Molly is their Penelope, as impure as Homer's Penelope was chaste, but just as much the fixed center of the wandering world. Around these three swirl scores of lesser figures from Bella Cohen, the Circe of Dublin's Nighttown, to the Citizen, the Polyphemus of Barny Kiernan's pub. The story, in eighteen episodes, takes us through the gradual process in which Stephen and Leopold are brought together as father and son. We begin with three episodes devoted to Stephen whose day opens with "stately, plump Buck Mulligan" (Oliver Gogarty) shaving at the tower they share at Sandycove. Stephen goes to his teaching job, to an interview with the headmaster of the school, and for a rambling walk by the shore. Meanwhile, Leopold begins his day with a trip to buy a kidney for his breakfast, a visit to a Turkish bath, and the long ride out to Paddy Dignam's funeral. Leopold and Stephen almost meet when their paths cross at a newspaper office and again at the National Library of Ireland, but their real meeting is delayed for many hours. Leopold goes on about his business, examines pornography in a bookstore, and gets into a quarrel in a pub. By late afternoon he is indulging in sexual fantasies at a beach, and in the early evening he happens to stop by a maternity hospital where a friend's wife is giving birth. There he again observes Stephen and, seeing him go off with some rowdy students, decides he ought to keep a paternal eye on him. They all go to Nighttown where Leopold rescues Stephen from a disturbance in a brothel, recognizing in him the surrogate of his own dead son. Together "father" and "son" go finally to Leopold's home, 7 Eccles Street, where Molly has spent the entire day resting before a tour (she is a professional singer) and dallying with her latest boyfriend, Blazes Boylan. When Stephen finally leaves, Leopold comes up to bed to tell Molly about him, and she drops off to sleep in more than eighty pages of almost unpunctuated prose reverie.

That, briefly, is what happens in *Ulysses*, but *Ulysses* hardly has a plot in the conventional sense. That does not mean that it has *no* plot; in fact, Joyce's narration of events is cunning and convincing. But so wholly is *Ulysses* an entity that it is almost impossible to separate mere action from character, setting, symbol, and technique. The characters are realized with amazing fullness, and we know an enormous amount of detail. About Leopold, for example, we know that he was born in 1866, the son of a Hungarian Jewish pedlar and moneylender who converted to Protestantism and committed suicide in Ennis in County Clare in 1886. We know the schools he went to, the places at which he was employed, all about how he met his wife, and even the date of their last sexual intercourse—November 27, 1893. We know that Leopold weighs 158 pounds, is shy, a voyeur, a masochist, generous to his friends but a little evasive, an acquaintance of Arthur Griffith, kind to animals, fond of organ meats, and ambitious to move from modest Eccles Street to the suburbs. If we read carefully we can, in fact, know a great deal more about him, Stephen, and Molly, but this obsessive attention to detail in character is matched by an obsessive attention to detail in setting. *Ulysses* is scrupulously accurate about that, and Joyce went to what may seem absurd lengths to be sure that he had totally re-created the actual facts of the Dublin of June 16, 1904.

All this makes *Ulysses* sound like a realistic novel, and so it is, but it is not only that. Details of character and setting are presented in a method of narration which would have terrified any conventional realist. The basic narrative method is a stream of consciousness in which spoken words, thoughts, and random associations join. As we read, clear patterns of conscious and unconscious significance gradually emerge.

Each of the eighteen episodes has its own distinctive style, styles which demonstrate Joyce to have been a master parodist. A visit to the newspaper office is peppered with headlines; Leopold's tea-time visit to the Ormond Hotel turns into a mock fugue; the scene at the maternity hospital appropriately recapitulates the development of English prose style from its origins in Anglo-Saxon to modern advertizing jargon; Leopold's exhausted conversation with Stephen at the end of the day turns into an extraordinary exercise in impersonal question and answer. Research on Joyce's manuscripts has shown that as he wrote the novel he became increasingly interested in parody and complex patterns of narration as a means of aesthetic distancing. The surrealist melo-drama of the Nighttown episode, the questions and answers at Eccles Street, and Molly's gigantic reverie all stretch the conventions of fiction to the break-ing point, but the methods of narration and the material narrated are so perfectly matched that we know instinctively the story could not be told in any other way. Still, the stream-of-consciousness technique can be frightening on a first reading, and the only way to get around that is to read *Ulysses* again.

In Joyce's world of intimation and remembrance, rereading is absolutely necessary and utterly rewarding. What may seem hopelessly confusing on a first try makes sense on the second and better sense on the third. It helps to know something about the Homeric parallel, but only as background, just as it helps to know something about Dublin, Catholicism, Judaism, aesthetic theory, Irish history, nineteenth-century music, theories of Shakespeare interpretation, and even horse-racing in 1904. As with any great work of art, the more the reader brings to it, the more he takes away from it. Still, all this makes *Ulysses* seem a daunting, even frightening, book, and that is hardly fair. For all its difficulties, it is an immensely rich comic vision. *Dubliners* had portrayed its city with scrupulous meanness; *Portrait* had described the artist with that plus painful psychological insight and almost suffocating symbolism. *Ulysses* has all those and the precious gift of comedy besides. Joyce's great discoveries in it are Leopold, Molly, comedy, and compassion. It is not difficult to imagine that Blooms as characters in *Dubliners*—shabby, frustrated little people living out lives of defeat and obsession. It is also not difficult to imagine how the Stephen of *Portrait* would have despised them. But the sympathy Joyce shows for both of them in *Ulysses* is, on his own terms, one of his great achievements. We know their failings, their inanities, and their vulgarities, but we come to love Leopold for his fundamental decency and goodheartedness, just as we come to love Molly for her earthy truthfulness and sordid sensitivity. *Ulysses* is, in the best sense, a profoundly loving book. It has the moral insight of *Dubliners* and the intensity of *Portrait*, but to these has been added something more— charity, the *sine qua non* of the greatest comic art, and something curiously lacking in much of the rest of Joyce and much of the rest of modern Irish literature.

For most readers, *Ulysses* was and is Joyce's masterpiece; he would go on from it to *Finnegans Wake* and an imaginative world so private that few could follow. The direction toward the *Wake* was already evident in the verbal and structural methods in *Ulysses*, and it is really not very far from the last episodes of *Ulysses* to the techniques of the later book. But *Finnegans Wake*, more than any other of his fictions, belongs to the "international" Joyce, the writer who puzzles and fascinates the scholars and means more to modern European writers of fiction than to ordinary readers in Britain, America, or Ireland. In spite of that, we must return to the *Wake* in a later chapter, for it, too, is a major work in the modern Irish tradition.

Finnegans Wake is a particularly significant work in the ancient Irish mode of fantasy, but the most popular Irish fantasist of Joyce's time was his friend, James Stephens. Stephens was also a significant poet, but his lasting reputation rests on a book he himself came to dislike, *The Crock of Gold* (1912), one of the finest of modern prose fantasies. His biographer, Hilary Pyle, believes that he wrote it as an expression of his own philosophy, a philosophy largely derived from his understanding of the ideas of the English poet and mystic of a century before, William Blake, but Stephens' own temperament and experience made him a natural fantasizer. He claimed not to know when he was born, though he said he and Joyce shared the same birth date (Miss Pyle believes he was born two years before). His stories about his childhood, stories of stealing a muddy piece of bread from a dog's mouth and being abandoned by his mother when he was three, may not have been literally true, but they were imaginatively accurate versions of a poverty-stricken Dublin childhood. Perhaps because he was begging on the streets, Stephens was sent to the Meath Protestant Industrial School for Boys when he was six, a school created according to its own description "to afford a refuge, and to give a Scriptural and industrial education to young children in cases where, either by the neglect or vice of their parents, they are driven on the streets to beg, or where they are left homeless and exposed not merely to misery and want but to every temptation to crime."[10] It all sounds very grim and earnest, but Stephens got a good education there, learned to love to read, and went from the school at about sixteen to a job as a clerk in a law office. The YMCA's library furthered his education, but Stephens himself best described his progress toward becoming a writer by saying, "The Dublin I was born to was poor and Protestant and athletic. While very young, I extended my range and entered a Dublin that was poor and Catholic and Gaelic—a very wonderworld. Then as a young writer, I further extended to a Dublin that was poor, and artistic, and political. Then I made a Dublin for myself, my Dublin."[11] His interest in the arts and philosophy brought him to AE and his interest in politics brought him to Arthur

10 Quoted in Hilary Pyle, *James Stephens* (London: Routledge, Kegan Paul, 1965), p. 6.
11 Quoted in *ibid.*, p. 3.

Griffith. His sense of the comic rejoiced in parodying AE's tendency to pontificate, but the older man provided much of his spiritual and artistic education, and Stephens was grateful. Griffith converted him to nationalism and gave him, too, an outlet for his writing in the nationalist newspaper, *Sinn Fein*. Even before he had published much creative work of value, Stephens had become a Dublin character. Although he was a fine athlete, he was very small with a large head and a shock of black hair. He was always dressed in shabby clothes and usually carried a pipe with the bowl almost worn away. He quickly became famous as a wit, storyteller, and conversationalist in a city which still valued the spoken arts. Stephens could discourse on the precision with which fleas jumped or the way in which the comic-strip "Mutt and Jeff" represented a new American art form, and often he was himself the butt of his own stories.

His first collection of poems, *Insurrections*, (1909) and his writing for *Sinn Fein* had already demonstrated his talent, but Stephens' two best works of fiction appeared in book form in the same year. *The Charwoman's Daughter* had, in fact, been printed earlier as a serial in an Irish magazine, but when Macmillan published it and *The Crock of Gold* in 1912, Stephens' reputation as an important writer of fiction was made almost overnight. *The Charwoman's Daughter* is a longish novella which focuses on a Mrs. Makebelieve, the charwoman, and her daughter, Mary, whom she wants to bring up to be prepared for a life of leisure as the wife of a rich man. Mary Makebelieve's chances of marrying wealth are, of course, nil, but Stephens wants us to respect Mrs. Makebelieve's fantasies and her earnest devotion to them, just as he wants to make us appreciate Mary's active imagination. The daughter, not yet working, spends her days wandering through Dublin. The contrast between the beauty created by her imagination and the seaminess of reality is very effectively handled, and there is something naively wonderful in Mary's first encounter with the tall policeman who turns her from a child to a woman.

All of *The Crock of Gold* is naively wonderful, but the wonder and naiveté should not blind us to the fact that the book is a profound and joyful account of our inner lives. One of the secrets of Stephens' art is his ability to mix all kinds of experience so that the ordinary and the astonishing touch, and that happens repeatedly in *The Crock of Gold*: men and gods converse freely, leprechauns complain to the police, philosophers marry fairy women, and the ancient gods of Ireland open the gates of a Dublin prison. In one sense, *The Crock of Gold* is a childrens' story, and it is full of the adventure and word play children love. But it is also an allegory of human experience which invites us to understand the Philosopher as the image of the intellect, his wife, the Thin

Woman, as the image of intuition, Caitlin as innocence, and Angus Óg as the lonely god who would restore us to joy if only we would pay heed to him. Yet the lasting joy in *The Crock of Gold* comes less from its adroit handling of the natural and the supernatural or its allegory of intellectual and emotional liberation than from its language. It is a wonderfully exuberant book as well as a wise one, and its slapstick and sentimentality are held in beautiful balance by its talk. When The Philosopher's brother decides to commit suicide, he explains his reasons by saying that he has "attained to all the wisdom which I am fitted to bear," and then adds: "My wife's face is the same for ever. I want to play with the children, and yet I do not want to. Your conversation with me, brother, is like the droning of a bee in a dark cell. The pine-trees take root and grow and die.—It's all bosh, Goodbye." And no reader of *The Crock of Gold* can forget the "wisdom" of the maxims of the Thin Woman and her sister:

> A secret is a weapon and a friend.
> Man is God's secret, Power is man's secret, Sex is
> woman's secret.
> By having much you are fitted to have more.
> There is always room in the box.
> The art of packing is the last lecture of wisdom.
> The scalp of your enemy is progress.[12]

Stephens wrote a great deal of fiction after the publication of these two books, but he never seemed to recover their breezy charm. *The Demi-Gods* (1914) comes close with its tale of two tinkers who are joined on their wanderings through Donegal, Mayo, and Kerry by three archangels, but there is really too much philosophizing and too much Theosophical speculation for the story to hang together or the fantasy to retain its freshness of invention. *Irish Fairy Tales* (1920) regains some of the old touch with a sense of enchanting make-believe in what is mostly a retelling of stories about Finn Mac Cumhaill and the Fianna, but *Deirdre* (1923) and *In the Land of Youth* (1924), retellings of *Táin* stories, both seem to bog down in an uncomfortable mixture of whimsy and legend. Perhaps that is not fair to Stephens, and certainly many readers have loved all these books. But one's feeling is that Stephens began to lose his touch after he moved to Paris in 1913, and that even a return to Dublin later on could not restore it fully. He lived on until 1950, still writing,

---

12 *The Crock of Gold* (1912; London: Pan Books, 1965), pp. 13–15.

compiling anthologies, and making some memorable broadcasts on the BBC as well as some remarkable lecture tours.

One of the attractions of *The Crock of Gold* is the sense that it gives us of listening to the voice of a master storyteller. That sense of a speaking voice is particularly valuable in the Irish short story, too. The realistic short story was a special triumph of Irish writing in the 1930s and later. Even earlier, though, writers of short fiction in Ireland were beginning to master the craft. Moore and Joyce provided them with models of how to write about rural and urban life. Gradually, the number of worthy stories began to build, and, even while Joyce himself remained in exile, a few novels of quality were written to go along with the stories. Yet the novel was not really a successful genre in Ireland during this period, particularly not the novel as we commonly understand it, a major narration dealing with real people in real situations. The novel has its origins in urbanized middle-class culture, and there it has always found its largest readership. Ireland still has no large urban middle class, and its great tradition in storytelling is rural and oral.

In the introduction to his excellent collection of Irish short stories, Professor Vivian Mercier reminds us that in the past oral storytelling in Ireland was a highly developed art: "In the dark fall and winter nights from Hallowe'en to St. Patrick's Day (March 17), an audience consisting mainly of older people would gather in some hospitable house around a turf fire to listen until bedtime to one or more storytellers. This gathering was usually called *céilidhe*. The ideal storyteller could entertain his listeners every night for $4\frac{1}{2}$ months without repeating a single story."[13] One storyteller of fairly recent times made a series of recordings that ran to more than half a million words, and another recorded 120 long stories. The storyteller who specialized in the shorter tales was called a *seanchái*, usually Anglicized as "shanachie." Most modern writers of short stories in Ireland have steered away from the supernatural elements which were the traditional shanachie's stock in trade, but the modern writers have often sought to approximate the tone of the shanachie, the tone of the speaking voice. The best writers of modern Irish fiction put words on the page as though they were saying them aloud to an audience. They *tell* stories using fluent and realistic language and developing characters with a few economical gestures. The best modern Irish stories are not symbol-heavy prose poems as so many modern stories from other traditions are, but that does not mean that they are naive or artless. The Irish writers learned valuable lessons

---

[13] *Great Irish Short Stories* (New York: Dell, 1964), p. 10.

from Checkhov, Maupassant, and the other masters of the European short story in the nineteenth century. Mixing the shanachie's tone and the conscious artist's sense of form, they created a fiction that stayed close to its Irish origins but has a universal appeal.

Stephens catches something very close to the tone of the shanachie in his fantasies, but it was left to other writers to show how traditional storytelling and modern technique could be blended to create the modern Irish short story. One of these writers was Padráic Ó Conaire, a native of Connemara who had the advantages of growing up in a Gaelic-speaking area and spending part of his life in the wider worlds of Dublin and London. Influenced by Maupassant and aware generally of the Continental story as a model, he was able to create beautifully observed stories in modern Gaelic. Moreover, Ó Conaire had the good sense to write about what he knew; his stories exploit the color and vigor of life in the west of Ireland, but his characters are real people whom we can understand and sympathize with. The charming statue of him in Galway shows him almost as a village storyteller, and he would have liked that, but he was also a fine artist. Ó Conaire wrote in Gaelic, though, and much of his work was not available in English translations during his lifetime (he died in 1928). Two other writers, both of whom came to prominence after 1910, Daniel Corkery and Seumas O'Kelly, did write in English, and their work was more important than Ó Conaire's in the continuing development of the realistic Irish story. Neither was a Dubliner, and perhaps that helped them find their distinctive voices. Both were Catholics and both identified with rural Ireland. Both, too, were avowed nationalists, and both were suspicious of the directions Irish writing in their time was taking in the hands of the Anglo-Irish masters. One, Corkery, through his writing and teaching, exerted an immense direct influence on other writers; the other, O'Kelly, had little direct influence, but he wrote one story, "The Weaver's Grave," which is one of the great pieces of fiction to come from Ireland in his time.

It is not entirely fair to call Seumas O'Kelly a "one book" writer, but "The Weaver's Grave" completely overshadows the rest of his large canon. Nevertheless, he had an active and important career as a newspaper editor, playwright, and novelist. He came from Loughrea in County Galway, and he was a characteristic member of that generation which matured in the provinces around the turn of the century, committed to nationalism and the preservation of an Irish Ireland. He edited newspapers in Skibbereen in County Cork and then at Naas in County Kildare and was too busy with that and work for Arthur Griffith's Sinn Fein movement to participate much in the exalted circles of literary Dublin, circles in which earnest, provincial nationalists were not exactly welcomed. Even so, he was a prolific imaginative writer, perhaps too prolific to sustain high quality. The Theatre of Ireland, a nationalist company of amateurs which played occasionally at the Rotunda or the Abbey in Dublin, produced several of his plays. One of these, *The Shuiler's Child* (1909) is a fine essay in dramatic realism, melodramatic but effective in its presentation of a poverty-stricken woman's efforts to provide a decent upbringing for her son. The strength of the play lies in its honesty and its sympathy for its characters as well as its fine command of ordinary speech. These qualities also mark the best of O'Kelly's fiction, these and a strong sense of the realities of country life. As one critic has observed, the childhood at Loughrea gave O'Kelly "intimate contact with the people of the West, with farmers, tinkers, fisher-folk, gombeen-men and the decaying ascendancy. He saw at first hand one of the bitterest upheavals in Irish history—the Land War; and he came to realize in that barren countryside why the land-hunger was such a fierce, integral part of the Irish peasant."[14]

All of this comes through in his best fiction, and he wrote a great deal of good fiction: an interesting novel, *The Lady of Deerpark* (1917); a fine set of ten short stories, *The Waysiders* (1918); and the great novella, "The Weaver's Grave," a story which deserves to rank beside the best of Conrad in that genre. The story itself is simple enough. An old weaver, Mortimer Hehir, is dead, and his young widow must find in the cemetery of Cloon na Morav, "the Meadow of the Dead," the gravesite to which he has a right. No one is exactly sure of the place, though, and so two old peasants are brought from the poorhouse to help find it. They argue over the location, thus reviving memories of more than half a century as they look for the spot. Meanwhile, the young wife becomes attracted to one of the gravediggers, but soon a gravesite is found, and the story ends. There is no melodrama here, only a kind of Hardyesque irony. The strength of the story lies in its characterizations of the two old men, the rightness of the dialogue, and the occasional moment of plainly beautiful description. O'Kelly's sureness of touch is demonstrated, to take one example, by his description of Cahir Bowes, the old stonebreaker who is brought to help find the grave: "Cahir Bowes followed the drifting figure of the nail-maker over the ground, his face hitched up between his shoulders, his eyes keen and grey, glint-like as the mountains of stones he had in his day broken up as road

[14] A. O'Hanlon, quoted in G. B. Saul, *Seumas O'Kelly* (Lewisburg, Pa.: Bucknell University Press, 1971), p. 18.

material. Cahir, no less than Meehaul, had his knowledge of Cloon na Morav and some of his own people were buried here. His sharp, clear eyes took in the various mounds with the eye of a prospector."[15] This is plain writing, but strong and subtle in its control of imagery and cumulative suggestion.

"The Weaver's Grave" was the first masterpiece of the kind of plain-surfaced and quiet-toned realism which was to make the Irish short story great, but Seumas O'Kelly was dead before it was published. The story could, and did, serve as a model for younger writers, but a stronger personal and artistic influence on several of them came from the Cork schoolteacher and writer, Daniel Corkery. One of his former students, a grubby boy named Michael O'Donovan who grew up to be Frank O'Connor, the great master of the Irish short story, remembered in his autobiography how "one afternoon, at three o'clock, when we should have been going home, he kept us in, wrote a few words in a mysterious script on the top of the blackboard, and went on to give us our first lesson in what he called in his monosyllabic articulation 'Eye Rish,' a subject I had never heard of, but which seemed to consist of giving unfamiliar names to familiar objects."[16] Daniel Corkery spent his life, literally and figuratively, in giving lessons in "Eye Rish" to anyone who would listen. O'Conner remembered that the most striking thing about his old teacher was his self-control, and Corkery was an intense, passionate man who seems almost to have battered himself into self-control. He had overcome a limp and a stammer, and he was determined that Ireland would overcome the limp and stammer in her creative imagination made by centuries of British domination.

Corkery's passion for all things Irish sometimes took him to extremes; his study of the survival of Gaelic literature in Munster in the eighteenth century, *The Hidden Ireland* (1924) badly overstates the case both for the survival and the literature, while *Synge and Anglo-Irish Literature* (1931) is an intemperate attack on an artist who loved peasant Ireland as passionately as Corkery himself, but loved it in a different way. Nevertheless, both books were significant in the development of the consciousness of a national literary tradition. Corkery's reputation must rest, however, on his work as a teacher and imaginative writer rather than on his somewhat erratic scholarship. If a teacher's reputation depends, ultimately, on the achievements of his students, then the man who taught Frank O'Connor and Sean O'Faolain must be ranked as a very fine teacher indeed. Corkery urged on his students the importance of

[15] "The Weaver's Grave," reprinted in *Age of Yeats*, edited by G. B. Saul (New York: Dell, 1963), p. 315.

[16] *An Only Child* (1961; London: Pan Books, 1970), p. 113.

constant revision in their work and the necessity of concentrating on what they wanted to say rather than merely how they said it. He insisted to them, too, that the attentive realism of a Turgenev with its emphasis of the significance of the commonplace would provide a better model for the Irish short story than the grinding and sometimes brutal determinism of naturalism.

Corkery's own real achievement as an imaginative writer lay in his mastery of the ordinary and his ability to draw close and convincing connections between character and environment. He was a very productive writer, and in several genres, but his best work consists of an extraordinary novel, *The Threshold of Quiet* (1917), and a fairly large number of fine short stories. *The Threshold of Quiet* does not please all readers, and many of them complain of its strained and sometimes clumsy style and its "middle-aged" tone. To the more sympathetic, though, the novel is a masterpiece of quiet realism and a superb study of those who, in Thoreau's phrase, "lead lives of quiet desperation." The death of Frank Bresnan, a young traveling salesman drowned in the River Lee at Cork, and the subsequent wake is the occasion for the exploration of the lives of his friends and relatives, and the story develops out of them and their relationships. As Bendict Kiely, a fine contemporary Irish novelist, says of the book: "The lives of the thoughtful men and virginal women in that novel are all bound together in a net that can be as black as despair and stronger even than the self-inflicted death that can be the only logical outcome of despair."[17] The novel has some serious weaknesses in plotting and narration, but it is a strong evocation of the sense of community that informs Irish life, and there is a kind of dulled power in its presentation of humdrum lives. Corkery does seem strained, though, by the problem of length in a novel, and his best work is probably found in his short stories, of which there are three major collections, *A Munster Twilight* (1916), *The Hounds of Banba* (1920), and *The Stormy Hills* (1929). The stories in *The Hounds of Banba* probably wear least well today, though they do present an effective picture of the days of the Anglo-Irish war from a strongly nationalist point of view. The best stories in the other two collections are powerful depictions of rural life. In stories such as "The Ploughing of the Leaca" and "The Stones," he seems to be almost a twentieth-century Carleton, superb in his presentation of a clumsy and groping rural life forever governed by the overpowering and sometimes menacing nature which surrounds it. In his concern with the effects of nature perceived as supernatural, Corkery seems a throwback to the earlier kinds of Irish fiction, but his

[17] *Modern Irish Fiction—A Critique* (Dublin: Golden Eagle Books, 1950), p. 2.

peasants are convincingly real as Carleton's seldom are, and his best work has a careful, earnest craftsmanship.

Craftsmanship, attention to detail, a plain style, a sympathy with ordinary people and their beliefs, these are all hallmarks of the Irish short story O'Kelly and Corkery helped develop. It may seem a long way from the still realism of *The Threshold of Quiet* to the elaborately busy world of *Ulysses*, but different as these two novels are, they have two things in common, things which run through much of the best of Irish fiction: a sense that significant meaning lies just beyond the edge of ordinary experience and is its logical extension, and a sense of the overwhelming importance of community. Both of these characteristics are among the strengths of Irish fiction from the first quarter of this century, and both are important parts of the continuing Irish experience. Past and present continuously intermingle in Ireland, and the feeling that the unremarkable experiences of everyday life may be more important than they seem superficially is constantly present. It does not take much imagination to feel the continuity of human experience in an Irish village, and it takes even less to be aware of the sense of community. The sense of the local, with all its implications, is very strong whether it expresses itself in a town's enthusiasm for its football team, an older person's feeling that nieces and nephews in America are closer that more distant relations in a village five miles away, or even the Dublin newspapers' resolute attention to Irish matters at the expense of world news. The significance of the ordinary and the concern with community are only general characteristics of Irish fiction, of course, but they are important ones nevertheless, and they are among the ones which give it its extraordinary strength. These emphases are two of the ways in which the best of Irish fiction mirrors the physical and emotional realities of Irish life. But Irish fiction also mirrors its writers: Joyce's intensity and innovativeness; Stephens' fantasizing and philosophizing; Corkery's earnest nationalism and attentive realism. For Irish readers, the Irish fiction of this time was also an effective mirror of their own concerns and attitudes; in the best of it, we, too, can find a mirror of ourselves.

Part III

phoenix imperilled

a nation once again?
Social and Political Contexts Since 1923

> A healthy nation is as unconscious of its nationality
> as a healthy man of his bones. But if you break a
> nation's nationality it will think of nothing else
> but getting it set again.
>
> George Bernard Shaw

> If, in the long view of history we Irish have thus
> far learned little, and that slowly, from our actions
> and our passions, we have at least begun to learn how
> to learn. We will, painfully, learn more.
>
> Sean O'Faolain

T HE RECENT HISTORY of Ireland began in the summer of 1923. In the new Irish Free State, the civil war had ended with the defeat of those who had opposed the Treaty and still wished to fight on for a republic. Yet the bitterness from that war would last for generations; de Valera had told his men to hide away their guns because they might be needed again, but he and the other Republican leaders were forced to admit the victory of the Free State's army. In six of the nine counties of Ulster, the new admininistrative unit was Northern Ireland, still an integral part of the United Kingdom. Ironically, the Protestant Unionists in Ulster who had so much opposed home rule for all of Ireland now had it for themselves because the only other option Britain would permit them was unification with the predominantly Catholic Free State. In 1922 the six counties had come close to anarchy as more than

200 people died in sectarian violence; after that, the politicians of the Protestant majority moved quickly to create their own local government, one which they could control totally. Northern Ireland would remain politically stagnant for more than forty years, with every election there nothing more than a referendum on the continuing union with Britain, a referendum the Ulster Unionists would always win, and the Catholic third of the population kept out of any kind of effective political power.

The situation in the Free State itself was not very encouraging. The twenty-six counties, from Donegal in the northwest to Wexford in the southeast, had won a large measure of political independence, but at a terrific price. The founders of the Free State, Arthur Griffith and Michael Collins, in different ways both men of real vision and common sense, were dead. In their place as leader of the new nation was William T. Cosgrave—competent, hard-working, and limited; the one brilliant political leader left, Eamon de Valera, adamantly refused to admit the legitimacy of the Free State, and the Republicans who followed him liked to pretend that their shadow government was, in fact, the rightful government of Ireland. Cosgrave and his ministers were faced with a staggering set of problems: the partition which separated their state from the six counties in Ulster; the necessity of creating governmental institutions from scratch among people who had a long tradition of being "agin the government"; the economic chaos which was the inevitable result of the years of fighting. The treaty their government had signed with the British in 1921 had provided for a commission to settle the problem of the boundary with Northern Ireland, and some Free State leaders had hoped that when the boundary was drawn in its final form, it would make Northern Ireland so small and weak that it would be economically unworkable, thus gradually leading to reunification. Instead, the boundary commission's report in 1925 left things precisely as they were, with Northern Ireland a going concern and many Catholic nationalists still under British rule. Cosgrave's government had greater success in establishing governmental institutions; departments, commissions, and authorities were created with surprising efficiency. The new Irish bureaucrats made some mistakes, but they demonstrated convincingly that they could provide responsible administration, and the Irish people showed that when they had their own government they could be as law-abiding as any other. In fact, the twenty-six counties have provided a model of good government which few other nations that have achieved independence in the twentieth century have been able to match—no coups, no dictatorships, no major scandals. Economic problems, on the other hand, were more difficult to deal with. Agriculture remained the fundamental industry, and for several reasons the agricultural situation was not good; too many farms that were too small for anything but subsistence farming, too slow a growth in production, too much reliance on export to Britain. The Cosgrave government, fundamentally conservative and farm oriented, employed an economic policy a Gladstone or a Coolidge would have approved. The economy gradually improved, but it was so gradual that social melioration was very slight. What the Cosgrave government demonstrated, in effect, was that it could perform the administrative functions the British had performed in the past and about as effectively.

Perhaps that was enough, and the Irish government of 1923–32 ought to be commended for restoring stability, but it all seemed rather dull and ordinary when compared to the political visions of Thomas Davis and Padraic Pearse or the economic visions of Fintan Lalor and James Connolly. Moreover, this holding action could not last permanently; for better or worse, things began to change when de Valera and his Republican followers decided they were ready to make their peace with the Free State. The great stumbling block for them was the oath of allegiance to the British king which the 1921 Treaty had required for membership in the Dáil, the Free State's parliament. The civil war had essentially been fought over this oath, and it was the oath with its implicit rejection of the ideals of a republic and a united Ireland that de Valera absolutely refused to acknowledge. Eventually, though, he began to realize that it was better to live with realities than to continue to serve an unattainable dream. In 1926 he broke with Sinn Fein, the Republican movement, then founded a new political party, Fianna Fail, and started a newspaper, *The Irish Press,* all signs that he and his followers were ready to join the established political process. In the general election of 1927, his Fianna Fail party won almost as many seats in the Dáil as Cosgrave's, and abstention from the Dáil seemed no longer a sensible policy. There followed one of the oddest events in Irish history: in spite of the civil war of only five years before, de Valera and his followers took the oath and entered the Dáil. They certainly entered the Dáil, but perhaps they did not take the oath. De Valera unquestionably signed a piece of paper with the oath written on it, but he insisted that he was taking no oath and merely writing his name on a page as one might do in giving an autograph. Call it chicanery or the workings of a very subtle mind, but whatever it was, it ended the civil war as the Free State's military victory had not, and it brought a vocal and important segment of Irish opinion into the mainstream of political life. Cosgrave's government survived a second election in 1927, but it was perfectly obvious from the time de Valera entered the Dáil that at some point in the future the former rebels against the Free State would become its rulers.

That happened in 1932 when Fianna Fail won a plurality of the seats in the parliament, and de Valera took office for what would turn out to be sixteen years of uninterrupted rule. The early thirties, with worldwide depression and social dislocation, were bringing new and aggressive leaders to many countries, Hitler in Germany, Roosevelt in the United States. Some in Ireland feared that de Valera would turn into a dictator, but that was hardly the case. He ruled firmly, imaginatively, and aggressively, but his failures and successes indicated even more sharply than Cosgrave's the problems of any government in the Free State. Irish self-esteem received a needed boost from de Valera's distinguished performance at the League of Nations, and he wisely resisted Catholic pressure to become involved in the Spanish Civil War on Franco's side. He also brought an admirable firmness to dealing with the continuing problem of threats to constitutional government in the Free State. Extreme republicanism was still a menace to the established order; as late as 1927, Republicans settling old scores from the civil war had murdered Minister of Justice Kevin O'Higgins, the man who had carried out the reprisals policy that had helped the Free State win. When the IRA, de Valera's old comrades, threatened the stability of the state, he moved quickly and harshly to suppress it. A rather silly Fascist movement, the Blueshirts, in which Yeats briefly participated, was also suppressed. Civil libertarians were sometimes distressed by de Valera's methods, and the military tribunals he used against the IRA were an extreme expedient, but with his incorruptible honesty, de Valera could argue that sometimes the liberties of the few must be abrogated to protect those of the many.

All this was to his credit, but he was less successful in winding up the two great problems left from the nineteenth century; the relationship with Britain and the problem of economic independence. He produced a new constitution in 1937 which virtually wrote out the last vestiges of British influence. The Free State became Éire, and the function of the governor general, the king's representative under the Free State, was given to a president. Douglas Hyde, then in his seventies and honored as the founder of the Gaelic League, took office as president. Ireland remained a part of the British Commonwealth, but like Canada she worked to loosen that relationship into nothing more than a free association of independent nations. The new constitution was written in such a way that it could be understood as applying to the six counties of Northern Ireland, but they remained as Unionist and as British as ever. The constitution was one more step toward complete independence, but its real importance was in its codification of the realities of the new Ireland: the family was enshrined as the basic unit of society and divorce was therefore forbidden; the Catholic Church was recognized as the religion of the vast majority, though it was not established as a state faith; Éire defined itself as being a mildly authoritarian nation with some tendencies towards state ownership in the common good but a strongly capitalist orientation. Éire's public policy was closer to that of Italy or Portugal than Americans or Britons might like, but de Valera was not a Mussolini or a Salazar, and the state remained healthily democratic.

The constitution of 1937 loosened some of the political ties with Britain, but it was more difficult to loosen the economic ones because Éire was thoroughly dependent on Britain as a market for its agricultural produce and dependent on Britain, too, as a supplier of all the manufactured goods the Irish did not or could not make for themselves. The limits of economic independence were clearly shown in 1932 when Éire and Britain quarreled over the payment to Britain of land annuities which were the interest on loans given the Irish tenants under the British Land Acts before independence. De Valera argued that this money belonged now to his government rather than the British and withheld payments. The British retaliated by declaring an economic war which lasted for six years; Britain imposed tariffs on agricultural imports from Ireland, and Éire retaliated with tariffs on imports from Britain. Éire was thrown back on its own resources, and the results were not entirely pleasing to anyone. Farmers, who were mostly in the cattle business, were encouraged to turn to tillage, and this shift was not a success; Irish industry was encouraged by the protective tariffs, but Éire was too small a country to produce all that a modern state needs, and Irish goods were often overpriced and of poor quality.

Even so, the economic war had an unexpected benefit in making Éire better able to sustain the rigors of the war which broke out in Europe in 1939. During that war, the country declared its independence and its isolation. When Britain went to war with Germany in September, all the British Commonwealth followed suit except Éire, and for the duration the country was rigidly neutral. It made for an odd situation. Many Irishmen went to fight with the British Army anyway, but the government's neutrality was so strict that de Valera even went to the German embassy to express his condolences after Hitler's death. Northern Ireland was as much at war as any other part of the United Kingdom, and Belfast became a major naval center. German bombs fell on much of the province, but south of the border, life went on much as usual in spite of what was called "the emergency." During the battle of the Atlantic, the British must have regretted that they had returned the three navel bases they had held in Éire in 1938, but the British were careful to respect Éire's neutrality. In what many people saw as a battle for civilization, there was something petty about de Valera's refusal to join the Allies, and in his speech after VE Day, Churchill chastized Éire for its neutrality, and praised his own government for its restraint in not violating it. The British government must have known, however, that any armed intervention in Éire would have had disastrous military results and that there would have been something very unseemly about a Britain that had gone to war to protect one small nation, Poland, attacking another. De Valera replied a few days later in the best speech of his career: "Mr. Churchill is proud of Britain's stand alone, after France had fallen and before America had entered the war. Could he not find in his heart the generosity to acknowledge that there is a small nation that stood alone, not for one year or two, but for several hundred years, against aggression; that endured spoliations, famines, massacres in endless succession; that was clubbed many times into insensibility but each time, on returning consciousness, took up the fight anew; a small nation that could never be got to accept defeat and has never surrendered her soul?"[1]

de Valera's invocation of the past as justification for action in the present was entirely characteristic of him, and surely most Irish people agreed that, of all countries, Éire was under no obligation to fight England's wars. Still, even aside from the moral issue of fighting the Nazi evil, Éire's wartime neutrality did as much harm as good. On the credit side, there were the facts that the country was spared bombing and possible invasion as well as the inflation of a wartime economy; on the debit side, Éire was very largely cut off from the rest of the world during those six years. The economy stagnated, and little improvement could come in social problems. In addition, the isolation and censorship of the press encouraged the intellectual and cultural provincialism which had always been a serious problem in the Free State. Ireland was becoming ever more a backwater; that could be shown by the fact that she was not admitted to the United Nations for several years after its creation, and it could also be shown by the stagnation in Irish culture. One observer has noted that "It is a paradox of all revolution that it paralyzes the creative impulse from which it sprang,"[2] and that is precisely what was happening in

---

[1] Quoted in Tony Gray, *The Irish Answer* (Boston: Little, Brown, 1966), p. 119.
[2] Quoted in *Ireland Since the Famine*, p. 470.

Ireland. The nationalistic impulse which had created its revolution and spurred its artistic creativity had become a formula, a formula with the power to choke.

In cultural terms, the newly independent Free State of the 1920s faced some serious problems. It was a small, poor, weak, English-speaking nation only a few miles from the most powerful English-speaking nation in the world; how could it assert its cultural independence with Britain so near? The simplest answer, of course, was to create a Gaelic state, as Gaelic in its popular culture as well as its serious creative work as, say, Denmark was Danish. But that simple answer, beloved of true believers in the Gaelic League, ignored two basic facts of Irish life: the Free State was overwhelmingly English-speaking and English-influenced in most of its traditions and institutions. Road signs in Gaelic or "Mna" and "Fir" on the doors of restrooms were one thing, but generations of communal experience could not be changed overnight. Beyond the problem of language, the Gaelic civilization which had ended in the seventeenth century really could not provide a model for a new Irish culture except in the most general terms. The desire to imitate the past was very strong, though, and the suggestion that Ireland return to the attitudes of the Anglo-Irish eighteenth century, an obsession with W. B. Yeats in the 1920s and later, was no more practical than extreme Gaelicism. Anglo-Irish culture represented all those things the Free State had been created to destroy, but Yeats's theory does point to a basic problem in Irish culture of the time: was it possible to make a society which reflected the wishes of most of the people without making one which would stifle creativity? The Free State's record at this is not particularly encouraging. It saved the Abbey Theatre with a financial grant and provided some aid for libraries and the preservation of national antiquities, but it was often inimical to free artistic expression.

The Irish Free State itself was the creation of men who had hated *The Playboy* fifteen years before, and the attitudes of those who found *The Playboy* unpatriotic, *The Countess Cathleen* irreligious, and *Ulysses* irredeemably obscene were the dominant tastes in the Ireland of the 1920s and 1930s. Before 1923, every Irish writer of quality came into conflict with nationalism and Catholicism or both, and that did not change with independence. Every good writer had to fight some sort of battle against Irish public opinion, and that, among other things, tended to provincialize most of them. The fate of AE's journal, *The Irish Statesman*, was one indicator that Ireland was not ready for the sort of disinterested criticism which any healthy culture needs. This was the best journal of arts and ideas Ireland had ever had, but its readership was embarrassingly small, it was frequently attacked by the Church, and it finally died in 1928 as the result of a silly libel suit.

The death of *The Irish Statesman* was not a good sign, but a far worse one was the institution of governmental censorship. In 1926 the Cosgrave government established an "Evil Literature Committee" to examine the threat to Irish public virtue from the British newspapers that specialized in sex scandals, and this led, three years later, to the Censorship of Publications Act which provided for censorship of books, magazines, and newspapers which might be conducive to "sexual immorality." The government was right to believe that British popular journalism was a threat, not because of the sex but because British popular culture at large was a threat to any kind of Irish Ireland, but the censorship was a disaster for Irish literature. It was the product of naive, puritanical men, one of whom observed in the debate over the Act: "We will not allow, so far as it lies within us to prevent it, any free discussion on birth control, which entails, on the one side, its advocacy,"[3] and so books dealing with birth control or books which were "in general tendency indecent or obscene" were banned. Aldous Huxley's *Point Counter Point* was the first book to be forbidden under the new Act, but over the years the list grew to include not only a fair amount of routine pornography but works of F. Scott Fitzgerald, William Faulkner, Thomas Mann, Ernest Hemingway, George Orwell, Somerset Maugham, Graham Greene, and Arthur Koestler. Among Irish authors, George Bernard Shaw, Sean O'Casey, Oliver Gogarty, George Moore, Frank O'Connor, Samuel Beckett, Brendan Behan, and John McGahern have all had the honor of being on the list at some point; by 1965 almost 10,000 books were forbidden. In 1946 the provisions of the censorship law were slightly modified, but it remained a blight. Films are also censored in Ireland, and the continuing power of the attitudes behind censorship was compellingly demonstrated as late as 1958 when the Dublin Theatre Festival of that year was wrecked by Church and public pressure against the performance of O'Casey's *The Drums of Father Ned* and a dramatization of parts of *Ulysses*. Yet the harmful effect of censorship lay not so much in the absurdities of what was forbidden as in its stifling of adult discussion and the harm it did to serious Irish writers.

For a time after World War II, Éire in general seemed a stagnant country. Well enough off to provide some aid to war-ravaged Europe, it still seemed just to limp along in those first postwar years. de Valera's party won more seats in the Dáil than any other in 1948, but a bizarre coalition of parties

---

[3] Quoted in Gray, *The Irish Answer*, p. 244.

representing everything from the old pro-Treaty forces to rampant republicanism did well enough to put him out of office. The coalition government was no
success, though; it rather stupidly bumbled into declaring Éire a republic at
last, but the declaration of the Republic of Ireland as the new name for the
twenty-six counties merely helped solidify partition from Northern Ireland.
An attempt to introduce a mother-and-child health plan was scuttled by pressure from the Church, and the coalition government failed to provide imaginative leadership or much change in an economic and social situation which had
forced emigration back to a high level. de Valera was returned to power in
1951, and ousted in 1954. The merry-go-round governments seemed to be
going nowhere until 1957 when de Valera's Fianna Fail party won the first
absolute majority in the Dáil in almost twenty years.

For more than thirty years, Irish politics had been dominated by the men
who led the Rising and the war against the British. It was time for a change
at last; the first sign of that change was a document on economic development
prepared by T. K. Whitaker and submitted to the government in May of
1958. The "Whitaker Report," as it has come to be called, was arguably the
most important government document to come out of Ireland since the proclamation of the Republic in 1916. It said that the Irish Republic needed a complete shift in economic policy: greater support for agriculture, especially animal husbandry; more state intervention in industry; reduction of tariffs; and,
most significant perhaps, heavy state efforts toward self-sufficiency were
thrown overboard in the First Programme for Economic Expansion which the
government introduced late in 1958. There were problems with this new
departure, of course, but in general, it was a success. Industrial output increased by almost 50 percent in only six years, and between 1961 and 1966
the population of the Republic increased significantly for the first time in its
history. It is too early yet to judge the long-term success of the new economics,
but its implementation was a significant shift, probably more significant than
the changes in political leadership which came at about the same time. Nevertheless, de Valera's retirement from the premiership in 1959 ended one phase
of Irish history; his successor, Sean Lemass, an old associate, had won the
title "General Manager of Ireland" for himself earlier on, and Lemass and
his successors have appeared to be a new kind of Irish politician, far more
interested in effective management than the old shibboleths of nationalism or
the enmities from the civil war. Lemass' successor, John Lynch, was born in
the year of the Rising and was only seven when the civil war ended; when he
took office in 1966, the fiftieth anniversary of the Rising, the old days seemed
very far away.

With its entry into the Common Market, the Republic of Ireland seems to be continuing the process of becoming a characteristic small western European state. The wealth of, say, Denmark, is not there yet, but there is no question that the Irish people as a whole are physically and economically better off than they have ever been. They complain about inflation, and the recent rate has been alarming, but to the traveler from abroad the Republic seems prosperous and even a little complacent, not a bad thing in the long view of Irish history. Britain remains the Republic's largest customer, and the two economies are still probably too tightly tied together with Irish agriculture so dependent on the British market. Agriculture remains underdeveloped in terms of what it could be, but farm life is getting better all the time, and Dubliners like to joke about Kerry farmers taking milk to the creamery in a Mercedes-Benz. A third of the work force is still involved in farming, but the industrialization process continues. Everything from Jacob's biscuits, Waterford crystal, and Guinness stout to pianos and transistor radios come from Irish factories for sale abroad. The economy remains a mix of capitalism and state management, and such state agencies as the Electricity Supply Board and the Turf Board, which markets peat (turf in Ireland) for fires have been among the real successes. Nevertheless, serious problems remain: poverty in some areas, bad labor relations, and, most distressingly, the violence in Northern Ireland.

There is also the problem, if it can be called that, created by a rising standard of living and rising expectations. Refrigerators and televisions in the kitchens of isolated farmhouses are no longer an oddity, and they are symptomatic of the new way of life. Educational institutions have been under constant pressure from parents and students wanting more, and the aftereffects of Vatican II have profoundly shaken the Catholic Church. The Church's teaching and the law's injunction against contraceptives, for example, are widely flouted, and that is indicative of a new permissiveness in the society as a whole. Unmarried mothers may still be denounced from the altar in some parishes, but Irish mores are changing quickly, especially in the cities. The Republic still has one of the lowest marriage rates in the world, however. As late as 1961, over 46 percent of the men between 35 and 44 in rural areas were unmarried, and the average age at marriage was almost 31 for a man and 27 for a woman. Even that is changing as the agricultural system shifts away from the tradition in which a man would wait to marry until after he had inherited the family farm. And in spite of changing mores, the Irish still seem to an outsider to be a curiously innocent people. Alcoholism, probably the product of celibacy and boredom, is a serious problem among men, but even for the "liberated" young people, life seems to revolve around sports, films (Dublin is remarkable for long lines of people waiting to buy tickets even for old movies), and show bands. Some critics complain that the country is becoming ever more a backyard of Britain, and there may be some truth in that. The language movement has never caught on, and there was widespread relief when Gaelic was removed recently as an obligatory subject in the schools. Thus the country remains English-speaking and wide open to a spillover from British popular culture. British magazines jam the newsstands, the British Sunday newspapers are read avidly, and the BBC seems to have about as many listeners and viewers as the RTE, the Irish radio and television network. The spillover is most evident in the cities, Dublin in particular, but even in the cities assimilation is far from complete. Dublin may look like an English provincial city, aside from the Gaelic on telephone booths and the destination signs on the busses, but only a very ignorant traveler would mistake Dublin for Leeds. London accents stand out sharply in pubs and restaurants, and the whole tenor of life is something certainly not English.

The signs of Anglicization are most evident in urban popular culture; they are much less apparent in rural life or in "high culture." There is an obvious continuity with a distinctly un-English past on the farms and in the market towns, while all sorts of groups and organizations in Dublin and elsewhere work to maintain a recognizably Irish culture. In some ways this is not altogether healthy, because it leads towards provincialization. The leading newspapers, *The Irish Independent, The Irish Press,* and *The Irish Times,* devote really too much attention to Irish matters, and they sometimes give the impression that the world centers on Ireland. On the other hand, the newspapers have done admirable work in sustaining modern Irish literature and culture. The *Times'* "Arts and Studies" page contains consistently able discussions of cultural developments, while the *Press's* Saturday page on Irish writing has published many important new writers of short stories and some excellent criticism. But if the presence of dispassionate critical examination is a sign of a healthy literary culture, and surely it is, then all is not well. The newspapers and *Hibernia,* the interesting journal of arts and ideas, publish too much criticism which is little more than gossip or mutual back patting. One of the serious problems for an Irish writer today is the problem of audience. The literate market in Ireland is too small to support much of a book-publishing industry, although the Dolmen and Mercier presses have done excellent work in the past, and the Poolbeg Press, Gallery Books, and the Writers' Cooperative will probably add to that in the future. Dublin has a disproportionately large number of good bookstores, too, but the market is necessarily dominated by the major British publishers. This means that Irish writers, especially the young and unknown, find it very difficult to publish their work, and this leads to frustration and boosterism. The resulting emphasis on local achievement is perfectly understandable, but it also creates cultural isolationism; one student at University College, Dublin, knew well the work of a score of recent Irish writers, but had to admit to me that he had never read Faulkner, Wallace Stevens, Albee, or Ted Hughes.

The literary isolation implicit in that may be breaking down, though, as heavy-handed censorship and the Sinn Fein tradition of Irish self-absorption slip into the past. Certainly, the physical isolation of Ireland is slipping away with entry into the Common Market and the influx of foreign tourists in the recent past. The influx of tourists, many of them attracted by the effective advertising of Bord Fáilte, the tourist board, Aer Lingus, the state's airline, and CIE, the national ground transportation system, is clearly changing Irish life. Remote towns now sport American-style motels, and Dublin seems to be falling in love with American-style fast food. Irish-Americans, "returned Yanks," make up a very significant part of the tourist trade. Some do no more than eat at the patently phony but entertaining "medieval banquet" at Bunratty Castle near the Shannon airport, take a look at Killarney, and go on to shop in Dublin's Grafton Street; others come to visit relatives in out-of-the-way places in Meath and Clare, check genealogies, participate in the various literary summer schools, or even look for a retirement home. For many of those who return, it must be a shock to realize that the poverty-stricken Ireland of their childhoods is largely gone; for others, it must also be a shock to realize that the land of thatched cottages and leprechauns their grandparents talked about has turned into a tidy little country of prosperous farms and light industry.

Yet for Irish-Americans, the return to Ireland is a search for roots, and Irish people at home sometimes forget the extent to which they are only the center of a people who have been spread to every corner of the earth. Millions of Irish left over the centuries, perhaps never expecting to see Ireland again; the monks of the remote past who spread their learning throughout Europe were only the beginning. Their successors were and are the missionary priests and nuns who helped create the Catholic Church in the United States and still work in Africa and Asia. The "wild geese" of the eighteenth century who left Ireland as British rule solidified created a remarkable record of soldiering and governing in Europe and its colonies:

one Irish emigrant, John Barry, fathered the American navy, and another, William Brown, the Argentine, while the son of an emigrant, Bernardo O'Higgins, became the founder of modern Peru. 200,000 Ulster Protestants left between 1730 and 1770 to come to America, mostly the victims of British economic policy, and from their stock came ten American presidents, Appalachian farmers and coal miners, and the backbone of the new frontier in the America of Andrew Jackson's day. Irish immigrants built the Erie Canal, and after the Famine, hundreds of thousands of them came to Boston, New York, and the other port cities of the northeast. The vast majority of them were farm people, but they became urbanized remarkably quickly, moving up the social ladder from jobs as manual laborers and parlor maids into the skilled crafts, the police, and politics, sending back money to bring relatives over and support the seemingly eternal battle of Irish nationalism against British rule. It was, curiously, a chief of the Chicago police who became the great collector of traditional Irish music in his time and compiled the book which is still the bible for performers of traditional music in Ireland itself. And it was an Irish-American lawyer in New York, John Quinn, who became one of the great modern patrons of literature and painting, supporting not only Yeats and Joyce but Joseph Conrad, T. S. Eliot, Picasso, Matisse, and Gaugin in a time when none of them had much recognition. Of all the "returned Yanks," though, none so much pleased Irish people as John Kennedy, all of whose great-grandparents had emigrated during a three-month period during the Famine. His visit to Ireland in 1963 was a heady experience for the Irish, and their grief at his death was painfully intense.

Violent death is still too much a part of the Irish experience, and no sketch of modern Ireland can ignore the continuing tragedy of Ulster. The situation there is immensely complex; to many Americans it is inexplicable tribal warfare, and to a surprising number of citizens of the Irish Republic it has become a battle about which they do not care. But the Ulster crisis is a fundamental part of the continuing history of Ireland. It appeared in the early 1960s that the two Irelands were learning to live with each other. Shoppers from the Republic often went to Belfast to take advantage of the lower prices there, while some northern Protestants discovered the Republic as an attractive vacation land. In 1965 the prime ministers of the Republic and Northern Ireland exchanged visits, and there was a good deal of confident talk of a new cooperation. Yet all this ignored the basic fact that Protestant Unionists ran Northern Ireland as a highly discriminatory society. Economic and political discrimination kept the old nationalism alive among the Catholic minority, and discontent with the situation was probably encouraged by the

commemorations in 1966 of the Easter Rising. With the potent rhetoric of
Ian Paisley, a Protestant clergyman and anti-Catholic agitator, the cautious
efforts of the Ulster government to give some voice politically to the Catholic
minority, and the gradual development of a nonviolent civil rights movement
among Catholics, all the elements were in place by 1968 for an explosion.

The inevitable happened in October of that year when civil rights march-
ers in Londonderry came into bloody conflict with the Ulster police. The
civil rights movement sought a fair political situation for the Catholic minority
and an end to inequity in such matters as jobs and housing, but the conflicts
with the police turned the entire situation toward violence. The whole story
is too long and complex to recount here, but, after eight years of violence, the
net result has been a disaster for everyone—Catholics, Protestants, and the
British. The passion for noble ideals—and for shoddy ones—has once again
proved that there is too much hate and too little room in Ireland. The policy
of trying to choke off support to all the gunmen by turning Catholic and
Protestant opinion against them may yet succeed, but it has led to increasing
desperation on their part. Ordinary life stumbles on in the six counties despite
it all, but the warfare is an especially ugly business of reprisal and counter-
reprisal, and the random murders seem to have almost nothing to do with the
sectarian and economic differences that began the whole hellish affair nearly
a decade ago. As one Irishman said to me recently, "It has nothing to do anymore with the churches or the jobs; it's no more than vicious gangsters with
the taste of blood in their mouths who pleasure themselves killing whomever
they can find."

At this point it is impossible to predict how, or even if, the Ulster crisis
will be resolved. For the moment, though, the crisis remains a hurt in Irish
life, bloody proof that the old angers over religious faith, nationalism, and
control of the economy are far from dead. Citizens of the Republic can take
pride in the way their country has demonstrated their ability to deal maturely
with serious political and economic problems over the last fifty years. On
balance, they have learned to handle the situation in which they find themselves; whether the same can be said of the rest of Ireland remains to be seen.
Until that happens, the broken bone of nationality Shaw spoke of will remain
a besetting pain. Sean O'Faolain, in 1947, was a better prophet than he knew
when he wrote that the Irish will, tragically, have to learn yet even more from
their actions and their passions.

vision and cliché
Anglo-Irish Drama, 1923–1940

The terrible beauty was beginning to lose her good looks.

Sean O'Casey

Cinderella has turned into the Free State.

Denis Johnston

O NE EVENING in the early summer of 1976, I stood in the lobby of the Abbey Theatre after a performance of the "Golden Jubilee" production of Sean O'Casey's *The Plough and the Stars*. It had been a fine production of a play that has long been an important part of the Abbey repertory; looking at the paintings of Lady Gregory, Yeats, and some of the great actors and actresses of the past which hang in the lobby, it seemed to me that all of them would have been pleased with what had gone on in their theater that night. As the crowd pushed its way out to the street, I happened to meet a friend, a Dublin businessman who knows and cares a great deal about Irish drama. I commented to him on the excellence of the performance, and he replied, "Ah, yes, this theatre always embalms the classics with only the best fluid, but there's really no life in this place, you know, no life." I agreed with him that too often the Abbey seemed to be no more than a competent provincial repertory theater, and as we walked up toward O'Connell Street he launched into a little sermon on modern Irish drama that ran something like this:

"Now the first thing you must remember is that *The Plough and the Stars* is exactly fifty years old, and it was the last important play that has had its premiere in the Abbey. Of course, it's a mistake to confuse the Abbey with Irish drama, but ever since the days of Synge and Yeats we've always assumed that what goes on at the Abbey is what goes on in Irish drama. Yeats, you know, liked to talk about an 'Irish dramatic movement,' but perhaps that's not really a very helpful idea anymore. The kind of collaboration he and Synge encouraged was useful enough in the early days, but the 'dramatic movement' has ended up being a straightjacket in which mediocrities are awfully comfortable and those who are more than mediocre are always squirming. Sean O'Casey squirmed right on out of it, and most good Irish dramatists since his time have done the same. Who's the greatest living dramatist born in this country? Samuel Beckett, surely, but who would ever think of Beckett as part of any 'Irish dramatic movement'? Yet most dramatists here are really quite comfortable inside their straightjacket. I've seen most of the 'new' Irish plays in the last thirty years, and at least two-thirds of them follow the same formula; they're either Ibsen problem-plays in some small town in the midlands or stupid farces in the same wretched town. In fact, they usually have the same plot and the same characters. There's a father who's a veteran of the Civil War and now is some minor flunky with the County Council. There's a mother who spends her life cooking chips and eggs, going to Mass, and sharpening her tongue on the neighbors. They have a daughter who gets pregnant by a visiting Socialist and a son who wants to be either a poet or an auto mechanic but because the parents want him to be respectable, he's off at university doing mediocre work in an easy subject. If the play's a comedy, son comes home, opens a garage, and buys out the town; daughter marries her Socialist, who is really just a nice boy from Rathmines, and they turn into Irish-speaking pub keepers. If it's a tragedy, mother tells father the children aren't really his, father, we learn, has had his hand in the till at the County Council, daughter is driven out of town by the priest, and son, poetically disillusioned by it all, shoots himself. Either way, there will be great talk about how everyone in Ireland is victimized by some impossible dream he cannot fulfill, and the minor characters, all great talkers, will include a priest who's not sure of his vocation, two Irish-Americans looking for their cousins, and the fellow next door who is always an amiable drunk."

My friend's analysis is hardly fair, but it does suggest some of the problems in Irish drama during the last half-century. It is easy to feel a disillusionment with a national drama which has dwindled down since the great days of Synge, Yeats, and O'Casey, but Lennox Robinson, who knew the best days as well as the worst, liked to observe that Irish drama is not what it used to be, and never was. The presence or absence of dramatic talent is, of course, a matter of luck, but it was more than bad luck that has afflicted Irish drama in the fairly recent past.

The 1920s and the early 1930s were really a second golden age of Irish theater. Sean O'Casey rapidly demonstrated that he was the most important dramatist to appear in Ireland since Synge; Yeats produced a series of plays which were valuable experiments in several modes, and the stable of regular Abbey dramatists, Lennox Robinson, T. C. Murray, George Shiels, Brinsley MacNamara, and others, contributed solid and interesting work. The Abbey probably never had a better group of actors and actresses than its regular company in the twenties: Sara Allgood, May Craig, Eileen Crowe, Barry Fitzgerald, F. J. McCormick, Arthur Shields, and the rest. The theater itself was showing wear after two decades of hard use, and its technical facilities seemed even more inadequate, but the grant from the Free State in 1923 which made the Abbey the first state-supported theater in the English-speaking world promised a new financial security after the bleak days of the Anglo-Irish and Civil Wars. Moreover, as the country recovered from the "troubles," there were signs of new theatrical activity all over Ireland, particularly in Belfast, Galway, and Cork. In Dublin itself, Lennox Robinson, with encouragement from Yeats, had founded the Dublin Drama League in 1918 to present experimental and continental plays that were not a part of the Abbey's reportory. The Drama League did good work through the twenties; the Abbey itself did some experimental productions and eventually opened a small theater, the Peacock, in its own building for experimental plays. The Peacock was the site of the first production (Ibsen's *Peer Gynt*) by the remarkable team of Micheál Mac Liammóir and Hilton Edwards who soon moved a few blocks away to the Gate Theatre to open their own important playhouse. Dramatic activity slowed perceptibly during the depression of the 1930s, but it remained healthy all over Ireland, and especially in Dublin, until the self-imposed isolation of Irish neutrality and an increasingly strident nationalism finally clamped the straightjacket of conventionality firmly in place during the war years. The recovery since the war has been slow, and the fire which destroyed the old Abbey in 1951 was a real disaster for Irish drama, but signs of vitality have been present all along in the work of a postwar generation of playwrights of whom Brendan Behan was the best known, the Dublin Theatre Festival, Mary O'Malley's courageous Lyric Theatre in Belfast, the continuing work of the Gate, the upsurge of amateur dramatic companies in the 1950s which produced at least one valuable playwright, John B. Keane, and even the gradually improving standards of the Abbey. If Irish drama remains disappointing, provincial, and old-fashioned in terms either of world drama or the work and ideals of the men and women who began the dramatic movement early in the century, it is still surprisingly healthy for a small and not especially rich nation.

Even so, theaters cannot survive without playwrights, and too often the best Irish playwrights, like the best Irish actors and actresses, have ended up as exiles in London, New York, and Hollywood. "The weak stay and the strong go" is too easy a formula, but the career of Sean O'Casey, the strongest Irish playwright of the last fifty years is obvious support for it. When O'Casey's first play appeared at the Abbey in 1923, it was perfectly clear that he was precisely what the theater and Irish drama needed, a good craftsman with the ability to appeal to a popular audience without debasing himself. It is significant that Lady Gregory was the first to recognize his talent, for he shared with her the ability to mix the popular and the serious, and, like her, he was an inveterate experimenter. The value to Irish drama of his three early Dublin plays was immense; the popularity of *Juno and the Paycock* (1924) helped save the Abbey from bankruptcy and all three of these plays helped establish an important new mode. O'Casey's *The Shadow of a Gunman*, the first of his plays to be produced, was given only at the tag end of the 1922–23 season at the Abbey, but it was unquestionably the best new play of the year. Lennox Robinson's *Crabbed Youth* and *Age* was an amusing little piece in that season, and George Shiels' *Paul Twyning* was an adequate essay in conventional Abbey comedy. But too many of the "new" plays were throwbacks to the old styles: George Fitzmaurice's tired *Twixt the Giltinans and the Carmodys*, R. J. Ray's thin *The Moral Law*, and J. B. McCarthy's *The Long Road to Garranbraher*. Fitzmaurice's play could have been done better by Lady Gregory, McCarthy's by Synge, and Ray's by almost any writer of melodrama. *The Shadow of a Gunman* has some serious flaws, the plotting is contrived, the characterization is sometimes diffuse, the language has little of O'Casey's later magic, but this is obviously the work of a playwright who has things to say and is learning to say them well. O'Casey's central characters, Donal Davoren and Seumas Shields, are alive as few characters since Synge's had been, and his handling of a recent situation, the Anglo-Irish War of only two years before, is extremely able. That topicality helped make the play popular during its short initial run, but it is the feeling of truthfulness about people and their experiences which the play conveys which gives it lasting importance.

O'Casey was, if nothing else, a truth-teller, and a kind of blunt honesty was one of his great strengths as an artist. Sometimes, like anyone with passionate beliefs, he tries too hard to tell us the truth he knows, but there is never any question of his burning sincerity. His three early plays about the Dublin slums and the terrors of the Irish "troubles" from the 1916 Rising to the Civil War convince us because they are so clearly truthful tales, and O'Casey knew the world he portrayed in them almost too well. Born into a Protestant family in Dublin in 1880, he was the last of thirteen children, eight of whom were already dead by the time he was born. After his father's death, John Casey, as he was then, grew up amidst the squalor of the Dublin tenements and saw the daily Gethsemane of the women like his mother who tried to bring a little decency into that filthy world. His eight dead brothers and sisters were pathetic statistics in the appalling records of infant mortality in Dublin, a city in which the rate of infant mortality was higher than in Calcutta and the general death rate higher than in any other city in Europe. Young Casey survived in this hell, but he was half-blinded from an ulcerated cornea which had to be endured because there was never enough money to pay for proper medical care. He had some intermittent schooling, but the great escape from slum life for him came in amateur theatricals. By the age of eleven he was going to the Queen's Theatre with his brother to see Boucicault and Shakespeare; in 1895, ironically enough, he played a minor role in Boucicault's *The Shaughran* in the decrepit Mechanics Institute, a building which later would house the Abbey itself.

He went to work at fourteen, first in the stockroom of a hardware store, later, for ten years, as a manual laborer on a railway. These jobs provided the money to buy books, and he gradually built up a little library of Shakespeare, Dickens, Scott, Shelley, Ruskin, and others of those writers who meant so much to the self-educated workingmen of his time. His schooling may have been slight, but the rhythms of some of those writers, and some of their ideas, became a part of his imagination, as did the rhythms and ideas of the Bible and the Prayer Book. Like so many Irish men and women of his generation, especially among Dublin's working poor, he became interested in both nationalism and socialism. His nationalistic enthusiasm led him to learn Gaelic, but socialism became an even stronger concern. James Connolly and "Big Jim" Larkin, the great labor leaders of the early days of the century, were his heroes, and he saw at first hand the cruelty of the terrible lockout of 1913. After that infamous encounter between aspiring labor and brutal business, O'Casey became the secretary of the Irish Citizen Army, the paramilitary organization founded to protect workers from harassment. His passionate socialism caused him to leave that group when he felt it was being infiltrated by persons who cared more about nationalism than socialism, and he played no active role in the Easter Rising, the Anglo-Irish War, or the Civil War. Nevertheless, his socialism provided the opportunity for some of his earliest published writing, a series of ballads and a history of the Citizen Army. Neither showed any remarkable talent, nor did the first three plays he submitted to the Abbey. The first, written on sheets of paper stolen by friends from the offices in which they worked with an ink made from boiling the leads of indelible pencils because O'Casey was too poor to pay for proper ink and paper, came back from the Abbey with the comment, "Not far from being a good play."[1] This rejection encouraged him to try again; he had not survived forty years in the Dublin slums to be fazed by a single failure. A second play went to the Abbey, and it, too, was rejected. A third play went, and again the rejection notice came, but by this time Lady Gregory was interested in this common laborer who was so persistent. "I believe you have something in you," she wrote to him, "and your strong point is characterization."[2]

The Shadow of a Gunman, the next play O'Casey submitted, showed how right she was, but it was *Juno and the Paycock* (1924) which said most emphatically that here was an important writer. Even more than *Shadow of a Gunman*, *Juno* is an utterly truthful play, honest in its characterization of ordinary, even sub-ordinary, people whom we should not particularly like but come to be deeply concerned about. Its topicality—it deals with the Irish Civil War—helped make it the most popular new play the Abbey had ever presented, and for the first time in history a run was extended to a second week because of the crowds that filled the house night after night. *Juno*'s popular appeal then may have rested on its topicality and its convincing depiction of Dublin slum life, but we would not care about the play today if those were its only strengths. Nevertheless, both of these factors are continuingly important to it. The Abbey, long oriented toward rural and small-town life and values, had rarely done a play about urban slum life before, and that helped begin an important shift in Irish drama; moreover, the topicality of his setting in the recent past was central to O'Casey's artistic method. *Juno* is a "popular" play in the best sense, full of sharply observed realistic characters and convincing situations. As popular art, it is unabashedly farcical and melodramatic, and that makes it tempting to describe it as Boucicault updated. It has some of Boucicault's sentimentality, but it also has a grippingly honest vision of life that Boucicault never dared. In addition, it is written with a brilliance and sensitivity that only Synge among the Irish playwrights can match. For sheer

---

[1] Quoted in David Krause, Sean O'Casey (1960; London: McGibbon and Kee, 1967), p. 34.
[2] *Ibid.*

linguistic invention, it may be the best of O'Casey's work. That inventiveness, the brilliantly fatuous talk of Captain Boyle and his "butty" Joxer, the sharp honesty of Juno, the whining of Johnny, the frustrated imaginativeness of Mary, is more than a mere record of Dublin dialect, though it is superb as that. It is thoroughly integrated into a dark plot of warfare outside the tenement and disillusionment inside. Mary's disastrous romance, Captain Boyle's delusions of grandeur, Juno's not always patient suffering, Joxer's blathering agreeableness, all add up to superb commentary on the emotional and spiritual conditions of an Ireland which has gained its freedom and, in brutal civil war, lost the idealism which made the freedom seem worthwhile.

O'Casey would go on to other things, but there are few scenes in modern drama more ironically crushing than the final one in *Juno*. Johnny is dead, murdered in reprisal by his fellow Republicans for betraying a comrade; Mary is pregnant by a man who has deserted her. The Boyles' expectations of wealth have vanished. As she goes out to arrange the burial of her dead son, suffering Juno intones a keen that is Synge-like in its power: "What was the pain I suffered, Johnny, bringin' you into the world to carry you to your cradle, to the pains I'll suffer carryin' you out o' the world to bring you to your grave! Mother o' God, Mother o' God, have pity on us all! Blessed Virgin, where were you when me darlin' son was riddled with bullets, when me darlin' son was riddled with bullets? Sacred Heart o' Jesus, take away our hearts o' stone, and give us hearts o' flesh! Take away this murderin' hate, an' give us Thine own eternal love!" Synge might have stopped there, but O'Casey drives on. Captain Boyle and Joxer, both thoroughly drunk, come back in after the women have left. They stumble around the empty room, saying inanities:

> *Boyle.* If th' worst comes . . . to th' worse . . . I can
> join a . . . flyin' . . . column. . . . I done . . . me bit
> . . . in Easther Week . . . had no business . . . to . . . be
> . . . there . . . but Captain Boyle's Captain Boyle!
>
> *Joxer.* Breathes there a man with soul . . . so . . . de
> . . . ad . . . this . . . me . . . o . . . wn, me nat . . .
> ive 1 . . . an'!
>
> *Boyle. (subsiding into a sitting posture on the floor).* Commandmant
> Kelly died . . . in them . . . arms . . . Joxer . . . Tell me
> Volunteer Butties . . . says he . . . that . . . I died for . . .
> Irelan'!
>
> *Joxer.* D'jever rade Willie . . . Reilly . . . an' his own

... Colleen ... Bawn? It's a darlin' story, a daarlin' story!
   Boyle. I'm telling you ... Joxer ... th' whole worl's
... in a terr ... ible state o' ... chassis![3]

Curtain. Curtain, after brutal irony. It is brilliant theater, but it is also a powerful commentary on human waste in the very jakes of idealism.

O'Casey's next play, *The Plough and the Stars* (1926), is even a bigger play, bigger in its range of characters, its temporal span, and its experience. In some ways, it is almost too big; we swing so far between farce and melodrama in it that it may seem to lack some of the genuine humanity of *Juno*, or so it would seem if it were not for Fluther Good and Bessie Burgess, the carpenter and the fruit seller who eventually show us that they have humanity and more to spare. *Juno* was an extremely popular play from the very first; the *Plough* was surrounded with controversy when it was first presented, though it has gradually been accepted as a classic and perhaps as O'Casey's masterpiece. Still, the row over it was second only to the one over the *Playboy* in the Abbey's long history. Before the play even went into rehearsals, George O'Brien, the government member of the Abbey's board, complained to Yeats and Lennox Robinson that the love scene in Act I was offensive and that the prostitute in Act II was more than that. Yeats and Robinson agreed that the language in the love scene was "most objectionable," but they were adamant about the prostitute: "O'Casey is contrasting the ideal dream with the normal grossness of life and of that she is an essential part."[4] Their one-sentence analysis of the play was precisely right, but there was enough of the "normal grossness of life" in it to continue dissension even after Professor O'Brien had been pacified. Eileen Crowe refused to play her original part because of the language she was made to use, and F. J. McCormick, another important member of the company, also complained. The first night's performance went well enough, but soon enough nationalists were enraged by what they saw as an insult to the memory of the 1916 Rising.

Certainly, there is powerful stuff in the play. Act I, with foolish Uncle Peter dressing in his absurd uniform to go out to a patriotic demonstration and Jack Clitheroe deserting the Citizen Army out of picque, is a sharp satire on the pretensions of the nationalist organizations of the years just before the rising. The pub scene, Act II, had plenty in it to offend any ardent nationalist: the high, nonsensical words of Padraic Pearse floating in through the pub window

---

[3] *Three Plays by Sean O'Casey* (1957; rpt. London: Macmillan, 1968), pp. 71–73.

[4] *The Letters of Sean O'Casey, Volume 1,* ed. David Krause (New York: Macmillan, 1975), p. 146.

to be equated with the brawling and intoxication inside; Rosie Redmond, the
prostitute, and her scathing commentaries on nationalism; the flags of the Irish
Volunteers and Citizen Army leaning against the bar while patriots drink to the
murderous ideal of Mother Ireland. The nationalists in 1926 especially objected
to these scenes, but the real assault on delusions of heroism comes in the last
two acts. In the third, the fighting during the rising provides Bessie Burgess
and Mrs. Gogan with a golden opportunity for looting the shops; in the fourth,
the high ideals and the fight for a glorious and bloody thing have reduced Norah
Clitheroe to madness. She raves on about the loss of her husband and her child
while the others cower in Bessie's attic room, the men playing cards, the women
caring for Norah. Bessie Burgess dies from a random bullet while trying to protect Norah; the men are marched off to internment, and the stage at the end
belongs to two British soldiers stupidly singing "Keep the Home Fires Burning"
while drinking the dead Bessie's tea. The nationalists who rioted in the Abbey
in 1926 were not wrong in seeing the play as an attack on the murderous ideals
of the rising, but Yeats was also right when he shouted to the seething throng
in the theater that it had disgraced itself again and that, just as with Synge's
Playboy, riots in the Abbey had proclaimed the birth of a work of Irish genius.

The *Plough and the Stars* is undoubtedly a work of genius, brilliant in its
theatrical impact, superb in its characterization, crushing in its dramatic
ironies. It is a play about ordinary people caught up in events and movements beyond their control. In that, in its antiheroism, it is a part of the
central movement of modern drama. Some things cannot be helped, the play
seems to say; consumptive children, like Mrs. Gogan's Mollser, will die no
matter how much idealism is in the air, and Jack Clitheroes will always leave
their little Norahs to go out to be bewildered into death. In Act III, Norah has
been searching the streets during the fighting for her Jack, and in her great
central scene she tells us what she has seen among the Irish guerrillas:

> I tell you they're afraid to say they're afraid! . . . Oh,
> I saw it, I saw it, Mrs. Gogan. . . . At th' barricade in
> North King Street I saw fear glowin' in all their eyes. . . .
> An' in th' middle o' th' sthreet was somethin' huddled up in
> a horrible tangled heap. . . . His face was jammed again th'
> stones, an' his arm was twisted round his back. . . . An' every
> twist of his body was a cry against th' terrible thing that had
> happened to him. . . . An' I saw they were afraid to look at it.[5]

5 *Three Plays by Sean O'Casey*, p. 185.

Like so many of O'Casey's women, Norah knows the terror and the suffering that lie behind the drunken idealism of the men, and Norah is one of O'Casey's great truth tellers. Like little Mollser who wonders if there is a titter of sense anywhere in Dublin, Norah is crushed by her existence, but O'Casey's theme in the play is something more than individual helplessness. Many modern dramatists have argued our helplessness, but O'Casey argues also a way beyond helplessness, the way of creating a decent community of support and sympathy, even in the worst of times. Uncle Peter's nationalism is a silly charade; the Young Covey's socialism is a front for his own insecurity; Jack's patriotism comes out of a mixture of motives, but Maisie Madigan and Fluther Good show us that decent realists can, in a small and limited way, make a better world than any Nationalist or Socialist dreamer. Maisie is the tenement scold, a raving Protestant and Unionist, always ready to assault her neighbors; Fluther is an amiable drunk, a sort of Joxer with basic decency. Together they protect and succor Norah, and with real effort they maintain a sense of community in the midst of the chaos, and the final failure of their efforts does not invalidate their worth. This makes *The Plough* sound grimly bleak, and so it is, and yet it is also intensely funny. The swings back from melodrama to farce are extreme, but the wildness, the exuberance, and the sentimentality are all parts of O'Casey's truth. Strong medicine every bit of it, and nothing stronger than the final scenes punctuated with songs, Norah's remembrance of her dead Jack's version of "When You and I were Young Maggie," Bessie Burgess gasping out "I do believe, I will believe/That Jesus died for me," the British soldiers and their "Keep the Home Fires Burning" as the curtain falls.

The songs come close to grotesque music hall, and they reflect one of the ways in which O'Casey was beginning to free himself from the norms of conventional realism. The pub scene, Act II, suggests another; it is realistic in superficial appearance, but its distortions of historical fact and its mechanical structure make it almost expressionistic in its technique. Expressionism, the literary method that distorts ordinary reality so as to show its essential truth more clearly, was a natural direction for O'Casey the truthteller, and, from the perspective of his later career, it is easy to see how even in the early plays he was chafing at the constraints of urban realism. O'Casey was always an experimenter, one who insisted that "Dramatists cannot go on imitating themselves, and, when they get tired of that, imitating others. They must change, must experiment, must develop their power, or try to, if the drama is to live."[6] Lady

6 *The Green Crow* (New York: Braziller, 1956), p. 165.

Gregory would have agreed with that, and it was characteristic of her that she was anxious to produce O'Casey's next play, *The Silver Tassie*, when it was submitted to the Abbey in 1928. *The Silver Tassie* represented a distinct change in O'Casey's method. Three of its four acts were still superficially realistic, and the characters were still drawn on Irish types, but the second act was an expressionistic dream sequence, and some of the characters and action in the other acts were closer to expressionistic than realistic depiction. By the time he had sent this play to the Abbey, O'Casey was living in London. The Dublin critics had been hostile to *The Plough and the Stars*, and life abroad seemed a marvelous release from all the narrow constrictions of Ireland. He had married a Dublin girl, taken her to London with him, and there he had made friends and found what seemed a good, new life.

Still, the Abbey was his home theater, and O'Casey confidently expected that *The Silver Tassie* would have its premiere there. When the Abbey's directors read it, they realized that it was a significant new departure for him, a play not about Dublin's recent past, but a study of the effects of World War I on an athlete-turned-soldier who is maimed in the trenches in France and returns to Dublin to drag out his life. Lady Gregory and Lennox Robinson were both willing to produce the play, but Yeats erupted when he saw it. O'Casey should write about what he knows, Yeats insisted, and that is the Dublin slums. The reasons behind Yeats's dislike of the play were complex, partially having to do with his attitudes toward World War I and the writers who depicted its horrors, partially having to do with his dislike of "modernist" literary techniques, but the final result was that, at his insistence, the Abbey rejected the play. O'Casey, infuriated, had Yeats's condescending letters to him and his own angry ones to Yeats published in a London newspaper, and cut himself off from the Abbey. Given the fact that it was only four years since *Juno* had helped save the theater from financial ruin, it was exceedingly ungenerous of the Abbey to refuse the play. Worse plays had their premieres there while O'Casey and Yeats were feuding, and the Abbey's unwillingness to take a risk on what was clearly an experimental play was a bad omen for its future.

Yet, to be honest, *The Silver Tassie* is not an especially good play. The expressionistic battlefield scene is a splendid idea that does not really work because the writing is not strong enough to sustain the conception. The first act begins well, with Harry Heegan, the athlete, in his triumph, but the characters around him even then seem stereotyped, and that becomes more of a problem in the final two acts with Harry paralyzed and the entire play collapsing into the bathos O'Casey had skirted but avoided in his earlier plays. The ironies crunch rather than crush; some of the dialogue feels warmed over, some of the language is inflated, and the play as a whole frustrates because it ought to be so much better than it is. After the Abbey rejection, *The Silver Tassie* had a fairly long run in London, but it was not a successful experiment, and it was not an entirely encouraging sign about the direction of O'Casey's career. O'Casey's characters would increasingly become mouthpieces for his ideas, and too often the ideas, at least in their dramatic presentation, would seem the cobbled-up opinions of the auto-didact. His theatrical instinct would remain sure, but after 1928 he found it increasingly difficult to get his new plays produced, and the lack of regular experience in the theater began to show. Occasionally he would make bad bumbles in stagecraft—in one late play a woman has time to write a long letter between the time she is shot and her death—but, more distressingly, too often the effective theatrical strokes would seem to exist for their own sake rather than as parts of a unified conception.

Even so, O'Casey was a great dramatic innovator, and every one of his plays after *The Silver Tassie* has something of interest in it. His next major play, *Within the Gates* (1933), moves fully into an expressionistic style with four tableaux full of stylized figures, walking abstractions for the most part. O'Casey himself thought of it as a film of London's Hyde Park, and it is essentially a morality play about the struggle for the possession of the soul of an ordinary woman. It is an interesting experiment in drama as prophecy, and it is interesting, too, as O'Casey's first real effort to write about something other than Ireland. Yet it does not work, and the basic problem seems to be language. O'Casey could do a good deal more than write Dublin dialect, but too much of the language here is inept, and so the ideas are clumsily presented. His increasing commitment to communism in the 1930s and after led him to create a piece of anti-Fascist propaganda in his next long play, *The Star Turns Red* (1940). O'Casey's communism was not the doctrinaire sort of the time, being rather a personal amalgam of economic theory, personal idealism, and a deep sympathy for the oppressed, all of this mixed with a strong, if anti-institutional Christianity, and there is no reason why this volatile mixture could not make strong drama. But *The Star Turns Red* fails badly because its dramatic possibilities are overpowered by invective and sentimentality. O'Casey's overriding beliefs—sympathy for the oppressed, hope for the possibility of creating a good community, hatred of English overlordism,

clerical oppression, and middle-class values—were turning into hardened opinion rather than creative ideas.

He was more fortunate when he turned to another mode, that of Arcadian
comedy which tries to present a vision of the way towards a perfect world.
Purple Dust (1940), in this mode, is one of his best later plays, a highly
amusing tale of the efforts of two Englishmen to make an old Tudor mansion
in a small Irish town into a "great house" so that they can live in the style of
the Anglo-Irish Ascendancy. O'Casey called it a "wayward comedy," and so
it is, at times reminiscent of Lady Gregory's farces in its shrewd manipulation
of characters. As a comedy of ideas, it is reminiscent of Shaw, but there is
also a strong dash of O'Casey's own sense of the magic of the Irish countryside. Of the later plays, though, a serious one, *Red Roses For Me* (1942) is
the most impressive. Using essentially the same background as *The Star Turns
Red*, it recaptures some of the energy and passion of the early Dublin plays.
Its setting is based on the 1913 Dublin strike, and much of it seems strongly
autobiographical, with Ayamonn Breydon, its hero, a young, self-educated
laborer, much like the young Sean O'Casey. The play certainly has its grim
side and its bitterness; Ayamonn is killed in a demonstration, and there are
plenty of attacks on O'Casey's usual rogues' gallery of self-deluding nationalists and aggressive ignoramuses, but the final effect is of a kind of glowing
nostalgia and glowing acceptance. It has some bad flaws, notably in the construction of the last act, but the first two acts have real life and passion, and
the third act is one of O'Casey's finest achievements. The scene is a quay and
a bridge across the Liffey, and it gradually develops into a powerful evocation
of Dublin, past, present, and future. We begin with an apple seller's complaint, "This spongy leaden sky's Dublin; those tomby houses is Dublin too—
Dublin's scurvy body; an' we're Dublin's silver soul," but before the act ends
Dublin has become, at least for those with vision, a possible new Jerusalem.
In Ayamonn's words:

> There's th' great dome o' th' Four Courts lookin' like
> a golden rose in a great bronze bowl! An' th' river
> flowin' below it, a purple flood, marbled with ripples o'
> scarlet; watch th' seagulls glidin' over it—like
> restless white pearls astir on a royal breast. Our city's
> in th' grip o' God![7]

7 *Three More Plays by Sean O'Casey* (London: Macmillan, 1965), p. 289.

Here, too, O'Casey seems to be in the grip of something more than his frequent obsessions. David Krause, in his fine study of O'Casey, calls this the playwright's "Ode to Joy in honour of the people of Dublin, his first and only love,"[8] and that is a good description. *Red Roses For Me* is an affecting play, honest in its vision and written with a new depth of sympathy. Too often, though, in his later plays, the powerful moral vision was not successfully translated into dramatic fact. Clumsy writing and inept stagecraft mar even *Red Roses For Me,* and they make *Oak Leaves and Lavender* (1946) a very bad play. The problem of a brilliant conception poorly worked out is also present in *Cock-a-doodle Dandy* (1949), but O'Casey's mastery of farce makes this the best of the plays from the last fifteen years of his life. It is a fantasy, the tale of a remarkable rooster who thoroughly upsets a crowd of Irish philistines in a small town. In some ways it is a bitter play, but it is also exuberantly funny, with the Cock providing a splendid symbol of joy, courage, and sensual ecstasy. It is an effective presentation of the perpetual conflict between those who affirm vitality and joy and those who would deny it, and, for O'Casey, it is surprisingly unsentimental. Strong satirist that he was by this point, he let the life-deniers defeat the Cock in the end, and we are reminded that the joyous imagination he represents must continue the dance of life even when it can be only a defeated affirmation. Too often, though, O'Casey himself failed to learn his rooster's lesson. His last two major plays, *The Bishop's Bonfire* (1955) and *The Drums of Father Ned* (1959), convey essentially the same message of vitality, but the message is obscured by rather obvious attacks on the Irish clergy and middle class. The effects of years of exile show in these plays; O'Casey seems to be battering away at the same old enemies, and some critics complained that he was attacking an Ireland that had long since ceased to exist. Yet the rows in Dublin over the attacks on the clergy in both plays made it evident that the clerical repression O'Casey hated was not exactly dead.

The old man's ability to affirm and infuriate lasted to the very end of his life. That ability informs his best plays, and it, as much as his constant experimentation, is part of his greatness. Sometimes the denunciations of fat businessmen or grasping priests go on too long, though, and we are left with the impression of a powerful imagination shackled by a more powerful set of obsessions. This is particularly true in his autobiography, a work which by its very size commands attention. Beyond the simple matter of bulk, some half a million words, the autobiography is a valuable work, a very full portrait of

---

[8] *Sean O'Casey,* p. 171.

the artist as a young man, a middle-aged man, and even an old man. It began
in a fragmentary way about 1930 and eventually stretched into six big
volumes, each but the last covering a decade or so of his long life. The lack of
interest in his plays after the mid-1930s probably stimulated the autobiographical impulse; certainly much of his income for years came from royalties
from the autobiographies. Yet the autobiography is an uneven achievement.
O'Casey's invitation to himself to thump the world with talk produced almost
too much of a good thing. The last two volumes, *Rose and Crown* (1952) and
Sunset and Evening Star (1954), covering the years from 1926 to 1953, have
too much self-indulgent talk—"yak" might be a better word—and too much
thumping of old enemies and old obsessions. Still, every volume is interesting,
and the first ones are superb exercises in the great Irish tradition of autobiography. In these the dramatic sense is strong and the narration is powerfully propulsive; they are clearly the work of a writer who knows how to use
dramatic techniques in narrative prose. In *I Knock at the Door* (1939), *Pictures in the Hallway* (1942), *Drums Under the Window* (1946), and *Inishfallen Fare Thee Well* (1949) we follow, in third-person narration, the career
of Johnny Casside from the reeking slums of his childhood through years as
a laborer and agitator to his triumph as a dramatist. As Roy Pascal, in his
study of autobiography, observes, "The four earlier books are not reminiscence,
but life regained, relived passionately with all the intensity of a man fiercely
engaged."[9] That engagement is especially strong in the recreation of childhood
with the powerful scene at his father's funeral, the encounter with the brutal
schoolmaster Slogan, and the wonderfully observed episode of the visit to
Kilmainham prison with an uncle after the death of Parnell. Sometimes the
narration between the dramatic set pieces lags or trips into invective or tedi-
ously Joycean word play, but every one of the big scenes comes off impres-
sively. None is more moving than the great emotional center of the fourth
volume, "Mrs. Casside Takes a Holiday," the painfully honest and moving
tale of his mother's death and funeral with its wonderful summation, "the
banner waving over every grave is silence."[10] Mrs. Casside is the presiding
genius of the autobiography, the archetype of every suffering and courageous
woman in his plays, the archetype of her generation of poor Irish women, and
her death, more than O'Casey's triumphs in the theater, seems the real emotional climax of the book.

The autobiography is a deeply flawed work. Some of the writing is very

---

9 *Design and Truth in Autobiography* (Cambridge, Mass.: Harvard University Press, 1960),
p. 151.

10 *Inishfallen, Fare Thee Well* (1949; London: Pan Books, 1972), p. 39.

bad indeed; some of the opinions are repeated *ad nauseam*. It has neither the perceptiveness of Yeats's autobiography nor the moving simplicity of Ruskin's *Praeterita*, and yet it deserves to stand, flawed as it is, among the dozen great autobiographies in our language. In a sense, it is characteristic of so much of O'Casey's work—flawed, powerful, commanding in a kind of rough greatness. As with Thomas Hardy, one feels that O'Casey is often not really in full control: the conceptions are superb but the presentation is distressingly amateurish. It is easy to catalogue the faults in his work, the clumsy dramatic constructions, the ham-fisted use of language, the omnipresent opinion-talking, and yet there is no question that he is the great Irish dramatist of the last half-century. It used to be confidently asserted that none of his plays after *The Plough and the Stars* equaled his earlier work; more recently, as the English-speaking theater has finally acclimated itself to the plays of Pinter, Stoppard, and Albee, his post-Dublin plays have come to be seen as important forerunners of much recent drama. Both opinions have some truth in them, and O'Casey surely deserves a place as an important experimenter in modern drama. But for the Irish theater, his final reputation must always rest on *Juno and the Paycock* and *The Plough and the Stars*, two plays of a greatness Ireland has not seen the likes of since.

Had O'Casey spent all of his life in Ireland, his presence might have encouraged more adventurousness in Irish drama or, alternatively, it could have stunted two generations of playwrights. As it was, from 1928 until his death in 1964, he remained the greatest living Irish dramatist but an insignificant force in Irish drama. His plays were presented in Ireland only sporadically, and he was largely out of touch, from his exile in Devon, with developments at home. For a time after his departure in 1926, Irish drama remained extremely healthy. Strong new plays continued to come from the Abbey and from smaller theaters around the country, and new names were on the Irish scene: Brinsley MacNamara, George Shiels, Teresa Deevy, Denis Johnston, Paul Vincent Carroll, Lady Longford, Micheál MacLiammóir. The Dublin Drama League, which used the Abbey on the two nights of each week the regular company did not play in the house, introduced Dublin audiences—and Irish playwrights—to the work of Strindberg, O'Neill, and Schnitzler. Micheál MacLiammóir and Hilton Edwards expanded on the work of the Drama League at their Gate Theatre with brilliant productions of classics and Continental plays. Orson Welles and James Mason were among their actors. Their patron, Lord Longford, went on to found his own company which specialized in Elizabethan and Restoration plays, and his wife wrote some bright and clever drawing-room comedies, a genre almost unknown in Irish drama. Increasingly, the Abbey was not the only outlet for Irish drama. It had had its competitors all along, of course; Edward Martyn, who had broken with it early, had helped sponsor a number of companies in Dublin, the most important being the Irish Theatre Company which, between 1914 and 1920, almost equaled the Abbey. An Taibhdhearc, a Gaelic-speaking company, sprang up in Galway; Cork had at one point a little theater, An Dun, that produced some of the early work of Lennox Robinson, T. C. Murray, and Daniel Corkery. Belfast, too, had a succession of little theaters doing good work; Joseph Campbell, Rutherford Mayne, and George Shiels were among the writers of merit who worked with them. Yet the Abbey remained the real focus, and its bread-and-butter repertory was strengthened by several new and good playwrights. George Shiels, adept at the sort of comedies which always went well with audiences but capable, too, of stronger work, became the most popular Abbey dramatist of the 1930s and after. Brinsley MacNamara, an actor turned playwright, provided one extremely funny comedy, *Look at the Heffernans!* (1926), and a long series of later plays which had a respectable place in the repertory. Lennox Robinson, too much literary man about town to fulfill his talent, did write one brilliant comedy, *Drama at Irish* (1933), about the effect of a visiting drama company on a small Irish seaside resort. It is excruciatingly funny, and it raises the question of why most of his other plays are not as good, but he could always be relied on to provide effective work. Teresa Deevy wrote two good studies of romantic young women, *The King of Spain's Daughter* (1935) and *Katie Roche* (1936), both interestingly done and remarkable in their dialogue, especially when we realize that Miss Deevy had been totally deaf since she was a girl.

She shared the prize in a play competition at the Abbey in 1931 with a man who seemed for a while as though he would be O'Casey's successor as the Abbey's great resident talent, Paul Vincent Carroll. Carroll was, however, an oddly frustrating playwright, a superb technician who always seemed about to write a better play than he actually created. Born in Dundalk in 1900, he discovered what he called his "spiritual home" in the Abbey as a teen-ager. Although he spent much of his career as a schoolteacher in Glasgow, and had some of his plays produced by little theater groups there, his most interesting work first appeared at the Abbey. His first play, *The Watched Pot* (1930), a grim study of a dying man, was done in the Abbey's experimental theater, the Peacock. *Things That Are Caesar's* appeared in the main theater in 1932. It was a conventional well-made play about a girl torn between her status-seeking mother and her idealistic father, but the dialogue was strong, and it proved a convincing study of the triumph of narrow Irish conventions over an individualistic free spirit. *Shadow and Substance* (1937), perhaps Carroll's best play, was much finer work. It has accurate, effective dialogue and some really memorable characters: Canon Skerritt, a proud, elegant, sophisticated priest with an abstract love of God; Dermot O'Flingsley, a cynical and anticlerical schoolmaster; Brigid, Canon Skerritt's simple and pious housekeeper. Brigid's religious visions provide the center of the play; at first, they embarrass Canon Skerritt, who has no use for emotion or mystery in religion, but they bring him eventually to accept his own need for a deeper humility and a deeper faith. A host of well-done minor characters, including two really obnoxious "modern" priests and two idiotic schoolteachers, give Carroll's fable the feel of reality and provide the opportunity for some biting satire. It is a strong play, thoroughly Irish at many levels, and it ought to have been the first of a series of important works. But the Abbey rejected Carroll's next play, *The White Steed*, although it was unanimously voted the best foreign play of the 1938–39 season by New York drama critics. The rejection by the Abbey was stupid, but it was a sign of the times. The play was judged to be anticlerical, and the Abbey's management was becoming "afeard of the priests" as well as afeard of the Free State which helped pay the bills. *The White Steed* is superficially similar to *Shadow and Substance*, but it is a strong play with some excellent characterization. In spite of the charges of anticlericalism, it offers an interesting study of conflict between a kindly but paralyzed priest and his ferocious curate. The older man, Canon Matt Lavelle, is a good part, but he is, as Robert Hogan says, "little more than a stage priest with a few lovable crotchets and a heart of gold,"[11] while Father Shaughnessy is close to caricature. Nevertheless, the play is tightly controlled and interesting. Unfortunately, *The White Steed* was as good as the end of Carroll's career; excluded from the Abbey, he continued to write, and produced a large number of plays, but by the time he died in England in 1968 he was almost forgotten as an Irish playwright.

That the Abbey would drive out its strongest younger playwright was a sign of the sickness that afflicted the theater towards the end of the 1930s and later. Yeats himself, the only survivor of the Abbey's founders among the management, had lost most of his influence by the time *The White Steed* was submitted. At least one of Yeats's own later plays, *The Herne's Egg*, was

---

[11] *After the Irish Renaissance* (1967; London: Macmillan, 1968), p. 57.

judged too strong for Abbey audiences. Yet in spite of the continuous bicker-
ing on the Abbey's board, Yeats himself played a major role in Irish drama
all through the twenties and thirties. He had virtually washed his hands of the
Abbey in 1919, writing a public letter to Lady Gregory in which he said that
the Abbey's success in developing a realistic drama in Ireland was, for him,
"a discouragement and a defeat."[12] That was true enough, for the Abbey had
long since failed to become the theater of passionate symbolism and poetic
drama that he had originally imagined. Moreover, by 1919 Yeats had discovered a new dramatic mode for himself in his imitations of Japanese Nōh
plays. These plays were intended only for an elite audience; their complex
metaphorical constructions, minimal action, elaborate choreography, and spare
stage settings made them unsuitable for a commercial theater. While Yeats
was working in this mode, no new plays of his appeared at the Abbey, and a
decade passed between the poetic version of *The Player Queen* in 1919 and
the drama-ballet, *Fighting the Waves* (1929). The Nōh plays, which were not
produced in Dublin, turned out to be some of his finest dramatic achievements.
At the Hawk's Well (1916) is an especially beautiful play, almost inert in
terms of action but marvelously unified through its verbal imagery. It and *The
Only Jealousy of Emer* (1919) are continuations of Yeats's series of drama-
tizations of the stories of Cuchulain, and both of these are really plays for
dancers, dramatically cold but powerful psychologically in their fusion of
mask, language, and movement. Yeats may have put the Abbey behind him,
and may have turned to a style which would have been incomprehensible to
most Dublin audiences, but these two plays remain Irish in their subject matter,
and the same is true of a third Nōh-based play, *The Dreaming of the Bones*
(1919), an eerily effective dramatization of the story of Dermot and Devorgilla, the lovers who first brought the English to Ireland. *The Dreaming of the
Bones* is a real masterpiece, closest of all his plays to the Nōh model, beautifully written, and surprisingly good theater in the conventional sense.

The fact of the matter was that Yeats was becoming what he had never
really been before, a master of dramatic craft. That shows in his recreations,
translations is hardly the word, of Sophocles' Oedipus plays which the Abbey
produced in 1926 and 1927, though the credit there must belong more to
Sophocles himself than to Yeats. Some of Yeats's plays from the 1930s, *The
Herne's Egg* is one, are too full of Yeats's own idiosyncratic ideas and also too
full of murkily obscure poetry, but each of the plays actually produced during

12 *Explorations* (London: Macmillan, 1962), p. 250.

that decade shows a master dramatist at work. *The Words Upon the Window-Pane* (1930) is a brilliant study based on two of Yeats's interests, spiritualism and Jonathan Swift. In it, a medium, Mrs. Henderson, calls up the ghost of Swift at a seance, or, rather, the ghost imposes himself, and the result is a brilliant theater piece with a superb final curtain. Beyond theater craft, the play is an extremely adroit handling of some complex ideas in a way worthy of them. *The King of the Great Clock Tower* (1935) is an even more disturbing play, a cruel, capricious, almost expressionist version of something like the Salome story which so fascinated Yeats's fellow poets, Arthur Symons and Oscar Wilde, in the 1890s. *The Resurrection* (1927) is perhaps better theater in its version of responses to the stories of Christ's return from the grave. Dealing with some of its author's most complex ideas about human history, the play centers on a debate between a Greek and a Hebrew, and later a Syrian, on the meaning of what seems to be a miracle. To the Greek, Christ was merely a spirit masquerading as a man; to the Hebrew, he was a man who deluded himself into thinking he was God. As they argue these rational theories, a frenzy of noise from the worshippers of Dionysus builds up outside. The Syrian enters to report Christ's appearance to his disciples, and the Greek and Hebrew both defend their rationalistic theories against this apparent miracle. In a brilliant *coup de théâtre*, the risen Christ silently enters the room; the Greek, insistent that "there is nothing here but a phantom," goes slowly to the figure and feels, to his astonishment, "The heart of a phantom is beating!"[13] This is a brilliant dramatic climax, and it is also precisely the right dramatic metaphor to reinforce the lesson of the play: the supernatural does enter our world when it chooses and changes it utterly.

The power of the supernatural also informs the last of Yeats's plays to be produced at the Abbey during his lifetime, *Purgatory* (1938), and that little play is almost the quintessence of the best in Yeats's drama. A ghost story in a way, it recounts the simple fable of how an old man and his son stopped one night near a ruined house, the house in which the old man had been born, the son of a great lady who had married a drunken groom. The wife died in childbirth; the groom had burned down the house when his son was sixteen; the son, in turn, had stabbed his father. Now, on this night, the old pedlar relives it all again and stabs his own son. It is an odd, shivery tale, but in Yeats's masterly handling, it becomes a spare, withered masterpiece like the tree on the stage that is its ruling symbol. The idea of the play is a

---

13 *Collected Plays of W. B. Yeats*, p. 593.

powerful one, and perhaps it is not wrong to see it as a fable of Ireland and the continuing pattern of Irish history. Beyond that, its language is precisely right, clotted sometimes, but often direct and hard. At the premiere of *Purgatory*, Yeats appeared for the last time on the stage of the Abbey to acknowledge the audience's applause. An old man then who would be dead in less than a year, he was the last survivor of the great triumvirate that had created the Abbey. With Synge and Lady Gregory, with the Fays and Annie Horniman, too, he had made the Abbey one of the great theaters of the world. One of the gifts reserved for old age was the knowledge that the Abbey in 1938 was a far lesser thing than he had dreamed of, but another was the greatness of his last plays, plays in which, in a curious and idiosyncratic way, he had really become the great dramatist he had dreamed of being forty years before.

By the time Yeats stood on that stage for the last time, much of the energy in Irish drama had gone elsewhere. O'Casey was an exile in Devon; Carroll's *The White Steed* would soon open in New York. For nearly a decade the Gate Theatre on the far side of O'Connell Street had shown as much life or more than the Abbey. The Gate has for long been the special project of Hilton Edwards and Micheál MacLiammóir, two excellent theater men, who have regularly given in it brilliant productions with superb casts. Because the Gate has produced all sorts of plays, from Aeschylus to Brecht, it plays a less important role in Irish literary history than its merits warrant, but it encouraged a number of good playwrights, none more valuable than Denis Johnston, surely the most remarkable Irish playwright to emerge after O'Casey. Johnston's great strength was his intelligence, and even his weaker plays are the work of a finely tuned critical and imaginative mind. Born in Dublin in 1901, he took degrees at Cambridge and Harvard before returning to Dublin as a lawyer in the 1920s. There he became involved in theatrical activities, writing some penetrating drama criticism and acting in several plays. Sometime along the way, he began writing a play—he called it *Symphony in Green* then— which was an exuberant parody of Irish high talk. The Abbey rejected it, Yeats, for one, not at all understanding what it was about, but the Gate produced it in a revised version in July of 1929.

Retitled *The Old Lady Says 'No!'*, it turned out to be a radical departure in Irish theater, a complex, allusive play, hilarious in its parody, and genuinely profound in its analysis of the Irish mind. A plot summary will hardly do for this extravaganza, but it might run something like this: a drama company is performing a play about Robert Emmet, the eighteenth-century patriot, and his beloved, Sarah Curran. They declaim romantic verse at each other until the

British come to arrest him. In the scuffle, Emmet is knocked unconscious, and the director of the production comes before the curtain to ask if there is a doctor in the house. The rest of the play takes place in the mind of the actor playing Emmet. He imagines himself searching through modern Dublin for Sarah; the quest for her provides the "action" for the remainder of the play, but the texture comes from a mass of allusions to all sorts of popular and serious elements in Irish culture. Emmet's journey into disillusionment takes him from a talk with the statue of Grattan in College Green, that interrupted by cackles from an old flower woman who is Kathleen ni Houlihan gone to seed, through encounters with arty ladies in an elegant salon, a blind beggar who claims to be descended from Brian Boru, six ghostlike shadows who are Mangan, Swift, Wilde, Yeats, Joyce, and Shaw, and finally back to Sarah's garden where it all began. *The Old Lady Says 'No!'* was like nothing else in Irish theater, too complexly allusive, perhaps, for a popular audience, but masterful in its contrast of the romantic patriotism of the past with modern Irish sentimentality and nationalistic obsession. It could be argued that it is more the work of a critical imagination than a creative one (Hilton Edwards once said it read like a railway timetable and played like *Tristan und Isolde*, a fair enough comment on its incredible allusiveness and its leitmotiv structure). If nothing else, it was a play Ireland needed in 1929. After all the political talk and the unthinking nationalism of the decade, someone needed to set off a firecracker under Irish pretensions, and *The Old Lady Says 'No!'* does it with a bang.

Johnston's next play, *The Moon in the Yellow River* (1931) represents a complete change in style, for it is a carefully made, realistic problem play focusing on the attempts of some Irish revolutionaries to blow up a power station. But in its origins, it was not so very much a change; Johnston began it as a parody of the conventional Abbey "serious play," and superficially it has all the earmarks of the class. The central figures are Darrell Blake, an IRA man and political obsessive who is also a classicist, musician, and student of oriental poetry. In his effort to blow up the power station he comes into conflict with Tausch, the German engineer who has built it and has great faith in material progress to save the world; Dobelle, a former railway engineer who has accepted, as Tausch will not, his inability to save the world through progress; and Lanigan, the efficient Free State Soldier who shoots Blake dead without a second thought. The plot does indeed sound like a parody of many Abbey plays, but it is developed with a sureness of touch well beyond the capabilities of most of the regular Abbey dramatists. It turns, in fact, into a complex argument about human capability and human freedom. In the end, the power station blows up anyway, but only after Johnston has given us an evening of intellectual tragicomedy which Shaw would have been proud to have written.

The Old Lady Says 'No!' and The Moon in the Yellow River remain Johnston's best-known plays, the one the only really good expressionistic play written in Ireland, the other a frequent popular success. None of Johnston's subsequent plays has been as well received as these, but he is a continuously interesting playwright. A Bride for the Unicorn (1933), for example, is a remarkable study of the conflict between the rhythm of ordinary life and the rhythm of the imaginative life. The basic idea for it owes much to the once popular theory of time of J. W. Dunne, but the play with its poignant portrayal of the career of a shy schoolboy who has one night of mystical passion with a masked lady, his spiritual bride, and spends the rest of his life frustrated by the memory of that imaginative adventure turns Dunne's theory into living theater. The Dreaming Dust (1940), a play on Swift, almost makes us forget Yeats's Words Upon the Window-Pane. A troupe of actors, performing a masque of the Seven Deadly Sins in St. Patrick's Cathedral, begins to speculate on the relations of Swift and Stella, his beloved. Eventually, the question so overpowers the actors that each projects the sin he has portrayed in the masque onto Swift, and the play turns into an elegant and complex dissertation on psychology and human relationships. Each of Johnston's plays, though, has an interesting idea, and each is stylishly developed.

But it is a long way from the best of Johnston's plays, or the best of Irish drama in this period, to the norm. The Abbey, the Gate, and other theaters continued to do some good work during the 1930s, but the Irish dramatic movement was gradually falling apart. Two of the best playwrights, O'Casey and Carroll, were driven out of the Abbey; Johnston and Yeats seem rather peripheral figures in terms of what was regularly staged in the Dublin theaters. A few interesting playwrights, notably Michael J. Molloy, emerged in the 1940s, but, for all practical purposes, the life was gone out of Irish drama by the beginning of World War II. Literary historians have quarreled over who is to blame for that. Some would say it was simply bad luck. Others have argued that there was a general collapse in standards towards the end of the thirties. Ernest Blythe, the main force in the Abbey's management after the death of Yeats, is often portrayed as the villain. All of these explanations probably have some truth in them, but two impersonal forces also played their parts, conventionality and fear. The audiences who patronized the theaters liked conventional drama. Far better, they would say, a good farce by George Shiels or Brinsley MacNamara than O'Casey's harsh expressionism, Yeats's obscure poetry, or Johnston's complexities. The desire for the safe and the conventional played directly to the fear of innovation and controversy so common in the Ireland of the time. The managements, and too many of the playwrights, were fearful of driving audiences away, offending the Church, offending the state. The crowds came to the Abbey and some of the other theaters mostly to see the sorts of plays my Dublin friend described; the crowds, good, decent people wanting to be amused, played their part, too, in ending a great movement. Given the chance, the ordinary will almost always drive out the remarkable. Or, as Yeats put it, in a tantrum over *Look at the Heffernans!*, a play he hated, "Every country likes good art until it produces its own form of vulgarity and after that will have nothing else."

14 *Letters of W. B. Yeats*, p. 713.

11

COME BACK TO ERIN
Anglo-Irish Fiction, 1923–1940

> Our demons may be mischievous, but they are every-
> where admitted to be as upright and pure in their
> manner of living as demons can be. The chastity of
> the Irish demon is well known and everywhere admitted.
>
> Mervyn Wall, *The Unfortunate Fursey*

> 'A what?' the old woman asked.
> 'A peasant—we're all peasants, are we not?'
> 'Faith, I never knew that until you came across
> the ocean to tell us,' the old woman said
>
> Seumas O'Kelly, *Wet Clay*

IN 1922, when Ernest Boyd published the revised edition of his *Ireland's Literary Renaissance*, the first major study of modern Irish literature, he devoted only one of fifteen chapters to prose fiction. He called it the "weak side of the movement," observed that "the absence of good prose fiction is noticeable,"[1] and intimated that the real genius of Irish literature lay in drama and poetry. By the time he made that judgment, James Stephens and James Joyce had already published enough to belie it, but Boyd was not entirely wrong in seeing that modern Irish fiction had developed slowly. Poetry and drama had dominated public attention during the earlier phase of the Irish Renaissance, but the years after 1923 were not an especially rich time for either. Of course, a drama boasting an O'Casey or a poetry boasting a Yeats

---

[1] *Ireland's Literary Renaissance*, pp. 375–385.

was not exactly impoverished, but it is difficult to think of more than two or three names to put beside each in his genre as figures of outstanding accomplishment. In fiction, on the other hand, there was a small legion of writers of diverse and remarkable accomplishment. Joyce was the great name, but he hardly stood alone. He, Samuel Beckett, and Brian O'Nolan made an impressive trio of experimenters with language and perception. Frank O'Connor and Sean O'Faolain became real masters of the realistic short story with Mary Lavin and Michael McLaverty as worthy heirs to that tradition, while Liam O'Flaherty, a fine writer of short stories, produced a series of naturalistic novels of powerful obsession.

If we could make a "map" of Irish fiction in this period, it would depict a very complex creative geography, stretching from the mythic phantasmagoria of Joyce's *Finnegans Wake* to the exacting realism of the best of Frank O'Connor's stories. Yet certain things would be constant enough that we could begin to be able to understand the lay of the land. Disillusionment and disaffection would present themselves as repetitive themes. More precisely, we would find those themes dealt with frequently in terms of the three great problems of nineteenth and early twentieth-century Irish history: the Church, nationalism, and the land. All sorts of novels and stories, in many different modes and techniques, deal with the Church, its power especially in rural society, and the puritanical attitudes it helped create. The question of who will possess the land, not completely answered even after the final expulsion of the British from most of Ireland in the 1920s, expresses itself in several ways. It is found in the studies of the collapse of the Anglo-Irish Ascendancy, the conflicts of rural and urban values, and the difficulties of the adjustment of the peasantry to new political and social independence. In the fiction of this period, there is disillusionment with both Church and peasant society, two of the great shibboleths of Romantic nationalism, but there is even greater disillusionment with nationalism itself. There is an entire subgenre of fiction about the Civil War and how it destroyed the illusions of national virtue held over from the past. There is another subgenre of disaffection from the Ireland created after independence was mostly won, Socialist protests against a situation in which no ideal society was to be found, agrarian protests against an Ireland rapidly falling under the control of the urban bourgeoisie. And out of the trauma of nationalism and warfare comes, too, almost a kind of fantasy literature which sees history itself as nightmare.

It is tempting to describe the 1920s in Irish fiction as a decade in which naturalism and fantasy predominated and the 1930s as the decade of a more cautious realism, but that description is too neat and ignores too much. Nevertheless, naturalism and fantasy were too important subgenres in the twenties, perhaps partially because Ireland itself was then coming to from a long bout with nationalism and political hysteria. There was a real feeling of hangover in the air, a feeling that the new Ireland was dull and headachey, and there were some sharp disagreements over who was to blame. Naturalism and fantasy are both fictional modes which assume that the causes for the way things are lies outside ourselves; both are modes which tend to avoid personal responsibility. Naturalism blames the grim state of real life on forces beyond our control which impel us to be what we are. Fantasy assumes that the way things are and the way things could ideally be are both functions of impersonal forces, too, forces we may come to personify in supernatural creatures, but forces over which we have little or no control. Realism, on the other hand, demands a greater sense of personal responsibility. The writer of realistic fiction may depict a world which is very unpleasant, but the assumption is that things are as they are because we are as we are. Greed, for example, is not an impersonal force we cannot control but a part of our makeup which we can learn to deal with well or badly. Realism demands a degree of maturity, in reader or writer, beyond either fantasy or naturalism.

Whatever the reasons, Ireland in the 1920s produced some impressive writers of naturalistic fiction. Brinsley MacNamara was one, a writer with some very serious flaws but, at his best, able to create a compelling vision of the meanness of rural Ireland. Born John Weldon in County Westmeath in 1890, he was a member of the Abbey company from 1909 until 1912 and later wrote some of its most popular plays, including *Look at the Heffernans!* That comedy of intrigue turns on the efforts of the Heffernans to keep up their reputation, and the strongest of MacNamara's novels use a similar provincial setting and have a similar concern with provincial issues. *The Valley of Squinting Windows* (1918) is a portrayal of the power of gossip in what is really an agricultural slum, while *The Clanking of the Chains* (1920) is a grim exposure of the seamy side of Irish politics in the years before and during the "troubles." *The Clanking of the Chains* is a thin novel with clichéd characters and too much flat prose, but it is a good study of revolution and its decay which plays on one of the central themes of Irish fiction, the perversion of idealism and patriotism into yet another excuse for meanness and the continuation of shabby things as they are.

MacNamara's feel for the Irish midlands seems real enough, but Peader O'Donnell's feel for County Donegal is even more impressive. That strong local sense allies itself to a clear, hard prose in his best work, and O'Donnell was one of the ablest of the Irish naturalists of his time. His novels have had less attention than they deserve, partially because O'Donnell himself has been better known in Ireland as a political figure than as a writer. Born in Meenmore, County Donegal, in 1893, he spent some time as a teacher before becoming involved in Socialist and Nationalist organizational work. From 1920 through the years of the Civil War and for much later, he remained an important propagandist for the IRA, editor of *An t'Oglach*, the Army's illegal newspaper between 1924 and 1926, editor of *An Phoblacht*, its official organ, for eight years after that. O'Donnell broke with the IRA in 1934, but he remained an important left-wing organizer and propagandist, a supporter of the Republican side in the Spanish Civil War in the 1930s, an opponent of American involvement in Viet Nam in the 1960s. Through all this, though, he was an active man of letters, publishing several novels, having a play produced at the Abbey, and aiding Sean O'Faolain in the founding of *The Bell*, the best journal of literature and ideas in Ireland in the 1940s. When O'Faolain resigned as editor of *The Bell* in 1946, O'Donnell succeeded him, editing the journal until it ceased publication in 1954.

All of this would seem to leave little time for writing fiction, but between 1927 and 1930 O'Donnell produced three important novels, *Islanders* (1927), *Adrigoole* (1929), and *The Knife* (1930). These are not his only novels, for O'Donnell was always a prolific writer, but they are probably his best. *Islanders*, written while O'Donnell was an inmate of a Free State prison after the Civil War, is particularly successful in its handling of an entire family of characters and its evocation of life on the western seaboard of Ireland. *Adrigoole* is a study of the human effects of the Civil War. The poverty and pride of the Dalachs are important thematic threads in the book, as poverty and pride were central themes in *Islanders*, but the Dalachs' pride is not strong enough to sustain them in a time of political crisis. They harbor Republican soldiers during the Civil War, sacrificing more than they can afford in the process; when the war ends, they are ostracized by their neighbors and reduced to poverty. Hughie, desperate for some income, brews illegal whiskey, *poteen*, but is caught before he can sell it. Unable to pay the fine for his crime, he is jailed for a year, and during that time his family starves. The plot may seem melodramatic, though it is based on fact, but the novel impresses by its portrayal of decent people caught in something beyond their control. The bog around Adrigoole, malevolent and life-destroying as it seems to Hughie, becomes the governing symbol in the novel, and O'Donnell adroitly uses it to suggest all those impersonal forces—poverty, civil war, village bias, rural decay, a ponderous legal system—that eventually destroy his characters and their dreams. *The Knife* is also impressive in its control of naturalistic techniques, and many critics consider it O'Donnell's best novel. In it the eternal tension between Protestants and Catholics in Ulster functions as an overwhelming force, but the novel is somewhat weakened by obvious melodrama and diffuse characterization. *Adrigoole* in its sense of inevitability, its precise portrayal of Donegal peasant life, and its angry compassion stands as representative of the best of Peader O'Donnell's valuable fiction.

It was Liam O'Flaherty who urged his English publisher to consider *Adrigoole*, and that is appropriate in a way, for only O'Flaherty was O'Donnell's superior among the Irish naturalists. Of O'Flaherty's fourteen novels, *The Informer* (1925) remains the best known, largely thanks to John Ford's great film made a decade after its publication. O'Flaherty himself has chafed at the idea of being a "one book" writer, and justly so, by claiming that *The Informer* was nothing more than an exercise in writing a cheap thriller. But that is hardly fair to one of the most powerful novels of its time and one that comes very close indeed to the naturalistic ideal of exacting depiction of relentless external forces. *The Informer* opens in the seedy Dublin of flophouses and brothels just at the time the Civil War had deteriorated into a vicious vendetta over badly understood causes. Its central figure is Gypo Nolan, a huge, dull-witted brute who stumbles through the entire book with a kind of awesome power. Gypo and his friend, Frankie McPhillip, have been expelled from their revolutionary group because they have killed the secretary of a farmers' union. Desperate for money, Gypo tells the police of Frankie's whereabouts. Frankie is killed, and the remainder of the story hinges on Gypo's act of informing. Through the long history of thwarted rebellions, informing has become an unforgivable Irish sin. Gypo knows that, but the enormity of his act dawns on him only slowly. The reward for his informing on Frankie is £20, and much of the story is given over to Gypo's wild use of his Judas-money as he tries to use it to expiate his evil. As Gypo's former comrades search for him, our attention is shifted to their leader, Dan Gallagher, an embittered idealist obsessed by his self-defined role as a cog in the machinery of human history. Gypo, the uncomprehending brute, has a debased-Romantic sense of guilt and a Romantic desire for purposeless freedom; Gallagher, the hard semi-intellectual, has a debased-Romantic sense of history and a Romantic desire for purposeful action. Like Conrad's secret sharers, he and Gypo need each other because neither can achieve self-definition without what the other has to offer, but it is Gallagher who must track Gypo down and destroy him. Eventually Gypo is caught, and in a tremendous scene he breaks down under questioning. Sentenced to death, Gypo, Samson-like, breaks out of his cell to run amok in the streets. There he is shot by Gallagher's men, and he dies on the floor of a church, his arms outspread, begging forgiveness from Frankie McPhillip's mother.

The Informer has some very serious flaws. The contrast between Gypo and Gallagher is not adequately drawn, much of the action is crudely melodramatic, and there is an unnecessary subplot of Gallagher's romantic interest in McPhillip's sister. Yet for all its obvious flaws, *The Informer* is a compelling conception and something close to a great novel. Carl Jung once shrewdly observed that some fictions work not because of their artistry but because they seem to deal with the psychological fundamentals of our experience. In its evocation of archetypes, *The Informer* provides one of the basic myths of modern Ireland, powerful in its sense of urban decay and in its description of two figures who between them seem to sum up much of the experience of their time. The thriller, so often a worthless kind of novel, is turned to a profoundly disquieting purpose, and in that *The Informer* prefigures some later tales by Graham Greene and Albert Camus.

Readers of *The Informer* are sometimes put off by its melodrama, and the ending is, surely, a grotesque exaggeration in terms of our ordinary expectations about fiction. Nevertheless, melodrama and violence are essential parts of O'Flaherty's imagination. In an autobiography, he tells us about the first story he ever wrote, a school exercise done when he was only seven. It described a man who killed his wife because she brought him cold tea: "The problem of the story was the man's difficulty in getting the woman, who was very large, to fit into the fosse. The schoolmaster was horrified and thrashed me."[2] The schoolmaster had good reason to be horrified, but even at seven O'Flaherty was already dealing with some of the things that would be central to most of his mature fiction, a grotesque situation, random violence, the idea that a story must solve a "problem." O'Flaherty wrote that story growing up on the Aran Islands, and the fact of his Aran birth, in 1896, is also central to his imagination. The world of his childhood was not very far removed from the Aran Synge knew, and O'Flaherty later recalled, "I was born on a storm-swept rock and hate the soft growth of sunbaked lands where there is no frost in men's bones. Swift thoughts, and the swift flight of ravenous birds, and the squeal of

2 "Autobiographical Note" in *Ten Contemporaries: Second Series,* ed. John Gawsworth (London: Joiner and Steele, 1933), p. 16.

terror of hunted animals are to me a reality."[3] There was not much chance of escape from the round of poverty, hunger, and isolation that was Aran life then, but O'Flaherty was one of the lucky. A visiting priest persuaded him to prepare for the priesthood, and when he was twelve he left Aran for a junior seminary at Cashel in County Tipperary. An excellent student, he went on to Blackrock College and the Dublin diocesan seminary. By 1914, though, he was already beginning to doubt his religious vocation, and he had become involved in the nationalist movement. He left the seminary then to study medicine at University College, but soon quit that to fight with the British Army in France. Shellshocked in 1917, he then wandered for several years before returning to Dublin to participate in the Civil War on the Republican side. That participation was brief, but he and some others occupied the Four Courts in Dublin for a few days, and that was enough to give O'Flaherty the reputation of a dangerous Communist. Eventually, in 1922, he drifted on to London where he began to write, and there he met Edward Garnett, literary adviser to a publishing company and friend of Joseph Conrad and D. H. Lawrence. O'Flaherty published his first piece of creative work only in January of 1923, but later in the year he published his first novel, *Thy Neighbour's Wife*, and under Garnett's tutelage he rapidly became an extremely productive writer. In the fourteen years between 1923 and 1937 he published twelve novels, several collections of short stories, a biography of Timothy Healy, a guide to Ireland, two autobiographies, an account of a trip to Russia, and several incidental items.

The best of O'Flaherty's novels date from this period of almost manic activity, and at least six of them, including *The Informer*, deserve to rate among the best written by an Irishman in his time. *The Black Soul* (1924), O'Flaherty's first really successful novel and one he always took pride in, is the powerful story of the experiences of an emotionally distraught veteran of World War I who goes to the Aran Islands. The account of the Stranger's gradual coming to terms with himself through coming to terms with the raw nature of the islands and the islanders is an impressive psychological study, but the novel is particularly memorable for its lyrical evocation of the natural world and its almost Lawrentian account of the struggle between civilization and nature. *Mr. Gilhooley* (1926) is another study of a man in crisis, this time a retired civil engineer who seems to be sinking into the dregs until he meets Nelly, a young woman who represents for him the purity that he thought was gone out of the world. His discovery that Nelly is a complex human being, not merely a walking symbol of innocence, leads Gilhooley to

[3] Quoted in Paul A. Doyle, *Liam O'Flaherty* (New York: Twayne, 1971), p. 8.

murder her, and it is that act which brings him to see the absolute emptiness of his life. William Troy used the phrase, "melodrama of the soul," to describe O'Flaherty's fiction, and the action in each of these novels is indeed melodramatic.[4] The attentive reader will see that for O'Flaherty melodramatic action is a means of depicting individual emptiness and frustration as well as a means of portraying extreme personal conflict. *The Puritan* (1931) is an especially intense study in personal conflict. Francis Ferriter believes himself to be a chosen weapon for attacking the evils of sensuality, and he eventually murders a prostitute in an excess of puritanical zeal, an action which then drives him into extreme humanistic atheism. *Skerrett* (1932) is the more satisfying story of a schoolmaster on the Aran Islands who, during the years between 1887 and 1902, finds himself in conflict with the parish priest and the society around him. O'Flaherty intended in *The Puritan* and *Skerrett* to argue his own theory of human evolution, a theory which holds that man must move beyond the impersonal forces controlling him by intense, self-defining action to reach the freedom that exists far beyond personal self-obsession and despair. The theory itself is valuable, and makes O'Flaherty almost an existentialist novelist long before existentialism developed as a popular philosophy, but the novels are marred by outrageous melodrama and moral judgments as intense as they are obvious. In all of these novels, as in so much of O'Flaherty's work, one feels a powerful imagination but a failure of technique to sustain fully the imaginative vision. In that sense, he is almost reminiscent of William Carleton a century before, another writer who knew the people he described intimately but often seemed to fail somewhere between the vision and the expression.

The same complaint could be made about *Famine* (1937), but there is also reason to argue that it is O'Flaherty's strongest novel, in spite of its very severe problems. On the debit side are a failure really to master the techniques of historical fiction (*Famine* is an account of the great famine of the 1840s in a small village in the west of Ireland), some absurdly melodramatic sequences, and too much anticlericalism. But this comes close to being a great novel, and Sean O'Faolain was hardly exaggerating when he called it an "almost Biblical" novel, an "Irish Exodus in which there is no Moses to lead out the people of Israel."[5] The novel has the power and the sweep of the Biblical narrative, allied to a moral vision reminiscent of the great Hebrew prophets, Amos in particular.

4 See "The Position of Liam O'Flaherty," *The Bookman*, LXIX (March, 1929), 7–11.
5 Quoted in Doyle, *O'Flaherty*, p. 106.

I remember the first time I read this novel, starting it late one night, intending to read only a few chapters before going to sleep. At four in the morning, bleary-eyed, I stumbled off to bed profoundly moved and disturbed by a book I could not put down. The novel argues out some of O'Flaherty's private theories, and we are asked to sympathize with Mary Kilmartin, the young wife who desperately tries to find means of survival in even the worst situations, but the most moving figure in the book is her father-in-law, old Brian Kilmartin. Passionately devoted to his land, doggedly willing to accept hunger and tribulation he cannot really account for, Brian is one of the great images of the Irish peasant, as much as archetype of his kind as Gypo and Gallagher were of theirs. Yet the book is full of archetypal figures: Chadwick the insatiable landlord's agent, Hynes the merchant more than willing to turn others' sufferings to his profit, Father Geelan the prorevolutionary curate crushed between his people's needs and his superiors' commands. None of these characters, though, is quite as memorable as the famine itself, a natural disaster man cannot explain or control. In no other of his novels does O'Flaherty quite match the conflict presented here between archetypal characters and a vast, impersonal force. We feel that all the way through the novel, nowhere more strongly than in the scene late in the book when a cloud of pestilence moves over the Valley to destroy another year's potato crop after the first season of hunger and suffering. The scene is described in spare, chiseled prose, but that is one of the great strengths of the novel all the way through; almost always O'Flaherty gives us prose of a hardness and rightness that Hemingway would have envied. In spite of some weaknesses, *Famine* seems O'Flaherty's finest work, right and true in the way that only great works of art are.

O'Flaherty was not just a strong novelist; he was also a major writer of short stories, and the finest of them have the same sense of absolute truthfulness that informs his best novels. His best stories are mostly found in his first three volumes, *Spring Sowing* (1924), *The Tent* (1926), and *The Mountain Tavern* (1929). In such stories as "The Cow's Death" and "The Hawk," O'Flaherty writes some of the finest animal stories of our century, and one feels a constant sympathy on his part with unspeaking nature. Many of the other stories are about peasants. Some are marred by melodramatic sequences that simply will not work in so small a form as the short story, and in others the ironies are heavy-handed. Yet others have an earthy gravity that befits their subjects. Like Conrad, O'Flaherty is determined to make us *see*, and Vivian Mercier has rightly observed that O'Flaherty, a native speaker of Gaelic, gives us surprisingly little sense of a speaking voice in his stories.[6] "Spring Sowing," for example, is a remarkable tale of the eternal ritual of farm life and full of subtle nuances, but essentially it is visual in its technique. The narration is impersonal and concrete; what the characters say is considerably less important than what we are made to see about them and their actions. Animals and peasants, often observed with a Wordsworthian sympathy for the interrelationships of man and nature, bring out the best in O'Flaherty. In these stories, as in some sequences in his novels, O'Flaherty depicts almost static action, and that mastery of meaningful stasis relates his work to one of the central qualities in the best of Irish writing.

Nevertheless, O'Flaherty's fiction is exceedingly uneven. Much of his work after 1937 was disappointing; the two big historical novels that followed *Famine* and were intended to make up a trilogy with it, *Land* (1946) and *Insurrection* (1950), were both unsatisfactory successors to that earlier masterpiece. By the mid-1950s O'Flaherty had virtually ceased to write, and it seemed evident that he had said what he had to say twenty or even thirty years before. Much of his work is frustrating because one feels that it ought to be so much better than it is. The imagination behind it often seems the most powerful in Irish fiction with the exception of Joyce, but the execution could sometimes be improved by almost any competent hack. Yet even as we mutter about his faults, we still remember that cast of obsessed characters he created: Gypo Nolan, Francis Ferriter, Mr. Gilhooley, Brian Kilmartin. They, together with the suffering animals and the silent peasants of the short stories, define the world of his fiction, and it is an important and serious world. Judged by the highest standards, O'Flaherty seems a distinctly lesser writer than, say, Dostoyevsky, but the very fact that it is possible to speak of the two of them together is a sign of his enduring value and even his approach to greatness.

The speaking voice that is usually absent from O'Flaherty's peasant stories can be found in some other books from this period, especially a remarkable trio of autobiographies by three natives of the Blasket Islands who were, like O'Flaherty, originally Gaelic speakers. The Blaskets, rocks in the sea off the Dingle Peninsula in County Kerry, are abandoned now, but fifty years ago they were still an outpost of Gaelic peasant culture. Tomas Ó Criomhtain's autobiography, *An tOileánach* (1929), was the first reminiscence of life on the Blaskets, and, to a certain extent, it set the model for the subsequent autobiographies of Maurice O'Sullivan, *Twenty Years A-Growing* (1933) and Peig

6 "The Irish Short Story and Oral Tradition," *The Celtic Cross*, ed. Ray B. Browne, William J. Roscelli, and Richard Loftus (Lafayette, Ind.: Purdue Univ. Studies, 1964), p. 105.

Sayers, *Peig* (1936). These books were one way of keeping a hold on the Gaelic past, but an entire peasant culture, English-speaking as well as Gaelic, was dying in Ireland in the twenties and thirties. Government efforts to save it and the Gaelic language were not really successful, partially because "official" Ireland wanted to save its idealization of peasant life rather than the real thing. The *reductio ad absurdum* of official and semiofficial attempts to deny the vitality of peasant life while praising what seem almost its shabby-genteel virtues came in 1942 with the publication of Eric Cross's *The Tailor and Ansty*. Cross was a young Englishman who recorded in that book his friendship with two great characters, the Tailor of Gougane Barra in County Cork and his wife, Anastasia. The Tailor was one of those natural philosophers, shrewd, wise, and bawdy; his wife was a warm-hearted, crafty scold. Cross's version of their conversation is full of the Tailor's earthy wisdom and Ansty's cackling commentaries on him and his ideas. But the censorship board found the book indecent, and the old people were assaulted by self-appointed defenders of the public morality. The book Eric Cross made about them is one of the best records we have of a peasant life now almost lost; genteel and pious Ireland's attack on them and their book was a painful indicator of how the country was forgetting its own virile, laughing heritage.

The Tailor and Ansty were victims of a specious gentility in the Ireland of their times, and perhaps it is not surprising that some writers of fiction took up the old weapon of Swift, satiric fantasy, to attack the new mediocrity that was becoming the norm in Irish public life after independence. Eimar O'Duffy had little of Swift's genius, but *King Goshawk and the Birds* (1926) was an effective attack on capitalism and urban gentility. Like all the best writers of Irish fantasy, O'Duffy gloried in verbal invention, and the book seems funnier now for that than for its actual satire, though there is a fine passage when Cuchulain, of all people, joins a tennis club in the suburbs. Lord Dunsany's *The Curse of the Wise Woman* (1933) was closer to conventional fantasy, and especially effective in its hunting scenes, but the novel turned on the conflict between Marlin, the peasant "wise woman" and the developers who want to exploit her beloved bog for financial profit. Much of the fantasy writing in this period had less overtly to do with political or social problems than these two books. Through the 1920s, James Stephens continued, too, his series of fantasies, of which *In the Land of Youth* (1924), a retelling of some tales from the ancient mythological cycle, is perhaps the most important. There are elements of fantasy, too, in Stephens' collection of short stories, *Etched in Moonlight* (1928), tales dealing with the encounter of the ordinary and the supernatural in everyday life. These are for the most part cruel stories, reminiscent of the tales the Philosopher hears in prison in *The Crock of Gold*, and they remind us that cruelty and whimsy are often more closely related than we like to admit.

The great fantasy of the period, though, was Joyce's *Finnegans Wake*, the work which occupied almost all his creative energy from the publication of *Ulysses* in 1922 until his death in 1941. It was, his wife Norah used to insist, the "big book," and thirty-five years and more after its publication it remains the great unread masterpiece of twentieth-century literature, terrifying in its complexity but tantalizing in its imaginative vision. The *Wake* took so long to write for two simple reasons, Joyce was going beyond any previous notions of fiction, and it was the work of an almost-blind man. Moreover his always complicated private life kept interfering with what was hopefully called during its process of composition, "Work in Progress." Family matters, especially the increasing madness of his daughter, quixotic projects like pushing the career of an ugly-voiced Irish tenor, and legal squabbles over *Ulysses* all interfered with the writing. Bits from the narrative appeared in *transition*, a little magazine, and some pamphlets published by Faber and Faber in London, but it took seventeen years to bring *Finnegans Wake* to completion. And before it was finally published, Joyce had carried the manuscript through revision after revision, regularly making what was already a complex work even more complex.

Although a few critics have tried to assure us that *Finnegans Wake* is really quite an easy book once you get the hang of it, there is no point in trying to wish away its difficulty. The language itself is intensely allusive and full of verbal jokes and extravagances; it helps if you have read everything Joyce read and are a congenital punster, but even that may not be enough. Essentially, *Finnegans Wake* is a dream, and like all meaningful dreams it is a complex blend of the trivial and the archetypal in which demonstrable significance is probably less important than total effect. It is, in one sense, a history of the human race based on the cyclical theory of history Joyce found in the writings of the eighteenth-century Neapolitan sociologist, Gianbattista Vico. Vico saw human history moving through four inevitable phases—the divine, the heroic, the human, and the chaotic which leads to the return of the first phase—and the four sections of *Finnegans Wake* reflect these four phases with the last sentence of the book being the beginning of its first sentence as a way to remind us of the inevitable repetitions of the cycle. To Vico's theory of perpetual repetition, Joyce has added the notion of dualism derived from the Renaissance philosopher, Giordano Bruno. Thus while the movement of the book is cyclical, the characters regularly appear in pairs and as dualistic projections of themselves. The central figure is a pubkeeper usually called H. C. Earwicker who also appears under a number of other guises—Oliver Cromwell, the Duke of Wellington, a big salmon in the River Liffey, Finn MacCool, and God the Father, among others—all projections of his essential characteristic as fathering male. His wife, Anna Livia Plurabelle, is also Eve, Lilith, the Liffey, Mrs. Noah, and several other projections of the all-mothering female. Their children are projections of themselves. The daughter, Isolde, is watered-down Anna Livia; their sons, Shaun and Shem, are man as commonsense go-ahead and impractical artist.

The plot, though that hardly seems the right word for it, begins with a retelling of the Irish-American ballad, "Finnegan's Wake," the story of a surprise resurrection from the dead which gives the fiction its title. That moves us into some stories about H. C. Earwicker (his surname refers to a nocturnal insect; his initials, H.C.E., easily turn into "Haveth Childers Everywhere"), the episode of Anna Livia as Belinda the hen trying to understand a letter from Boston, and then the lyrical evocation of the Liffey, put into the mouths of two washerwomen, with which this section concludes. This presentation of the "divine" stage of human history, man as myth and mythmaker, is followed by a presentation of the "heroic" in the squabbles of Shem and Shaun, mock-heroic entertainments and discussions in Earwicker's pub, and Earwicker's dream of sailing the high seas accompanied by four figures who seem very much like the evangelists of the New Testament. The heroic moves to the merely human, and we see the decay and collapse of Shaun the pillar of social order in his parable of the "Ondt and the Gracehopper," his sermon (Shaun is now Jaun, a "liverish" lover) to some schoolgirls which is full of idiotic sententiousness, and his final transmogrification into a yawn. After a dreamy interruption in the dream, we move finally into an episode of confusion and re-creation, ending with Anna Livia Plurabelle's final monologue. Dream stuff that, and more dream stuff in Joyce's kaleidoscopic language as puns, realignments, and repetitions converge to delight and infuriate the reader.

Finnegans Wake is the most audacious fiction in the English language, and it is the sort of work about which there can be no middle view. One either loves it and wades into it rejoicing or wants to have nothing to do with it. Conservative readers, raised to understand "fiction" as meaning Austen, Balzac, Dickens will probably think it ought to be labeled with the warning, "Abandon hope, all ye who enter here." Other readers find in it a life-affirming richness and a profound myth of contemporary experience. As Robert Adams says,

"*Finnegans Wake* answers to and expresses a fundamental bind in the modern consciousness, which, in becoming infinitely deep, complex, and cosmopolitan, has only shackled itself more terribly to the sense of universal meaningless-ness."[7] Indeed, and yet a nagging little voice keeps asking, "If the work is so central to our experience, why do we not read it?" That, perhaps, is the funda-mental difficulty with the *Wake*, its privacy to Joyce himself—and thus its seeming impenetrability—is as great as its potential universality. One could argue that, metaphorically at least, the *Wake* is the most Irish of all of Joyce's books; not Irish as a portrayal of literal reality, but Irish in its mythic con-sciousness, its sense of history, its sense of the ebb and flow of personality.

The publication of the *Wake* marked the effective end of Joyce's career as a writer; he began no new work, and two years after it appeared in finished form he was dead. With Joyce, as with Yeats, there is the feeling, though, that death was not an interruption but a logical termination. By the time of his death in 1941, his fame as the greatest writer of fiction in English of the first half of the century was secure, and one wonders if there was anywhere for him to go creatively after the *Wake*. His lasting achievement was remarkable. More than sixty years after its publication, *Dubliners* still seems the finest col-lection of short stories in our language; *Portrait* remains, for every new genera-tion, a remarkable novel of self-discovery. *Finnegan's Wake* continues to baffle and obsess its readers, and whole new ways of understanding fiction have had to be created to cope with it. Yet if all his other books were lost, *Ulysses* would be enough to guarantee Joyce's lasting reputation. Even more of an innovation in many ways than *Finnegans Wake*, more exact in its realism than *Dubliners*, more thorough in its range of symbolism than *Portrait*, *Ulysses* has one quality all other books seem to lack, a quality Joyce himself had in a double measure—humanity. In all his fiction, but especially in *Ulysses*, Joyce turns Ireland and some ordinary Irish men and women into living symbols of all our experiences. His fictional world, fuller, more real than the world of our ordinary experience, enriches us and makes us more fully human. There is no more an artist can do.

Joyce's contemporary, Yeats, so towered over Irish poetry in his time that most other Irish poets became his disciples and imitators, and died creatively for their trouble. Joyce had no real disciples in Ireland; he was unique, and there could be no imitation. Yet his innovations with language and perception point us toward the work of two other Irish writers of fiction, Samuel Beckett and Brian O'Nolan; one, like Joyce, an exile who even more than Joyce belongs to "inter-

---

7 *James Joyce: Common Sense and Beyond* (New York: Random House, 1966), pp. 215–16.

national" literature rather than Irish, the other so utterly Irish that his work
has never exported well. It is often said that Beckett was Joyce's secretary, and
some literary historians have tried to use that to draw close connections between
the two. In fact, this is not true; Beckett, like many others who knew Joyce
while he was writing *Finnegans Wake*, read for the nearly blind master, and
he translated one part of the *Wake* into French. There are characteristics
Beckett and Joyce have in common, an obsession with the processes of time, a
sense of individual guilt, an impatience with the traditional forms of literary
discourse, a remarkable ability to create complex "high art" out of the detritus
of popular culture. But there is an exactness, an aridity, and a judgmental
attitude in most of Beckett's work that sharply delineate him from the Joyce of
Ulysses and the *Wake*. Hugh Kenner, one of Beckett's ablest critics, describes
him as "a unique moral figure" and "a cultivator of what will grow in the waste
land, who can make us see the exhilarating design that thorns and yucca share
with whatever will grow anywhere."[8] The moral authority and the significant
innovations with literary form and perception have made Beckett one of the
most important figures in modern literature, but it is characteristic of his position vis-à-vis Irish literature that at least one Dublin newspaper found that it
had no information on him in its files when the news came in 1969 that he had
joined Yeats and Shaw as one of the Irish-born winners of the Nobel Prize for
Literature.

In a way, though, that is entirely understandable. Beckett had left Ireland
in 1932, when he was twenty-six, returning only for occasional visits. Although one of his most important novels, *Watt* (1953), was finished in Dublin
and his first collection of stories, *More Pricks Than Kicks* (1934) had been
written about a Trinity College student, Beckett is an Irish writer only by birth.
Born into a well-off Protestant family in Foxrock, near Dublin, in 1906, he took
his B.A. at Trinity College in 1928 and later spent four terms as a lecturer in
French there. Most of his important work has been published in both French
and English and, as in his most famous play, *Waiting for Godot* (1952), his
imaginative landscape is some desolate place inside ourselves, neither French nor
English nor Irish. Nevertheless, *More Pricks Than Kicks* is a distinctively Irish
work, Irish in its setting, but Irish, too, in its concern with ennui and stasis. The
central figure in the stories, Belacqua Shuah, moves through a trivialized Dublin
Stephen Dedalus would have understood, and Belacqua is clearly the prototype
for Beckett's long list of spiritually immobilized, inert figures. *More Pricks Than*

---

[8] *A Reader's Guide to Samuel Beckett* (New York: Farrar, Strauss, and Giroux, 1973), p. 194.

Kicks is not, to be honest, a very successful volume; most of the stories are too imitative of Joyce, and, in view of Beckett's later career, the entire volume is obviously 'prentice work. Nevertheless, one story, "Dante and the Lobster" achieves real greatness in its description of a world of random and meaningless actions. It leads up to its superb conclusion as Belacqua's aunt prepares to boil a lobster alive:

> She lifted the lobster clear of the table. It had
> about thirty seconds to live.
> Well, thought Belacqua, it's a quick death, God help
> us all.
> It is not.[9]

That, as Yeats said of *Ulysses*, has the Irish cruelty and the Irish feline grace.

There is even more feline grace in the works of Brian O'Nolan. O'Nolan's novels deal in multiple layers of perception, and so it is appropriate that he himself is known under three names. Born Brian O'Nolan, he became Flann O'Brien for his novels and Myles na Gopaleen for his brilliant series of essays in the *Irish Times*. O'Nolan's own life was as unremarkable on the surface as that of many of his characters. He was born in Strabane in 1912, educated at University College, Dublin, and employed as a civil servant in the Irish government. He published his first novel, *At Swim-Two-Birds* (the title is a literal translation of a Gaelic place name) in 1939. It sank almost without a trace. In 1941 he published a second novel, this time in Gaelic, *An Béal Bocht*. Later, he began writing a column in the *Irish Times*, "Cruiskeen Lawn," but until 1960 it was almost an Irish secret that *At Swim-Two-Birds* was one of the great comic novels of the century. It was reissued in that year, and the enthusiasm for his work it created then led him to publish three more novels, *The Hard Life* (1961), *The Dalkey Archive* (1964), and *The Third Policeman* (1967), the last coming out after his death in 1966. An unremarkable life, then, but as O'Nolan's novels regularly remind us, glorious craziness always lies just below the surface of the unremarkable.

All of O'Nolan's work could be described as a series of brilliant farragoes of distinctly Irish experience. Like Joyce, he was a great parodist and punster, the sort of writer whose parodies are so good that they send you back to the original and whose puns are so outrageous that you quickly come to hate their

---

9 *More Pricks than Kicks* (London: Chatto and Windus, 1934), p. 20.

author out of sheer jealousy. The columns for the *Irish Times*, collected by his brother Kevin as *The Best of Myles* (1968) are consistently acute in their delineations of the foibles and idiocies of Irish life; they are also absurdly funny. A constant critic of the narrowmindedness of the Gaelic movement but a fluent writer of the language, O'Nolan printed one column in Gaelic using the Greek alphabet. The puns turn up constantly, especially in the anecdotes about two pranksters, Keats and Chapman; there is, one tells the other, when he finds himself in charge of some performing bears which he proceeds to anesthetize, "safety in numb bears." *An Béal Bocht*, O'Nolan's second novel (translated into English as *The Poor Mouth*, 1973), is the finest of his parodies, a hilarious send-up of the autobiography of the Gaelic-speaking innocent. O'Nolan tells us the "pathetic" tale of Bonaparte O'Coonassa whose "autobiography" is well summarized as "a bad story about the hard life." From the very beginning O'Nolan maintains exactly the right tone of the naive narrator: "I cannot truly remember either the day I was born or the first six months I spent here in the world. Doubtless, however, I was alive at that time although I have no memory of it, because I should not exist now if I were not then and to the human being, as well as to every other living creature, sense comes gradually."[10] The story is full of absurd incidents including a disastrous first day at school and a ridiculous Gaelic *feis*, and we quickly note that in addition to parodying the tone and form of the naive Gaelic autobiography, O'Nolan is also having wonderful fun taking pot shots at some of the sacred cows of the Gaelic language movement.

This superb parody is, however, the slightest of O'Nolan's novels. *The Third Policeman*, written in the 1940s but not published until 1967, is just as full of parody, especially of scholars' quarrels over the meaning of the work of the great thinker and theoretician, De Selby, the creator of a remarkable number of fatuous ideas. The novel itself focuses on a murder and its consequences, and it is typical of O'Nolan's work that two such disparate elements should go together to make a very funny book. *The Hard Life* is almost Swiftian in its satire on ecclesiastics, madcap inventors, and social improvers (one character wants to install ladies' urinals in Dublin and goes to see the Pope about it), while one of the characters of *The Dalkey Archive* is James Joyce, a pious barman who writes tracts for the Catholic Truth Society and insists that *Ulysses* was put together by a crowd of pimps and ruffians in Paris. This sort of inspired nuttiness keeps all the novels going, but *At Swim-Two-Birds*, O'Nolan's first

---

10 *The Poor Mouth*, trans. Patrick C. Power (1973; London: Pan Books, 1975), p. 11.

novel remains his most enduring achievement. It owes, for its structural strategies and verbal tricks, a good deal to the Joyce of *Finnegans Wake*, and Joyce himself praised it as "a really funny book," while Dylan Thomas said it was "just the book to give to your sister, if she is a dirty, boozy girl."[11]

The plot of *At Swim-Two-Birds* defies any summary, but it runs something like this. A narrator (we never know his name) is writing a book about a writer named Dermot Trellis who is writing a book, too. The characters in Trellis' novel are desperately anxious to be left alone by their creator, and so do what they can to keep him asleep as much as possible. During one of his few periods of wakefulness, Trellis creates a female character, Sheila Lamont, with whom he then falls in love. He seduces her, and the birth of their child, Orlick Trellis, provides an opportunity to bring two more characters into the story, the Good Fairy and the pooka, MacPhellimey. Sheila Lamont's father is Finn MacCool, and the plot thickens, if that is the word for it, when another of Trellis' characters, Shanahan, introduces two cowboys, left over from some western stories a former employee of Shanahan's once wrote. Eventually, the characters in Trellis' book get Orlick Trellis, who is something of a writer, to produce a counterstory as an act of revenge against their creator. In this story, Dermot Trellis is brought to trial for his manifold evils before a court made up of minor characters from his own work. Eventually, there is a sort of resolution to all this, but long before the end we realize that O'Nolan is doing a good deal more than pulling his reader's legs with a vengeance. For all its hysterical humor, *At Swim-Two-Birds* is a serious and even profound commentary on the nature of fiction. Fiction is, well, fiction, but truth too, and more than truth. As Lorna Sage writes of this novel, its author "distrusts absolutely the timid, prurient pieties of home, but he cannot believe in the literary orthodoxy (which says that the writer re-creates his world) either. Inertia is the answer. The changeless unreason in people seems to him awfully true, the truest thing about them."[12]

The sense of inertia is a theme O'Nolan and Beckett share with several other novelists. The theme has been one of the major ones in modern fiction in general, and it has frequently been expressed through the tradition of psychological analysis derived in the English novel from Henry James. But Jamesian analysis has found few practitioners in Ireland. An honorable exception in this period was Elizabeth Bowen, one of the finest of James' heirs. Born into an old

---

[11] Quoted on the dust jacket of *At Swim-Two-Birds* (1939; Harmondsworth, Middlesex: Penguin, 1967).

[12] "Flann O'Brien," *Two Decades of Irish Writing*, ed. Douglas Dunn (Cheadle, Cheshire: Carcanet Books, 1975), p. 201.

Ascendancy family, she was an acute critic of the Anglo-Irish, a class she liked to describe as being like only children, alone, independent, and secretive. But only one of her superb novels, *The Last September* (1929), deals directly with the Anglo-Irish experience, and even in it the "big house" setting is used primarily as background for the story of her young heroine, Elizabeth Farquar. Elizabeth, waiting for her own personal life to begin during the time of the Anglo-Irish War, is a working out of what Edwin Kenney in his study of Bowen has called "the recurrent theme" of her fiction, "man's primary need for an illusion, an image of himself, in order for him to be."[13] *The Last September* is, technically, an extremely fine novel, and it is always a pleasure to encounter in Bowen's fiction the workings of a shrewd and penetrating mind. Joyce Cary, an Anglo-Irishman from Derry and like Bowen one of the really distinguished novelists of his time, wrote two novels about Ireland, *Castle Corner* (1938) and *A House of Children* (1941). Both are valuable for their portrayals of the life of his class, but neither is among his best work. The presence of these novels by Bowen and Cary raises the question of why there is so little Ascendancy fiction of real merit from the last fifty years. The decay of Anglo-Irish life could, it seems, have provided the material for fine work, but the novels were never written.

On the other hand, the novels of Francis Stuart provide some indication of what a disillusioned and thoroughly modern Catholic mind could do in the Irish situation. In his life and work, Stuart is a characteristic modern man of the kind Arthur Koestler or Camus could understand, but perhaps not of the kind ordinary Ireland can. Born in Australia in 1902, he came to Ireland as a child, married Maud Gonne's daughter, Iseult, in 1920, fought on the Republican side in the Civil War, and, after it was over, settled in County Wicklow. There he devoted himself largely to writing, while fighting off a series of psychological crises. In 1940 he left Ireland to teach modern English and Irish literature in Berlin, and it was there that he spent the war, officially as a neutral, though the French thought he had collaborated enough with the Germans to imprison him for several months after the war ended. Long separated from his wife, he spent many years in Paris and London before returning to Ireland in 1958. That brief biography sounds almost like the synopsis of a novel on the condition of the modern writer-intellectual, and Stuart has turned his story into a powerful autobiographical fiction, *Black List, Section H* (1971). That is probably his finest work, though *The Pillar of Cloud* (1948), a parable of the human spirit's

---

[13] *Elizabeth Bowen* (Lewisburg, Pa.: Bucknell University Press, 1975), p. 18.

ability to survive and find meaning in the midst of chaos, is also impressive. Of Stuart's overtly Irish novels, two published in 1932 are especially interesting, *Pigeon Irish* and *The Coloured Dome*. Both seem characteristic works of their period now—intense, probably overwritten, but, like Aldous Huxley's novels, effective as arguments of important theses about life in their time. Both novels have obvious flaws; as with O'Flaherty, there seems to be a gap between Stuart's conceptions and his execution, and the conceptions themselves are of a lesser order. Nevertheless, he is an interesting figure, one of the few Irish novelists of his time to be able to sustain a convincing novel of ideas in the Continental mode.

Stuart's parables, like Bowen's psychological analyses, really stand outside the mainstream of Irish fiction in the period. It could be argued that naturalism and verbal experimentation have been the major modes of modern Irish fiction, but that argument would be satisfactory only for dealing with novels. And, to be honest, the novel is not a form that has been practiced with any more than sporadic success in Ireland. Many reasons could be brought forth to explain the shortage of good Irish novels: the lack of a clearly defined class system, something that almost always strengthens English fiction; the conservatism and rigidity of Irish society; the lack, in postrevolutionary Ireland, of any really compelling and big themes. Whatever the reasons, the novels are in short supply, but the short stories are there in abundance. The old tradition of oral storytelling supports short fiction. So, too, does the fact that the realistic short story has always been an effective way of dealing with rural and small-town life, and Ireland has plenty of both. Moreover, the realistic story offers an artist the opportunity to illuminate the significance of the ordinary, and that often seems a special genius of the Irish writer. Frank O'Connor sums up the situation of the Irish short-story writer of his generation by saying of his own stories: "They describe for the first time the Irish middleclass Catholic way of life with its virtues and its faults without any of the picturesqueness of earlier Irish writing which concentrated on colour and extravagance. The latter was the work of romantics acting on a supercharged nationalism. These little stories, I feel, came out of a nationalism that had achieved its result and was ready to look at everyday things with a new respect."[14]

O'Connor has been dead for ten years now, and perhaps his reputation is suffering some of that decline that almost always affects a writer's work after his death. Nevertheless, his fame as one of the masters of the realistic short

---

[14] *Stories by Frank O'Connor* (New York: Vintage, 1956), pp. vii–viii.

story seems more than likely to endure. "My Oedipus Complex," a story from fairly late in O'Connor's career, gives us some indication of his worth. It is the disarmingly simple tale of a child's view of his parents. Father has been away in the army almost since the time Larry was born, and, like a good boy, Larry has been praying for his safe return. "Little, indeed, did I know what I was praying for!" he tells us, and soon we learn why. When Father returns, he becomes the obnoxious intruder in Larry's life with Mother: Larry must be quiet while Mother is "talking to Daddy"; Larry must be quiet in the morning so as not to wake Daddy; Daddy seems to always be asleep in what used to be only Mummy's bed just when Larry needs conversation and a good snuggle. Larry prays for God to take Father back to the war, but Mother explains that God does not make wars, bad people do, and Larry feels that "God wasn't quite what he was cracked up to be." Father and Larry eventually become avowed enemies, both fighting for Mother's attention. To Larry's great pleasure, a new baby, Sonny, comes along. Larry has wanted that, and it satisfies him immensely that Mother still pays some attention to his wishes. But, as Larry explains, Sonny was a calamity: "Mother was simply silly about him, and couldn't see when he was only showing off. As company he was worse than useless. He slept all day, and I had to go round the house on tiptoe to avoid waking him. It wasn't any longer a question of not waking Father. The slogan now was 'Don't-wake-Sonny!' " One day, while playing trains in the front garden, Larry simply explodes with a solemn warning to Father, "If another bloody baby comes into this house, I'm going out." But Father, it turns out, is not so enthusiastic about Sonny either. One morning Larry awakes to find Sonny howling in the next room and Father in his bed, "wide awake, breathing hard and apparently mad as hell." It dawns on Larry that now it is Father's turn: "After turning me out of the big bed, he had been turned out himself. Mother had no consideration now for anyone but that poisonous pup, Sonny." Larry soothes Father, tells him to put his arm around him ("He was very bony but better than nothing"), and the story ends with the marvelous final line, "At Christmas he went out of his way to buy me a really nice model railway."[15]

One could say that the story is only slight whimsy, but it is hardly that, for it is really a masterpiece of the storyteller's craft. O'Connor gives us the perceptions of a small child filtered through the language of an adult, but the fact that we never doubt the reality of Larry's experience is one of the story's achievements. Another is its exact control of implication. The point of view is

15 Jbid., pp. 249–62.

that of a child; the implications are far-reaching. The story is called "My Oedipus Conflict," after all, and it is about a profound psychological experience. But there are no profundities to mar the control of surface, only some spare details and a crystalline prose style. The mixture of innocence, honesty, and a wry sense of human limitation that underlies this story is characteristic of O'Connor at his best. So is the exactly right prose and the deft manner. O'Connor was one of the great modern masters of English prose style, but he never insists on it. "Less is more" could have been his motto, as it could have been the motto of Mozart or Jane Austen, two artists he admired.

There is a slight touch of autobiography in "My Oedipus Complex," and it is not surprising that O'Connor wrote one of the finest of all Irish autobiographies, *An Only Child* (1961). Like "My Oedipus Complex," it deals with deep emotions and experiences, but it is masterful in its tonal control. Beginning with historical fact, "I was born in 1903 when we were living in Douglas Street, Cork, over a small sweet-and-tobacco shop kept by a middle-aged lady called Wall,"[16] it moves quickly to the imaginative re-creation of memory. Frank O'Connor was born Michael O'Donovan (he took the other name only when he began to write), and we see the boy growing up between the powerful personalities of his parents. Minnie O'Connor O'Donovan was a gentle, patient woman whose happiest memories were of the orphanage in which she grew up and the well-to-do-house in which she worked before she met her husband. Michael O'Donovan, Frank O'Connor's father, was an ex-soldier, hard-drinking, passionate, usually out of work. "One of the things," their son tells us, "I have inherited from my mother's side of the family is a passion for gaiety. I do not have it myself—I seem to take after my father's family, which is brooding, melancholy, and violent—but I love gay people and books and music."[17] Books and music early become a world of very real fantasy for him, part of his mother's unselfconscious program for making her son something more than yet another poor boy in a provincial city. They are his secret life, especially after he leaves school for a series of menial jobs. Daniel Corkery, who had once been his schoolmaster, becomes a supporting friend. Gradually, the outside world closes in, the world of nationalism, politics, and civil war. A Republican in the Civil War because Corkery was, O'Connor soon finds himself the censor of the local newspaper and before long the prisoner of the Free State army. After nearly a year in internment, he is released when the war ends, free to return to Cork to his mother's greeting, "It has made a man of you." It had, and the autobiography ends with Michael O'Donovan a man,

16 *An Only Child* (1961; London: Pan Books, 1970), p. 9.
17 *Ibid.*, p. 11.

disillusioned, uncertain about himself, adult. This is, of course, a "portrait of the artist as a young man," but it has little of the aching intensity of Joyce's great novel. O'Connor becomes disillusioned with Church and State, as Stephen Dedalus was, but the disillusionment is in another key, a knowing regret for innocence lost, a gentle acceptance of things as they must be.

In 1923 O'Connor was, like so many young men of his generation in Ireland, a man with a history and apparently no future. Finding work was the first imperative, so he became a librarian. That took him, eventually, to Dublin where he began to find himself. Some essays and poems appeared in AE's *Irish Statesman* and Seumas O'Sullivan's *Dublin Magazine*, and he began to write short stories seriously. Through AE, he began to meet some of the right people, Yeats, Lady Gregory, others. In 1931 he published his first collection of short stories, *Guests of the Nation*, and that volume indicated that he was already an important writer in the genre. A less successful novel, *The Saint and Mary Kate*, followed the next year. O'Connor wrote one other novel, *Dutch Interior* (1940), and several plays, some based on his fiction, were produced at the Abbey, but his great strength was in the short story, and he never abandoned the form for long. Even so, the Dublin of the 1930s had plenty of distractions for a young writer, and one of the worst was the aging Yeats. It was Yeats who encouraged him to continue his translations from Gaelic poetry into English. O'Connor's own poetry showed no particular talent, but his translations are another matter indeed, fluent, unsentimental, marvelously alert to the possibilities of rhythm and form. Yeats did O'Connor less of a favor by making him a director of the Abbey Theatre at the time it was falling away from its former greatness. O'Connor made some mistakes, but he fought hard to keep up the company's old standards against the new philistinism. After Yeats's death in 1939 that battle was lost, and O'Connor resigned from the board in 1941. The combative streak from his father's family could never be suppressed, though, and he remained a powerful critic of Irish public life. During World War II, part of which he spent as a radio broadcaster in London, he wrote a long series of articles in the *Sunday Independent* under the name "Ben Mayo," many sharply critical of mediocrity in government and narrowness in Irish attitudes. O'Connor sometimes seemed to have a talent for making enemies, but with his fierce integrity that was almost unavoidable. His fourth collection of short stories, *Crab Apple Jelly*, published in 1944, solidified his reputation as a master of the form, and when the war ended, he was able to go abroad to teach at Stanford and Harvard and play a role as an important man of letters until his death in 1966.

O'Connor once commented that he wrote about Ireland and Irish people merely because he knew exactly, to a syllable, how everything in Ireland could be said. There is a touch of arrogance in that, but truth as well; no writer of his time came closer to understanding the middle-class Catholic Ireland that was the natural milieu of his stories. His first collection, *Guests of the Nation,* shows that ability already well developed. "The Procession of Life," the story of how a boy discovers the adult tastes of liquor and tobacco, is a good example; so is "The Patriarch," an exceedingly fine story about an old man, his veneration of Gaelic, and a small boy. The boy narrates that story, and O'Connor often found children effective narrators for his particular blend of innocence and experience. The most famous story in the first collection is the title piece, "Guests of the Nation." All of the stories in this volume turn on the disillusionment of an Ireland grown out of its nationalistic adolescence into a less satisfying adulthood, but "Guests of the Nation" seems to provide an almost mythic statement of the experience. Two British soldiers are being held hostage by the Irish against the execution of some Irish soldiers in a distant city. Slowly, inevitably, the plot develops; the two Englishmen, Belcher and Hawkins, are decent enough chaps and become friends with their Irish captors. Then word comes that they must be shot. The two men are taken to the nearby bog. The Irish almost botch the job of shooting Hawkins; Belcher goes over "like a sack of meal, and this time there was no need for a second shot." The Irishmen go back to the house where all have been staying; the woman of the house prays for the dead men, and the narrator tells us, "And anything that happened to me afterwards, I never felt the same about again."[18] It is a grim, powerful story, the more powerful for its flat, uncomprehending narration, and it seems to sum up in a dozen pages a whole range of experience. Ideals, Jeremiah Donovan the Irishman's nationalism, Hawkins the Englishman's socialism, mean nothing in the face of brute reality. The eternal silence of the infinite spaces is all we can hear at the story's end.

Guests of the Nation was a remarkable achievement, though O'Connor himself tended to discredit it later in his career by observing that it was written too much under the influence of Isaac Babel. Perhaps that is true; in any event, something more of O'Connor's permanent voice is heard in his next collection, *Bones of Contention* (1936). O'Connor was often a severe critic of his own work, and he later said that in this volume he was merely fumbling for a new style. Even so, "In the Train," "The Majesty of the Law," and "Peasants," to choose only three stories from the volume, are impressive achievements. The

---

[18] *Stories by Frank O'Connor,* p. 16.

last two show his ability to write about the peasantry with just a touch of sentimentality but also with a wry sense of humor. "In the Train" is even more impressive in its tonal control and penetrating observation. Yet O'Connor was probably right in his feeling that he was working toward something else. Some of the stories have too much melodrama, and sometimes the invention is just a bit obvious. *Crab Apple Jelly* (1944) represents a remarkable advance on this earlier work. In "The Mad Lomasneys," for example, the narration is rather diffuse, but this story of romantic misunderstanding is the stronger for it, and that story, together with several others in the volume, is most impressive for its range of characters and sympathies. O'Connor was a man of strong opinions, and those opinions sometimes walked right into his stories, but they rarely walked away with them. There are things O'Connor clearly disliked, abstract forces such as empty nationalism or puritanism, for example, and such living realities as meddling priests, but the stories rarely degenerate into diatribe. Instead, many of the stories in *Crab Apple Jelly* and in O'Connor's later collections achieve a rare balance. Their world is, in Thomas Flanagan's description, "a substantial, dowdy and unbreakably provincial world of publicans, doctors, priests, small merchants, builders, chemists and solicitors," but it is described "without a shade of condescension; the narrator always identifies himself as part of that society, even when he laughs at it or rebels against it."[19] There is something almost Mozartian about O'Connor's later stories. Like his beloved Mozart, O'Connor had a superb sense of form and the genius to turn a work full of elegance and sentiment. It is an extremely rare gift, especially in Ireland where gentleness is not a common literary attribute, but there it is in story after story: "The Luceys," "The Custom of the Country," "The Masculine Principle," "The Stepmother," "The Pretender." He found his own best voice in *Crab Apple Jelly*, and the stories from the next twenty years showed a continuing control of that voice.

O'Connor's importance as a master of the short story should not make us forget his other work. Neither of his novels is quite up to the best of his stories, and a number of critics have noted that *Dutch Interior* would work better broken into short pieces. But *The Mirror in the Roadway* is a valuable study of the novel as a genre, old-fashioned perhaps but sensible and thought provoking. *The Lonely Voice* is even better as a study of the short story. It, too, could be called old-fashioned, and O'Connor never had much patience with Joycean experimentation, but it is an effective reminder of the possibilities of the realistic

---

19 "The Irish Writer," *Michael/Frank*, edited by Maurice Sheehy (New York: Knopf, 1969), p. 158.

tale and the craft that must go into its making. As an imaginative writer, O'Connor was thoroughly aware of the world beyond Ireland, and his criticism shows a healthy lack of provinciality, but Ireland was the constant theme of his creative imagination. That imagination extends to *Irish Miles* (1947) and *Leinster, Munster, and Connacht* (1950), two admirable travel books, the latter still the best armchair guide to the Republic. One of the things that makes the travel books good is their mixture of sharp criticism of the present and a strong sense of the past. O'Connor pays tribute to the Irish literary past in *The Backward Look* (1967), a history of Irish literature based on some lectures given at Trinity College towards the end of his life. The book is far from conventional literary history; too personal by half, a scholar might sniff, and the sections on early Gaelic literature demand more knowledge of the subject than most readers can bring. But Frank O'Connor brought distinction to everything he did. Brendan Kennelly described him well by saying that "he was a man of greatness and generosity, a man who loved laughter, who escaped bitterness although meeting with disappointments; a passionate man who made himself vulnerable in order that he might inspire."[20]

As the years pass, O'Connor's position as the greatest of Irish realists seems increasingly secure, but the period that produced his first collection of stories was a fine one for realistic fiction. It brought Kate O'Brien, whose *Mary Lavelle* (1936) and *The Land of Spices* (1941) are the impressive work of a quiet but passionate imagination, and it also brought Sean O'Faolain. After a writing career that stretches back more than forty years, O'Faolain is now the most distinguished man of letters in Ireland, the last great survivor of his generation. He and Frank O'Connor were born in Cork within three years of each other, and they had a good deal in common in addition to Cork childhoods. Both were protegés of Daniel Corkery; both fought on the Republican side in the Civil War; both first achieved reputations with strong collections of short stories out of that experience; both have been valuable critics of Irish society. O'Faolain, born John Whelan in 1900, grew up in a Cork more genteel but no less restrictive than the town O'Connor knew. His father was a policeman; his mother was a pious, narrow woman who constantly urged her sons to better themselves in the world. At about the time O'Faolain entered University College, Cork, he joined the Irish Volunteers, and he served in the Civil War as censor for the *Cork Examiner* and later as publicity director for the IRA. Embittered by the Republicans' loss, he drifted for several years in the 1920s,

---

20 "Oration at Graveside," *ibid.*, p. 167.

finishing an M.A. in Irish from University College, teaching school for a year in Ennis, spending two years at Harvard as a graduate student.

Gradually, the writer in him began to come out. American-style graduate training began to bore him just as writing began to fascinate. By 1930 he was living in England, teaching but hard at work on his first collection of stories, *Midsummer Night Madness*, published in 1932. That collection, like O'Connor's *Guests of the Nation*, established a reputation for him as an important short-story writer and thoughtful interpreter of the Civil War and its aftermath. During the thirties, O'Faolain wrote three novels, *A Nest of Simple Folk* (1933), *Bird Alone* (1936), and *Come Back to Erin* (1940); several novellas; a number of short stories; biographies of De Valera, Constance Markievicz the revolutionary leader, and Daniel O'Connell; a play produced at the Abbey in 1937, *She Had to Do Something*, and a collection of translations from old Gaelic poems, *The Silver Branch* (1938). This was, by anyone's standards, a substantial achievement, but O'Faolain added to it in the 1940s by six years as editor of the best Irish literary magazine of its time, *The Bell*. *The Bell* gave splendid support to Irish writers when Ireland was, by its neutrality, largely cut off from the rest of the world, and its authors included Brian O'Nolan, Frank O'Connor, O'Flaherty, Patrick Kavanagh, Austin Clarke, and many others. Moreover, *The Bell* brought a healthy adventurousness to Irish life. O'Faolain lustily attacked the censorship, defended *The Tailor and Ansty* (which *The Bell* first published), and firmly chastized Irish politicians and civil servants for their provinciality and narrow-mindedness. And *The Bell* deserves some of the credit for the fact that during the isolationist days of the 1940s, when the narrowest kind of nationalism and clericalism were in the ascendancy, a valuable Irish literature kept going in spite of it all. Nevertheless, by 1946 O'Faolain was tired of the journal. He resigned the editorship, turning it over to Peader O'Donnell, to give himself more time to write. Since then, his publications have included several collections of short stories, among them *The Man Who Invented Sin* (1948), *I Remember! I Remember!* (1961), and *The Heat of the Sun* (1966); an autobiography, *Vive Moi!* (1964); *The Irish* (1947), a "character study" of Ireland's people; travel books; a study of Cardinal Newman; and two works of literary criticism, *The Short Story* (1948) and *The Vanishing Hero* (1956).

O'Faolain has shown remarkable development as a writer of short stories, and that has led him sometimes to criticize his own early work. But *Midsummer Night Madness* is an impressive first collection, written almost too beautifully, but striking in its evocation of a sense of place and its command of disillusioned attitudes. All seven stories deal with the "troubles," and all have the feel of reality. The action is tense; the emotions are intense. Yet they are more than skillful reporting of experience, and each is an interesting experiment with the techniques of the short story. "Fugue," for example, is overtly the story of two young Irish soldiers fleeing from the Black and Tans. In one of the houses in which they find refuge, the narrator encounters a farm girl he had seen earlier. Alone together briefly, they have a brief moment to express their love before a knock is heard at the door and the narrator again has to flee into the night. The incidents of the story are surely things that happened regularly during those times, but the story's distinction comes from the adroit handling of the material. The interweaving of images and motifs make it formally like the fugue of its title. This is a particularly sophisticated exercise, but it is typical of the book in its exacting craftsmanship.

O'Faolain himself has complained that this first collection romanticizes the anger and disillusionment he felt after the Civil War, and his next collection of stories, *A Purse Full of Coppers,* seems a conscious effort to avoid that romanticization. The stories deal with the late 1920s and early 1930s, the dull aftermath of revolution and civil war. The writing is plainer, the point of view more objective, and both are appropriate to the subject. The first story in the collection, "A Broken World," one of O'Faolain's very best, is characteristic of his new point of view. We have only three characters and very little incident. Three men are thrown together by accident in a railway car traveling through the countryside during a snow storm. One of the three, a priest, recounts some of his experiences as a young clergyman in a remote part of County Wicklow, turning his story into a little sermon on the need for a sense of moral unity among the Irish country people. The narrator, an unnamed "intellectual" and the other character, a farmer, are drawn into the priest's tale very strongly. When the priest leaves the train at the next station, the narrator asks the farmer if he knows the priest, and the farmer explains that the priest has been silenced by Church authorities because he had urged the peasants to take possession of the deserted estates in their district. The farmer seems irritated by the narrator's questions about the priest; he goes to sleep for awhile, then gets off the train, leaving the narrator to sort out the experience. The plot of the story is utterly unremarkable; what is remarkable is the way in which O'Faolain pulls us into the situation, making us understand the priest's frustration with poor farm people who will not try to better themselves and rich ones who will not help them. But he also makes us understand that the old farmer in the train is a symbol of the peasant mentality that defeats the priests—permanent, inflexible, wrong perhaps, but utterly a part of the Irish experience.

O'Connor was a storyteller who took strength from the natural compulsion of his narrative. O'Faolain is a storyteller of a different order, less willing to tell a story seemingly for its own sake, more interested in drawing out significances. As O'Faolain himself puts it, "I would . . . try to write, however tangentially, about those moments of awareness when we know three truths at one and the same moment: that life requires of each of us that we should grow up and out whole and entire, that human life of its nature intricately foils exactly this, and that the possibility of wholeness is nevertheless as constant and enormous a reality as the manifold actuality of frustration, compromise, getting caught in some labyrinth, getting cut short by death."[21] That complex program for his writing tells us something fundamental about O'Faolain; it tells us, of course, that he has a finely honed mind, but it also tells us that he is essentially an observer and commentator. In O'Connor's stories we rarely lose the sense that the narrator is a participant in the world he depicts; O'Connor in his fiction is, in that sense, an insider. O'Faolain is usually an outsider. He knows Ireland and the Irish intimately, but the Ireland he portrays is an exemplary world, not "exemplary" in the sense of "perfect" but merely in the sense of "an example." He explains, describes, illuminates, but it is almost always with the voice of a detached observer pointing us toward significant detail and potential meaning. His study of his countrymen, *The Irish*, is characteristic of his method, though the method there is applied to fact rather than fiction. In giving the history of Ireland, he ignores many of the facts professional historians would emphasize to focus on significant details, and he goes on then to describe what he calls the "six representative types" of the Irish: the peasantry, the Anglo-Irish, the rebels, the priests, the writers, and the politicians. The emphases on process, detail, and representative types in that little book are entirely in line with the techniques of his fiction.

O'Faolain's ability to illuminate representative types is one of his great strengths as a writer of short stories. It makes the rebels of *Midsummer Night Madness* thoroughly convincing and the ordinary folk of *A Purse Full of Coppers* perhaps even more true. It makes "The Man Who Invented Sin" with its cast of monks and nuns and its puritanical priest a gently right account of evil in the eye of the beholder. In some later stories, especially those in *I Remember! I Remember!*, autumnal memory becomes a new means for the depiction of exemplary characters and situations. This is, in a way, an old man's book, but it is the work of an old man still ready to grow. "The Sugawn Chair," one of the best stories in the collection, is an especially beautiful nar-

---

[21] Quoted in Maurice Harmon, *Sean O'Faolain* (Notre Dame, Ind.: Notre Dame University Press, 1967), p. 63.

rative about memory and the attempt to recapture the past through the attempt
to remake an old rocking chair. The story could turn maudlin, but O'Faolain
carefully skirts that to leave us with a sense of the richness of the remembered
past and our inability to recapture it. Yet the ability to illuminate the meaning
of exemplary types and situations served O'Faolain less well in the three novels
he published in the 1930s. All are worth reading, but each gives the feeling
that their author is not quite in command of the longer form. Exemplary characters tend to become stereotypes as in *Come Back to Erin* where, for a novel,
at least, it is a bit too neat to play an aging rebel off against his two half-
brothers, one a priest, the other a successful businessman. The novel deals ably
with the theme of the revolutionary who has outlived his cause and the conflicts
between Irish and Irish-Americans, but there is too much padding and too
much reliance on mechanical plotting to keep the story going. As with
O'Connor's *Dutch Interior*, one senses a series of fine short stories trying to
escape from an uneven novel. Commenting on these novels, John Kelleher says
of O'Faolain, "as a novelist he was beaten not by lack of talent—he has always
had talent to spare and fling away—but by his too great demand upon a society
intimate, homely, compact and too rigidly narrow."[22]

Sometimes the same complaint could be directed against his short stories;
the sophistication of his technique seems too great for the people and situations
he chooses to portray. But in the best of his stories, there is a fascinating
balance between his own ingenuity and the Ireland he describes. With Frank
O'Connor and James Joyce, he stands as one of the great masters of the Irish
short story. All three were able to use specific Irish experiences to illuminate
broader themes and problems. Yet Joyce, O'Connor, and O'Faolain are only
the best writers in an admirable movement, and Ireland has been fortunate in
having many able writers of short fiction in recent years. The tradition that
began early in the century found further expression in the 1940s in the work
of Mary Lavin and Michael McLaverty, both distinguished exponents of the
realistic tale. There was, perhaps, a slowing down in Irish fiction after the mid-
1940s, but by then no one could say, as Ernest Boyd had in 1922, that fiction
was the "weak side" of modern Irish literature. The novels of Liam O'Flaherty,
the stories of O'Connor and O'Faolain, *Finnegans Wake*, *At Swim-Two-Birds*,
and other works of experimental fantasy had all contributed to making fiction
something very close to the strong side.

---

22 Quoted in Paul A. Doyle, *Sean O'Faolain*, (New York: Twayne, 1969), p. 71.

∂oors open on exile
Anglo-Irish Poetry, 1923–1940

In my land nothing stands at all,
But some fly high and some lie low.
                    Louis MacNeice, "Eclogue from Iceland"

No System, no Plan,
Yeatsian invention
No all-over
Organisational prover.
Let words laugh
And people be stimulated by our stuff.
                    Patrick Kavanagh, "Mermaid Tavern"

THE IRISH RENAISSANCE began with poetry. It found its first expression in the work of Yeats, AE, Katharine Tynan, and others, and up until the time of the First World War, poetry and drama seemed to be its dominant genres. "Irish poet" meant W. B. Yeats in all his many manifestations, and after Yeats's death in 1939, W. H. Auden wrote that the "Irish vessel" was "Emptied of its poetry."[1] So it seemed then, though Yeats himself, compiling the *Oxford Book of Modern Verse* only four years before, had made some extravagant claims for some of his younger Irish contemporaries. Yeats dominated Irish poetry for half a century, and, outside Ireland, his reputation probably helped other Irish poets gain more attention than they would have had otherwise. Yet the presence of Yeats was not exclusively a blessing. As Donald Davie remarks:

1 "In Memory of W. B. Yeats," *Collected Shorter Poems* (London: Faber, 1966), p. 142.

"When a poet so great as Yeats is born to a country as small as Ireland, this is a wonderful windfall for everyone in that country *except the poets*. For them it is a disaster."[2] "Disaster" is a strong word, and it may be an exaggeration. Nevertheless, it is difficult to think of any Irish poet who was Yeats's contemporary who was not affected, even damaged, by the presence of the master. Austin Clarke, a fine poet thirty years Yeats's junior, was one, and he later remembered the situation when he began to write: "Young poets stared through the windows of the Dublin bookshops and saw his volumes displayed in them, with covers that were a blaze of gold. . . . In the art shops his best known lyrics . . . all hand-printed, illustrated and framed, were on sale; and we saw those framed poems hung on the drawing-room walls of every house with any pretensions to good taste."[3]

The 1920s was not an especially memorable decade in Irish poetry. Yeats published *Michael Robartes and the Dancer* and *The Tower*, two of his finest achievements, but few new figures appeared on the scene. Some established poets, Joseph Campbell, Padraic Colum, James Stephens, continued work, but rather erratically. Campbell's active republicanism led to his internment for a long period, and in 1924 he emigrated to the United States. Although he returned to Ireland in 1935 and lived near Glencree in County Wicklow until his death in 1944, his best work was already done before he emigrated. Colum left Ireland in 1914, and spent most of the rest of his long life outside the country. He remained an immensely productive writer, publishing collections of childrens' stories, plays, folklore, and poems. As late as the 1960s there was an important new development in his work in a series of Irish plays on historical personages using the Nōh form, but Colum had made his lasting contribution to Irish poetry with *Wild Earth* in 1907, though *The Poet's Circuits* (1960), a gathering and rearrangement of his Irish verse into a remarkable "saga" of peasant life is a fine achievement. James Stephens, too, had said much of what he had to say in verse before the twenties. In 1924 he moved to London, where he spent much of the remainder of his life, often haunting Euston Station looking for old friends coming in on the Dublin boat trains. He continued to write, but the poet in him had died before the man himself left the scene in 1950.

Stephens, Colum, and Campbell were born within three years of each other, just at the turn of the 1880s. They were representative of what should have been a generation of mature poets in the Ireland of the 1920s; instead, all were exiles by the middle of the decade, and none had fulfilled his rich initial

---

2 "Austin Clarke and Padraic Fallon," *Two Decades of Irish Writing*, p. 41.

3 *Poetry in Modern Ireland* (Dublin: Three Candles Press, 1961), p. 47.

promise. Their contemporary, James Starkey, stayed in Ireland, and continued to write under the name of Seumas O'Sullivan. A significant volume, *The Lamplighters*, appeared in 1929, but Seumas O'Sullivan's talent, while real, was a distinctly minor one. At his best as a poet in impressionistic sketches, his services to Irish writers and Irish writing were more important than his own creative work. No service he performed was more valuable than the founding of the *Dublin Magazine* in 1923. Ireland in the midst of civil war was an unlikely place for a literary magazine, but for thirty years the *Dublin Magazine* provided an outlet for writers and a high standard of editorial judgment. Like Colum, Stephens, and so many others, O'Sullivan was one of AE's discoveries, and it constantly galled Yeats that it was to AE rather than to him that the new poets seemed to turn. Yeats's discovery in the 1920s was Oliver St. John Gogarty, though by the time Gogarty came under Yeats's influence he hardly needed discovering. Born in 1878 and educated at Oxford and Trinity College, Gogarty earned one kind of literary fame by appearing in *Ulysses* as Buck Mulligan. He and Joyce had briefly shared the martello tower at Sandycove in 1904. Joyce came to detest him, but Gogarty went on to become a celebrated figure in the Dublin of his time, medical doctor, wit, raconteur, and sometime poet. It was Gogarty who helped arrange Yeats's election to the Senate of the Free State, and Yeats loved his courage and grace. Captured by Republicans during the Civil War, Gogarty escaped by diving into the Liffey. Swimming the river in a hail of revolver bullets, he swore to give the river two swans if he survived. He did, and Yeats and other notables were there later on when Gogarty fulfilled his vow, though the swans were none too enthusiastic about the entire affair. That adventure gave the title for Gogarty's *An Offering of Swans* (1924), a volume Yeats praised inordinately. But Yeats was given to excessive praise of Gogarty's work. He printed more of his poems than any other poet's in his *Oxford Book of Modern Verse*, a remarkable judgment in a volume that also included the work of T. S. Eliot, Auden, Pound, and Yeats himself, and he called him "one of the great lyric poets of our age."[4] Gogarty's poetry really will not stand up to that judgment, and Yeats himself admitted that he sometimes flattered Gogarty's work out of friendship for the man and sometimes helped him with lines or even recastings of whole poems. Gogarty's best book was not poetry at all but the marvelous set of reminiscences, *As I Was Going Down Sackville Street* (1937). It started a notorious libel action at the time of its publication, but from today's perspective it is valuable for its vivid picture of

---

4 *The Oxford Book of Modern Verse* (Oxford; Clarendon, 1936), p. xv.

Dublin in the days of revolution and literary renaissance; perhaps it is more valuable for the sense it gives us of Gogarty himself—insouciant, irresponsible, vibrantly alive.

In the 1930s, Yeats had other protégés. Frank O'Connor was one, and it was partially with Yeats's encouragement that he turned to making his brilliant series of translations from Gaelic poetry. If all his stories were lost, his translation of Merryman's "Midnight Court" would still mark him as an important figure in the Irish movement. It was F. R. Higgins, O'Connor's sometime friend, though, who became Yeats's most favored protégé in the 1930s, and it is still open to question whether that was a good thing or not. Higgins, born in 1896, was the first poet of his generation, the generation after that of Stephens and Colum and two generations after Yeats himself, to make a real mark. A contemporary of O'Connor, O'Faolain, and O'Flaherty, like them he had matured during the "troubles," and he shared a good deal of their disillusionment with post-independence Ireland. Higgins' disillusionment, though, was of a simpler kind. He was, especially during the earlier part of his career, almost a throwback in his attitudes to the poets of the Celtic Twilight, ready to glorify Ireland as a mystical land of continuous revelation and the Irish peasantry as a spiritual aristocracy. Attitudes like those had motivated the rioters at the premiere of *The Playboy of the Western World* in 1907, and perhaps it is not surprising that Higgins was one of several young writers (Austin Clarke and Liam O'Flaherty were others) who attacked O'Casey's *Plough and the Stars* in letters to the *Irish Statesman* in 1926. There was, as Richard Loftus comments in his study of Higgins in *Nationalism in Modern Anglo-Irish Poetry*, something very close to nineteenth-century racialism in Higgins' views of the Irish peasant: "In Yeats's verse the peasant is praised for his subservience, in Pearse's for his fighting spirit, in Colum's for his lowly virtue and his righteousness, in A.E.'s for his godliness; in Stephens' for his vitality and good humor. In Higgins' poetry, although the peasant ideal encompasses fighting spirit, lowly virtue, and, in some measure, vitality, it is vaguer and, in a romantic sense, more mystical than the verse of Stephens, Colum, or Pearse." Loftus observes too, that in some unpublished lecture notes Higgins went so far as to imagine the Irish as predecessors of a race of supermen.[5]

That all sounds very much like the views of some of the poets of the nineties, and, like Yeats, Hyde, and AE of the earlier generation, Higgins was born a Protestant but worked hard to identify himself with Catholic, Celtic

[5] *Nationalism in Modern Anglo-Irish Poetry* (Madison and Milwaukee: University of Wisconsin Press, 1964), p. 237.

Ireland. A poem of Padraic Colum's and Douglas Hyde's *Love-Songs of Connacht* inspired him to write verse. Three volumes appeared in the twenties, *Salt Air* (1924), *Island Blood* (1925), and *The Dark Breed* (1927). The poems showed a remarkable talent, undisciplined perhaps and given to an uncritical glorification of the peasantry, but genuine. The man could put words together as no other Irish poet of his time except Yeats. Higgins' problem, in fact, was his fluency; the phrases were memorable and the verbal music gorgeous, but sometimes the overall form was uncontrolled. Like his friend at the time, Austin Clarke, Higgins was fascinated by the techniques of assonance in Gaelic poetry, and he used these to create poems of lush sensuality, beautiful often in the way that the poetry of the Celtic Twilight was beautiful, but more intense, specific, and passionate.

By the early 1930s Higgins' obsession with the peasantry and his native Mayo led him to move to a cottage near Loch Conn, not far from his birthplace at Foxford. What was to have been a year there stretched out to three, and it was 1935 before Higgins and his wife returned to Dublin. *Arable Holdings* (1933), an important book of poems, was published during this period, and it showed a real change in Higgins' work. He was slowly excising sentimentality and with it some of his voluptuous imagery. *Arable Holdings* drew some excellent reviews, and after Higgins returned to Dublin, Yeats began to take an active interest in his career. Together they prepared a series of broadside ballads which the Cuala Press printed, and each began to influence the other. Yeats taught Higgins something about disciplining his art, while Higgins helped Yeats catch something of the authentic voice of folksong in his later poetry. A huge, gregarious man, careless in his friendships and enmities, Higgins in the later 1930s was in the center of all sorts of literary cooperations and quarrels. He fell out with two early friends, Austin Clarke and Frank O'Connor; in a famous brawl, he assaulted another poet, Padraic Fallon. Brinsley MacNamara, the novelist and playwright, remained a good friend and drinking buddy, as did R. M. Smyllie, the editor of the *Irish Times* and an important maker and breaker of Irish literary reputations. The literary pub world of those days was very much like the one Patrick Kavanagh later satirized in "The Paddiad," and it did not do Higgins' poetry much good.

His last volume, *The Gap of Brightness* (1940), had some valuable work in it, but the influence of the later Yeats was almost too strong, and, as Richard Loftus observes, the volume fails because, unlike Yeats, Higgins never developed a coherent aesthetic.[6] He died in 1941. He was as prodigal with his

6 *Ibid.*, p. 255.

imagery as Dylan Thomas, and his poems are always striking for their musicality. Yet all that talent seems to add up to a good deal less than the sum of its parts, and the reasons seem clear enough: a lack of intellectual grasp in his early work and too much imitation of Yeats's mannerisms in his later. Even so, some of his poems, "Repentance," "Father and Son," "Changeling," "A Tinker's Woman," are remarkable achievements, and his elegy for his friend Padraic Ó Conaire, the Gaelic short-story writer, begins and ends with two of the great stanzas in Irish poetry. It is characteristic of Higgins that the middle stanzas fail to sustain their argument, but the last stanza would serve well as his own epitaph:

> Alas, death mars the parchment of his forehead;
> And yet for him, I know, the earth is mild—
> The windy fidgets of September grasses
> Can never tease a mind that loved the wild;
> So drink his peace—this grey juice of the barley
> Runs with a light that ever pleased his eye—
> While the old flames nod and gossip on the hearthstone
> And only the young winds cry.[7]

Higgins is an especially interesting example of the problems of the Irish poet in his time. It seemed that an Irish poet of his generation could choose between two distinct manners. There was the intellectual passion of Yeats, aristocratic in its sympathies and at least aware of the international modernist movement of Eliot, Pound, and, later, Auden. Or there was the anti-intellectual, peasant-oriented nationalism of Colum, Stephens, Campbell, and AE. Higgins began with the latter, gravitated toward the former, and was probably damaged by both. His case was not untypical of his generation, but there was, in fact, a third option, to move fully toward the styles of English and even European modernism. T. S. Eliot's *Waste Land* had remarkably little effect on Irish poetry; it took forty years and Thomas Kinsella's "Nightwalker" before it was integrated into Irish poetry as it had been integrated long before into British and American. The traditional concerns of Irish poetry and the bias in Irish poetry toward song both worked against an Irish assimilation of Eliot's earlier work or Pound's. On the other hand, the disillusioned modernism, politically

---

[7] "Padraic O'Conaire Gaelic Storyteller," *The Mentor Book of Irish Poetry*, p. 165.

oriented but oriented too toward individual values, that Auden, Spender and others in England in the 1930s came to represent, had more effect on Irish verse. A good young poet, Charles Donnelly, for example, died in his twenties fighting with the Republican forces in Spain in the civil war that was the great cause of the left-wing English poets of the thirties. With Denis Devlin, Donagh MacDonagh (both to become important poets in the 1940s), and Brian O'Nolan, he was part of a brilliant circle at University College, Dublin, in the 1930s, and the poems he wrote before his early death showed real talent. Ewart Milne, an older contemporary and for a time a committed Marxist, expressed almost apocalyptic politics in some powerful rhetoric. Lyle Donaghy, too, made some interesting experiments with free verse, a form Irish poets had generally avoided, though some of his best-known poems, "A Leitrim Woman," for example, ally the free verse form to the garrulous rhetoric of the poets of *The Nation* almost a century before.

The most impressive young poet to come out of Ireland in the 1930s was Louis MacNeice, born in Belfast in 1907. MacNeice wrote a critical study of Yeats, the first one of any lasting distinction, but he was hardly a poet in the Yeatsian mould. A sophisticated, intelligent man, MacNeice became a celebrator of the ordinary and the everyday. He was a friend of Auden's, and to some extent his early poetry is similar to Auden's work in the thirties, but MacNeice was his own man, ready to argue that poetry should not be divorced from life but ready, too, to write poems of tentative discovery which often have as their theme the incomplete relationships of life and art. In an interesting essay on his work, an important contemporary Irish poet, Michael Longley, argues that MacNeice's Irishness, especially his childhood in Protestant Belfast, was central to his work.[8] While MacNeice certainly took pride in his Irishness and probed the problems it involved in a major poem, *Autumn Journal* (1939), and an autobiography, *The Strings Are False* (1966), his place in modern Irish poetry has been somewhere just inside the periphery. Valuable work, MacNeice's poetry seems only sporadically Irish, and a definition of Irish poetry broad enough to include it all would be too diffuse to be meaningful.

It is to Yeats, then, that we must turn for greatness in Irish poetry in this period, and the greatness is astonishing. Not every poem Yeats wrote was a masterpiece, and some of the work from the last years of his career fell sharply below his usual standard, but even his failures were evidence of a continuing desire to experiment and grow. That itself is a remarkable thing in an aging

8 See "The Neolithic Night: A Note on the Irishness of Louis MacNeice," *Two Decades of Irish Writing*, pp. 98–104.

poet, but then few poets have made the experience of old age so engrossing a theme. In 1923 Yeats was fifty-eight, married finally, father of two children, and a world-famous figure. A senior poet in the English-speaking world then, he looked with some dismay on his younger contemporaries, Eliot and Pound in particular, and it would have been easy for him to have settled into complacent old age, respected, honored, and out of touch. Instead, something nagging and insistent in his imagination kept asking, "What then?" That question prodded him to write more than 170 poems in the last sixteen years of his life in addition to revisions of much of his early work. It prodded him also to eight plays, translations of Sophocles' Oedipus plays, essays, volumes of autobiography and a reworking of his philosophical book, *A Vision*.

All this work did not take place in a vacuum. During the years between 1923 and 1939 he served in the Irish Senate, took an active hand in the management of the Abbey Theatre, edited a major anthology of modern English poetry, gave many lectures, including dozens on a long tour of America, and read at everything from studies of philosophy and religion to cowboy stories. From early in the 1920s until close to the end of his life he spent much of his time in Dublin, and his homes, first at 82 Merrion Square, and later in the suburb of Rathfarnham, were gathering places for writers and artists. Dublin sometimes laughed at his manner and was sometimes shocked by his public pronouncements. The old man in the soft gray suit with the incantatory voice and the sweeping gestures who occasionally appeared on the stage of the Abbey was like a creature from another planet in the fussy Dublin of de Valera's 1930s. When in 1934 he underwent an operation for sexual rejuvenation, Dublin sniggered at the "Gland Old Man," and his continuing interest in the occult earned him the nickname, "Willy the Spooks." Stories of his eccentricity went the rounds in Dublin pubs: his sweeping judgments on men and movements some of which he knew nothing about, his ludicrous attempts at golf, his devastating comments on the latest upstart poet. Yet the man who could absentmindedly sign checks, "Yours sincerely, W. B. Yeats," never became the addled character Dublin gossip liked to make him. The abstracted manner came as much from shyness and partial blindness as from arrogance, but any man who was making poetry of his quality had some cause to be arrogant.

Yeats had spent a decade mostly outside of Ireland when he returned to live in Dublin in 1922. By accepting a seat in the Irish Senate he put himself on the side of the Free State during the Civil War, a dangerous act in those days. An armed guard was assigned to his house in Dublin for a while, and in the summer of 1922 the bridge at Thoor Ballylee was blown up by Republicans.

In spite of the danger, his tower there in the Galway countryside near Lady Gregory's Coole Park, which he used as a summer home, was an important place to him emotionally. He had bought it before his marriage, reconditioned it, and found in it a powerful personal and poetic symbol. Even so, the experiences there during the Civil War made the terror of fraternal warfare frighteningly real. The end of the war brought better times, and in 1923 Yeats was honored by the award of the Nobel Prize for Literature. He thoroughly enjoyed the ceremonial of the Swedish court, and his acceptance speech gave the opportunity to pay tribute to his coworkers at the Abbey Theatre, Lady Gregory and Synge. For several years in the 1920s he participated actively in the work of the Irish Senate, usually allying himself with enlightened political conservatism. His public life stimulated his imagination, but that imagination was working under full pressure in those days. The frenzy of public and creative energy gradually began to take its toll, though. A staunch believer in the necessity of a firmly regulated society, he was appalled in July of 1927 by the assassination of Kevin O'Higgins, the Free State's minister of justice and the strong man in the government. In October, during a trip to France and Spain, he became seriously ill. When he had partially recovered, he and his wife went on to Rapallo in Italy to spend the winter with Ezra Pound and his wife. Yeats's term in the Irish Senate ended in 1928 as ill-health and disillusionment led to a partial disengagement from Irish affairs. He would still spend much of his time in Ireland, but most winters found him in warmer and drier climates, and Mrs. Yeats had to be increasingly careful about his gradually deteriorating health.

Ireland, civil war, and old age are some of the themes in *The Tower*, the collection of poems Yeats published in 1928. This is the bleakest and perhaps the most powerful volume he ever wrote. It contains some of his most famous poems, "Sailing to Byzantium," "The Tower," "Leda and the Swan," "Among School Children," and others, but it is more than a collection of fine poems. Yeats sought to make each of his volumes a collection in which the sum is more than the parts, and in that *The Tower* succeeds triumphantly. It opens with "Sailing to Byzantium," a meditation on the conflict between the real world we know and the ideal world of art, both seen from the point of view of an aging poet only too conscious of his own mortality, and it is one of the finest poems we have on the conflict of life and art that so obsessed the later Romantics. Yet in terms of the volume as a whole, "Sailing to Byzantium" is only a prologue. In it, the poet seeks the mosaic-like dream world of his own imagining, meaningful and complete; in the three poems that follow, "The

Tower," "Meditations in Time of Civil War," and "Nineteen Hundred and Nineteen," private dream worlds meld into public nightmares. The three poems (or sets of lyrics, for each is a set of diverse lyrics united by common themes and images) were written in reverse order from that given in the collection. "The Tower" extends the discussion of the intersection of life and art from "Sailing to Byzantium" in the poet's personal terms. He stands on the battlements of his own tower at Ballylee looking at the countryside around while he imagines the memories it contains. Both tower and countryside are permanent, but the poet, feeling old age as caricature and absurdity, knows that he is not, and the lyrics in "The Tower" gradually develop into a subtle and beautiful descant on the themes of age, memory, and imagination. The intersection of the private imaginative world of the poet and the world of public events provides the matter of the following poems, "Meditations in Time of Civil War." These were mostly written at Ballylee during the war, and they move back and forth between concern about the present and nostalgia for the past. The present seems meaningless and chaotic; the emblems of the past, ancestral houses, a Japanese sword, pass judgment on the futility of modern experience. The meditations find an achingly beautiful resolution in the next to last lyric, "The Stare's Nest by My Window," where the last stanza invites bees, emblems of the meaningful activity that yields the sweetness of honey and the light of wax, to build their nests in the loosening masonry of our civilization:

> We had fed the heart on fantasies,
> The heart's grown brutal from the fare;
> More substance in our enmities
> Than in our love; O honey-bees,
> Come build in the empty house of the stare.[9]

But the last poem in the sequence contains a vision of the phantoms of hatred that destroy the goodness the bees suggest, and that takes us into the world of the next poem, "Nineteen Hundred and Nineteen." Yeats never wrote a more brutally pessimistic poem than this, and no poet of our century has given us a more terrible vision of the meaning of our times. "The Second Coming" had expressed the poet's sense of apocalyptic change in the world, but this later and greater poem is his fullest meditation on the theme. It begins with a sense of nostalgia for the "Many ingenious lovely things" that time and change have destroyed, but that quickly leads into a bitter recollection of the nineteenth-century belief in perpetual progress which World War I ended forever: "O what fine thought we had because we thought/That the worst rogues and rascals had died out." In the broken world of 1919 that sort of naive faith has been replaced by the knowledge that "Man is in love and loves what vanishes." There follow two superb sections, one equating the public nightmare of the modern world with oriental dancers, the other equating the private imagination with the swan. But neither image is adequate to describe the sense of our world, and so then follow two blackly bitter lyrics, one comparing us all to weasels fighting in a hole, the other inviting us to mock the great, the wise, and the good. But that utterly pessimistic section concludes by inviting us to mock mockers especially, for we all "Traffic in mockery."[10] The final section yields a series of violent images of our world, horses, crazed dancers, and, finally, the repulsive but bone-true figure of Robert Artisson, a demon lover created by the magic of a witch. That final image, like many of Yeats's, is an arcane one, and some might say it is too private to make sense. But really that is not true in this case; even more than the sphinxlike creature of "The Second Coming," Robert Artisson is a compelling image of the spirit of our times: humanoid but inhuman, our creation but perfectly capable of destroying us, stupid, insolent, and utterly commanding. He could be Hitler, Stalin, or our own worst selves.

"Nineteen Hundred and Nineteen" is as intense a poem as Yeats ever wrote, but the poems that follow it in *The Tower* gradually distance us from the terror of apocalyptic change so that we begin to understand it as part of a larger pattern of human experience. "Two Songs from a Play" and "Leda and the Swan" cast the pattern of cultural transformation into a classical context. The two songs, equating Dionysus and Christ as god-men who defined the worlds that grew out of the imaginations of their devotees, insist that "Everything that man esteems/Endures a moment or a day"[11] because every system of belief is our own creation. Like the two songs, "Leda and the Swan" deals with moment of historical transformation, here the encounter of the god in the form of a swan and the girl, Leda. The poem is valuable thematically and reflects Yeats's interest in the patterns of history, but the poem is even more valuable formally; has a more astonishingly controlled sonnet been written in our century? These distancing poems lead us then to "Among School Children," one of Yeats's finest meditations. The terrors of apocalypse

10 *Ibid.*, p. 432.
11 *Ibid.*, p. 438.

and modern madness are now gone, but the poem continues the volume's theme of the intersection of imagination and memory with old age. We begin with the poet as Senator, observed by children who see him as "A sixty-year-old smiling public man," on the day the great man visits to inspect their school. They have their image of him, and that image begins a long series of images: his imagining of Maud Gonne as a child, his image of her as an old woman, his image of himself as a comfortable scarecrow, images of youthful mothers and their children grown old, images nuns adore, images, brilliantly conceived, of the world as perceived by Plato, Aristotle, and Pythagoras. All this culminates in that wonderful final stanza and those culminating figures of tree and dancer, symbols of perfected life, but perfected life we can only question, not fully comprehend:

> O chestnut-tree, great-rooted blossomer,
> Are you the leaf, the blossom or the bole?
> O body swayed to music, O brightening glance,
> How can we know the dancer from the dance?[12]

We cannot, for we are human, all too human, and the later poems in the volume are subtle and allusive commentaries on our humanity. By the time we reach the end in "All Soul's Night," the poet with his comprehensive vision of human experience admits that even wisdom is the stuff of the dead. *The Tower* takes us to painful depths of experience, admits the irrational while insisting there must be explanation, and reminds us that even in the worst of times there is meaning, public and private. It is a distressing and bitter collection of poems, and painfully true to the experience of our times, but black darkness never fully overwhelms. There is always the perfection of art that the gold mosaic of "Sailing to Byzantium" signifies and the perfection of life signified by the tree and dancer of "Among School Children." We may be able to touch neither finally, but even when we become the weasels of "Nineteen Hundred and Nineteen," they remain.

Shortly after its publication, Yeats wrote about *The Tower* to an old friend: "I was astonished at its bitterness, and long to live out of Ireland that I may find some new vintage."[13] After 1928 there was some disengagement from Ireland, but Yeats could never exorcise Ireland or bitterness completely. Still, the work of revising *A Vision*, which was not published in its final form

---

12 *Ibid.*, p. 446.
13 *Letters of W. B. Yeats*, p. 742.

until 1937, provided one way of coming to terms with his experience in a broader context. In 1929 he published *The Winding Stair*, a collection of poems that were almost a response to *The Tower*, gentler, more emotionally generous, less distraught. What he called the "bird songs of an old man" became another collection, *Words for Music Perhaps*, and the two were eventually published together as *The Winding Stair* in 1933. By that point, illness had again intervened, as had the death of Lady Gregory.

In the last decade of his life, Yeats moved between extreme emotions, joy and despair, an almost classical acceptance of fate and warfare against it. New friends, Dorothy Wellesley, Frank O'Connor, F. R. Higgins, provided satisfactions; the establishment of the Irish Academy of Letters in 1932 gave a sense of formalizing the achievements of the literary movement he had nurtured and chastized for generations. Yet there were quarrels and unhappinesses in Dublin. To Yeats, the development of the Free State was a constant source of bitterness. It was, he felt, mean-minded, vulgarly commercial, subservient to clerical pressure, and he reflected angrily on his own nationalistic idealism of forty years before. He insisted that the proper model for modern Ireland was the Anglo-Irish eighteenth century, aristocratic and swashbuckling, imbued with the philosophical idealism of Berkeley and the patriotic anger of Swift. But the ideal society Yeats proposed had almost nothing to do with the realities Irish politicians in the 1930s understood, and his political and social theories were ignored. As political and social theories, they deserved to be; as metaphors for poetry, they were another matter entirely. By 1935 and his seventieth birthday, he seemed to be pulling the threads of his life together for a final time. Collected editions of his poems and plays were published in that year as was another installment of autobiography, *Dramatis Personae*. The last work on *A Vision* was done soon thereafter. A year later his anthology of modern poetry, *The Oxford Book of Modern Verse* was published; it gave him the chance to pass final judgments on the lyric achievement of his age.

His life was gradually winding down, or so it seems in retrospect, but that ignores the astonishing energy of his last years. He continued to write at an almost furious pace, and he remained wide open to new experiences and ideas. In preparing the *Oxford Book of Modern Verse* he gave himself a crash course in modern poetry; he found a good deal of poetry he did not like, but by the time he came to write the brilliant and quirky introduction to the anthology, he was an expert on the subject. He read widely in social theory and philosophy, and after he was seventy began again to study Indian philosophy with a swami. The sense of experiment and innovation comes directly into

The Winding Stair and *Words for Music Perhaps* as well as the poems published as *A Full Moon in March* in 1935.

If we come to *The Winding Stair* directly from *The Tower*, what is most striking is the new sense of acceptance and self-forgiveness. "In Memory of Eva Gore-Booth and Con Markiewicz" makes the poet's peace with two lives he believed wasted and does it in passionate speech, deceptively simple and intricately made. "A Dialogue of Self and Soul" is his great poem of self-acceptance, while the poems on Coole Park and "Stream and Sun at Glendalough" reinforce that theme with nostalgia. *The Winding Stair* is also remarkable for its openness. The hieratic Yeats, poet of apocalypse and private mythology, is still present, but most of the memorable poems in the volume find him almost walking naked. "At Algeciras—A Meditation on Death" faces the final reality straight on, while the sequence, "Vacillation," takes us very close to the core of Yeats's personal experience. And in "Byzantium" we come even closer to the core of his creative experience; that great poem on death and the origins of creativity is intensely private and beyond any full explication, but instinct, if nothing else, tells us that its metaphors of transformation and rebirth were crucial to the generative process of Yeats's imagination. *Words for Music Perhaps* is an even more innovative volume, memorable for "Crazy Jane" and her randy wisdom; a series of exquisite lyrics; "Speech After Long Silence;" "Lullaby;" and the marvelous sequence, "A Woman Young and Old." *Words for Music Perhaps* are small poems, not great meditations, and almost always perfectly made with their haunting refrains and flickering allusions. The political ballads from *A Full Moon in March* represent another innovation, this one perhaps less happy. They would never do as popular marching songs, as Yeats once intended, and they sometimes come too close to angry rhetoric. Even so, making them seems to have kept the lyrical vein open, and that made for better poems elsewhere. The "Supernatural Songs" contained in this volume represent a different Yeats, difficult and utterly unpopular. Compressed and packed, these little poems achieve both public and private resonance; like the poems in *The Wind Among the Reeds*, their mythology is arcane, but comprehending them can be exciting work. The popular and the supernatural of this volume are combined in "Parnell's Funeral," a complex and perhaps unbalanced meditation on mythology and Irish history.

The poems of *A Full Moon in March* are erratic in quality, and so are the poems Yeats wrote in the last years of his life, eventually published together simply as *Last Poems*. Some are thin and overly private, graffiti on the walls of the poet's mind, but taken together these last poems would make a worthy achievement for a lifetime for most other poets. The political ballads and commentaries are not especially impressive and the farewell poem, "Under Ben Bulben" is oddly unsatisfactory, too garrulous and too compressed at the same time. On the other hand, the poems on art and personality, "Lapis Lazuli," "The Statues," "Long-Legged Fly," "The Circus Animals' Desertion," and "The Man and the Echo," show an unfailing command of Yeats's art and a continuous probing of his experience. "The Circus Animals' Desertion" is rightly read as a summing up of his career, though one must be careful not to sentimentalize it, but "Lapis Lazuli" and "The Man and the Echo" are even finer poems, both wonderfully sustained, one a profound commentary on the function of art in the world, the other a bleakly moving dialogue of the selves in the face of death. The rage against old age is largely gone from this volume. It has become a wry complaint in "Why Should Not Old Men Be Mad?" or "John Kinsella's Lament for Mrs. Mary Moore" with the latter's refrain, "What shall I do for pretty girls now my old bawd is dead?"[14] Old age now brings more nostalgia, more recollection: the persisting question of "What then?", the private images of "Beautiful Lofty Things," the moving tour of the images of a life in "The Municipal Gallery Revisited." These last two edge on sentimentality, but in Yeats's very last poems, "The Black Tower" and "Cuchulain Comforted," sentimentality is altogether banished in favor of heroic defiance and heroic acceptance. Those are extremely difficult poems, and so are many of these late lyrics. Yet the difficulties and the urge to puzzle out the private significances should not prevent us from seeing the glorious mastery of the poet's craft. No modern poet can equal Yeats's control of traditional stanzaic forms; few approach his ability to create and sustain breathtaking patterns of imagery. And few poets indeed have quite equaled his ability to turn the utterly right phrase.

Yeats died at Mentone, in the south of France, on January 28, 1939. Before slipping into a final coma, he dictated corrections for his last play and poem. At the funeral, one mourner remembered gravediggers working in another part of the cemetary: "Standing in the bitter wind of the mountain range, the words of the Protestant Burial Service were scattered far and wide by the blast; 'I heard a voice from Heaven saying unto me, 'Write!' The rest seemed blown away."[15] Now the rest is blown away; Yeats has become his poems and his admirers. Only a few weeks before his death, he wrote in a letter, "Man can embody truth; he cannot know it."[16] That, in nine words, is

[14] *Variorum Poems*, p. 620.

[15] Dorothy Wellesley, ed., *Letters on Poetry from W. B. Yeats to Dorothy Wellesley* (1940; London: Oxford Univ. Press, 1964), p. 195.

[16] *Letters of W. B. Yeats*, p. 922.

the story of his life. The quest for ultimate truth that took him to studies of Blake, the occult, Theosophy, philosophy, and, ultimately, to *A Vision* was a failure; that sort of truth he never knew, as none of us can. But his poems embodied truth as no other poet's in our centuries have. Intellectually, the truths may be partial and incomplete, but the fifty or so best of his poems are poetic truth as it has been revealed to no other Irish poet. Moreover, he had a heroic life, full, rich, and passionate. He created the Irish Renaissance and if sometimes later he erred in his judgments on Irish writers and their works, he was also the presiding genius of a golden age, the "onlie begetter" not only of great poems but of a great literary movement. Amy Stock, near the end of her fine study of Yeats, observes that he rejected most of the things the modern world values, "but found and synthesized what answered to certain enduring qualities in himself: joy in heroic greatness, indifference to mere sublunary defeat; faith in eternity and love of passionate life, not at war with each other but inseparable as two sides of a penny; love of his own ancestral roots, a deep conviction that mind is the source of all things."[17] His greatness lies in his ability to answer those qualities in himself; it lies in the variety of his achievement, the fulness of his vision, and the enduring sense that poetry matters because life matters. He wrote his own epitaph, a coldly chastening one in "Under Ben Bulben," but a slight poem, "A Prayer for Old Age" provides a better commentary on the later Yeats:

> God guard me from those thoughts men think
> In the mind alone;
> He that sings a lasting song
> Thinks in a marrow-bone;
>
> From all that makes a wise old man
> That can be praised of all;
> O what am I that I should not seem
> For the song's sake a fool?
>
> I pray—for fashion's word is out
> And prayer comes round again—
> That I may seem, though I die old,
> A foolish, passionate man.[18]

---

17 *W. B. Yeats: His Poetry and Thought* (Cambridge: Cambridge Univ. Press, 1964), p. 240.
18 *Variorum Poems*, p. 553.

By the time of Yeats's death, the Irish Renaissance as a coherent phenomenon was diffusing. The great years of Irish drama had been over for a
decade; Irish fiction remained strong, but it found its strength in reaction
against Ireland, and, indeed, in reaction against much of what the Irish
Renaissance had stood for. The situation in Irish poetry was a bit different,
though. Already some young poets, Thomas MacGreevy and Dennis Devlin,
for example, were finding in Paris and international modernism a new imaginative home. But other figures remained physically and creatively a part of
Ireland and a part, really, of the Irish Renaissance. Two, Austin Clarke and
Patrick Kavanagh, were to prove important connectors between the Renaissance and contemporary poetry in Ireland, and, although it violates chronology
to some extent, both need to be discussed here. Clarke's first volume appeared
as early as 1917; Kavanagh's in 1936, although he had published poems in
newspapers and magazines before that. Each did some of his best work as late
as the 1960s, and in very different ways both became presiding figures over
the Irish poetry of our own time. The two had little in common superficially;
Kavanagh heartily disliked Clarke, and the feeling must have been returned,
though Clarke was never as flamboyant in his dislikes as Kavanagh. But both
made remarkable poetic pilgrimages, Clarke from the Celtic Twilight to bitter
satire, Kavanagh from rural impressionism and angry satire to life-affirming
lyricism. Between them, they defined some of the main trends in Irish poetry
of the last thirty or forty years, and each provided, too, an exemplary demonstration of the condition of the Irish poet.

One of Austin Clarke's later poems, *Forget Me Not* (1962), begins with
a childrens' rhyme about a horse:

> Up the hill,
> Hurry me not;
> Down the hill;
> Worry me not;
> On the level,
> Spare me not,
> In the stable,
> Forget me not.

There then follows a prosodist's learned explanation of the verse:

> Trochaic dimeter, amphimacer
> And choriamb, with hyper catalexis,

Grammatical inversion, springing of double
Rhyme. So we learned to scan all, analyse
Lyric and ode, elegy, anonymous patter,
For what is song itself but substitution?[19]

An odd introduction for what proves to be an important poem, but entirely characteristic of Clarke. Poetry for him began with the commonplace, the ordinary, especially in his later work, and one of the strengths of the enormous amount of poetry he wrote in his old age is its placement in the ordinary experience of Irish life. Dublin buildings, schoolchildren, nuns, missionaries en route to Africa, politicians, all the stuff of newspapers and popular culture, provide the topics for his verse. But as the childrens' rhyme is turned quickly into prosodic analysis, so Clarke regularly turns from ordinary experience to complex analysis. The basis for the analysis is his strong moral sense; the method involves all the techniques of the learned and utterly professional poet: puns, assonance, inversions, grammatical substitutions, and the rest. As in W. H. Auden's later poetry, we are constantly reminded that Clarke is a craftsman who knows all the skills of his trade, but where Auden's technical learning is lightly worn, Clarke's is not. He can be pedantic about it; he is never less than learned. He once told Robert Frost that his way of writing a poem was to "load myself with chains and try to get out of them,"[20] and the metaphor shows an exact self-knowledge.

Clarke was born in 1896 into an old Dublin family, respectable and bourgeois. A Catholic, he was strengthened and brutalized by his faith. Like James Joyce, he went to Belvedere College, experienced a Joyce-like crisis of faith there, and went on to University College, Dublin, the successor to Joyce's university. There, in the time around the Easter Rising, he came under the influence of Thomas MacDonagh, a lecturer in English literature at UCD who, in 1916, would die for his part in the rebellion. MacDonagh was a thoroughgoing nationalist, but he was also a literary critic of real distinction, and his *Literature in Ireland*, published after his death, embodies his notion of an Irish Mode in Anglo-Irish literature, a poetry based on the themes and the techniques of Gaelic poetry but those transferred into English.

After MacDonagh's death, Clarke, still in his early twenties, was for four years his successor at UCD. He lost his position in 1921 when the authorities

19 *Collected Poems* (Dublin: Dolmen Press, 1974), p. 237.
20 *Ibid.*, p. 545.

learned that he had married, not in a church but in a registry office. That was one of several incidents that helped alienate Clarke from institutional Catholicism, and the marriage itself helped bring on an emotional crisis which led to a breakdown and a period of wandering which kept him out of Ireland for many years. Between 1923 and 1937 he was a book reviewer in London. Nevertheless, Clarke became a prolific poet early on. His *Vengeance of Fionn* (1917) earned a long review in the London *Times Literary Supplement* and went into an early second edition, astonishing notice for an Irish poet hardly yet legally an adult. This long poem, based on the old story of Diarmuid, Grainne, and the vengeance of the cuckolded Finn Mac Cumaill, seemed to suggest that Clarke's basic affinities were with the Celtic Twilight of the 1890s. Later volumes, *The Sword of the West* (1921) and *The Cattledrive in Connaught* (1925), with poems based on ancient legend, reinforced that impression. But the impression is superficial. Clarke did retell some of the stories that had fired the imaginations of the poets of the nineties, but his verse had little of their gauzy lyricism. Even in this early work, his quick intelligence is obvious in the puns, elaborate verbal constructs, and complex patterns of assonance and internal rhyme modeled on the techniques of Gaelic poetry. There are also some serious problems with the poems. Clarke tended always to be garrulous, and even the first sentence of *The Vengeance of Fionn* runs to eleven lines of contorted grammar and syntax. Sometimes the technical mastery in these poems is impressive, but sometimes it turns to an Irish imitation of Swinburne. Bits and pieces of the retellings of legend are impressive, but the wholes rarely satisfy, and the best of his early work is found in the dramatic lyrics scattered among the longer poems. "The Scholar," in *The Sword of the West*, and "The Frenzy of Suibhne," in *The Cattledrive in Connaught*, are both fine dramatic lyrics, and Clarke seems gradually to have realized that this sort of poetry, more personal than a retelling of legend but still at a distance from subjective statement, was his natural form.

By the late 1920s he was clearly looking for a new method and a new matter. A poem on Moses, *The Fires of Baal* (1921), had been one attempt to find a new theme, but it was not a success. In 1927, though, he published a three-act verse play, *The Son of Learning*, based on the medieval *Vision of Mac Con Glinne*. The medieval text itself is one of the great Gaelic satires, sharply critical of the Church, and Clarke seemed to find himself both in satire and in the medieval setting. No other writer had really taken up the theme of medieval Ireland, not the Ireland of heroic antiquity, but the Ireland of the Danish and Anglo-Norman invasions and after, still Celtic but increasingly a part of a larger European civilization. As Ben Bulben, the haunted mountain near Sligo, became a fundamental part of Yeats's poetic geography, so the Rock of Cashel, the great eruption in the Munster plain crowned by the ruins of a medieval cathedral, became a part of Clarke's. The Catholic piety, more Celtic than Roman, the unabashed learning, and the tough view of life of medieval Ireland all appealed to him. His next collection of poems, *Pilgrimage* (1929) reflected some of that interest, and it contains some fine work. There are no verse-narratives here; instead, we find powerful lyrics, personal yet distanced. The title poem is an important exercise in the new mode, the account of a medieval pilgrimage to Cashel and its significance. "Celibacy" is an even finer monologue of a cleric torn between passion and asceticism. The great poem on sensuality in the collection, though, is "The Confession of Queen Gormlai," the monologue of a passionate medieval queen "Murmuring of the sins / Whose hunger is the mind." This is balanced by "The Young Woman of Beare," another lyric of a passionate woman, this one a reversal on the Old Woman of Beare who, bitter but still alive, speaks one of the great lyrics of medieval Gaelic poetry. But every poem in the volume is an achieved statement, impressive proof of the way Clarke had found his imagination and a unique poetic voice. The same interest in medieval Ireland also inspired a good one-act play, *The Flame* (1930) and an even better prose romance, *The Bright Temptation* (1932). The latter is a wonderful recounting of the adventures of an Irish monk, Aidan, about the time of the Danish invasions. With something of the fantasy of James Stephens, Clarke sends Aidan through all sorts of scrapes, including being kidnapped by the Sidhe, before he is finally reunited with Ethna, his almost magical, preordained beloved. The story lets him exploit his interest in medieval Ireland and his bent for satire, the two inextricably mixed at this point; while it makes some bitter observations of Irish puritanism, it ends up being a celebration of the innocence of the senses and a delightful tale.

The Bright Temptation was Clarke's most successful *sustained* effort to that point in his career, and it was characteristic of him that he would turn to the prose romance after writing a series of verse-narratives; he had a strong storytelling urge and a desire to achieve in the longer forms. Eventually, he would turn away from lyric poetry for a long period to devote himself to poetic drama, but before that happened he published his *Collected Poems* (1936), a summation of his work to that point, and one further volume of shorter poems, *Night and Morning* (1938). This was the first volume to be published after his return to Ireland from the long period in London, and it came at a point at which Clarke was receiving little attention in his native country. As Donald Davie notes, Yeats ignored him in his *Oxford Book of Modern Verse,* while making room for many other Irish poets, and *Night and Morning,* like many of his later volumes, was published in a small edition under the imprint of his own Bridge Press. Clarke almost seemed to be seeking obscurity by doing that, and the poems in *Night and Morning* are themselves difficult and obscure. Nevertheless, this volume is one of Clarke's great achievements, a collection of superb dramatic lyrics, perhaps the finest religious poems written by an Irish Catholic in the century. Yet the poems, all intensely personal, are hardly conventional religious verse. Some are meditations on Passion Week; others focus on the poet's unhappiness with a faith he cannot give up and a Church he cannot fully accept. The speaking voice is a painfully honest one whether observing the mystery of the Mass in "Night and Morning," meditating in the dark shadows of faith in "Tenebrae," or fighting with itself in "Repentance." Perhaps the most remarkable poem in the volume, for its sympathy and intensity, is "Martha Blake," observations on a pious woman at communion, but every poem in the collection is masterful.

In spite of the accomplishment of *Night and Morning,* this was to be Clarke's last collection of poems for seventeen years. He turned to verse drama, and in 1940 founded, with Robert Farren, another poet and playwright, the Dublin Verse-Speaking Society to produce verse plays for radio. Irish radio is often given to a stifling kind of provinciailty, but it has a good record in encouraging verse and especially verse drama. Padraic Fallon and Padraic Colum wrote some impressive work for the medium later on, and the radio network also presented the first of Brendan Behan's plays. Clarke himself ended up writing some work for radio; a short play, *As the Crow Flies,* was broadcast in 1942, but he was really more comfortable with a more conventional theater. The Lyric Theatre Company grew out of the Verse-Speaking Society, and for several years it would rent the Abbey for a week or two at a time to present poetic drama. There is, of course, a certain irony in a group of outsiders having to rent the Abbey to present the sort of plays that the theater itself was originally created to perform, but such was the situation at the Abbey and in Ireland in the 1940s. As it turned out, Clarke's experiments with verse drama never really became much more than experiments, although he wrote enough plays to fill two volumes. Some of them, *Sister Eucharia* (1939), for example, have fine poetry in them, but banal or undramatic situations. Others, *The Plot is Ready* (1943) is one, are effective dramatic ideas which are damaged by inept stagecraft. Nevertheless, Clarke and his group helped keep verse-drama alive in

Ireland. That helped make possible some more impressive work in the form later: Donagh MacDonagh's excellent *Happy as Larry* (1947) as well as the radio plays of Fallon and Colum.

The verse plays were a noble experiment, but the most remarkable phase of Clarke's career began in 1955 with the publication of *Ancient Lights*, a new volume of poems and the first of nearly a dozen volumes he would publish before his death in 1974. The poems from this last phase of his career take up nearly two-thirds of the pages in his *Collected Poems* in the 1974 edition, and, to a considerable extent, they represent a new departure. Many are openly topical in their satire; many are bitter, but few show the exhaustion of invention one might expect in an aging poet. In fact, Clarke enjoyed almost a rejuvenation. He remained the complexly learned poet, but he also learned to take chances. Some of the later poems fail because of that; they become too prolix and personal. Yet the best of them are a remarkable achievement, none more than a very late sequence, *Mnemosyne Lay in Dust* (1966), a superb set in the confessional mode made popular in the United States by much younger men, Robert Lowell, John Berryman, W. D. Snodgrass. That Clarke in old age would adopt a method which seems peculiarly a part of our own time rather than the time in which he first matured is characteristic of him; he never lost the ability to grow. Maurice Harmon describes Clarke's later work well by saying: "Many of these poems are concerned with the conflict between the desire for freedom of action and self-expression and the regulations of the Church. The most personal, dominated by religious images and the contrasting images of natural freedoms, are the result of a genuine spiritual need. Clarke is inescapably attracted to the idea of sin, guilt, and damnation; he cannot ignore conscience and feels the need for repentance. . . . But his work is not limited to a self-centered interest. It is human and passionate in its concern for the dignity of man. . . . He is concerned with the outcast, the misfit, the mistreated, and with the individual who does not conform or blend with his environment."[21]

Ancient Lights, subtitled "poems and satires," contains a good many of both, none more moving than "Three poems about children," harrowing commentaries on children burned to death in an orphanage fire and a bishop's smug assurance of their immediate entry into Heaven. The poems are worthy of Swift at his most acid and horrified, though the craftsmanship is better. Satiric comment on the local Irish situation also dominates the next collection, *Too Great*

---

[21] "The Later Poetry of Austin Clarke," *The Celtic Cross*, p. 48.

a Vine (1957). In a note to the volume, Clarke mentions a Dublin ancestor who amused himself by wearing different colored wigs and writing satiric squibs, a good metaphor for Clarke himself here. The poems range from comments on the Abbey Theatre fire and a plan to reenact the trial of Robert Emmet to a powerful personal confession, "The Loss of Strength." Encouraged by support from Liam Miller and his Dolmen Press, the press that has done more for Irish poetry in our time than any other, Clarke continued to publish at an astonishing rate through the 1960s. *The Horse-Eaters* (1960), his first book to come from Dolmen rather than his own Bridge Press, upset some readers by seeming to devote an inordinate amount of space to various schemes to exploit the Irish horse-raising industry. It seemed an odd, even slightly silly, theme, but the next book, the remarkable *Forget Me Not* (1962), demonstrates that Clarke was finding in man's inhumanity to horses a potent metaphor for his dismay at the almost sacrilegious way we exploit the natural world and cut ourselves off from the natural order. *Forget Me Not* is a great poem, nostalgic in one sense, but unforgettable in its evocation of the horse as perpetual symbol. In some of Clarke's later poems the Swiftian savage indignation carried him almost too far. "Precautions" in *Flight to Africa* (1963) is simply a nasty little verse, but "Burial of an Irish President" is a powerful comment on the poisonous effects of religious intolerance in Irish life, a theme employed with sympathy and even pathos in the moving "Street Game."

That poem is a fine example of Clarke's sympathy with the victimized and his iron contempt for those who harm them. Yet the most lasting of his later poems may well prove to be the poems of private confession, "From a Diary of Dreams" in *Flight to Africa*, equivalent poems in other volumes, and *Mnemosyne Lay in Dust*. This last, based on personal experience but distanced by third-person narration and the *persona* of Maurice Devane, is the extraordinary narrative of a mental breakdown, incarceration in an asylum, and final release. It is, in one sense, a poem on the loss of memory (hence the title), but it is also a poem on the inability to escape from memory. The sequence could become pathetic as some confessional poetry does, but Clarke's powerful craftsmanship prevents that. Other confessional poets have given us searing accounts of mental collapse, but none has quite equaled Clarke's control of the experience; because of that, we share Devane's experience almost completely and stand apart from it at the same time, a remarkable achievement. Confession is an important part of Clarke's later work, and so is satire, and so is an almost nostalgic reverence for the recent Irish literary past. *Old Fashioned Pilgrimage* (1967) is a collection of poems about travel to America and Yugoslavia, those mixed with bitter satires on priests encouraging exhausted women to have yet more babies and customs' house officials censoring imported books on painting. The voice in the travel poems is gentler than in the earlier satires, and a gentler voice yet emerges in *The Echo at Coole* (1968), an interesting group with effectively ruminative poems on Yeats, Stephens, and, especially, F. R. Higgins. The moral imagination and the satiric voice are not gone; "Above Party," a poem of Eamon de Valera shows that. Age, perhaps, was catching him, though; the ruminative spirit is attractive in this volume, but in some of his very last work, *A Sermon on Swift* (1968) and *Orphide* (1970), the imaginative grip seems loosened. Even so, *Tiresias* (1971), the story of the ancient figure turned from man to woman here given as "a cheerful account of the experiences of Tiresias as wife and mother,"[22] is astonishing in its poetic inventiveness and even its sense of the absurd. And perhaps it was appropriate that Clarke ended where he began; *The Wooing of Becfola* (1974), nearly sixty years after *The Vengeance of Fionn*, is an account from Irish legend, brief and finally controlled.

Clarke's was, then, a remarkable creative achievement, and it was not entirely confined to poetry. His plays add something to it, though his literary criticism adds rather less. More substantial, though, are *The Bright Temptation* and his other prose romances, *The Singing Men at Cashel* (1936) and *The Sun Dances at Easter* (1952), both fascinating as evocations of the Irish medieval past and as commentaries on puritanism and sensuality. His other important prose work, an autobiography, *Twice Round the Black Church* (1962), is a fine example of a genre in which many Irish writers have excelled. In sum, then, Clarke was an important if erratic artist, too personal and quirky perhaps to ever have a wide readership, but for those who care, addictive.

In many ways, Patrick Kavanagh was the opposite of the patrician, private Clarke. A rambunctious countryman from County Monaghan, he was a famous quarreller in pubs, perfectly willing to tell another writer that he had read his book and it was no good. His life was often a dishevelled mess, and one famous Dublin story recounts how another poet, seeing a load of manure go by, said, "Ah, I see Paddy Kavanagh's moving lodgings again!" He came on the Dublin scene in the 1930s as a professional bumpkin, the real peasant out to upset all the genteel poets who liked to write about the peasantry but could not stand the stench of the barnyard. Yet the image of Kavanagh as a poetic naif and loudmouthed stage-Irishman is unfair. Especially in his later work, he demonstrated that he was the most able Irish lyricist since Yeats, and under the rough

[22] Austin Clarke, *Collected Poems*, p. 557.

facade there was poetic cunning, a sharp intellect, and a bruised soul. Like Clarke, whom he detested personally, he played the ancient role of the satirist, and, again like Clarke, his early career was stunted by the Ireland of his time. The 1940s were a bad time to be an Irish writer, and Kavanagh suffered from his time and place as much as anyone. As Darcy O'Brien puts it: "Having seen the nationalist myths dissolve, disheartened by the values of the developing society, the better Irish writers had by 1940 turned caustically critical. Most got themselves banned. Sean O'Faolain used his editorial columns in *The Bell* to attack the Government and the Church. The most talented novelist of the period, Flann O'Brien, ended one of his novels with a meditation on suicide, another with a purgative gush of vomit; a third is in its entirety a psychic map of Hell."[23] Such poems of Kavanagh's as "The Great Hunger" (1942) and "The Paddiad" (1949) reflect his own intense bitterness, but he found a way to integrate that anger into a more complete vision of experience. His unique vision—gay, simple, and self-consciously parochial—made him something very close to a great poet. It made him, too, especially in Ireland, a poet's poet, and his influence on recent Irish poetry has been enormous.

In an essay called "Suffering and Literature," Kavanagh wrote that the basic experience of the poet was a journey "from simplicity back to simplicity."[24] That journey began for him in 1904 in Inniskeen, County Monaghan, where he was born the son of a shoemaker and small farmer. Kavanagh remembered his birthplace as "a traditional Irish cabin, wedge-shaped, to trick the western winds," surrounded by a neighbor's field with the bog beyond and "little hills all tilled and tame." It was a world in which "The Parish Priest was the centre of gravity, he was the only man who was sure to go to Heaven. Our staple diet was potatoes and oatmeal porridge. Porridge had only recently taken the place of potatoes and buttermilk as the national supper. Though little fields and scraping poverty do not lead to grand flaring passions, there was plenty of fire and an amount of vicious neighbourly hatred to keep us awake."[25] He began to write poetry about the time he left school in 1916, but until 1930 and beyond he earned his living as a hired hand, apprentice shoemaker, and farmer. His early poems, influenced by Thomas Moore and Mangan, were good enough for the poets' corners of such small town newspapers as the *Dundalk Democrat*, but, in 1929, AE accepted some of his work for the *Irish Statesman*. That impelled him to want a wider world than Monaghan, and a year later he walked

23 *Patrick Kavanagh* (Lewisburg, Pa.: Bucknell University Press, 1975), pp. 18–19.
24 *Collected Pruse* (London: MacGibbon and Kee, 1967), p. 278.
25 *The Green Fool* (1938; Harmondsworth, Middlesex: Penguin, 1975), p. 11.

to Dublin to make his reputation. AE, always the friend of young and hungry Irish poets, took him in, lent him some books, and helped him introduce himself to Dublin literary society. Kavanagh played the role of the rustic bard, and that is reflected in the title of his first collection of poems, *The Ploughman* (1936). It was an uneven collection, but the best of Kavanagh's early work already showed the direction he would take in his best poetry. The poems had surprisingly little to do with what had been going on in Irish poetry for half a century. Like Colum's early poetry, for example, Kavanagh's had a rural energy to it, but Kavanagh was already a better craftsman, fresh, direct, and genuinely innocent.

Even so, Kavanagh's early work had more promise than achievement, and the enemies of promise were almost omnipresent. One was poverty. Believing that he might make more of a reputation in London than Dublin, Kavanagh went there briefly after the publication of his first book, but he failed to crash the London literary scene and ended up selling souvenirs at the coronation of George VI before he returned to Monaghan. He then wrote an autobiographical novel, *The Green Fool* (1938), a charming evocation of his childhood and youth on the farm and his attempt to make himself into a poet. It is, as Seamus Heaney observes, a mediation between his rural origins and his sophisticated audience "with a knowing sociological wink,"[26] and it is a charming and obliquely revealing book. The innocence of his early poems is all through it, but one bit of innocence got him into considerable trouble. Telling of his arrival in Dublin, he describes his ignorant assumption that Oliver Gogarty's maid was his mistress. The self-depreciation is perfectly obvious in the comment, "I expected every poet to have a spare wife,"[27] but Gogarty took offense and sued for libel. That led to the withdrawal of the book, and the furor over *The Green Fool* marked the beginning of a period of intense bitterness for Kavanagh. Through the 1940s and after he became an increasingly strident critic of Irish life and letters.

Controversy continually followed him. His most important poem from this period, "The Great Hunger," was banned in Ireland after its publication in Cyril Connolly's journal, *New Horizons*, in 1942. Seven years later, in "The Paddiad," Kavanagh excoriated the smugness and mediocrity of Irish poetry in his time, telling how Paddy Whiskey, Rum and Gin, Paddy of the Celtic mist,

26 "The Poetry of Patrick Kavanagh: From Monaghan to the Grand Canal," *Two Decades of Irish Writing*, p. 109.

27 *The Green Fool*, p. 228.

Paddy Frog, and all the other poetic Paddies gathered to croak nightly in the bog that was their favorite pub as they puffed each other's wares and decently interred any real Irish talent. It was a mean satire, too true for comfort if not true enough to be a great poem, and it, together with many other satiric poems on the state of Irish letters, helped make Kavanagh plenty of enemies. In 1952, he and his brother, Peter, added to the melee by producing, for thirteen too-short issues, a newspaper, *Kavanagh's Weekly*. Full of tough, hardheaded, nasty comment, *Kavanagh's Weekly* was in the best tradition of eighteenth-century satiric pamphleteering, and it made the Kavanaghs even more unbeloved. Three months after *Kavanagh's Weekly* folded, *The Leader* ran a "profile" on him. It was written anonymously (though rumor has always said that Brendan Behan had a hand in it), and it began by paying tribute to Kavanagh's talent. That lasted for a paragraph, but the remainder of the essay was a vicious attack, no worse, perhaps than what Kavanagh had said about other writers and not necessarily untruthful, but cruel nevertheless. Kavanagh was portrayed as a malevolent alcoholic given to praising himself, accepting the praise of sycophants, and damning everyone else. Kavanagh sued for libel, and the case, one of the great *causes célèbres* in modern Irish literary history, came to trial in February of 1954. A former prime minister, John A. Costello, was the chief counsel for the defendants, and the transcript of the trial, printed in Kavanagh's *Collected Pruse*, is still extremely entertaining and a little pathetic. He lost the case, but it gave him a good deal of public attention and the chance to air his views before a larger audience than usually cared about poetry, and perhaps that, as much as his damaged reputation, was his point in bringing suit.

The satirizing and the pamphleteering took much of Kavanagh's energy between 1938 and 1955, but not all of it. His most important work from this period was a long poem, "The Great Hunger," and a novel, *Tarry Flynn* (1948). Both have their settings in the rural Ireland Kavanagh knew so well, and each deals with a man who wants something more from life than the poverty and routine that peasant life can provide. The central figure in "The Great Hunger" is a farmer, Patrick Maguire, the prisoner of his mother, his farm, and his own lack of initiative. "Watch him, watch him," the speaker of the poem tells us, "that man on a hill whose spirit/Is a wet sack flapping about the knees of time."[28] Maguire's is one of those lives in which nothing happens. He works his land, waiting for his mother to die so that he may marry. She

---

[28] *Collected Poems* (1964; London: Martin Brien and O'Keeffe, 1972), p. 35.

dies, finally, at ninety-one, but by then Maguire himself is sixty-five, too old for marriage, for sensuality, for the imaginative life. He has stumbled through a lifetime of trivia, quarrels with his sister, card games, sexual fantasies, masturbation. The theme of the poem is the tension, perhaps dysfunction is a better word, between the institutions of Church and peasant life and the natural world. Unnatural because Church, family, and peasantness have made it that way, Maguire's life becomes barren repetition even as nature's cycle of birth, death, and rebirth goes on all around him. Kavanagh himself later dismissed the poem by saying, "There are some queer and terrible things in *The Great Hunger*, but it lacks the nobility and repose of poetry."[29] Perhaps, but it comes close to being a great poem. It is too long, too repetitious, and sometimes self-indulgent, but no other Irish poem quite captures the real condition of the peasant so fully. Section XIII of the poem demolishes fifty years of adulaton of peasant virtues in Irish poetry, but the entire poem seems a liberation of something crucial in the Irish imagination, something the Anglo-Irish agricultural tourists like Yeats and Higgins had never understood. Dark and brooding over ordinary experience, it, and others of Kavanagh's poems like "Spraying the Potatoes," helped give rise to a new mode in Irish verse. "The Great Hunger" is the phrase commonly used in Ireland to refer to the Famine of the 1840s, and the analogy between physical and sensual hunger is an important one in much recent Irish poetry, too, but the poem's real importance is, finally, in its language. There is the famous Biblical introduction:

> Clay is the word and clay is the flesh
> Where the potato-gatherers like mechanised scarecrows move
> Along the side-fall of the hill—Maguire and his men.

Sometimes there is too much rhetoric and too much insistence, but Kavanagh is often at his best in a simplicity that would be absurd if it were not somehow *right*, as in the description of Maguire at thirty-four or thirty-five.

> Sitting on a wooden gate,
> Sitting on a wooden gate,
> Sitting on a wooden gate
> He didn't care a damn.[30]

29 *Collected Prose*, p. 37.
30 *Collected Poems*, pp. 34 and 43.

The cursing failure of Maguire's life is his failure to escape; *Tarry Flynn*, Kavanagh's second autobiographical novel, takes an almost Maguire-like figure, farm boy but a bit of the poet, and lets him escape. Unlike Stephen Dedalus, Tarry becomes a real poet, but only after a series of adventures with the Church and the senses that recall Stephen's career. But this is a country book with Dargan, County Monaghan, in place of Dublin and a rustic's open innocence in place of Stephen's furtive guilt. The terrors of sermonizing religion are real enough, but it is a far cry from the Jesuit retreat in *Portrait of the Artist* to the absurd Redemptorist mission in *Tarry Flynn*. Tarry eventually leaves the village world of matchmaking and piety, but only after a series of hilarious adventures and half-adventures. For the bitterness of "The Great Hunger," Kavanagh here gives us gaiety, laughing acceptance. The satiric barbs are there in plenty, but they are not an end in themselves; instead, they are part of a full and life-affirming comic vision.

That vision governs the best of Kavanagh's later poetry. *Tarry Flynn* was written several years before "The Paddiad" or the furors over *Kavanagh's Weekly* and the article in *The Leader*, but the balance and vision of the novel came into his poems only after a traumatic experience in 1955, an operation for lung cancer. As Kavanagh says, "I lost my messianic compulsion. I sat on the bank of the Grand Canal in the summer of 1955 and let the water lap idly on the shores of my mind. My purpose in life was to have no purpose."[31] After that experience (the "Grand Canal," incidentally, is Dublin's, not Venice's), satire became a less important element in his work. Making his own return to simplicity, Kavanagh found a new poetic voice in celebrating himself, the ordinariness of his experience, doing that through poems that seem casual and almost slapdash. At his later least, self-celebration led to the self-pity of "Sensational Disclosures (Kavanagh Tells All)" and the unsustained satire of "Who Killed James Joyce?" At his best, though, the later Kavanagh cut out an important poetic world for himself. As Darcy O'Brien puts it, "Kavanagh tried to be parochial without being provincial, he wrote of the universal particular. 'Parochialism and provincialism,' Kavanagh used to say, 'are direct opposites. A provincial is always trying to live by other people's loves, but a parochial is self-sufficient.'"[32] That distinction is important because it permitted him freedom from the norms of the Irish poetic tradition. Good, bad, or indifferent, his poetic voice is always his own and no one else's. It is at its most substantial in

31 *Ibid.*, p. xiv.
32 *Patrick Kavanagh*, p. 14.

such wonderful sonnets as "Miss Universe," "Come Dance with Kitty Stobling," and "Winter." The formal demands of the sonnet brought out the best in him, but many of his later poems are superbly controlled personal statements. His imagery may seem plain and unremarkable to those accustomed to Yeats's wild-fire or Clarke's intricate chains, but the images are sharp, clean, and precisely used. The patterns of rhyme and half-rhyme are in the best manner of Anglo-Irish poetry; in that, if in not much else, he showed his affinities with the past, for the best Irish poetry has always been scrupulously alert to the possibilities of interlocking sound and sense. Beyond technical expertise, the best of the later poems are informed by a genuine comic vision, not always laughing by any means, but always affirming the possibilities of life and the sense that some of its meaning is there for the taking. These poems sometimes seem far distant from the Kavanagh of popular memory, an angry, rude man holding forth in McDaid's or the Bailey to whomever would listen and buy a round. Yet it is Kavanagh's poems that endure, and his importance in Irish poetry was already well established before his death in 1967. As much as any poet, he liberated Irish poetry from the ghosts of the past, the powerful ghost of Yeats in particular. That liberation had its dangers; too many young poets mistook his casualness for sloppiness. He was, unquestionably, an erratic talent. Seamus Heaney phrases it well by saying that there is a feeling of "prospector's luck . . . about many of his best efforts,"[33] but even so he demonstrated that a poet, even an Irish poet, could be a poet simply by being himself. An obvious lesson, a liberation into ignorance as one successor has said, but an important one in his time and his country. As Kavanagh himself put it:

> The main thing is to continue
> To Walk Parnassus right into the sunset
> Detached in love where pygmies cannot pin you
> To the ground like Gulliver. So good luck and cheers.[34]

The title for this chapter comes from a translation of St.-John Perse by Denis Devlin, "doors open on exile." What exile? the reader may well ask, for almost every poet mentioned here did his most significant work in Ireland, not in exile. Yet exile is a state of mind as well as a state of the body, and every valuable Irish poet in this period became some sort of exile. Higgins, for ex-

[33] *Two Decades of Irish Writing*, p. 107.
[34] "Dear Folks," *Collected Poems*, p. 151.

ample, exiled himself in the west of Ireland, but his real exile was in a land Yeats had created, the mists of the Celtic Twilight, and that was his undoing. Some of the young poets of the 1930s found exile in the anonymous world of modernism, giving up Ireland for Auden's world. Yeats himself, physically often a wanderer, found early on an exile in his imagination. Whether imagining himself in Byzantium with the sages or on a back-country road with Crazy Jane, he exiled himself, as only the greatest creative artists can, fully into his own imagination. He was, as Thomas Parkinson reminds us, a great poet who happened to have lived in the twentieth century and in Ireland, neither fully a modern poet nor fully an Irish poet, yet more wholly modern and perhaps more wholly Irish than any contemporary. Clarke and Higgins found exiles, too; Clarke in medieval Ireland and in the study of his house, Templelogue. Kavanagh, when he wandered off from the pubs to the banks of the Grand Canal, found exile and himself. The doors were open on exile for all the poets. The weak ones shut the doors completely to become what Kavanagh would have called Paddy-poets, safe by the Irish fire. Stronger ones passed through the doors into self-created isolation, the beginning of greatness even in that most social land called Ireland. The fullness of the exile chosen was in direct proportion to the fullness of the poetic vision accepted and the final greatness of the achievement.

since the irish renaissance
Recent Irish Writing

I will feel lost,
Unhappy and at home.

Seamus Heaney

Irish proverb

Is cuma no muc fear gan seift (The man without
an expedient is of no more account than a pig.)

I T IS DIFFICULT to say when a literary phenomenon like the Irish Renaissance began; it is even more difficult to say when it ended. Rather
arbitrarily, I have chosen 1885 as a date for the beginning because a certain
sequence of events began in about that year; even more arbitrarily, I have
chosen 1940 as a date for the end, though the previous chapters have in some
cases gone well beyond 1940 in discussing figures who seem to me to be part
of the Irish Renaissance, even though they were writing as late as the 1970s. A
case could be made, of course, for the idea that the Irish Renaissance never
ended, that it is still with us. Perhaps the case would stand up—certainly
literary work of very high merit is still being done in Ireland—but it seems to
me that things began to change sharply enough around 1940 to justify that date
as a terminus. The original impetus in drama was lost by then. In fiction, the
realistic short story remained for years after 1940 a form in which there was
continuing achievement, but, by the 1950s, the scene in fiction was changing,
too. Since then, the realistic short story has tended to give way to the novel.
In poetry, too, the situation has changed enough to differentiate recent work in

Ireland from the techniques and themes of the Renaissance, although poetry is a particularly complicated case.

Since 1940 Ireland has produced a remarkable amount of distinguished literature; as in the decades before, no comparable nation or region in the English-speaking world with the possible exception of the American South can quite equal the small island's achievement. Yet recent Irish writing is not well known outside Ireland, and names that count for much there mean almost nothing elsewhere. That problem cuts both ways; Ireland remains startlingly provincialized. The lamentable condition of the Irish book-publishing industry has not helped Irish writers make reputations abroad, nor has the stereotype of the Irish writer—verbally fluent with more passion than brains, probably drunk. Americans in particular assume that every Irish writer ought to be like Brendan Behan. Stereotypes, economics, and the vagaries of literary puffing have kept many intelligent readers in Britain and America from knowing anything about recent Irish writing. This chapter tries to do something about that, if only in an extremely sketchy way. Irish writing since 1940 deserves a book to itself, and there is not room here for more than a rapid survey. Nevertheless, a rapid tour seems useful for the sake of basic information and also to provide some sense of how the Irish Renaissance itself helped create and direct the more recent literary culture.

By the time World War II began, Irish drama was entering what was to prove to be a long and barren stretch. New playwrights kept coming, the best of them Michael J. Molloy, author of a series of strong plays about peasant life, but the old energy in Irish drama seemed to be almost gone. Molloy's *The King of Friday's Men* (1948) came close to being a genuine masterpiece, but the Abbey Theatre in which it was presented was a shabby and threadbare place. The smell of decay was in the air, as it was in Irish drama in general. Isolation during the war years was no help, and there was, quite simply, a shortage of real talent. With Yeats dead, the Abbey was under the firm control of men like Ernest Blythe, a former treasury minister who was sure that the Abbey would fulfill its real function only by producing unexceptionable plays about the ordinary realities of Irish life. Blythe meant well by his own lights, but it was characteristic that among the great successes of his regime was a series of Christmas childrens' pantomimes in Gaelic. One can well imagine Synge's or Yeats's comments on that! Louis D'Alton and some of the older playwrights gave the Abbey decent work, but a real upswing in quality came only at the end of the decade with plays by Bryan MacMahon and Seamus Byrne. The latter's *Design for a Headstone* (1950), a strong, realistic play about the IRA after the Civil War, broke no new ground, but it was a solid work.

Still, it was a sign of a generally bad situation when, in 1947, two young writers rose to protest during a performance of the *Plough and the Stars*. Their protest was not against the play itself, as others had protested years before, but against a shoddy performance which, they believed, did violence to a masterpiece. On the night of July 17, 1951, the curtain came down on another performance of the *Plough*. Late that night a fire began in the dressing rooms, and soon it spread through the entire theater. The famous pictures in the lobby were saved, but by the next morning the old Abbey was only a burnt-out shell. The show went on, in the best theatrical tradition; later that day Seaghan Barlow, who had built the first sets for the Abbey back in 1904 and still built them, was making up sets for the evening's performance in a borrowed theater. There was much talk of a phoenix rising from the ashes, but no phoenix ever rose as slowly. For thirteen years the Abbey made do in borrowed theaters, most of the time in the Queen's, a huge and ugly building. The company languished during those years; the Queen's was too big for its distinctive style; without a permanent home, the management seemed to stumble along. It took ten years just to knock down the remaining walls of the old building, and another five before the new theater was in its place. Finally, though, in 1966, the new building opened. Externally, it is a stark block, and some have complained that its stage facilities are not as good as they should be, but from the audience's point of view, it is a fine house. The sight lines are good, the acoustics acceptable, and it has the intimate feel that a theater like the Abbey should have. Yet even in its new house the Abbey has not really been the sort of theater its reputation demands. Productions are usually professionally competent, but they often do not rise above that, and the theater has not done enough to encourage new playwriting talent. Of course, its stringent budget prevents it from trying every kind of experimentation, but the management seems committed to playing it safe at all times. A recent series of Boucicault revivals in indicative of the current situation; expensive productions which do well at the box office, plays like *Arrah-na-Pogue* and *The Shaughraun* are harmless entertainment except that they keep new playwrights' works off the stage.

Nevertheless, the very existence of the Abbey is good for Irish drama, even if it is sometimes nothing more than a whipping boy. Especially during the years when the Abbey was in the wilderness at the Queen's, other companies, some of them not even professional, showed some real vitality. An Amateur Drama Council, formed in 1953, has given direction to the amateur movement by sponsoring festivals all over the country. The Southern Theatre Group in Cork has used John B. Keane's plays and others to build a solid repertory and an able company. Gael Linn, an organization to encourage the Gaelic language, sponsored some interesting original plays in Dublin; the Peacock has continued to take an interest in drama in Gaelic, and An Taibhdhearc in Galway has survived as Ireland's only permanent theater for plays in the language. In Dublin, the universities have done good work at the amateur level, with Trinity College's drama group providing some of the city's most vital drama, while a whole series of little theaters have done important experimental work. But all Irish dramatic activity has not been confined to the Republic, and especially since World War II, Belfast has enjoyed a dramatic renaissance. The religious and political tensions in the province have sometimes done real harm; the Ulster Group Theatre of the 1940s broke up over a production of a play about religious intolerance, Sam Thompson's *Over the Bridge*. But the Belfast Arts Theatre, founded in 1947 by Hubert Wilmot did good experimental work before it became essentially a commercial company. During the recent troubles, Wilmot has led a new company, Interplay, which has brought mobile theater to all parts of the province. The great success story in Ulster, though, has been the Belfast Lyric Theatre, founded in 1951 by Mary O'Malley as a medium for poetic drama. Mrs. O'Malley is an indomitable woman, and the standards in her theater have always been high. It holds the distinction of being the only company in Ireland, the Abbey included, to have produced all of Yeats's plays, and the productions of some of the later verse plays were notably loving and effective. The Lyric Theatre is now housed in a handsome building on the outskirts of Belfast, hopefully far enough away from the bomb-throwers to keep it safe. In its first quarter-century it has established an enviable record of theatrical achievement and simple courage.

Increasingly, it has been these theaters, rather than the Abbey itself, that have carried the burden of innovation in Irish drama. The Dublin Theatre Festival has been helpful in producing plays by foreign playwrights and in encouraging local talent, though it is, quite frankly, a tourist attraction. Nevertheless, the Festival and the little theaters have helped to break down some of the gentility, sense of isolation, and smug provinciality that have been the enemies of real Irish dramatic achievement since World War II. It takes more than a little national arrogance to claim Samuel Beckett as an Irish dramatist, but the very fact that he is an Irishman did no harm to self-esteem among local dramatists, and successful productions of his plays, especially *Waiting for Godot* at the Pike, have helped open a few doors for experimentation. Beckett and the kind of drama he represents will probably never be popular in Ireland, but *Come and Go* and *Play* both had their first productions in English at the Peacock, and Jack McGowran, a remarkable Abbey actor, became a splendid interpreter of Beckett's work before his untimely death.

The great original in recent Irish drama from a Dubliner's point of view, though, was Brendan Behan. In some of his old drinking spots, Behan seems very much alive, and it is difficult to separate "Brending Behing," the great roistering character, from Behan the writer. Yet the separation must be made because it is entirely too easy to turn him into a boozy version of the lovable, irresponsible stage-Irishman, and that is hardly fair to his genuine achievement. Behan lived an immense and sloppy life; his art has some of its immensity, a bit of its sloppiness, and a good deal more besides. Some biographical details may be helpful. He was born in Dublin in 1923 while his father was a Republican prisoner in Kilmainham; one uncle was Peader Kearney, author of the Irish national anthem and employee of the Abbey, an uncle by marriage was the manager of the Queen's Theatre. Behan liked to portray himself as the child of poverty, diehard republicanism, and Guinness, and there is truth in that, but his father, a housepainter, was an important union official for many years, and there was more than a little respectability in his family. Even so, he began early on an outrageous career. At sixteen, in 1939, he was arrested in Liverpool while on an IRA errand to blow up a British battleship. That led to three years in a British borstal, a prison school for juvenile offenders. Returning to Ireland, he was again imprisoned for IRA activities, this time by de Valera's government. After his release he tried for a while to make a living as a housepainter, but the IRA and writing were both more important than mere income. By the early fifties he was an established Dublin character. Some broadcasts of Irish radio brought him some attention as a writer and balladeer, but much of his energy went into writing poems and short stories, one story, "The Communion Suit," coming close to being a masterpiece. Meanwhile, he had started work on a play based on his prison experiences; the Abbey rejected an early draft of it, but Behan kept working, and in 1954 the Pike Theatre agreed to stage it. That play, *The Quare Fellow*, announced resoundingly that a major playwright was on the scene, not perhaps a great literary artist, but a man with brilliant instincts for the theater. Joan Littlewood, the English director, picked it up for her Theater Workshop in 1956, and Behan's reputation spread well beyond Ireland. An Abbey production of the play followed, and two years later, on a commission from Gael Linn, Behan produced another play. *An Giall* was a far cry from the usual farces and melodramas in Gaelic; with Joan Littlewood's urging, Behan

"Englished" it and revised it for production in London. The English version was a great success, and *The Hostage* (1958) remains one of the most astonishing theater pieces by an Irishman of recent decades. By this point Behan was a famous man, famous especially for some drunken broadcasts on the BBC, and the fame ended his best work as a writer, though not before he had published *Borstal Boy*, a rough and touching account of his experiences in the British prison school. Nothing that came after that was especially remarkable, though, and in 1964 he was dead of liver and kidney troubles, diabetes, and jaundice, all complicated by alcoholism.

Behan's reputation as a dramatist must rest on his two major plays, *The Quare Fellow* and *The Hostage*. The center of his imaginative achievement, though, is *Borstal Boy*, the autobiography. It falls into a special subgenre of Irish literature, the prison memoir, and it, with John Mitchel's utterly different nineteenth-century autobiography, are the two great works of the kind. *Borstal Boy* swings back and forth between the grim and the hilarious. The entire book is crafted with the control of a superb dramatist, but certain characteristics of it are especially relevant to Behan the playwright. One is its prison setting; prison becomes a metaphor for the world and rebellion against authority becomes a means of self-authentication, but also an inevitably futile act. Young Brendan has a good deal of cunning (the message he sends back to Ireland after his arrest shows that), but his stance is that of the knowing innocent, wide-eyed but experienced. As a prisoner, he is part of one community of social outcasts; as an Irishman, he is part of another. The sense of a community of outcasts and the sense of knowing innocence are both crucial to *The Quare Fellow* and *The Hostage*. *The Quare Fellow's* prison setting and its random plot of preparations for a hanging make it appear to be a tract against imprisonment and capital punishment, and so it is, but it is more than that. It is fundamentally a play about human relationships—relationships that survive even when prisoners are nameless men and the dead are buried under epitaphs consisting only of numbers, and those misstated so as to make them easier to carve. Prisoners and warders, the omnipresent screws, make up each other's world, and their world is *the* world, a world in which survival is the fundamental good. Identity in the prison, identity period, seems to be reduced to what appears on the card of each prisoner's cell: name, religion, and length of sentence.

That description makes the play seem to be a grim exercise in existentialist drama, but shot through all of this is a macabre humor which comes especially in the songs. *The Hostage* has even more macabre humor and more songs. Comparisons between the two often end up in favor of *The Quare Fellow*, partially because many critics believe *The Hostage* worked largely because of Joan Littlewood's brilliant production. Yet *The Hostage* is the more remarkable play, perhaps more conventional in its stagecraft, but marvelously vital. The scene is a slum rooming house presided over by a veteran of the "troubles" and full of a motley assortment of boarder, prostitutes, homosexuals, and others from Behan's world of social outcasts. The action revolves around Leslie, the young English soldier taken by the IRA as hostage for an IRA man about to be executed in Belfast. By the end of the play Leslie is dead, by accident rather than reprisal, and the plot has given Behan an opportunity for some swipes at all sorts of segments of Irish life, an IRA gone seedy and mean, puritanical Catholicism, decaying Anglo-Irishry, expedient nationalism, ignorant English imperialism. Leslie himself has no idea why he is in Ireland, but the IRA men have no better idea about why they want him and his kind out of Ireland. As a satiric view of the Irish scene in the 1950s, the play is convincing, but it is more convincing as a variation on Behan's theme of the community of outcasts. And it is most convincing as vital theater, a brilliant extravaganza that sweeps us along from the wild Irish jig at the opening to the stunning chorus at the end:

> The bells of hell
> Go ting-a-ling-a-ling,
> For you but not for him,
> Oh death, where is thy sting-a-ling-a-ling!
> Or grave thy victory.[1]

The language of his plays is a very long way indeed from the langorous beauty of the Celtic Twilight, and that is one of their strengths. It is genuine Dublin talk, not the Dublin of O'Casey's tenements, but the Dublin of the working class, pious but not above a "Jesus, Mary, and Joseph," devoted to the IRA but contemptuous of the "bog men," everyone who is not a Dubliner. Behan's talk has a real authenticity, and that is always a basic requirement for good Irish drama. Often, though, Irish dramatists of his generation and later have not found that authenticity. Too many recent Irish plays have a modern version of the "PQ," "peasant quality," that old Abbey Actors were often told to put into their work. And too often, recent Irish plays have seemed fundamentally fraudulent, formally uninteresting, unsure in characterization, second-hand in theme. A kind of "chips and eggs" gentility afflicts too many

---

[1] *The Hostage* (1958; London: Methuen, 1973), p. 97.

of them; others, which toy with the international styles of absurdity and free theater, seem merely imitative. Nevertheless, there are still distinctive voices in the Irish theater, and none at the moment is perhaps more distinctive than John B. Keane. Keane is a pub-keeper in Listowel, County Kerry, and there are worse places to see the world than from behind the bar of a public house in that most flavorful of Irish counties. His career as a dramatist really began with the Listowel Drama Group, one of those many amateur drama groups. His first important play, *Sive* (1956), has been among the most popular written in Ireland in the last two decades. Its plot is one of the most used in Irish drama: a young girl is forced into marriage with an elderly farmer by avaricious relatives. Nevertheless, it is an honest play and true to the rural experience, particularly in its range of real characters. Too often the characters in this sort of play are stereotypes, but Sive herself, her grandmother, Mena, Sean Dota, and even the traveling tinkers all have the thickness of reality. So does the language, and only George Fitzmaurice, another Kerryman, has come as close to capturing the rhythms and idioms of country people in their fullness.

Keane is an able playwright and interesting in terms of the local Irish scene. His work is characteristic of what has been the mainstream in Irish drama for more than seventy years. Like Colum, Murray, Molloy, and a host of others, he writes truly and effectively about the realities of the ordinary Irish experience, especially that of rural Ireland. Yet none of their plays really travels well, and the non-Irish reader and playgoer may well find more satisfaction in plays that are technically more sophisticated. Ireland has produced a number of such plays in recent years and some able playwrights. Bryan MacMahon, like Keane a Listowel man, has done some dramatic work not at all intended for export, patriotic pageants and the like, but he is also a substantial dramatist and an able man of letters in several genres. He has written some fine short stories; *The Lion Tamer and Other Stories* (1948) is a collection that plays a bit to Irish stereotypes, and the stories are sometimes overwritten, but the collection was extremely popular, especially in the United States. His most impressive work, though, is found in his serious plays, two of which, written very close together, have special merit. *The Songs of the Anvil* (1960) deals with an old theme in Irish drama, the desire for a touch of romance in a drab world, but is a fine variation on the theme. Even better is *The Honey Spike* (1961), a richly imaginative play nominally about tinkers trying to reach a hospital before their baby is born.

Like MacMahon, Brian Friel has written both stories and plays. But Friel is an Ulsterman, and his work often portrays the divided self inherent in that schizophrenic province. Born in 1929, Friel is one of several writers of his generation—many are poets—who have helped create a real literary renaissance in Ulster over the last twenty years or so. He worked as a teacher until 1960 when a contract from *The New Yorker* encouraged him to turn to writing full time. *The New Yorker* has for long been a good friend to the Irish short story, and many of his early stories appeared there. A first collection of them, *A Saucer Full of Larks* was very well received when it was published in 1962, and for good reason. Friel makes little change in the received tradition of the Irish story, but he handles his rural and small-town material exceedingly well, and he is especially sensitive to the incongruities of Ulster life. A second collection, *The Gold in the Sea,* followed in 1966, but by that point Friel was already moving toward playwriting. After several pieces which were really 'prentice work, he spent some time with Sir Tyrone Guthrie's theater in Minneapolis. This experience seemed to help him move from staged fiction to real dramatic presentation. *Philadelphia, Here I Come!* (1964), written soon after the period in Minneapolis, is an interesting and innovative play. It deals with the problems of Gareth O'Donnell as he reluctantly decides to take the risk of emigrating to America, and it gains a great deal in its treatment by using two actors to portray Gar's inner and outer selves. The technique emphasizes the sense of personal division, an important theme in Friel's plays as in his fiction. The escape theme of this play and the commentary on the restrictiveness of Irish life are also found in *The Loves of Cass Maguire* (1966), the story of an elderly Irish woman who returns home after years in America, but this latter play seems a good deal less effective in its mix of naturalism, satire, and something close to fantasy. *Lovers* (1967) is more innovative technically with its impersonal commentator on the action and its two separate units, "Winners" and "Losers." But *Lovers* points to a recurring problem in Friel's work; the plays still tend to be staged short stories with an overlay of theatrical experiment. The same could be said of two later plays. *The Mundy Scheme* (1969) and *Freedom of the City* (1973), but both are interesting if flawed works. *The Mundy Scheme,* a farce based on a plan to turn the west of Ireland into an international cemetary, is obviously the work of an intelligent satirist. *Freedom of the City,* on the other hand, is a sad and grim commentary on Northern Ireland in its current troubles. The flashback method (we begin by being told that the central characters in the action are killed) makes the play undramatic in the conventional sense, but the lack of suspense forces us to focus on the action, the situation, and the implications. In this play, as in almost all his work, Friel makes his intelligence and his sympathy manifest. We sense an able mind and a strong ability to arrest the meaning of experience; what we may not sense is a first-class dramatic ability.

A number of other playwrights, Hugh Leonard, Eugene McCabe, and Fergus Linehan among them, have found in television work a steadier income than the legitimate theater can provide, and one wag has suggested that the real successor of the traditional Abbey play is the popular Irish television serial, *The Riordans*. It could be argued that Hugh Leonard's work on the English television serial, *Me Mammy*, should exclude him from serious consideration as a dramatist, but that is a snob's view and unfair to a highly professional theater man. Now the artistic advisor to the Abbey, he also writes a very acute page of personal observation in *Hibernia*, the Irish journal of contemporary affairs, arts, and letters. His plays include a number of strong original works, but he is probably best known for *Stephen D*, a brilliant dramatization of Joyce's *Portrait* and *Stephen Hero*. Other significant Irish plays of the recent past include John O'Donovan's *The Less We Are Together* (1957) and *The Shaws of Synge Street* (1960) and Thomas Murphy's *Whistle in the Dark* (1961). Irish drama does not seem especially healthy these days. "Competence" and "craftsmanship" are the words that come most easily to mind; both imply praise, but both imply something less than genius. Perhaps the commercialization of the urban theaters and the proliferation of amateur companies are part of the problem; neither commercial theaters nor amateur groups are very likely to welcome experimentation, and of all the literary arts, drama most thrives on experiment. There are playwrights in Ireland who have absorbed the lessons of Beckett, Ionesco, absurdist drama, and free theater, but absorbing lessons and creating out of them are radically different things. In any event, it is possible to admire the competence of a number of writers and their continuing ability to respond to Ireland and the Irish experience while still wondering where the next Synge or O'Casey is hiding.

If the contemporary dramatic achievement seems less considerable than that of the past, the achievement in fiction seems in better balance. There are no writers of the towering authority of Joyce in today's Ireland, but there are many substantial and important figures. Some, Sean O'Faolain, Mary Lavin, and Michael McLaverty, have had reputations established for three decades and more, and each is best known as a writer of short stories. Virtually every Irish writer of fiction has written realistic short stories at some point, and that includes most recent writers, but every literary mode eventually grows old and even hackneyed, and that may now be true of the realistic story.

Brian Friel, for one, has been accused of writing formula stories, an unfair accusation against his best work, but one which reflects a feeling that the mode is exhausted. The short story seemed particularly relevant for the discussion of disillusionment and its implications; Joyce, O'Connor, and O'Faolain all used it for that. Yet the realistic story seems almost an anachronism when practiced by the contemporary writer. The publishing market for realistic stories, in Ireland and abroad, is much smaller than it was thirty years ago. Moreover, a host of writers, Borges perhaps the most important, have shown that many other things can be done with short fiction in addition to what Checkhov, Turgenev, Katharine Mansfield, O'Connor, and O'Faolain tried. In other words, history seems to be passing the realistic story by, for better or worse. In Ireland it remains a major medium, but one of diminishing importance. Increasingly, younger writers have turned to the novel as a basic fictional mode. To some extent that may reflect the publishing situation in Britain and America, both potentially important outlets. If we assume that the tale is essentially a rural fictional form and the novel an urban one, it may also reflect the gradual urbanization of Irish life. Whatever the reasons, the Irish short story now seems to belong to an older generation.

Mary Lavin is one of several Irish writers who have worked primarily in the short story, but, like two other story writers, Michael McLaverty and Benedict Kiely, she has also tried the novel. Her considerable reputation, however, rests primarily on her stories, and justly so, for her stories are among the best to come from Ireland in the last thirty years. She was, in fact, born in the United States, but her family returned to Ireland when she was a child. Educated at a convent school, she went on to University College, Dublin, where she wrote an M.A. thesis on Jane Austen and started work on a doctoral dissertation on Virginia Woolf. Like Austen, she often writes about personal relations in a small, closed society; like both Austen and Woolf, her frequent theme is personal freedom or its lack. A good many of her stories reflect her personal experiences, growing up as the daughter of the manager of an estate, marriage to a lawyer, the problems of adjustment after his death and the responsibilities of raising young children alone, remarriage to a former Jesuit. Yet she does a good deal more than write disguised autobiography, however much personal experience and life on her farm are transfigured in her fiction.

Her great strength as a writer of short stories comes in her ability to imply more than she states and thus to use the medium for more than mere sketching. As she writes in the introduction to her *Selected Stories* (1959):

". . . it is in the short story that a writer distills the essence of his thought. I believe this because the short story, shape as well as matter, is determined by the writer's own character. Both are one. Short-story writing—for me—is only looking closer than normal into the human heart. The vagaries and contrarieties there to be found have their own integral design."[2] That word "design" is important, for the reader of Lavin's stories rarely feels that he is not reading thoroughly controlled work. Even in a story which is essentially subjective monologue, "The Nun's Mother," for example, the feeling of authorial control remains strong. That means, then, that she can deal with even macabre material without giving the impression of seeming simply to work for shock value. Her regular theme of the tension between personal freedom and social or institutional restriction finds expression in several ways: the anecdotes of soured marriages as in "A Cup of Tea," a superbly managed story; the tales of girls headed for or in convents who have no vocation for the religious life; the black humor and pressing sensuality of such a story as "A Visit to the Cemetary." Lavin has published two novels, *The House in Clewe Street* (1945) and *Mary O'Grady* (1950), but her best work is found in the long series of collections of stories: *Tales from Bective Bridge* (1942), *The Long Ago* (1944), *The Becker Wives* (1946), *At Sallygap* (1947), *A Single Lady* (1951), and others. Her work is not without its detractors; many critics have agreed with her own judgement that the two novels are not really successful and that material in both would have made better short stories. Others have complained of a lack of development in her work, a repetitiousness of themes and techniques. Yet she began as a considerable artist, and so she has remained. To charges of repetition or plotlessness, she might reply that life is both repetitious and plotless; the writer of realistic stories has no choice but to reflect those facts.

In many ways, Michael McLaverty is a different artist from Mary Lavin. He has the ability to sustain a long fiction convincingly and has written several successful novels, most notably *Call My Brother Back* (1939). Moreover, he is an Ulsterman with all that implies about settings and themes. The world of Lavin's stories is often a splashy and eccentric one; McLaverty's tends to be gray, sullen, defeated. The sense of lost innocence is a frequent theme in his work, and, appropriately enough, he often uses children as narrators, or adults reminiscing about childhood experiences. Like Lavin, he is a master of the use of significant detail for telling effect, and his collection of stories, *The Game*

<hr/>

2 Quoted in Zack Bowen, *Mary Lavin* (Lewisburg, Pa.: Bucknell Univ. Press, 1975), pp. 43–44.

Cock (1948), contains a series of finely controlled tales, sometimes dismal in tone but never less than impressive. "Pigeons" is a superb story on the condition of Northern Ireland's Catholics, bitter and frustrated, while "The Poteen Maker," like "Pigeons" a story about childhood, is a little tour de force in the control of point of view. Benedict Kiely is also an Ulsterman, but of a different cast of mind from McLaverty. For McLaverty's sense of the worrying dangers of urban complexity, Kiely gives us an exuberant celebration of the continuities of Irish life. Sometimes he seems almost too slick in his Irishness, a throwback to the writers of earlier periods who liked to praise the virtues of whiskey, ballads, Dublin gossip, and Irish eccentrics. His first significant publication was a study of William Carleton, and often there is a feeling that he wants to write his own *Traits and Stories of the Irish Peasantry*, and the Irish middle class, too. Even so, as his stories and his critical study of modern Irish fiction show, he is alert to the character types—peasants, rebels, immigrants—who fill so much of Irish fiction and Irish life. His stories are full of types, even stereotypes, but the anecdotal narrative method carries many of them well, none better than "A Journey to the Seven Streams," a wonderful fantasia on a Sunday outing, full of specific and tiny details that alert us to the fact that what we really have here is a journey toward death. It is the title story in Kiely's first collection (1963); a second collection, *A Ball of Malt and Madame Butterfly*, was published in 1973. Like many other Irish story writers, Kiely remains a fairly frequent contributor to *The New Yorker*. He has also written a number of novels, the best of which is *The Captain With the Whiskers* (1960).

It is much too soon to write "finis" to the Irish short story, but Lavin, McLaverty, and Kiely represent now an older generation in Irish fiction, a generation that began to publish in the heyday of O'Connor and O'Faolain. Kiely, the youngest of the three, is almost sixty. A good many younger writers, as well as some figures from the older generation, have found themselves more at home in the novel than the short story. Perhaps it was indicative of a changing social and literary situation in Ireland that the 1960s saw the publication of a good many historical novels in Ireland, novels of considerable literary craftsmanship, but books directed toward the new middle class. That middle-aged middle class, actively involved in the economic expansion that marked Irish life during the decade, had matured after the years of the "troubles," and perhaps it found satisfaction in big novels on the Irish past. Walter Macken, a Galway-born actor and playwright, produced three very popular historical novels before his death in 1967. *Seek the Fair Land* (1959) deals with the Cromwellian invasion of the seventeenth century; *The Silent People* (1962) is a novel about the Famine, while *The Scorching Wind* (1964) handles the period of the struggle for independence. The focus in each is on the common people, their faith and persistence, and perhaps the novels' popularity stemmed from the impression they give of creating imaginary ancestors for modern, middle-class Irish people gradually becoming urbanized and out of touch with their own long communal history. Macken was, in fact, a prolific novelist whose best work is not his historical trilogy but two novels set in his native Galway, *Rain on the Wind* (1950) and *The Bogman* (1952). The latter is a particularly fine book, not a great novel but impressive as the study of a youth's return to his native village, a fundamental theme in Irish fiction. James Plunkett published in 1969 *Strumpet City*, a sprawling but highly readable novel about the Irish labor movement in the years before World War I. Again, the historical novel serves the local purpose of creating an imaginary past, and *Strumpet City* is characteristic of its time in its focus on the labor movement, Irish socialism, and the experience of the urban working class, all themes of considerable importance as industrializing Ireland tries to come to terms with the significance of a new culture. *Strumpet City* is by no means an innovative fiction (historical novels rarely are), but Plunkett is a good artist whose best work is probably found in a collection of stories, *The Trusting and the Maimed* (1959). An official in the Workers' Union of Ireland in the years just before Jim Larkin's death in 1947, he has written a number of works besides *Strumpet City* dealing with the vicissitudes of the labor movement around the time of the great strike of 1913; a radio play on Larkin became *The Risen People*, a play successfully produced at the Abbey in 1958. Historical novels are by no means the only popular form of fiction in contemporary Ireland, but according to one Dublin bookseller, they make up a considerable part of his business. This bookseller also observes that the novels of Francis MacManus remain steady sellers, partially because they are sometimes required reading in schools. That is appropriate because MacManus was for many years the director of talks and features on Irish radio and was the creator of the "Thomas Davis Lectures" which have done much to educate Irish people about their country and literature, but MacManus was a solid novelist on his own merits. *Stand and Give Challenge* (1935) and *Men Withering* (1939) are both fine books, but all MacManus' novels reflect a kindly acceptance of the Irish people with all their faults, as well as sensitive craftsmanship.

The division between "popular" and "serious" fiction is often an arbitrary one, Macken, Plunkett, and MacManus all writing work of lasting merit. The categories become even more confused with such a novelist as Brian Moore, a good artist with the ability to attract a substantial audience and an Irish-Canadian to boot. Moore was born in Belfast, but emigrated to Canada in the 1940s. His first novel, *Judith Herne* (1955), is a study of a lonely spinster in Belfast, and some would say almost an allegory of the spiritual condition of Northern Ireland of its time. *The Feast of Lupercal* (1957) is also valuable as a study of Ulster society, an exceedingly unpleasant society in this case, while a more recent work, the novella *Catholics* (1972), is a fantasy set on an island off the coast of County Kerry, the last place in the world to celebrate Latin Mass. But a good deal of Moore's fiction, all of it very professional, some of it more than that, deals with non-Irish themes and settings. It could be argued, of course, that only an Irishman could portray New York as nothing more than a provincial city, as Moore does in *I am Mary Dunne* (1968), but the question of his Irishness is difficult to pin down. Irish by birth, yes; Irish in his way of perceiving the world, perhaps; an Irish novelist, then? Not really, but a characteristic figure of his time—nonexperimental, mid-Atlantic in his manner.

John Broderick has returned to a traditional setting for Irish fiction, the restrictive provincial town and village, for two strong novels, *Pilgrimage* (1961) and *The Waking of Willy Ryan* (1965). Kevin Casey's *The Sinners' Bell* (1968) deals with another traditional situation in Irish fiction, the Catholic sense of damnation, and it is also a strong study of the awesome restrictiveness of the Irish family. So is Christy Brown's best seller, *Down All the Days* (1970), a courageous and gritty book. Thomas Kilroy also handles a recurring theme, religious intolerance, in *The Big Chapel* (1971), turning the form of the historical novel into a vehicle for some good psychological analysis. The fact that many of these recent novels deal with traditional themes in Irish fiction does not imply that they are old-fashioned books or that their authors do not have distinctive voices. It may imply, though, a certain conservatism in narrative technique, and one of the oddities of Irish fiction since Joyce is a general lack of technical experimentation. There are exceptions, of course, but functional realism seems ingrained in many of the novelists. One exception to that generalization, and an interesting one, is Aidan Higgins' *Langrishe, Go Down* (1966), an elaborately stylized novel on the decay of the Anglo-Irish gentry, not unlike Virginia Woolf's *The Waves* in technique. Higgins's stylistic mastery, extending even to the use of the heroic simile, is better seen, though, in his collection of stories, *Felo de Se* (1960). The work of Bernard

Share and Anthony Cronin, the latter also an interesting poet, also show some Joycean effects.

Of the recent Irish novelists, though, John McGahern may well eventually seem to be the most substantial. Born in Dublin in 1935, the son of a police official but raised in the west of Ireland, McGahern used provincial police life as the setting for his first novel, *The Barracks* (1963), one of the finest Irish novels of its decade. The story focuses on Elizabeth Reegan who marries a police sergeant in a small town after years of freedom and lovelessness. She eventually dies of cancer, but only after a grim and powerful novel has unfolded. The fearfulness and fascination of regimentation is a central theme for McGahern, and the novel carefully explores that theme, but its real greatness lies in the rightness of McGahern's prose, bare and hard. The dialogue seems always accurate, and details are tellingly used, nowhere more so than at the end when we are given a count on the number of cars at Elizabeth's funeral, a respectable number, thirty-three, but only about a sixth as many as came to the best attended funeral in the district. *The Barracks,* in manuscript, won the AE Memorial Award for McGahern, but his second novel, *The Dark* (1965), set off a furor that shows that narrow-mindedness is not yet gone from the Irish literary scene. It is a bleak and powerful novel, but the sexual references in it, especially to masturbation, caused it to be banned by the Censorship Board and lost McGahern his job as a schoolteacher. If *The Dark* is an obscene book, it is obscene because the world it portrays is obscene. Like *The Barracks,* its theme is repression and the urge to death-in-life, this time expressed through the story of a boy whose piety and adolescent sexuality come into appalling conflict as he prepares for the priesthood. For part of the way *The Dark* reads like a rural, contemporary version of Joyce's *Portrait of the Artist,* like Joyce's masterpiece, it is a study in some particularly Irish kinds of deprivation. McGahern's mastery of prose style rarely falters, and in these novels, *The Leavetaking* (1974), and his collection of short stories, *Nightlines* (1970), he seems the most assured writer of fiction of his generation in Ireland. The ability to give Irish themes and conditions universal significance has been a characteristic of all the best Irish writers, and McGahern seems in the great tradition.

Edna O'Brien has also written successfully about sexuality and restrictiveness, and her novel, *The Country Girls* (1960), ranks with McGahern's novels among the most important from Ireland in the last fifteen years. Like McGahern, O'Brien has the ability to make one of her special themes, the shattered naiveté of Irish country girls in a big city, represent a universal situation in our time. She is in some ways a less satisfactory novelist than McGahern, less assured in her prose style, a little slapdash, sometimes too willing to retell the same tale. Nevertheless, she is an important figure in contemporary fiction because she is one of several writers now giving voice to the experience of women in our time. That she comes from Ireland, in so many ways a male-dominated culture, makes her the more remarkable. Yet O'Brien has largely avoided the various stereotypes of "women's fiction" from the past, and that is another of her strengths. Several of her novels, *The Country Girls*, *The Lonely Girl* (1962), and *Girls in Their Married Bliss* (1964), deal with the experiences of an Irish woman, Caithleen Brady, as she moves from adolescence through work in a Dublin grocery, flight to England, a bad marriage, and the problems of being an independent and disillusioned adult. Each to some extent reiterates the same pattern: a romantic perception of reality is upset by ordinary and even ugly experience before the heroine finds a new maturity and sense of personal resolution. *Casualties of Peace* (1966) continued the theme of the perils of love and lust, but two more recent novels, *A Pagan Place* (1970) and *Night* (1972), while retaining a thematic concern with the condition of the disillusioned woman, have been marked by a much more subjective and experimental narrative method. It is a cliché in Ireland that "Edna O'Brien = sex," and the cliché is unfair. Irish readers may find her honesty disturbing and may not like her blunt presentations of emotional experience, but in the novels with Irish settings and characters, as in the others, she creates a significant fictional record of the discontent of our time and the emergence of a new consciousness among women.

The list of significant writers of fiction in Ireland could go on at greater length, but McGahern and O'Brien seem appropriate stopping places simply because each is representative of new attitudes and methods, demonstrably related to the Irish tradition and experience but innovative, nevertheless. Still, Julia O'Faolain, Sean O'Faolain's daughter, deserves attention for her excellent short stories, while mention ought to be made of Sam Hanna Bell, author of the fine *December Bride* (1951), one of the best novels from Ulster in its time. Mention should be made, too, of Mervyn Wall, a valuable writer who does not quite fit into neat organizational categories. His *Leaves for Burning* (1954), in spite of a sprawling plot, is a fine study of the mental state of Ireland about 1950, grim but often funny in a bleak sort of way. But Wall's most readable book is *The Unfortunate Fursey* (1946), a hilarious fantasy set in the Irish Middle Ages. Fursey is an overweight, utterly mediocre lay brother in the monastic community of Clonmacnoise who is sent out into the world armed with a half-knowledge of sorcery and much cheerful ignorance. Like all good satire, the story can be read as innocent hilarity, but the book is a fine send-up of a good many of Ireland's favorite sources of self-congratulation, the purity of the clergy and chastity being only two of them. Any fiction that can range from Fursey to McGahern's Elizabeth Reegan is a broad and rich one indeed. Perhaps, a detractor might add, not one of great depth, and there is some truth in that. There may be too many writers of fiction satisfied with able professionalism and the reworking of old themes. But the same could be said of British and American fiction in our time. What is impressive in recent Irish fiction is the sense of maturity; the writers are technically able, and the best know how to be distinctively Irish without being either mere exploiters of local color or thorough-going provincials. On the whole, nationality means less to them than it did to their predecessors, and that in itself is a significant sign. If fiction is particularly a mirror of reality, then the recent writers of fiction in Ireland are doing an impressive job of reflecting their worlds, and not only in green-tinted glass.

Like fiction and drama, poetry is often a reflection of reality, but the lyric poem, personal and private as it so often is, reflects a singular reality more than a general one. Nevertheless, it could be argued that much of the best recent Irish poetry reflects the broad concerns of recent Irish experience: the lingering frustrations of the early 1950s, the economic development with its attendant dangers in the later part of that decade and the 1960s, the bloody dilemma of Northern Ireland in more recent years. In a good essay on "New Voices in the Fifties," Maurice Harmon finds in the generation of poets who gained a reputation during that decade evidence of a profound generational shift in Irish poetry. For these poets, the most intense memories were not of the "troubles" or the politics of the past, but "the gutted cities of Europe, the massed skeletons of Buchenwald, the 'rose illumination of thighs' in Hiroshima, the futile heroism of Cyprus or Algiers, and Krushchev's angry shoe. Where the previous generation had sought protection from outside influences in the areas of culture and commerce, the new generation looked outward to Europe and to America and were consciously part of the cosmopolitan, post-war era."[3] As evidence for this view, Harmon cites Richard Murphy's *The Battle of Aughrim* with its television image of the reburial of Roger Case-

<hr>

[3] "New Voices in the Fifties," *Irish Poets in English*, ed. Sean Lucy (Cork: Mercier, 1973), pp. 186–187.

ment and Thomas Kinsella's deflation of heroic names from the past in "A Country Walk." The irony of turning the rising into business names and seeing rebels as tottering elder statesmen does obviously reflect a generational change, and Harmon's emphasis on the cosmopolitanism of recent Irish poetry is correct. Nevertheless, Murphy's poem is a series of meditations on the implications of a crucial event in Irish history, the Battle of Aughrim of 1691, while Kinsella's is also, in part, a meditation on the interrelationships of the Irish past and present. In other words, to use Yeats's phrase about his own private vision, Ireland does still provide metaphors for poetry, and recent Irish poets have derived much of their strength from the sense of Irish place while deriving another strength from the knowledge of being part of a wider world.

The achievement in Irish poetry over the last twenty years or so is genuinely remarkable. The poets who found themselves and reputations in the fifties, Kinsella, Murphy, John Montague, and several others, found ways of being Irish but not provincial, while several poets from Northern Ireland who came to prominence in the sixties, Michael Longley, Derek Mahon, Seamus Heaney among them, have intensified the sense of a genuine renaissance in Irish verse. As David Marcus writes in the introduction to his anthology of recent Irish poetry, Ireland is "thick with poets, real and self-styled; its paths are strewn with broadsheets and pamphlets; its byways blocked by hand-presses and mushroom publishers."[4] Marcus exaggerates only slightly. The number of poets, even just of good poets, is astonishing and so is the quality of their work. At least in terms of poetry, right now seems a new Irish Renaissance.

The new Renaissance began about the middle of the 1950s; the Dolmen Press and such periodicals as *Envoy*, *Arena*, and *Poetry Ireland* had a good deal to do with its coming. Until then, Irish poetry still seemed lost in the shadow of Yeats, but one sign that the poets were coming out of that shadow was the new vitality of Patrick Kavanagh and Austin Clarke, both survivors from Yeats's time but poets who did their most important work in the fifties and sixties. Moreover, Irish poetry was also finally absorbing some of the method of poetic modernism, absorbing it without being overwhelmed. The international and cosmopolitan qualities of modernism had, perhaps, made it seem foreign to poets so rooted to local place as the Irish, but as early as 1934 Samuel Beckett had issued a monitory essay on the backwardness and

4 *Irish Poets, 1924–1974* (London: Pan Books, 1975), p. 4.

provinciality of Irish poetry. That warning was largely ignored in Ireland, but Beckett's friend, Thomas MacGreevy, like Beckett part of the network of friends and friends of friends around James Joyce in Paris, wrote what could be called the first modernist Irish poetry. Two other young Irishmen friends from University College, Dublin, were part of the Joyce network, Brian Coffey and Dennis Devlin. Together they had published a volume of their work in Dublin in 1930. Devlin is an especially interesting figure because he was, as John Montague observes, "the first poet of an Irish Catholic background to take the world as his province."[5] Born in Scotland in 1908, the son of an Irish businessman, Devlin was brought to Ireland as a child, and his parents' home became a meeting place for Irish political leaders around the time of the "troubles." That, together with his interest in Gaelic (an interest which was intensified by a visit to the Blasket Islands), could have turned him into a "conventional" Irish poet. But the interest in Gaelic led to a project to translate Verlaine, Rimbaud, and Baudelaire into that recalcitrant tongue, and that seems characteristic of Devlin. He was a man of wide culture who made his career in the Irish foreign service, serving in the embassy in Washington and later as minister and then ambassador to Italy. He was a careful, exacting poet, fully aware of the international creative world in which he lived as his translations of St.-John Perse and his friendships with Robert Penn Warren and Allen Tate demonstrate. Devlin's poetry is often Irish in setting, but even in his fine "Lough Derg," a meditation on the annual religious pilgrimage in Donegal, the imagery and tone are those of a man of the world. There was a good deal of bonhommie in Devlin the man, but what is striking in his verse is its sadness as well as its precision. In terms of the international scene, Devlin may not seem a particularly important poet; he was one of many in a distinguished school, but in terms of Ireland he occupies an important place as the first poet of strong talent to bring the modernist doctrine home. Like Devlin, his friend Brian Coffey has spent most of his life in exile from Ireland, and that shows in his poetry's American tone and manner. A younger man, Valentine Iremonger, is another interesting poet strongly influenced by the urge toward precision and impersonality in the modernist movement. He has insisted that eloquence is the greatest Irish fault, and his collection, *Reservations* (1950), eschews the clichés of Irish verse without, perhaps, quite finding a distinctive voice because the slangy idiom mixes oddly with his fine craftsmanship.

[5] "The Impact of International Modern Poetry on Irish Writing," *Irish Poets in English*, pp. 148–49.

These poets, each as much a part of an international movement as an Irish one, all show the dangers of the loss of an individual identity when a poet participates in a stylistic movement. Just as the manner of the Celtic Twilight tended to blur the individuality of some earlier Irish poets, so the modernist manner, colloquial, low-keyed, and exact, tends to blur theirs. Yet by the middle of the 1950s, Ireland had produced a number of poets who seemed able to write in something like a modernist manner without losing their identities. Thomas Kinsella is the most important, a poet who in off-moments seems too much like Auden, but a poet of very substantial achievement nonetheless. Kinsella was born in Dublin in 1928, and spent nineteen years in the Irish civil service. In the 1960s he emigrated to the United States, and has served on the faculties of Southern Illinois University and Temple. He is, then, fully aware of a world beyond Ireland, but he remains unquestionably an Irish poet in tonality and point of view. Like a number of other poets, he received early encouragement from Liam Miller's Dolmen Press, and it was Dolmen which published his first collection, a group of love poems, in 1956. Two years later Dolmen published a second volume, *Another September*, the volume which indicated Kinsella's real importance. It is a strong collection, technically very assured and informed by a discriminating imagination. Of the several excellent poems in it, "In the Ringwood" is notable for its balladesque treatment of poisoned romance, while "Clarence Mangan" is an equally potent poem of knowing madness. The extravagance of those poems is not all that typical of Kinsella's best work, however; "Baggot Street Deserta," a confessional poem on the theme, "*Endure* and let the present punish" is his first fully sustained effort in what becomes a major type in his work, the semiprivate meditation. *Moralities* (1960) contained a fine sequence of short, almost epigrammatic observations, but *Downstream* (1962) was more notable for two fine meditations, the title poem and "A Country Walk." The mode of semiprivate meditation reaches its full development, though, in "Nightwalker," the title poem of a collection published in 1968. Something close to a Dublin *Waste Land*, "Nightwalker" is "sad music" on the spiritual state of modern Ireland. In his meditational bent and his tendency to focus on the significance of specific locales, Kinsella resembles Austin Clarke, and his *Butcher's Dozen* (1972), poems on the Ulster crisis, are in some ways reminiscent of Clarke's angry satire. Similarly, Kinsella's *Wormwood* (1966), a sequence of poems on breaking love, despair, and possible renewal have characteristics in common with Clarke's *Mnemosyne Lay in Dust* and *Night and Morning*, but Kinsella finds a brief intensity Clarke seldom achieved. Unlike many Irish poets, Clarke included, Kinsella is rarely prolix, and he rarely uses some of the "Irish" devices, assonance or song-rhythms, for example, common in the work of earlier genera-tions. Yet Kinsella is unquestionably a major Irish poet in his feeling for the Irish locale and his strong sense of personal isolation in the midst of an in-clusive community. The state of Ireland and the vicissitudes of love are two of his most common themes; his moral imagination and technical mastery mark him as among the best poets of our time.

Kinsella was only one of several excellent poets who came to prominence in the 1950s. John Montague, Brooklyn-born but raised in Ulster, is another, and he shares with Kinsella a strong moral imagination as well as great technical facility. Montague impresses as having an especially quick mind, and an early collection, *Forms of Exile* (1958) contains some acute observations on the cheapness and transience of American culture gained while Montague was a student at the University of Iowa. "Like Dolmens round my Childhood" in *Poisoned Lands* (1961) shows the strength of his lyricism, though, and *The Rough Field* (1972) is an important long poem on his Ulster background which illuminates through its juxtapositions of past and present. Past and present also mean much to Richard Murphy, as his sequence of lyrics, *The Battle of Aughrim* (1968), shows. Originally created as a radio script, these lyrics reiterate the significances of place, history, and their interconnections. History for Murphy is an especially important concern. Born into an Anglo-Irish family and educated at good English schools and Oxford, Murphy wanted from childhood, nevertheless, to be "truly Irish." *Sailing to an Island* (1963) partly deals with his attempts to make himself that, one poem, "The Last Galway Hooker," celebrating his ownership of the last survivor of Galway fishing boats, and "The Cleggan Disaster" recounting in vivid language and meter the sinking of a ship in 1927. Both poems, and especially the latter, are exercises in a popular style John Masefield would have admired, but Murphy can write more complex and thoughtful poetry as the poems on Wittgenstein and Theodore Roethke show. For Brendan Kennelly, now a professor at Trinity College but a native of Ballylongford in County Kerry, there seems to be no concern about being "truly Irish." Kennelly *is* Irish, whether satirizing the Dublin scene or meditating on his dark Kerry fathers who "skeletoned in darkness . . . could not understand/The giant grief that trampled night and day."[6] An admirable translator of Gaelic poetry, Kennelly is in some ways closer to the aesthetic of some earlier poets than his contemporaries. In spite

---

6 "My Dark Fathers," *Selected Poems* (Dublin: Figgis, 1969), p. 15.

of the fact that he can be a sharp satirist, there is almost an old-fashioned romanticism in Kennelly, rich language, a comic sense in the poems in which he takes the *persona* of Moloney, and an admirable attention to the imaginative possibilities of ordinary life. Not all of Kennelly's poems work, but the best have a real imaginative energy. And there are a number of other good poets in this approximate generation in the Republic, Richard Weber, James Liddy, Michael Hartnett, Pearse Hutchinson, to name only a few.

Yet the remarkable phenomenon in Irish poetry in the 1960s was the emergence of a group of poets from Northern Ireland. Northern Ireland had had its poets before, of course, but the province had for long suffered from a lack of poetic self-identity. Irish yet largely Scottish in cultural orientation and Anglophile in politics, Northern Ireland has often seemed a lost province. During the 1940s, partially because of World War II when Northern Ireland fought the Axis powers with Britain while the south remained neutral, there were some serious attempts to develop a sense of provincial identity. An anthology of poetry from the province, *Northern Harvest*, appeared in 1944, and there was a good deal of brave talk about a Northern Renaissance. The period produced a substantial figure in John Hewitt, a sophisticated and able poet. Interested in Ulster regionalism as a counterpart to the growing Scottish regionalism of that period and after, Hewitt was involved with two important periodicals, *Lagan* and *Threshold*, both devoted primarily to encouraging new writing in Ulster. Earlier, in the 1930s, Hewitt had produced some fine nature poetry, and he remains best known for those and some longer poems from the 1940s. At about the same time, W. R. Rodgers, a Presbyterian clergyman, received a good deal of attention for a collection, *Awake!*, published in 1941. Rodgers went on to become a broadcaster with the BBC and compiler of a brilliant series of conversations about Irish writers, published after his death as *Irish Literary Portraits*. Those conversations, full of valuable reminiscence about Yeats, Joyce, AE, and others, may well be Rodgers' most lasting accomplishment, and perhaps that is not inappropriate, for his poetry often seems brilliant conversation, too, verbally exciting but, like good conversation, not necessarily going anywhere in particular.

Still, it was the work of Michael Longley, Derek Mahon, and Seamus Heaney which brought more than local attention to poetry in Northern Ireland. Each was in his late twenties when the violence in Northern Ireland began yet again, and, at the risk of cliché, it may be that violence and pressing nationalism are useful catalysts for Irish poets. All have been affected by the situation in the North, but none is a propagandist. Longley's first important collection, *No Continuing City* (1969), was notable for its tightly controlled verse, almost Audenesque, its intellectual wit, and clever artifice. A second collection, *An Exploded View* (1972), shows an intensification of his powers and a strong response to the situation in Northern Ireland. The images of violence in this volume have, as D. E. S. Maxwell notes in a valuable essay on contemporary poetry in Northern Ireland, "a touch of Grand Guignol," but, Maxwell adds, "the poet keeps his head, not aloof but composed."[7] Derek Mahon, whose *Night-Crossing* was published in 1968, shares with Longley a sense of the fluid disorder of Northern Irish life. Mahon joins to that a particularly strong visual sense; his images are often startling, and the more startling in their juxtapositions: sheep huddled on a golf course, the dead of Treblinka and Pompeii. "Ecclesiastes" from *Lives* (1972) is not only a remarkable virtuoso performance but an extremely moving poem, and one of Mahon's strengths is his inventiveness which is well used in a clear, grim poetic vision.

Seamus Heaney's four volumes have received even more attention than the work of Longley and Mahon. All are fine poets, but Heaney seems particularly strong. There are relatively few surface difficulties in his poems, and for American readers, Heaney sometimes is reminiscent of Robert Frost. There is the same interest in common experience, the same ability to make the ordinary significant, and the same genius for closing the trap on the reader. As D. E. S. Maxwell comments, the great achievement of Heaney's first volume, *Death of a Naturalist* (1966), is the way in which Heaney registers "the energies of a scene in its physical being."[8] The first poem, "Digging," turns on an analogy between the poet writing a poem and his father digging potatoes:

> The cold smell of potato mould, the squelch and slap
> Of soggy peat, the curt cuts of an edge
> Through living roots awaken in my head.
> But I've no spade to follow men like them.
>
> Between my fingers and my thumb
> The squat pen rests.
> I'll dig with it.[9]

The image of digging is particularly appropriate, for much of Heaney's poetry involves digging into the earth, literally in "At a Potato Digging," metaphorically in the extraordinary series of archaeological poems in *North* (1975). *North* also

---

7 "Contemporary Poetry in the North of Ireland," *Two Decades of Irish Writing*, p. 178.
8 Ibid., p. 171.
9 *Death of a Naturalist* (London: Faber, 1966), p. 14.

contains a sequence on the situation in Northern Ireland, but it is more characteristic of Heaney to preface another collection, *Wintering Out* (1972), with a single, powerful poem on the violence, then follow that with a sequence of poems on the imaginative roots of his province. Roots, digging, burial, recovery are recurring themes and metaphors in his work, and they reflect an imagination which likes rough incompleteness. When *Door into the Dark*, his second collection, appeared in 1969, a few critics were disappointed by what they felt was a lack of development in his work. Because *Death of a Naturalist* was an extraordinary first book, and because critics too often assume that poets must develop, they missed the fact that Heaney was doing something more than developing in a neatly explainable way. He was, in fact, going deeper in his dig into himself and his place. That ability to control and recapitulate as he comes closer to fully realizing his imaginative world indicates an important poet.

But the same could be said of a number of his contemporaries; Kinsella, Murphy, Montague, Longley, Mahon, Kennelly, others, are all exceptional talents, and among even younger poets there are fine talents, too. Eavan Boland, Ciaran Carson, Eiléan Ni Chuilleanáin, Tom McGurk, Paul Muldoon, and William Peskett are only a few distinctive voices in a remarkable crowd. The host of poets, the fine novelists, the smaller group of playwrights all attest to the continuing vitality of Anglo-Irish literature. Ireland is a small island, smaller than many American states. Yet no American state, no equivalent region in the English-speaking world has produced more writers of merit. The matter of quantity is of some significance, yet what really counts is the intensity and the fullness of the imagination. No plentitude of able writers can quite outbalance the weight of a single genius. Ireland has been blessed with single and singular geniuses, Yeats, Joyce, Synge, O'Casey, all irreplaceable. Still the process, not of replacement but of renewal, goes on. The good writers, the Augusta Gregorys, the Daniel Corkerys, the Joseph Campbells, play important roles; they help create, define, and sustain a literary culture. They become the worthy norm against which the shoddy and the incompetent must be judged. But greatness always comments on the limitations of the good. So Yeats, Joyce, and the others comment on the present; no figure now towers over Irish poetry as Yeats did in his time, none over fiction as Joyce. But that may change, may very well change, and in the meantime the energy and achievement of contemporary Irish writing remains a discernable wonder in a world too full of the ordinary.

SUGGESTIONS FOR FURTHER READING

Because of the limitations of space, this book can provide no more than a sketch of Irish literary history and brief introductions to the important writers. The following suggestions for further reading are provided for those who wish to know more. This is by no means a comprehensive bibliography of materials on Irish history, literature, and writers, but it is a selection of useful, readable studies which I believe will interest the ordinary reader or beginning scholar. For more comprehensive reviews of research, see *Irish Historiography*, ed. T. W. Moody (1971), *Anglo-Irish Literature: A Review of Research*, ed. Richard J. Finneran (1976), and *A Bibliography of Modern Irish and Anglo-Irish Literature*, ed. Frank Kersnowski, C. W. Spinks, and Laird Loomis (1976).

GENERAL STUDIES OF IRELAND AND IRISH LIFE

The best general introduction to Ireland is probably still Sean O'Faolain's *The Irish* (1947), a little classic of social analysis. It might well be supplemented by Frank O'Connor's *Leinster, Munster, and Connaught* (1950) and Tony Gray's *The Irish Answer* (1966). All of these are now somewhat outdated, but they are useful impressionistic studies, especially for those who have never visited Ireland.

The standard geography is T. W. Freeman's *Ireland* (rev. ed., 1964); the most thorough guidebook is *The Blue Guide to Ireland*, ed. L. Russell Muirhead (1962). *The Encyclopaedia of Ireland*, ed. Victor Meally (1971), is an enormously useful compendium. Two useful collections of essays are *Conor Cruise O'Brien Introduces Ireland*, ed. Owen Dudley Edwards (1969), and *The Shaping of Modern Ireland*, ed. Conor Cruise O'Brien (1960).

Dublin in the Age of William Butler Yeats and James Joyce by Richard M. Kain (1962) is especially good for giving a sense of the city in the heyday of the Irish Renaissance. Herbert A. Kinney's anecdotal *Literary Dublin* (1974) covers a wider period. *A Literary Guide to Ireland* by Thomas and Susan Cahill (1973) is especially useful for the tourist. A good visual sense of the Ireland of the Renaissance may be derived from two picture books, Maurice Gorham's *Ireland From Old Photographs* (1971) and Cyril Pearl's *Dublin in Bloomtime* (1969).

There are two splendid studies of Irish rural life, Conrad Arensberg's *The Irish Countryman* (1937) and E. Estyn Evans' *Irish Folk Ways* (1975); the latter is much more detailed.

For the visual arts in Ireland, Bruce Arnold's *Concise History of Irish Art* (1969) is useful, while Breandán Bréathnach's *Folkmusic and Dances of Ireland* (1971) is a helpful introduction to its subject.

IRISH HISTORY

Two standard histories, both solid and detailed works by reputable scholars, are *A Short History of Ireland* by J. C. Beckett (1952) and *A History of Ireland* by Edmund Curtis (1936). Both are now somewhat outdated by subsequent research, and both are rather ponderous. The ordinary reader of literature will probably find all he needs to know in *The Story of Ireland* by Brian Inglis (1956), an excellent piece of popularizing. Also good is *The Course of Irish History*, ed. T. W. Moody and F. X. Martin (1967). In this, excellent pictures and photographs supplement text prepared by a number of Irish scholars. *A Concise History of Ireland* by Maire and Conor Cruise O'Brien (1972) also has good pictures, but the text is extremely sketchy.

For Irish history since 1840, the standard work is *Ireland Since the Famine* by F. S. L. Lyons (rev. ed., 1973). Superbly detailed and controlled, Lyons' book offers a full political and economic history and an able discussion of the Irish Renaissance in its social contexts. Oliver MacDonagh's *Ireland* (1962) is a trenchant, shorter history, with the focus on nationalism and politics. *The Politics of Irish Literature* by Malcolm Brown (1972) is effective on literary nationalism in the nineteenth century, but it is marred by a polemical tone.

Some topics in fairly recent Irish history deserve special attention. The standard study of relations between Britain and Ireland for its period is Nicholas Mansergh's *The Irish Question, 1840–1921* (rev. ed., 1965). The tragic story of the Famine is splendidly told in Cecil Woodham-Smith's *The Great Hunger* (1962). Conor Cruise O'Brien's *Parnell and His Party* (1957) is the best study of Parnell's political career; for a detailed account of its end, see F. S. L. Lyons, *The Fall of Parnell* (1960). Max Caulfield's *The Easter Rebellion* (1964) is a detailed account of the rising. Three important collections of essays also cover the revolutionary period: *Leaders and Men of the Easter Rising*, ed. F. X. Martin (1967); *The Making of 1916*, ed. Kevin Nowlan (1969); and *The Irish Struggle, 1916–1926*, ed. T. Desmond Williams (1966). The classic account of the making of the Anglo-Irish Treaty is Frank Pakenham's *Peace By Ordeal* (1935); the subsequent Civil War is described in Calton Younger's *Ireland's Civil War* (1968). On the continuing Ulster crisis, Liam de Paor provides good background in *Divided Ulster* (1970), while *Ulster* by the London *Sunday Times* 'Insight' Team (1972) is reasonably objective on events up to its date of publication.

LITERATURE IN GAELIC

There is much commentary available, but Robin Flower's *The Irish Tradition* (1946) is still the best introduction to the field. Aodh de Blacam, in *Gaelic Literature Surveyed* (rev. ed., 1973) offers an old-fashioned but thorough over-view. *Early Irish Literature* by Myles Dillon (1948) is especially useful for its summaries of the sagas and tales.

Among the collections of translations from Gaelic poetry, three stand out: Gerard Murphy's *Early Irish Lyrics* (1956), Frank O'Connor's *Kings, Lords, and Commons* (1959), and Douglas Hyde's *Love-Songs of Connacht* (1893). The best modern translation of the Ulster material is Thomas Kinsella's *The Tain* (1970).

ANGLO-IRISH LITERARY HISTORY

There is, unfortunately, no general literary history of Ireland, nor is there a full-scale history of Anglo-Irish literature. Patrick C. Power's *Literary History of Ireland* (1969), while useful on the Gaelic tradition, is too brief to be more than a sketch. Frank O'Connor's *A Short History of Irish Literature: A Backward Look* (1967) offers some stimulating interpretations, but it is far from complete, and the sections on Gaelic literature may be confusing to the non-specialist. Stephen Gwynn's *Irish Literature and Drama* (1936) is a competent general survey, but badly outdated. *The Irish Comic Tradition* by Vivian Mercier (1962), on the other hand, is extremely good on its topic.

The standard history of the Irish Renaissance remains Ernest A. Boyd's *Ireland's Literary Renaissance*, but even the revised edition dates from 1922, and, obviously, Boyd does not tell the entire story. Some of his critical judgments are also naive. A more helpful book, and often quite stimulating in its judgments, is Herbert Howarth's *The Irish Writers, 1880–1940* (1958). Howarth's is not a general history; instead, it offers essays, often brilliant, on the effects of Parnellism on some major writers of the Renaissance. A vivid sense of some of those writers' personalities, and some fine anecdotes, may be found in *Irish Literary Portraits* by W. R. Rodgers (1972).

On Anglo-Irish poetry, there is a general survey by Robert Farren, *The Course of Irish Verse in English* (1947); it is competent but extremely impressionistic. Russell Alspach's *Anglo-Irish Poetry from the English Invasion to 1798* (1954) is good on its period; Patrick C. Power's *The Story of Anglo-Irish Poetry, 1800–1922* (1967), while sketchy, is useful for its emphasis on the influence of Gaelic verse. Richard Loftus, in *Nationalism in Modern Anglo-Irish Poetry* (1964), deals effectively with more recent poetry from his particular point of view, while Frank Kersnowski's *The Outsiders* (1976) is a useful catalogue of contemporary poets marred by confusing organization and some inaccuracies. Some of the better commentary on Anglo-Irish poetry appears in *Irish Poets in English*, ed. Sean Lucy (1973); all of the essays in this collection are good, and some are brilliant. In spite of some omissions and overlappings, it is probably the best available survey. The essays in *Two Decades of Irish Writing*, ed. Douglas Dunn (1975), are more erratic in quality, but many of them deal with fairly recent poets.

There are several histories of Anglo-Irish drama, but Andrew E. Malone's *The Irish Drama* (1929) remains the best, even after almost half a century. The book is valuable for its full account, its general lack of bias, and for the fact that Malone had seen virtually every play he discussed; its coverage ends, of course, in the late 1920s. For a survey of developments since then, see Robert Hogan's *After the Irish Renaissance* (1967). Hogan is at times almost indiscriminately enthusiastic, but his is a useful and informative book. Micheál Ó hAodha's *Theatre in Ireland* (1971) is a rapid and fluent survey of all of Irish drama. Hogan and James F. Kilroy are in the process of publishing *The Modern Irish Drama, A Documentary History*, and this should become an important aid in future research and criticism.

There are several histories of the Abbey Theatre, none entirely satisfactory. Gerard Fay's *The Abbey Theatre: Cradle of Genius* (1958) is much the best, but it deals with only the first ten years or so. Lennox Robinson's *Ireland's Abbey Theatre* (1951) is useful for factual information, but almost devoid of meaningful interpretation. On the other hand, Peter Kavanagh's *The Story of the Abbey Theatre* (1950) offers some convincing interpretations but is often biased and inaccurate. There is some good backstage gossip in *The Story of the Abbey Theatre*, ed. Sean McCann (1967), while Micheál Ó hAodha's *The Abbey—Then and Now* (1969) has many attractive photographs. James W. Flannery's *W. B. Yeats and the Idea of a Theatre* (1976) provides a valuable introduction to Yeats's intentions for the Abbey and a reliable history of the theatre's early days.

Some of the participants in the early days of the Abbey have left interesting memoirs; *Our Irish Theatre* by Augusta Gregory (1913), *The Fays of the Abbey Theatre* by W. G. Fay and Catharine Carswell (1935), and *The Splendid Years* by

Máire nic Shiubhlaigh and Edward Kenny (1955) are among these. The great first-hand account of doing at the Abbey, though, is contained in the voluminous dairies of Joseph Holloway. He was regularly wrong in his judgments, but Holloway had a superb eye for detail and ear for gossip, and his opinions often reflected those of Irish audiences. *Joseph Holloway's Abbey Theatre*, ed. Robert Hogan and Michael J. O'Neill (1967) probably contains the best of his observations, but it should be supplemented by the three volumes of *Joseph Holloway's Irish Theatre* (1968–70), also edited by Hogan and O'Neill.

On theatres other than the Abbey, see Micheál MacLiammóir's reminiscences, *All for Hecuba* (1946) and Sam Hanna Bell's *Theatre in Ulster* (1972).

There is a real need for some general studies of Anglo-Irish fiction. Thomas Flanagan's *The Irish Novelists, 1800–1850* (1959) covers its period admirably and often with sharp insight. Benedict Kiely's *Modern Irish Fiction—A Critique* (1950) is also good for its coverage of the period roughly between 1918 and 1950.

The most thorough study of the early days of the Irish Renaissance is *Yeats and the Beginning of the Irish Renaissance* by Phillip L. Marcus (1970). The classic description of the rise of Celticism is John Kelleher's "Matthew Arnold and the Celtic Revival" in *Perspectives in Criticism*, ed. Harry Levin (1950). Ann Saddlemyer also provides some good articles on Celticism, Yeats, and Irish nationalism in *The World of W. B. Yeats*, ed. Robin Skelton and Ann Saddlemyer (1965). The contexts and effects of the 1916 rising are the subject of William Irwin Thompson's controversial *The Imagination of an Insurrection* (1967); some of Thompson's views are highly debatable, but this is an exciting and provocative book.

INDIVIDUAL WRITERS

The items listed under each writer's name are secondary materials, many of them of an introductory nature. Items marked with an asterisk are in the extremely useful series of monographs on Irish writers published by the Bucknell University Press.

AE (George William Russell).

*George Russell (AE)** by Richard M. Kain and James O'Brien is a good introduction. Henry Summerfield's *That Myriad-Minded Man, AE* (1976) is an excellent full-scale biography. A strong sense of AE's personality comes through in the reminiscences of him in W. R. Rodgers' *Irish Literary Portraits*. Alan Denson is the editor of *Letters from AE* (1961).

SAMUEL BECKETT

The ordinary reader will find Hugh Kenner's *Reader's Guide to Samuel Beckett* (1973) very helpful; Kenner's *Samuel Beckett: A Critical Study* (1961) is valuable for the more advanced student. On Beckett's early fiction, see Raymond Federman's *Journey to Chaos* (1965).

BRENDAN BEHAN

There is a lively biography of Behan by Ulick O'Connor, *Brendan* (1970), and Dominic Behan's *My Brother Brendan* (1965) and Rae Jeffs' *Brendan Behan, Man and Showman* (1966) are interesting memoirs. Among the critical studies, Ted E. Boyle's *Brendan Behan* (1969) is useful.

ELIZABETH BOWEN

Edwin J. Kenny's *Elizabeth Bowen** (1975) is a good introduction.

WILLIAM CARLETON

Benedict Kiely's *Poor Scholar* (1948) is a full, sympathetic study, but some of the most acute criticism of Carleton's work appears in Thomas Flanagan's *The Irish Writer's, 1800–1850.*

PAUL VINCENT CARROLL

Paul A. Doyle has written a solid introduction in *Paul Vincent Carroll** (1971), but there is also some good commentary in Robert Hogan's *After the Irish Renaissance.*

AUSTIN CLARKE

Susan Halpern's *Austin Clarke* (1974) is a good study. M. L. Rosenthal offers some interesting comments in his *The New Poets* (1967). There is a fine essay by Maurice Harmon in *The Celtic Cross*, ed. Ray B. Browne, *et al.* (1964) and a good essay on Clarke and Padraic Fallon by Donald Davie in *Two Decades of Irish Writing*, ed. Douglas Dunn (1975).

PADRAIC COLUM

The best general study is Zack Bowen's *Padraic Colum* (1968).

DANIEL CORKERY

George Brandon Saul's *Daniel Corkery** (1973) is relatively unsympathetic but factually informative.

EDWARD, LORD DUNSANY

There is a full-scale biography by Mark Amory, *Lord Dunsany* (1972); there has been little intelligent criticism of his writing.

MARIA EDGEWORTH

The best study of Edgeworth's work is O. E. M. Harden's *Maria Edgeworth's Art of Prose Fiction* (1971), but Thomas Flanagan also has an able discussion in *The Irish Novelists, 1800–1850.*

SIR SAMUEL FERGUSON

Malcolm Brown's *Sir Samuel Ferguson** (1973) is a good introduction.

GEORGE FITZMAURICE

Fitzmaurice has yet to receive the attention from scholars and critics he deserves, but Howard K. Slaughter's *George Fitzmaurice and His Enchanted Land* (1972) is probably as full a biography as can be written of this reclusive man, while Arthur E. McGuinness's *George Fitzmaurice** (1975) is a competent introduction.

BRIAN FRIEL

D. E. S. Maxwell's *Brian Friel** (1973) is an enthusiastic introduction.

AUGUSTA, LADY GREGORY

After years of neglect, Lady Gregory is finally beginning to receive deserved attention. This revival has been much encouraged by the publication of the *Coole Edition of the Collected Works of Lady Gregory* (1970–) by Colin Smythe. The only full biography is Elizabeth Coxhead's *Lady Gregory: A Literary Portrait* (rev. ed., 1966), a readable if not entirely satisfactory book. The best introduction to Lady Gregory, though, is Hazard Adams' *Lady Gregory** (1973). Ann Saddlemyer's *In Defense of Lady Gregory, Playwright* (1966) is also sympathetic and extremely able. There are good chapters on her work in Herbert Howarth's *The Irish Writers, 1800–1940* and Una Ellis-Fermor's *The Irish Dramatic Movement* (1939).

OLIVER ST. JOHN GOGARTY

Ulick O'Connor's *The Times I've Seen* (1964) is an enthusiastic biography, better on Gogarty's personality than his creative work.

DOUGLAS HYDE

Douglas Hyde: President of Ireland by Diarmid Coffey (1938) is the standard biography.

DENNIS JOHNSTON

Harold Ferrar's *Denis Johnston's Irish Theatre* (1973) is a very fine biographical and critical study.

JAMES JOYCE

There are several good introductions to Joyce for the novice reader. Among these are Robert M. Adams' *James Joyce: Common Sense and Beyond* (1966), S. L. Goldberg's *James Joyce* (1962), A. Walton Litz's *James Joyce* (1966), and John Gross's *James Joyce* (1970). Richard Ellmann's *James Joyce* (1959), by far the best biography, was a landmark in Joyce scholarship, and anyone seriously interested in Joyce's work should read it. Don Gifford's *Notes for Joyce* (1967) provides very helpful annotations, while Anthony Burgess's *Re Joyce* (1965), quirky though it sometimes is, is probably the best running commentary on Joyce's work for the beginner. Hugh Kenner's *Dublin's Joyce* (1956) remains a highly influential, and very sophisticated, critical study of Joyce's achievement.

On *Dubliners* and *Portrait* an informative study is *Time of Apprenticeship* by Marvin Magalaner and Richard M. Kain (1959). Probably the best guide to *Ulysses* is Harry Blamires' *The Bloomsday Book* (1966); it is considerably better balanced than Stuart Gilbert's *James Joyce's 'Ulysses'* (1930), long the standard commentary. Among the many critical studies of *Ulysses*, Richard M. Kain's *Fabulous Voyager* (1947) and S. L. Goldberg's *The Classical Temper* (1961) are outstanding. There are many problems with *A Skeleton Key to 'Finnegans Wake'* by Joseph Campbell and Henry M. Robinson (1944), but it remains widely used as an introduction to that book. Clive Hart's *Structure and Motif in 'Finnegans Wake'* (1962) is a very able critical study, but James S. Atherton's *The Books at the Wake* (1960) is also important.

Among the scholarly tools, *A Bibliography of James Joyce* by John J. Slocum and Herbert Cahoon (1953) is the authoritative guide to Joyce's own writings. Robert H. Deming's *Bibliography of James Joyce Studies* (1964) lists and describes books and articles on Joyce, but it should be used with caution and supplemented by the checklist of Joyce studies prepared by Maurice Beebe, A. Walton Litz, and Phillip F. Herring and published in the special Joyce issue of *Modern Fiction Studies* in 1969. In *Anglo-Irish Literature: A Review of Research*, Thomas F. Staley provides a more recent guide to secondary materials.

A. Walton Litz describes the composition of *Ulysses* and *Finnegans Wake* in *The Art of James Joyce* (1961); there are concordances or word indices to *Dubliners* (by Gary Lane, 1972), *Portrait* (by Leslie Hancock, 1967), *Ulysses* (by Miles L. Hanley, 1937), and *Finnegans Wake* (by Clive Hart, 1963). The published versions of Joyce's works have often failed to give us his final intentions, and the various available versons of *Ulysses* remain notoriously corrupt. *Dubliners*, ed. Robert Scholes and A. Walton Litz (1969); and *Portrait*, ed. Chester G. Anderson (1968), both in the "Viking Critical Library," provide sound texts of those works and good collections of critical essays. *The Letters of James Joyce,* ed. Stuart Gilbert and Richard Ellmann (1957; 1966) gather much of the best of his correspondence.

PATRICK KAVANAGH
Darcy O'Brien's *Patrick Kavanagh** (1971) is a good introduction, but the fullest study of Kavanagh's work is Alan Warner's *Clay is the Word* (1972).

BENEDICT KIELY
There is an able monograph by Daniel Casey, *Benedict Kiely** (1975).

THOMAS KINSELLA
David R. Clark is the author of a good introduction, *Thomas Kinsella** (1972).

MARY LAVIN
Zack Bowen's *Mary Lavin** (1975) is a solid introductory study.

LOUIS MACNEICE
MacNeice has received considerable attention; one of the better books on his poetry is D. B. Moore's *The Poetry of Louis MacNeice* (1972).

JAMES CLARENCE MANGAN
James Kilroy's *James Clarence Mangan** (1970) is a sensitive and sympathetic study, rightly emphasizing Mangan's technical expertise.

EDWARD MARTYN
The devastating portrait of Martyn in George Moore's *Hail and Farewell* (1911–14) is a classic of its kind, but for serious consideration of Martyn's work, see Denis Gwynn's *Edward Martyn and the Irish Revival* (1930) and Jan Setterquist's *Ibsen and the Beginnings of Anglo-Irish Drama: Edward Martyn* (1960).

JOHN MONTAGUE
There is a monograph by Frank Kersnowski, *John Montague** (1974).

BRIAN MOORE
Jeanne Flood's *Brian Moore** (1975) is a helpful, brief study.

GEORGE MOORE
The standard biography of Moore remains Joseph Hone's *George Moore* (1936), but Malcolm Brown's *George Moore: A Reconsideration* (1955) uses biographical

information more effectively in interpreting Moore's writings. Although less full than it might be on Moore's involvement in Irish matters, Brown's book remains the best general study. The reader seeking a shorter introduction might well investigate A. Norman Jeffares' short *George Moore* (1965). Moore's own *Hail and Farewell* is, of course, an indispensable book, while Herbert Howarth, in *The Irish Writers, 1800–1940*, is very good on the Irish phase of Moore's career. Two collections of essays do much to illuminate Moore as man and artist, *George Moore's Mind and Art*, ed. Graham Owen (1968); and *The Man of Wax*, ed. Douglas Hughes (1971).

EDNA O'BRIEN

Grace Eckley's *Edna O'Brien** (1974) is an able introduction.

SEAN O'CASEY

O'Casey has received considerable scholarly and critical attention, and that material is very thoroughly described by David Krause in *Anglo-Irish Literature: A Review of Research*, ed. Richard J. Finneran. Of the many general studies of O'Casey, Krause's own *Sean O'Casey: The Man and His Work* (rev. ed., 1975) is outstanding for its sympathy, balance, and enthusiasm. Bernard Benstock's *Sean O'Casey** is a very good brief introduction, while Robert Hogan's *The Experiments of Sean O'Casey* (1960) is good on O'Casey's stagecraft and especially interesting in its defense of the later plays. Thomas Kilroy has edited a good collection of essays on O'Casey in the "Twentieth Century Views" series (1975).

There is no full-scale biography, and readers should remember that in his massive autobiography O'Casey made little attempt to give a balanced account. Gabriel Fallon's *Sean O'Casey, the Man I Knew* (1965) contains much interesting biographical information but is often hostile; Eileen O'Casey's *Sean* (1971) is very good on the years after her marriage to O'Casey in 1926. A strong sense, not altogether attractive, of O'Casey's personality comes through in his letters, edited by David Krause. A first volume appeared in 1975; two more are promised, and these should provide a great deal of significant information.

FRANK O'CONNOR

O'Connor has received much less than his due from scholars and critics, but there is a solid introductory monograph, *Frank O'Connor** by James H. Matthews (1974) and a fairly good collection of essays and reminiscences, *Michael/Frank*, ed. Maurice Sheehy (1969; contains a useful bibliography of O'Connor's writings).

PEADER O'DONNELL

Grattan Freyer is the author of an excellent monograph, *Peader O'Donnell** (1973).

SEAN O'FAOLAIN

There are two solid critical studies, both entitled *Sean O'Faolain*: Maurice Harmon's (1966) is the more ambitious, but Paul A. Doyle's (1969) is, for the beginning reader, perhaps the more useful. The Spring, 1976, issue of the *Irish University Review*, ed. Maurice Harmon, was devoted entirely to O'Faolain and his work. O'Faolain's autobiography, *Vive Moi!* (1964) is also well worth reading.

LIAM O'FLAHERTY

James H. O'Brien's *Liam O'Flaherty** (1973) is a good introduction to this important writer's life and work. Paul A. Doyle's *Liam O'Flaherty* (1972) is a fuller account, while John N. Zneimer's *The Literary Vision of Liam O'Flaherty* (1970) is more ambitious critically.

STANDISH O'GRADY

Phillip L. Marcus has provided an excellent introduction in his *Standish O'Grady** (1970).

SEUMAS O'KELLY

George Brandon Saul's *Seumas O'Kelly** (1971) is virtually the only extended study of this neglected figure.

BRIAN O'NOLAN (FLANN O'BRIEN)

The best introduction to O'Nolan's fiction is "To Write for my Own Race: The Fiction of Flann O'Brien" by John Wain in *Encounter*, XXIX (July, 1967); it is largely concerned with *At Swim-Two-Birds*. *Myles*, ed. Timothy O'Keeffe (1973) contains interesting memoirs and reminiscences of the man himself.

PADRAIC PEARSE

Raymond J. Porter's *P. H. Pearse* (1973) is a thorough study of Pearse as a writer; there is also some acute commentary in William Irwin Thompson's *The Imagination of an Insurrection*.

LENNOX ROBINSON

Michael J. O'Neill's *Lennox Robinson* (1964) is a solid study of Robinson's writings, though more information is still needed on his career in the theater.

W. R. RODGERS

*W. R. Rodgers** by Darcy O'Brien (1975) is an attractive introduction and memoir.

SOMERVILLE AND ROSS

The most detailed biography is by Maurice Collis, *Somerville and Ross* (1968); John Cronin's *Somerville and Ross** (1972) is an intelligent and fair critical introduction.

JAMES STEPHENS

The most complete biography is *James Stephens* by Hilary Pyle (1965); it should be supplemented by *Letters of James Stephens*, ed. Richard J. Finneran (1974), an excellent selection with informative supplementary information.

FRANCIS STUART

J. H. Natterstad's *Francis Stuart* (1974) is an able introduction.

JOHN MILLINGTON SYNGE

Because Synge was a particularly interesting example of the way an artist transforms personal experience, one good way to begin to learn about him is by reading biographies. *J. M. Synge, 1871–1909* by David H. Greene and Edward M. Stephens (1959) is the standard biography, based largely on Stephens' (Synge's nephew) memories and research. Robin Skelton's *J. M. Synge and His World* (1971) offers a much briefer text, but it has some excellent photographs.

There are several good studies of Synge's work. Alan Price's *Synge and Anglo-Irish Drama* (1961) is thorough and perceptive, while Donna Gerstenberger's *J. M. Synge* (1964) is also an able study. Robin Skelton's *The Writings of J. M. Synge* (1971) is critically acute and has the virtue of covering almost everything Synge wrote. Denis Johnston's *J. M. Synge* (1965) is much shorter—virtually a pamphlet—but it displays a high level of critical acumen. The same, though with some eccentricities, may be found in the introductions and notes in T. R. Henn's edition of *The Plays and Poems of J. M. Synge* (1963).

Henn's edition is a good reading text, but the authoritative edition of Synge's works is *The Collected Works of J. M. Synge* (4 vols., 1962–68), ed. Robin Skelton, Alan Price, and Ann Saddlemyer. Saddlemyer's treatment of the plays, in particular, is exemplary. Paul Levitt's *John Millington Synge: A Bibliography of Published Criticism* (1974) is a reasonably complete list of secondary materials, and Weldon Thornton's annotated guide in *Anglo-Irish Literature: A Review of Research* is thorough and judicious.

KATHARINE TYNAN

The most thorough discussion is found in *Katharine Tynan** by Marilyn Gaddis Rose (1974).

WILLIAM BUTLER YEATS

For the beginning reader, Gayatri C. Spivak's *Myself Must J Remake* (1974) is a useful introduction, but there is an enormous amount of significant commentary on Yeats's life and work, almost all of it ably evaluated by Richard J. Finneran in *Anglo-Jrish Literature: A Review of Research.*

Of the several fairly basic studies, Richard Ellmann's *Yeats: The Man and the Masks* (1948) remains outstanding for its fine balance of biographical detail and critical commentary, although Ellmann devotes rather heavy attention to Yeats's earlier career. Balachandra Rajan's *W. B. Yeats: A Critical Jntroduction* (1965) and Amy G. Stock's *William Butler Yeats: His Poetry and Thought* (1961) are both able books, while Edward Malins' *A Preface to Yeats* (1974), in spite of some errors and odd organization, contains a good deal of useful background information. John Unterecker's *Reader's Guide to William Butler Yeats* (1959) is a helpful poem-by-poem handbook; there is also a great deal of factual information on the poems in A. Norman Jeffares' mis-named *Commentary on the Collected Poems of W. B. Yeats* (1968).

Joseph Hone's *W. B. Yeats, 1865–1939* (1943) remains the standard biography, although it is now out-dated. There is more detail in A. Norman Jeffares' *W. B. Yeats: Man and Poet* (1949), but a modern biography is badly needed. In the meantime, *W. B. Yeats and His World* by Micheál MacLiammóir and Eavan Boland (1971) may be recommended for its fairly accurate brief text and its excellent pictures. In some ways, the best sense of Yeats's life comes in *The Letters of W. B. Yeats*, admirably edited by Allan Wade (1954). This is, however, only a selection from Yeats's letters; Eric Domville and John Kelly are preparing a collected letters, while Richard Finneran, George M. Harper, and William Murphy are preparing an edition of letters to Yeats. These should help prepare the way for thorough biographical study.

Among the more advanced studies of Yeats's poetry and thought, Denis Donoghue's *William Butler Yeats* (1971), T. R. Henn's *The Lonely Tower* (1950), Richard Ellmann's *The Jdentity of Yeats* (1954), and Harold Bloom's *Yeats* (1970) are of particular importance. On more specialized topics, Edward Engelberg's *The Vast Design* (1964; Yeats's aesthetics), T. R. Whitaker's *Swan and Shadow* (1964; Yeats's theory of history), Thomas Parkinson's *W. B. Yeats: The Later Poetry* (1964), Allen R. Grossman's *Poetic Knowledge in the Early Yeats* (1969; on *The Wind Among the Reeds*), Frank Kermode's *Romantic Jmage* (1957; on symbolism), and Robert Beum's *The Poetic Art of William Butler Yeats* (1969; on poetic technique) are all of great value.

Yeats's plays have attracted considerable attention. Peter Ure's *Yeats the Playwright* (1963) is a good introduction, while David R. Clark's *Yeats and the Theatre of Desolate Reality* (1965), Leonard E. Nathan's *The Jragic Drama of*

W. B. Yeats (1965), and John Rees Moore's *Masks of Love and Death* (1971) are other important studies.

On Yeats's methods of composition, an extremely important topic, see Curtis Bradford's *Yeats at Work* (1965) and Jon Stallworthy's *Between the Lines* (1963). *The Permanence of Yeats,* ed. James Hall and Martin Steinmann (1950), gathers most of the significant early essays on Yeats's work, including a number of brilliant pieces.

A Bibliography of the Writings of W. B. Yeats, ed. Allan Wade (revised edition, ed. Russell K. Alspach, 1968) is the authoritative guide through the complexities of Yeats's publications. The authoritative texts for the plays and poems are the *Variorum Edition of the Poems of W. B. Yeats,* ed. Peter Allt and Russell K. Alspach (1957) and the *Variorum Edition of the Plays of W. B. Yeats,* ed. Russell K. Alspach (1966). M. L. Rosenthal's *Selected Poems and Two Plays of W. B. Yeats* (1962) is a good student's text. Most of Yeats's important prose may be found, in fairly reliable texts, in *Autobiographies* (1955), *A Vision* (1962), *Essays and Introductions* (1961), and *Explorations* (1962). There is a concordance to Yeats's poems by S. M. Parrish and J. A. Painter (1963) and to his plays by Eric Domville (1972).

index

the irish renaissance

was composed in Linotype eleven-point Weiss, leaded two points,
with display type all hand-set in Libra, Weiss, and Lombardic initials,
and printed letterpress by Joe Mann Associates, Inc.;
Smyth-sewn and bound over boards in Columbia Atlantic Vellum
by Vail-Ballou Press, Inc.;
and published by

SYRACUSE UNIVERSITY PRESS

SYRACUSE, NEW YORK 13210